What Really Matters

CHURCH OF SWEDEN
Research Series

Church of Sweden Research Series (CSRS) is interdisciplinary and peer-reviewed. The series publishes research that engages in topics and themes in the intersection between church, academy, and society.

Editor of the CSRS: Jonas Ideström

1. Göran Gunner, editor,
   Vulnerability, Churches and HIV (2009)

2. Kajsa Ahlstrand and Göran Gunner, editors,
   Non-Muslims in Muslim Majority Societies (2009)

3. Jonas Ideström, editor,
   For the Sake of the World (2010)

4. Göran Gunner and Kjell-Åke Nordquist,
   An Unlikely Dilemma (2011)

5. Anne-Louise Eriksson, Göran Gunner, and Niclas Blåder, editors,
   Exploring a Heritage (2012)

6. Kjell-Åke Nordquist, editor,
   Gods and Arms (2012)

7. Harald Hegstad,
   The Real Church (2013)

8. Carl-Henric Grenholm and Göran Gunner, editors,
   Justification in a Post-Christian Society (2014)

9. Carl-Henric Grenholm and Göran Gunner, editors,
   Lutheran Identity and Political Theology (2014)

10. Sune Fahlgren and Jonas Ideström, editors,
    Ecclesiology in the Trenches (2015)

11. Niclas Blåder,
    Lutheran Tradition as Heritage and Tool (2015)

12. Ulla Schmidt and Harald Askeland, editors,
    Church Reform and Leadership of Change (2016)

13. Kjell-Åke Nordquist,
    Reconciliation as Politics (2017)

14. Niclas Blåder and Kristina Helgesson Kjellin, editors,
    Mending the World? (2017)

15. Tone Stangeland Kaufman,
    A New Old Spirituality? (2017)

16. Carl Reinhold Bråkenhielm
    The Study of Science and Religion (2018)

What Really Matters

*Scandinavian Perspectives
on Ecclesiology and Ethnography*

JONAS IDESTRÖM
and
TONE STANGELAND KAUFMAN
editors

Foreword by Christian Scharen

PICKWICK *Publications* · Eugene, Oregon

WHAT REALLY MATTERS
Scandinavian Perspectives on Ecclesiology and Ethnography

Church of Sweden Research Series 17

Pickwick Publications
An Imprint of Wipf and Stock Publishers
199 W. 8th Ave., Suite 3
Eugene, OR 97 401

www.wipfandstock.com

PAPERBACK ISBN: 978-1-5326-1811-6
HARDCOVER ISBN: 978–1-4982-4339-1
EBOOK ISBN: 978-1-4982-4338-4

Cataloging-in-Publication data:

Names: Ideström, Jonas, editor. | Kaufman, Tone Stangeland, editor.

Title: What really matters : scandinavian perspectives on ecclesiology and ethnography / edited Jonas Ideström and Tone Stangeland Kaufman.

Description: Eugene, OR : Pickwick Publications, 2018 | Series: Church of Sweden Research Series | Includes bibliographical references and index.

Identifiers: ISBN 978-1-5326-1811-6 (paperback) | ISBN 978-1-4982-4339-1 (hardcover) | ISBN 978-1-4982-4338-4 (ebook)

Subjects: LCSH: Church. | Ethnology—Europe, Northern. | Ethnology—Religious aspects—Christianity. | Christianity—Europe, Northern.

Classification: LCC BV600.3 W4 2018 (print) | LCC BV600.3

Manufactured in the U.S.A.   06/08/18

Contents

Tables and Figures

Contributors

Eileen Campbell-Reed is an ordained minister, practical theologian, and co-director of the Learning Pastoral Imagination Project, a national, ecumenical, and longitudinal study of ministry in the U.S. (2009-present). Her book *Anatomy of a Schism* (2016) brings together qualitative research, history, theology, psychology, and gender analysis to demonstrate the stakes of a religious split in America's largest protestant denomination. Campbell-Reed is Associate Professor of Practical Theology and Coordinator of mentoring, coaching and internships for Central Baptist Theological Seminary's Tennessee campus. She blogs at www.eileencampbellreed.org.

Ninna Edgardh is Professor of Ecclesiology with an emphasis on social and diaconal studies, at Uppsala University, and an ordained minister in the Church of Sweden. Her research is focused on ecclesiology and social change, with particular attention to gender. This is for example reflected in her chapters in the edited volumes *Welfare and Religion in 21st Century Europe: Volume 2 Welfare and Religion in 21st Century Europe: Gendered, Religious and Social Change* (2011) and *Ecclesiology in the Trenches: Theory and Method Under Construction* (2015).

Tron Fagermoen is Senior Lecturer in Practical Theology at MF, Norwegian School of Theology since 2009. He is director of the Master Program of Diaconia and Christian Social Practice. His research interest is folk church ecclesiology, and his publications include the articles "Etter folkekirken?" [After the Folk Church?] (2014) and "Et valg mellom visjoner" [A Choice Between Visions] (2016).

Sune Fahlgren is Associate Professor of Practical Theology at Stockholm School of Theology, where he teaches Practical Theology. His dissertation *Predikantskap och församling* [Preachership and Congregation] is an empirical och historical study of preachership as a fundamental ecclesial practice within the Free Church traditions in Sweden. His ecclesial practice-concept is discussed, evaluated, and extended in several studies, for example in *Ecclesiology in the Trenches* (2015). Fahlgren is editor and co-author of *Shalom Inshallah: Encountering Jews, Christians, and Muslims* (2013).

Kirsten Donskov Felter is Assistant Professor (PhD) at the Centre for Pastoral Education and Research in Aarhus. She is ordained pastor in the Evangelical-Lutheran Church of Denmark. Her primary field of research is ethnographic ecclesiology and the interplay between theology and practice, understandings of ordained ministry, religious and pastoral education, and the role of the church in contemporary society. Some of her publications, individual as well as co-authored articles, include "Doing Ethnographic Ecclesiology. The Challenges of Scholarly Situatedness" (2015) and *Hvad vil det sige at være præst?* [What does it Mean to be a Pastor?] (2016).

Marianne Gaarden (PhD) is recently appointed bishop in the diocese of Lolland-Falster in the Evangelical Lutheran Church in Denmark. She has previously taught homiletics at the Pastoral Institute in Copenhagen and Aarhus University in Denmark (2006–2014) and at The David G. Buttrick Certificate Program in Homiletic Peer Coaching, at Vanderbilt Divinity School, USA (2014–2016). She has contributed to several books and authored numerous publications in the field of homiletics, the latest being *The Third Room of Preaching* (2017).

Tim Hutchings is a sociologist of digital religion. His PhD (Durham University, UK, 2010) was an ethnographic study of five online Christian churches, and his postdoctoral research has included studies of online evangelism, digital Bibles and digital pilgrimage. He is now a postdoctoral researcher at the Department of Media Studies at Stockholm University, where his work explores the religious dimensions of death and grief online (for more information, see et.ims.su.se). His recent publications include *Creating Church Online: Ritual, Community and New Media* (2017) and the edited volume *Materiality and the Study of Religion: The Stuff of the Sacred* (co-edited with Joanne McKenzie, 2016).

Jonas Ideström is Associate Professor of Ecclesiology at Uppsala University and a researcher at the Church of Sweden Research Department. He is an ordained minister in the Church of Sweden. His main area of research is in ecclesiology and ethnography with a focus on local expressions of the Church of Sweden. In his latest book, *Spåren i snön* [Tracks in the Snow] (2015), he explores the life of local parishes in two rural areas in northern Sweden. He is also the editor of *For the sake of the world* (2009) and co-editor of *Ecclesiology in the trenches* (2015).

Tone Stangeland Kaufman serves as Associate Professor of Practical Theology at MF Norwegian School of Theology, Oslo. She is the author of numerous publications on spirituality, ecclesial practices, and practical theology, including *A New Old Spirituality? A Qualitative Study of Clergy Spirituality in the Nordic Context* (2017). She has recently directed an empirical study on preaching to children and adults, which is in the process of being finalized as a book. Kaufman is also the co-editor of a forthcoming volume on spirituality in the Christian education reform within the Church of Norway. Her research interests include questions of normativity, reflexivity, and various methodologies in practical theology and ecclesiology.

Kristina Helgesson Kjellin is a researcher in Cultural Anthropology at the Church of Sweden Research Department. Her research interests include migration, integration, church belonging, identity, and cultural and religious diversity. She works in the intersection between anthropology, mission studies, and theology, and is involved in the research field "Anthropology of Christianity." Her latest book is on diversity work in the Church of Sweden: *En bra plats att vara på* [A good place to be at] (2016).

Knut Tveitereid is Associate Professor of Practical Theology at NLA University College in Bergen and Oslo, Norway. In his PhD thesis (2015) he investigated various ambiguities in the use of discipleship-vocabulary on a strategic level in ten Christian Youth Organizations. Before entering into academia, Tveitereid worked for 10 years as an ordained (youth) minister in the Church of Norway. As a researcher, he is interested in questions related to ecclesiology, spirituality, and homiletics in popular culture, often at the intersection between classic, textbased theology and qualitative research methods.

Pete Ward is Professor of Ecclesiology and Ethnography and teaches at Durham University and at MF Norwegian School of Theology. He is Co-Director of the Ecclesiology and Ethnography Network. His recent publications include *Liquid Ecclesiology: The Gospel and the Church* (2017) and *Introducing Practical Theology: Mission Ministry and the Life of the Church* (2017).

Natalie Wigg-Stevenson is Associate Professor of Contextual Education and Theology at Emmanuel College, Victoria University (Toronto). She is particularly interested in how ethnographic research methods cannot only be reconstituted for theological contexts, but also how they might help us reimagine what the nature, tasks, and norms of contemporary academic theology should be. She is also interested in adapting diverse types of ethnographic approaches for use in transformative theological education. She is the author of *Ethnographic Theology: An Inquiry Into the Production of Theological Knowledge* (2014) and a number of articles on these topics.

Foreword

B riefly, I wish to tell you as a potential reader of this volume something not about its contents, something the editors do in the introduction with admirable clarity in style and substance. Rather, I want to say clearly how the volume matters in a broader context of academic work at the intersections of faith, church, and culture today. I can say it in summary here, and unpack it below, for those wanting to hear me out: in theology this book is cutting edge, untimely, and fruitful. The following paragraphs unpack each of these, but hopefully just long enough to entice you into the book, while not impeding your diving in.

The book you hold in your hands is, in the most obvious sense of the term, cutting edge. The cutting edge is the sharp edge of a tool's blade—the sharpened length of a knife blade, for example. It evokes the sense of a tool that can do particular work, and often denotes something like a vanguard, an innovating or pioneering effort. This volume includes a group of scholars in Europe and North America whose work has been cutting a new path forward for theology. The movement variously named, and that for shorthand here I call theological ethnography, offers perhaps the most robust response to the so-called "turn to culture" in theology over the past decades. Its deeply contextual mode allows asking questions of God in the lived, and unfolding within particular worlds of meaning at once deeply real and yet in important ways inaccessible by traditional philosophical means of doing theological work. When so many of the challenges God's beloved world, and its varied peoples, face today—from climate change to political unrest and mass migration and more—are thickly particular in their manifestations, the church's effort at participation in God's mission of love and mercy to this world requires just the sort of grounded theological work this volume helps to develop and extend.

This book might be thought of, just because of its character as cutting-edge, to also be timely, a counter to the long-standing effort of theologians to write timeless works of theology. Yet, a second key feature here, as in so much academic work, is its untimeliness. Especially in the broad sense of what the Germans call *Wissenschaft*, that is, study that entails systematic research, academic work requires a kind of produced distance from the present marking it off from, say, popular opinion or journalism. The research techniques academics deploy in their research—concepts and methodological tools—are designed in order to produce that distance, and potentially, for the insight only such disciplined research can accomplish. The deep engagement with reflexivity, one of the three "matters" taken up in the book, is in fact a way to exemplify this practice of distance from the timely and commonplace, for the sake of not only truer understandings of social realities, but also avoidance of the histories of racism, colonialism and asymmetrical power relations that historically accompanied both European theological and ethnographic projects.

Finally, the book is fruitful because it comes, as good theology should, from a life of prayer and the practice of Christian community. The writers, each, and as a collective, live a life of vital faith, a fact which shines through in what often are quite personal accounts throughout the chapters. But more than that, as an invitation to the reader, the volume is structured in such a way that the reader is drawn into that community of scholars and made part of the conversation. That the book emerged from a generative network of friends and colleagues working together over years, and specifically from days spent together in Uppsala, Sweden, would not necessarily lead to a book embodying the fruitful character of such shared conversation. Yet, here, one feels as if the book is much like Pierre Bourdieu's seminar on social science as craft, where sharing about trial and error, about practice and learning over time, is shared as part of a collaborative effort seeking to together accomplish something greater than any of the parts alone could accomplish. This process has changed the authors; I am quite sure the book, if readers engage it deeply, would change them as well. As one writer in the book puts it so beautifully, "The use of ethnography for theological research takes us so close to what really matters, so close to the life that God animates into the places where we find faith in that God, that how can we not be changed by it?"

Christian Scharen
Auburn Theological Seminary, New York

Abbreviations

CofN   Church of Norway
CofS   Church of Sweden
ELCD   Evangelical Lutheran Church of Denmark

1

Introduction

JONAS IDESTRÖM AND TONE STANGELAND KAUFMAN

W hat really matters? In any conversation that goes into depth on a certain issue or theme the question must be raised. This volume is about ecclesiology and ethnography, or rather the very interaction and juxtaposition of these two phenomena. This is a book on what one could describe as theological and ecclesiological ethnography and what really matters in such academic work. How does material from field studies matter in a theological conversation? How does theology, in various forms, matter in analysis and interpretation of field work material? How does method matter? The conversation that takes place on the following pages is part of a broader scholarly conversation within the Network for Ecclesiology and Ethnography. This network exists through meetings, conferences, publications, and relationships between scholars.

Over the years, several scholars working in a context have become part of this network and ongoing conversation. It has become obvious that the ecclesial context of the Scandinavian countries—clearly shaped by folk church tradition and theology—makes an interesting case for reflections on theological and ecclesiological ethnography. There is also a need in the Scandinavian context to create spaces and arenas for a deepened and widened scholarly conversation on qualitative research and theology. Therefore, organizing a meeting place in Sweden seemed like a good idea. The Church of Sweden Research Unit invited a group of scholars from Sweden, Norway, and Denmark for a symposium with the aim of publishing this volume. In order to weave our Scandinavian perspectives into the wider international network and conversation, we also invited non-Scandinavian scholars to participate in the symposium: Pete Ward, Natalie Wigg-Stevenson, and Eileen Campbell-Reed. For the same reason, Christian Scharen was asked to write a preface to the volume. The symposium was to a large extent funded by grants from *Riksbankens Jubileumsfond*.

The seminars and conversations at the symposium played a crucial role in the process of generating the chapters in this book. Our aim as editors has been to publish a volume that mirrors and embodies a conversation rather than simply placing texts next to one another between the two covers of a book.

The volume offers perspectives that grow out of a specific context, yet it should not be read as only relevant for Scandinavian scholars. Ecclesiology is always contextual. What is thought, articulated, and argued always comes from somewhere. There is a place where it happens. In this case, the place is the Scandinavian context. In one sense, then, this is to a certain extent a book about church in Denmark, Norway, and Sweden and what matters there. Yet, at the same time, this is a book about ecclesiology and ethnography that has relevance in many other places and hopefully the conversation and arguments in this volume will contribute to the broader conversation.

The structure of the book emerged from our conversation at the symposium, where we were able to identify the three themes of *reflexivity*, *normativity*, and *representation* as central to this ongoing conversation on ecclesiology and ethnography. Reflexivity concerns the crucial role played by the researcher in research inspired by ethnographic approaches. In the interaction between empirical material and theological reflections questions of normativity sooner or later have to be dealt with—which voices in the material or in the tradition are allowed to play a role in the conversation? And which roles are they allowed to play? Representation has to do with how ecclesial life worlds are presented and represented in written texts and research results.

The themes now make up the three parts of the book. Each part includes an introduction that briefly introduces the chapters. It was clear in the conversations at the symposium that the three themes cannot be separated from one another. They are rather to be seen as aspects or dimensions of one and the same research process in which the researcher is incorporated. Through all of this there were also other themes and questions that kept reoccurring: What do we mean by theology? How do we integrate methods from social sciences into a theological conversation?

The volume is, as already mentioned, not just an anthology in the traditional sense. Therefore, each main part of the book ends with a shorter response chapter that seeks to bring the contributions in that particular part of the book on speaking terms with each other, thereby adding yet another perspective.

In this introductory part we introduce the Scandinavian context—both the academic and the ecclesial—in two chapters. This will give the reader some contextual background information to the conversations in the chapters that follow. The present volume is written to serve students and researchers in the field of ecclesiology and ethnography, systematic and practical theology, and especially those who work empirically or ethnographically, broadly speaking. The book might be particularly helpful to those are interested in and have to deal with questions of methodology in these academic disciplines.

2

The Scandinavian Ecclesial Context

Kirsten Donskov Felter, Ninna Edgardh, and Tron Fagermoen

INTRODUCTION

A key insight for ethnographic ecclesiology and theology is that in theological conversations, both the particular and the contextual matter. Therefore, it is necessary to say something about the context of the conversations that led to this book. The aim of this chapter is to present a few significant themes in the Scandinavian ecclesial context. The presentation is far from complete, but the chapter still gives a sense of the particularity for the reader who may be, more or less, unfamiliar with ecclesial life in Denmark, Norway, and Sweden.

THE HISTORICAL ECCLESIAL CONTEXT

The ecclesial history of the Scandinavian countries goes back to early ninth century, with the first organized attempts to Christianize the Danish tribes from the South. During the following centuries, the new faith expanded to the East and the North through what is today Norway and Sweden. The church organization process reached an important point during the twelfth century with the establishment of the archbishoprics of Lund in Denmark[1] (1104), Nidaros in Norway (1153), and Uppsala in Sweden (1164).[2]

The church in the North was, from its beginnings, geographically based. According to Norse tradition, the religion of the tribe followed that of its leader, and the central position of the leader also became formative for the ways that religion and politics were intertwined in the young Scandinavian churches. Whereas the High Middle Ages, in general, were characterized by attempts to centralize clerical power in Rome over against secular rulers, the churches in the area kept a rather high level of autonomy under their respective kings. As the power of the kings increased, the geographical division of the church into parishes that centered around a church building became an important instrument for both religious and secular leadership. The movement towards national churches was completed by the Lutheran Reformation in the sixteenth century, which meant that the king officially gained the role of the head of the church. In Sweden the transition to the Evangelical-Lutheran faith, strongly inspired by Catholic and reformed Bible humanism, was officially declared in 1527 by King Gustav Vasa. In Denmark, the reformation process, inspired by a more orthodox Lutheran interpretation, was completed in 1536 and was politically extended to Norway by a decree from the Danish King Christian III.[3]

In the new national churches, the clergy, who mainly stayed in their positions, played an important role, both as propagators of the evangelical faith and as state officials who were to preach the gospel on Sundays, take care of the Christian education of the children and adults, and uphold church morals and discipline. Upholding discipline had not only religious but also civil consequences like, for instance, the right to marry. When new laws were passed, it was the duty of the local vicar to see to it that they were implemented in his parish. Economically, the clergy were dependent on their parishes, as their income was based partly on farming and partly on tithe paid by the parishioners.

Alongside the parochial structure and the clerical office, independent religious revivals have played an important role in the church life of the Nordic countries. A common trait of these revivals has been to stress the importance of both lay people and forms of organization that are based on conviction rather than on geography. Among the most influential of these were a range of pietistic revivals during the eighteenth century that were

1. According to the borders of that time. Lund is today in Sweden.

2. Balling and Lindhardt, *Den nordiske,* 14ff.

3. Ibid., 112, 163, 179. What today is Norwas was then under the rule of the Danish king.

more or less critical towards the established church. In some areas, especially in Sweden, free churches were established alongside the state church
and remained influential from that period onwards.

Between the seventeenth to the nineteenth centuries during the period of absolute monarchy in the Scandinavian countries, the churches were
consolidated as state churches led by the king. In 1848, Denmark instituted
a new constitution which decreed that citizens became members in the
state church through baptism and not by birth, as had previously been the
case. However, the Danish church (ELCD) is still closely linked to the state.
The clergy are employed by the state; the church is governed by the ministry for Ecclesiastical Affairs, and it is financed by taxes collected by the
state. Until recently, the churches in Norway and Sweden followed similar
models. However, in Sweden the relations between church and state were
fundamentally changed in 2000. Contrary to Denmark, the Church of Sweden (CofS) has its own leading organ in Kyrkomötet, that is, the national
church synod, yet the identity of the church is still regulated in Swedish
law. The church tax has been replaced by a church payment; however it is
still collected by the state, and the Church of Sweden employs the clergy. In
Norway, church and state were separated in 2017. As in Sweden, the Church
of Norway (CofN) has its own board, Kirkemøtet, but the state still supports
the church economically. The church employs the clergy.

Freedom of religion has been legally guaranteed in Denmark since
1848, in Sweden since 1951, and in Norway since 1964.[4]

The national churches in the Scandinavian countries were among the
first in the world to ordain women to ministry. In Denmark, the law for
women's ordination was passed in 1947, and already in 1948 the first female pastors were ordained. In 2018, 57 percent of the clergy in Denmark
are women. In Sweden the first female pastors were ordained in 1960, and
in 2014, 46 percent of the clergy were women. In Norway, the first female
pastors were ordained in 1961, and in 2014, 30 percent of the clergy were
women. When it comes to church leadership, the rate of women is also increasing. Norway elected its first female bishop in 1993 and today six of
twelve bishops are women. In Denmark the first female bishop was elected
in 1995, and today five of eleven bishops are women.[5] Sweden elected its
first female bishop in 1997, and today five of fourteen bishops are women.
In 2014, the first woman was installed as archbishop in CofS.

---

4. Den store danske, "Religionsfrihet," http://denstoredanske.dk/Samfund,_jura_
og_politik/Jura/Danmarks_statsforfatning/religionsfrihed [accessed 06.05.2017].

5. Including the Church of Greenland, Kalaallit Nunaanni Ilagiit, that was the second diocese that appointed a female bishop in 1995.

THE CONTEMPORARY ECCLESIAL CONTEXT

Europe, and the Scandinavian countries in particular, is often characterized as highly secularized. In the cultural map created by the global World Values Survey, the countries of the Nordic region live in a cluster in the upper right corner; this position is characterized by the extreme privileging of, on the one hand, secular-rational values over traditional values (the map's y-axis) and, on the other, self-expression values over survival values (the map's x-axis).[6] The map may be interpreted as an expression of the Scandinavian countries leading the world forward towards freedom from the bonds of both religion and other forms of collective traditional values.

Taken at surface level, this interpretation might mirror the fact that the Evangelical-Lutheran Scandinavian majority folk churches share an experience of steady decline in parishioners' adherence to doctrinal beliefs and attendance at regular church services. As church statistics are not collected in the same ways across the three countries, numbers are not directly comparable. However, a few examples indicate that the tendencies mentioned here are shared phenomena. In 2015, only 3 percent of the Norwegian population attended a church service on an ordinary Sunday.[7] In the same period, 10 percent of the Danish population reported that they had attended a Sunday service during the last year[8]. In Sweden the percentage of attendees has not been in the same manner, but church statistics show that between 1990 and 2016 the number of attendees in the Sunday service decreased with more than 50 percent.

However, as opposed to the low attendance in ordinary Sunday worship, the figures for membership and participation in life rites in Lutheran majority churches are still quite high. Recent statistics show that the majority of each country's population is still registered as members in the respective Lutheran majority churches: 61 percent in Sweden, 72 percent in Norway, and 76 percent in Denmark. Another way of measuring adherence is through rates of infant baptism. In 2016, 55 percent of the newborns in Norway were baptized. In the same period in Denmark, the baptismal rate was 73 percent. In 2015, the rate of baptism of newborns in Sweden was 45 percent, a decrease from 73 percent in 2000.[9]

6. Data from the WVS survey may be found at: WVS, "World," http://www.world-valuessurvey.org/WVSContents.jsp [accessed 28.08.16]. See more about the results from the study in the chapter by Ninna Edgardh in this volume.

7. Church of Norway. (2015a). Basics and statistics. Retrieved 3/25/15, from http://kirken.no/nb-NO/church-of-norway/about/basics-and-statistics/.

8. http://teol.ku.dk/cfk/undersoegelser/, Dåb og livsstil (2014) and Kirkebrug og livsstil (2015)

9. Data are from 31 December 2015. Svenska kyrkan, "Statistik," https://www.

These figures may be contrasted with the situation a hundred years ago, when living in the Scandinavian countries was tantamount to being a member of the national church and vice versa. The national churches served an important social role in providing what the American sociologist of religion, Peter Berger, has termed a "sacred canopy": an overarching sphere of meaning covering both private and public life.[10] Today, Christian faith is, in some ways, in retreat across Europe, especially when compared to other parts of the world. However, as the complexities of the situation have come to the fore, secularization has appeared as an insufficient and even misleading labeling of the complex processes of transformation of faith and tradition in "a late modern service society where the preconditions of modernity are being renegotiated."[11] In the beginning of the twenty-first century, German philosopher and sociologist Jürgen Habermas, convincingly argued for a new "post-secular" situation, where "religion maintains a public influence and relevance, while the secularistic certainty that religion will disappear worldwide in the course of modernization is losing ground."[12]

An increasing public interest in issues of faith, both in politics and media, seems to support the argument of Habermas and others for a post-secular condition. While secularization attests to the univocal decrease in religious faith and practice, it does not catch the contradictory aspects of the wider process.

One of the leading theorists in describing the ongoing changes is the renowned sociologist Grace Davie. Struggling with describing the situation in Britain during the last decades of the twentieth century, she coined the concept "believing without belonging."[13] The phrase caught on, as it seemed to summarize much of the European religious situation at the time. The Scandinavian countries, however, did not fit as neatly into the characterization. "Belonging without believing" seems a better way of catching the specific Scandinavian situation of large folk churches still gathering a vast majority of populations whose religious practices have radically decreased.

---

svenskakyrkan.se/statistik [accessed 13.05.17].

Statistisk, "Den norske kirke," https://www.ssb.no/kirke_kostra [accessed 27.06.17].

Kirkeministeriet, "Dåbstal," http://www.km.dk/folkekirken/kirkestatistik/daabstal/ [accessed 06.05.17]. As infant baptism is the far most frequent way of becoming a member of the church, the membership rate among the one-year-old is a good indicator of how many of these have been baptize

10. Berger, *Sacred Canopy*.

11. Bäckström, Edgardh and Pettersson. *Religious Change*, 22.

12. Habermas, "A 'post-secular' society."

13. Davie, *Religion in Britain*.

Grace Davie even argued that "what the Scandinavians believe in is, in fact belonging."[14]

The interest of this book is quite similar to Davie's interest in the relation between the broad sections of the European populations and the mainstream churches. Increasingly, however, Davie has left the wordplays with "believing" and "belonging" behind, observing that the focus on either-or tended to pull the two aspects apart, while in fact the relationship between them was more interesting. Davie suggested that the concept "vicarious religion" might in fact better characterize the ongoing religious development in large parts of Europe, as it has a greater capacity to catch "the subtle and complex relationships that continue to exist between these two variables."[15]

Davie defines the vicarious role of religion as "the notion of religion performed by an active minority but on behalf of a much larger number, who (implicitly at least) not only understand, but, quite clearly, approve of what the minority is doing."[16] The relative steadiness in number of members and continued economic support, the widespread use of the churches' life rituals, and general positive attitudes to the folk churches among the public indicate a general approval, even if the majority do not attend church regularly. Also, the public importance of the churches becomes visible on special occasions, not least in relation to large national crises. One example of this was the sinking in 1994 of the Baltic ferry Estonia, in which 900 lives were lost. The Swedish people suddenly gathered *en masse* in the churches they seldom visited when things were normal.[17] A similar Norwegian example would be the memorial ceremonies in Norway following Anders Behring Breivik's attack on the government building in Oslo, where he killed eight, and his subsequent murder of 69 young people on Utøya, on July 22, 2011.[18] Also in Denmark, large numbers of people gathered in the city churches to light candles and commemorate the victims of a terror shooting in Copenhagen in 2015.

The retreat of the public role of the folk churches has been clearly linked with increased religious freedom. As described earlier, the dominant state churches in the Scandinavian countries had to deal, in various ways, with internal revival movements, sometimes creating new denominations. Today these denominations are also in retreat, while there is an influx of

14. Davie, *Religion in Modern Europe*, 3.

15. Davie, "Vicarious Religion," 22.

16. Ibid., 22. For a debate around the concept see Bruce and Voas, "Vicarious Religion"; and Davie, "Vicarious Religion."

17. Bäckström, Edgardh, and Pettersson. *Religious Change*, 125–34. See also Danbolt og Stifoss-Hanssen, "Gråte min sang."

18. Danbolt and Stifoss-Hanssen, "Når kirkeledere."

new and rapidly growing churches and other religious bodies related to increased immigration. Since the 1990s the amount of citizens born outside Scandinavia has increased significantly, contributing to cultural and religious diversification. In 2015, 16 percent of the population in Sweden was born in another country and the figures in Norway and Denmark were, respectively, 13 and 11 percent.[19] In spite of differences between the Scandinavian countries, the three largest immigrant faith communities are the Roman Catholic Church and Orthodox and Oriental churches. There is also a relatively small number of practicing Muslims. For instance, the Swedish commission for government support for faith communities (SST) counted 110,000 practicing Muslims in Sweden in 2014. In addition to that number, there are, of course, people with a Muslim background who are not practicing, living in the Nordic countries.[20]

THE THEOLOGICAL CONTEXT

The idea of the church being a *folk church* has been a central aspect of the self-understanding of the Scandinavian Lutheran majority churches. In both Norway and Denmark the notion *folk church* [folkekirke] is explicitly mentioned in the Constitution, and in Sweden it is mentioned in Swedish law. Also in the other Nordic countries the term is frequently used in the self-presentations of the majority churches. Even in the current religious climate where the hegemonic position of the Scandinavian Lutheran churches is challenged, the term *folk church* keeps returning in the ongoing discussion of the future of the church.[21]

So, what is a folk church? What does a folk church ecclesiology look like? On a more popular level, *folk church* is often used to designate a majority church which is open to everyone and does not demand too much in terms of active engagement and articulated faith from its members. In the Scandinavian countries folk church primarily designates the former or present national Lutheran majority churches. When it comes to the more explicit theological interpretation of the term, things get more complicated,

19. Nordiskt. "Norge," http://nordisktvalfardscenter.se/sv/integrationnorden/Fakta/Landfakta/Landfakta—Norge/ [accessed 08.06.17]; "Danmark," http://nordisktvalfard-scenter.se/sv/integrationnorden/Fakta/Landfakta/Landfakta—Danmark/ [accessed 08.06.17].

20. The figures are from 31.12.14. Nämnden, "Nämnden," http://www.sst.a.se/ [accessed 13.05.17]. As will be discussed in Edgardh's chapter in this volume, that group matches the majority of people belonging to CofS, which sees its membership more as a form of cultural belonging than a direct expression of faith.

21. See for example Claesson, *Folkkyrka Nu?*; Dietrich et al., *Folkekirke Nå*; Hegstad, *Real Church*, 109–16.

however.[22] There are many different folk church ecclesiologies in circulation, just as the contextual conditions for holding on to or rejecting the folk church idea differs greatly between different parts of the Scandinavian countries. This said, we believe it is fair to say that there is one version of the folk church idea which over the last century has been given more attention than the others, and that is the "classical folk church idea" of, among others, the Swedish theologians Einar Billing (1871–1939) and Gustaf Wingren (1910–2000)—an understanding of the church which in turn is heavily influenced by the work of the Danish theologian, pastor, poet, and politician Nikolaj Frederik Severin Grundtvig (1783–1872).[23]

The governing notion in the classical folk church idea is that the offering of the gospel to the entire people is seen to be the primary task of the church. Billing's slogan, "the forgiveness of sins to the people of Sweden," is typical in this regard. The folk church idea is in other words explicitly theologically motivated: the *mission* of the church, to proclaim the gospel to every person within a certain geographical area, is also what constitutes the church as *folk church*. It is thus neither the majority position itself, nor the level of democratic participation, which defines the folk church character of the church.[24] The best way of realizing the folk church idea is thus to organize it in accordance with the so called parochial system, where parishes are defined as territories. Only in this way is it possible to do justice to the nature of God's grace—which needs to be freely offered to everyone to reach its determination, regardless of how it is received.[25]

Another central aspect in the folk church idea, at least as Wingren develops it, is that the church is situated within in the context of the first article of faith. God the Creator is seen as active in and with the world in promoting good and opposing evil, prior to and independent of the church. The presence of God is thus not restricted to the church. Rather, God's relation to human beings is given with life itself.[26] This means on the one hand that the church should not be allowed to understand itself as a distinctive

---

22. In a study on the theological identity of CofS, five different models of folk church ecclesiology are identified, spanning from models emphasizing the national character of the church to models drawing on contemporary feminist theology. Ekstrand, *Folkkyrkans*. For an example of the latter, see Edgardh Beckman, *Folkkyrka*. Similarly, an analysis of the campaign leading up to the 2015 general election in CofN, demonstrates that several mutually exclusive versions of the folk church idea are in play in the ecclesiological discourse. Fagermoen, "Et valg."

23. Wingren, *Demokrati,* 10; Elstad, "Folkekyrkeomgrepet," 25.

24. Wingren, *Demokrati,* 8–13.

25. Wingren, *Living Word,* 186–87.

26. Wingren, *Creation and Law,* 20.

community with fixed boundaries vis-à-vis its surroundings. On the other hand it means that the fellowship of the church is located in the everyday life of its members, as every individual is called to work for the sake of their neighbor.[27]

Similar to—and a great source of inspiration for—Wingren, N. F. S. Grundtvig stresses the continuity between the human and the religious dimension by virtue of God's spirit that is active in the world. Against the notion of Christianity as a set of abstract ideas, Grundtvig coined his famous dictum, "first human, then Christian."[28] To Grundtvig, the Nordic history and its myths make up an unavoidable—and positive—background for being a Christian, which lead him to a high degree of cultural openness. According to Grundtvig, each human being carries the image of God, in spite of the Fall, which means that human life at its best bears witness to God's Kingdom.[29] To Grundtvig, becoming a Christian, so to speak, grows out of the national soil and from the historical communities that have carried the gospel along. Rather than speaking of conversion, he prefers to speak of animating or raising people to receive life as God's gift.[30] Another key feature in Grundtvig's view of the church is a strong emphasis of freedom, both with respect to matters of faith and to ways of organizing society and congregational life.[31]

Although the folk church idea traditionally has enjoyed a central position within Scandinavian Lutheran theology, it has also been disputed. Not least from the influential revivalist movements it has been accused of giving to little attention to the notion of the church as a fellowship of believers. During the last couple of decades this kind of criticism has been intensified and given a new twist. The focus is now directed towards whether or not the folk church idea is able to give guidance to the Scandinavian folk churches in an increasingly pluralistic and post-Christian context. It has been argued that the folk church idea is unable to challenge the nationalistic tendencies underlying most folk church ecclesiologies—an argument informed by theologians such as Stanley Hauerwas, William T. Cavanaugh, and Graham Ward. In response to this, it has been argued that the folk church idea still represents a valid concept, if further developed. Such a development would, however, need to take the current pluralistic context into account, and thus

27. Ibid., 93.
28. Grundtvig, *Sang-Værk*, 296; Bugge, "Menneske," 127.
29. Grundtvig, *Sang-Værk*,145–46; Iversen, "Grundtvigs," 19–26.
30. Iversen, "Grundtvigs," 29.
31. Pedersen, "Grundtvig," 15–18.

articulate a folk church ecclesiology that is relevant for a post-hegemonic situation.[32]

It is, moreover, important to note that at the level of practice, there is a broad variety of theological expressions and experiences within the folk church context in the Scandinavian countries. The ethnographic approach to ecclesiology and theology, exemplified and reflected upon in this volume, can therefore contribute with important material and perspectives to the conversations on Scandinavian folk churches and their ecclesiologies.

32. Aldén and Lundberg, "Skapelsen"; Fagermoen, "Etter folkekirken?"

3

Mapping the Landscape of Scandinavian Research in Ecclesiology and Ethnography— Contributions and Challenges

TONE STANGELAND KAUFMAN

INTRODUCTION

T his chapter seeks to contribute to the ongoing conversation in ecclesiology and ethnography (see below) by mapping the landscape of qualitative empirical or ethnographically oriented research in the field of practical ecclesiology and theology (broadly defined) in the Scandinavian context.[1] What characterizes some Scandinavian approaches to this field, and how can they contribute to—and be challenged by—the international ecclesiology and ethnography conversation?

One key question in this regard is how to define and not least how to delimit the field of study. Internationally, the two volumes *Perspectives to Ecclesiology and Ethnography* and *Explorations of Ecclesiology and Ethnography* as well as the articles published in the journal *Ecclesial Practices*,[2] the ecclesiology and ethnography network related to the annual Durham

---

1. While the Nordic countries include Iceland, Greenland, Finland, Denmark, Sweden, and Norway, and the territories of the Aland and Faroe islands, Scandinavia is limited to Denmark, Sweden, and Norway.

2. Brill, *Ecclesial Practices*, http://www.brill.com/products/journal/ecclesial-practices.

conference,[3] and the Ecclesial Practices Program Unit at the American Academy of Religion[4] have contributed to shaping a specific network or "brand" and a scholarly conversation.[5] In the following chapter I will refer to this specific discourse as *the conversation of ecclesiology and ethnography*, as has been suggested by Pete Ward.

On a broader and more general level this specific conversation relates to what has been termed *practical ecclesiology* (Hegstad and Ideström),[6] *ethnographic ecclesiology* (Ideström), *concrete ecclesiology* (Hawksley), *ethnographic theology* (Wigg-Stevenson), and *empirically oriented practical theology* (Kaufman). The diverse terminology referring to *ethnographically-oriented ecclesiology and practical theology* signals that this is indeed a young field that has not yet been subject to strict definitions. In the following, I will use the shorter term "practical ecclesiology" when denoting the broader field of study whereas the term "the conversation of ecclesiology and ethnography" designates a more specific scholarly discourse.

Both the broader field of practical ecclesiology as well as the specific conversation of ecclesiology and ethnography have emerged as theologians and ecclesiologists sensed a need for studying the church as it concretely appears and is experienced by real people. They then sought to bring these experiences and practices into conversation with doctrinal theology.[7] Further, most of these scholars have integrated resources and methodological tools from the social sciences in their theological work in order to be able to offer thick descriptions of churches, congregations, and Christian communities in all their complexities. However, most theologians committed to both the specific conversation of ecclesiology and ethnography as well as the broader field of practical ecclesiology still self-identify as theologians. So how is this identity maintained when engaging in ethnography and other qualitative approaches? In short, how is and how should theological knowledge be produced?[8] Finally, this turn has raised methodological and

---

3. The Network for Ecclesiology and Ethnography, http://www.ecclesiologyandethnography.com/.

4. The Network for Ecclesiology and Ethnography, "AAR Annual Meeting," http://www.ecclesiologyandethnography.com/event/aar-annual-meeting/.

5. See for example Ward, *Perspectives*; Scharen, *Explorations*; Scharen and Vigen, *Ethnography*. See also the footnotes above.

6. Hegstad, "Menighetsutvikling," 10.

7. Hawksley, *Concrete Church*; Hegstad, "Ecclesiology"; Hegstad, *Folkekirke og trosfelleskap*; and Hegstad, *Real Church*. See also Ward's chapter in this volume.

8. See, for example, Wigg-Stevenson, "From Proclamation"; and Kirsten Donskov Felter's chapter in this volume.

epistemological questions, including reflections on reflexivity, normativity, and representation.[9]

In the Scandinavian context there has recently been an increased interest in the approaches and perspectives offered by the ecclesiology and ethnography network, and a number of Scandinavian scholars have joined this conversation. There is also an increase in practical theologians who have turned to empirical and ethnographic approaches. There seems to be a shared understanding that empirical or ethnographically oriented studies of the church and ecclesial practices are necessary in order to be able to *rescript*[10] these phenomena and practices in a way that is helpful to both practitioners and academics. Yet, these ecclesiologists and practical theologians also have various approaches to the field. While some of them are primarily located in systematic theology and ecclesiology, others self-identify as practical theologians and often possess a stronger inclination toward the social sciences. Hence, recent studies of various ecclesial practices undertaken by Scandinavian theologians and other scholars differ in terms of how the theological dimension of the work is expressed and how questions of ontology and epistemology are understood and addressed. While only some of these scholars relate to the specific conversation of ecclesiology and ethnography and are more explicitly theologically oriented, the work of others might also enrich this conversation with approaches and perspectives rooted in the Scandinavian context.

This chapter, therefore, seeks to map some of these contributions. In order to describe and discuss Scandinavian approaches to this conversation, I first offer an extended, though by no means exhaustive, literature review of recent Scandinavian publications as well as an overview of ongoing research, as this is a young field in our context. Secondly, I seek to relate to the three main themes of this volume and ask how the Scandinavian perspectives might contribute to and also be further developed by employing resources offered by the conversation of ecclesiology and ethnography.

9. See for example Henriksen, *Difficult Normativity*; Wigg-Stevenson, "Reflexive Theology"; *Ethnographic Theology*; "From Proclamation"; Kaufman, "Normativity as Pitfall"; Kaufman, "From the Outside."

10. Drawing on Hans Harbers, I intentionally use the term rescript rather than describe. To me, a rescription also implies an act of interpretation as well as acknowledging that what is rendered carries with it an inherent normative dimension. See Kaufman, "From the Outside," 147–49. For another practical theological work using this terminology, yet a bit differently, see Cartledge, *Testimony*.

SCANDINAVIAN RESEARCH IN ECCLESIOLOGY AND ETHNOGRAPHY

In my mapping of Scandinavian research in ecclesiology and ethnography, I have used the following criteria to select the works: (1) I look at *recent qualitative* studies of ecclesial practices conducted in the Scandinavian countries or by Scandinavian scholars that might contribute to the network and conversation of ecclesiology and ethnography.[11] Ecclesial practices should be widely understood, and they are not limited to a certain religious sphere in spatial terms. (2) I primarily attend to research undertaken by theologians (especially ecclesiologists and practical theologians) who have engaged in or related their work to this conversation of ecclesiology and ethnography.[12] (3) Yet, I also include ethnographic work by other theologians and also some contributions by scholars who do not self-identify as theologians but whose work can add to the ecclesiology and ethnography conversation in that it implicitly discloses theological or ecclesiological themes. My intention is not to address these contributions in detail; I only seek to tease out tendencies and overarching patterns in order to be able to characterize the Scandinavian approach.[13]

Studies of Ecclesial Practices in a Folk Church Context

As was further explained and discussed in the previous chapter, the folk church situation in the Scandinavian countries constitutes a particular ecclesial context. This context not only calls for specific approaches to the study of ecclesiology but also might have something to offer to the wider study of ecclesiology and ethnography.

---

11. I thus delimit myself from discussing quantitative approaches and studies of the church, and only include various forms of qualitative research, as this also seems to be the scope of the previously published books and articles in the field.

12. I also use and refer to some of my own (and co-authored) publications as examples of the points I am trying to make, which is also an attempt to include and reflect on my own empirical work as part of this volume.

13. With such wide criteria I will necessarily miss out on important works, and my sampling will also be biased by my own academic, ecclesial, geographic, and personal location. I am an ordained pastor in the Church of Norway and self-identify as a practical theologian. I have completed my doctoral training in a setting with an emphasis on the importance of interdisciplinary work; which is to say, I also needed to be accountable to social scientists. Thus, I must admit that my own scholarly identity is perhaps more colored by this consideration than by being accountable to traditional systematic theologians and ecclesiologists.

Text Studies—The Church as Body

Over the last decade an impressive number of textual and empirical eccle-siological studies have been published in the Scandinavian countries. Swed-ish scholars have contributed with systematic theologically oriented works exploring the folk church situation following the separation of church and state in 2000.[14] Several of these theologians critique a certain folk church position and point to the necessity of understanding and interpreting the church as a body.[15] Some of them have turned to other ecclesial traditions to find resources for a more embodied ecclesiology, such as William Cava-naugh's Eucharistic ecclesiology and Nicholas Healy's understanding of the church as being a pilgrim church *in via*.[16] In the edited volume, *Between the State and the Eucharist*, the authors facilitate a conversation between Swed-ish Free church theology/ecclesiology and Cavanaugh's work.[17] The contri-butions vary from Finnish theologian Patrik Hagman's essay that expresses a highly critical attitude toward the folk church to Jonas Ideström's chapter that asks "What's the point of being different" [from the state and society]?[18]

Danish missiologist Jeppe Bach Nikolajsen has recently published a study on the identity of the church, building on the post-secular theologies of Lesslie Newbegin and John Howard Yoder.[19] Drawing on Charles Taylor and Amos Yong, Norwegian systematic theologian Silje Kvamme Bjørndal points to the possibilities offered by Stanley Hauerwas's ecclesiology when reconstructed through a pneumatological lens. In her recent PhD work she makes the case that such a particularistic (and pneumatological, I would add) ecclesiology should also be considered a possible resource for the church in a secular age in the Scandinavian context.[20]

As an alternative to some of these approaches, Norwegian theologian of social practice (diaconia) Tron Fagermoen questions Hagman's critique of the Scandinavian folk church model, arguing that Gustav Wingren and Einar Billing actually offer important perspectives and resources for a viable folk church ecclesiology in our specific context.[21] Similarly, Swedish sys-

---

14. Eckerdal, *Folkkyrkans kropp*; Hagman, *Efter folkkyrkan*; Ekstrand, *Folkkyrkans gränser*; Ideström, *Folkkyrkotanken*.

15. Cf. Eckerdal's critique of Einar Billing in Eckerdal, *Folkyrkans kropp*; Sigurdson, *Return of the Body*.

16. See Healy, *Church*. See also Ideström, *Lokal kyrklig identitet*.

17. Halldorf and Wenell, *Between the State and the Eucharist*.

18. Hagman, "Constantinianism"; Ideström, "What's so Great."

19. See Nikolajsen, *Distinctive Identity*.

20. See Bjørndal, "Church in a Secular Age."

21. See Fagermoen, "Etter folkekirken."

tematic theologians Thomas Ekstrand and Johanna Gustafsson Lundberg express a critical attitude toward understanding the church as a social body, as argued for by Jan Eckerdal and Hagman.[22]

Some of these contributions, then, identify a deficit in terms of the church being an embodied community, as the folk church might appear as a social entity lacking a robust body. Looking for resources as to what it entails to be church in a post-Christian context, there has been a turn to postliberal theological contributions in the Scandinavian countries as well, which has raised a discussion of what it means to be church, not only in a post-Christian situation but also in a context with a significant folk church heritage. Yet, very few of these publications have engaged ethnographic methods.

The Empirical Turn and Studies in Ecclesiology

During the last ten to fifteen years, however, a major empirical turn in ecclesiology and practical theology has taken place in the Norwegian (and partly also the Scandinavian) context. This also includes doctoral and post-doctoral work in ecclesiology and practical theology. PhD programs receive an increasing number of applications for empirical projects including studies framed in ecclesiology and practical theology. In all the Scandinavian countries, PhD students are working on dissertations that explore ecclesiological issues by taking an empirical or ethnographic approach. A common characteristic of several of these projects is that they research ecclesial practices in a multi-cultural context.[23]

Already in 1996 Harald Hegstad empirically explored three different congregations in the Church of Norway (CofN).[24] The study resulted in

22. See Ekstrand, *Folkkyrkans gränser*; Aldén och Lunderberg, "Skapelsen."

23. One example is Norwegian theologian Sunniva Gylver's work on ecclesial community dynamics in two multicultural and multireligious parishes in Norway, which draws on resources from the field of social capital as her analytical framework. Swedish theologian Andreas Holmberg is researching congregations related to the network "Framtiden bor hos oss" [The future resides with us, FBHO] in urban, multicultural, and multireligious areas in Sweden for his PhD thesis. Norwegian PhD student Stian Eriksen explores migration congregations in the Norwegian context. His work is part of the larger research project "Cracks and Inbetweens" directed by Norwegian anthropologist and theologian Tomas Sundnes Drønen and missiologist Kari Storstein Haug at VID Specialized University, located in the department in Stavanger. VID, "Cracks," http://www.vid. no/en/research/research-groups/cracks-and-in-betweens/. See also Gyrid Gunnes's PhD work. Gunnes, "Hvem er folkekirkens folk?"

24. Hegstad, *Folkekirke og trosfellesskap*.

a typology of three types of congregations[25] as well as an understanding of the relationship between folk church and faith community as dynamic and interrelated.[26] His model has been both embraced and critiqued, and it has been frequently referenced. More recently, Hegstad has offered a more theologically-oriented ecclesiology that makes the case that the real church is the empirical, visible church that is made up of real people.[27] In this contribution Hegstad does not explicitly draw on empirical studies, yet my hunch is that the overall argument is implicitly informed by his previous empirical work.[28]

Hegstad's contribution is also included and further developed in the larger project *Menighetsutvikling i folkekirken [Congregational Development in the Folk Church]*.[29] A research team directed by Hegstad seeks to combine research with a transformative move, not far from John Swinton and Harriet Mowat's vision of practical theology, in which they understand practical theology to be partly overlapping with action research.[30] Hence, Hegstad and colleagues have described their work as being at least partly an action research project.[31]

Drawing on ethnographic fieldwork in the contemporary and growing churches Hill Song in London and Pinsekirken in Copenhagen, Norwegian Pentecostal Theologian Karl Inge Tangen asks why people identify with late modern churches and whether this identification leads to transformation.[32] This empirical work also relates ecclesiology to spirituality and congregational studies. Another Norwegian contribution to the field of ecclesiology, one which only partly draws on empirical studies, is religious educator and theologian Birgitte Lerheim's article-based dissertation where she reflects on the intersection of ecclesiology and ecclesial practices.[33]

Jonas Idestrom's ecclesiological work has primarily focused on the identity of the folk church studied empirically from the ground as expressions of *implicit ecclesiology*. In his doctoral work he explores the

25. Folkekirkemenigheten [the folk church congregation], bedehusmenigheten [the prayer house congregation], and arbeidskirka [the activity oriented congregation].

26. Hegstad, *Folkekirke og trosfellesskap*.

27. Hegstad, *Real Church*.

28. However, this claim might have to be further justified by an in-depth study of Hegstad's work.

29. Birkedal, Skorpe Lannem, and Hegstad, *Menighetsutvikling*.

30. Swinton and Mowat, *Practical Theology*.

31. Hegstad, "Reflections." From the view of the field of action research, this claim could be problematized, but that is not my aim in this text.

32. Tangen, *Ecclesial Identification*; Ward, *Perspectives*.

33. Lerheim, "Vedkjenning og gjenkjenning."

multicultural congregation of the suburb Flemingsberg outside of Stockholm. Ideström argues that the body of the local church is constituted by three identity structures, which are shaped around the employees, the worship services, and the geographical space of the parish.[34] In his 2015 book *Spåren i snön* [The Tracks in the Snow] Ideström studies what it entails to be church in rural parishes in Northern Sweden.[35] Employing Actor-Network Theory (ANT) as part of his analytical lens and approach, he makes the case that the church is actually present at places where one would not expect it, and that the presence of the church constitutes a hope for rural parishes and areas that experience depopulation and the closing down of public services. Hence, this is an argument for the significant possibilities of the folk church as being an agent of hope in the midst of everyday life. Moreover, the specific sociomaterial sensibility offered by the ANT approach allowed him to disclose ecclesial practices and an ecclesial presence in unexpected places.[36]

In the 2015 volume *Ecclesiology in the Trenches*, researchers from the Ecclesiology Research Seminar at Uppsala University, Sweden, present and reflect methodologically on their research, while three international scholars respond to their work.[37] One major point with this work is to make explicit the messiness of the research process, which is so often hidden or made invisible through the neat writing and reporting of most studies. Thus, this volume seeks to contribute to the field by showing the thorny path that our research might take us down and how some scholars have traversed it. The point is not to copy their processes or strategies but to lay open some of the challenges that young scholars might encounter when conducting research within the field of ecclesiology, including ethnographically oriented projects. This volume explicitly contributes to increased researcher reflexivity as well as to issues of normativity. It also reflects a general interest for methodological questions in the Scandinavian context.

Migration in general and the refugee situation in Europe in particular have also sparked recent research related to ecclesiology. Danish theologians Marlene Ringgaard Lorensen (homiletics), Kirsten Donskov Felter (practical theology), and Gitte Buch-Hansen (biblical studies) researched the encounter between converting refugees and an Evangelical Lutheran congregation (part of the Danish folk church) in Copenhagen.[38] Their con-

---

34. Ideström, *Lokal kyrklig identitet*.

35. Ideström, *Spåren i snön*; "Loving Gaze"; "Mediators of Tradition."

36. For a further reflection on the significance of taking a sociomaterial approach, see below.

37. Fahlgren and Ideström, *Ecclesiology*.

38. Buch-Hansen, Ringgaard Lorensen, and Felter, "Ethnographic Ecclesiology."

tribution is also valuable in terms of researcher reflexivity, as the researcher team was significantly challenged when confronted with their identity as white, academic, middle-class females. Moreover, Swedish anthropologist Kristina Helgesson Kjellin studied diversity work in congregations related to the network "Framtiden bor hos oss" [The future resides with us] in urban, multi-cultural, and multi-religious areas in Sweden.[39] Focusing on narratives in these contexts, she asks what can be learned from these practices. Norwegian and Swedish theologians Trygve Wyller and Cecilia Nahnfeldt have studied how a local congregation collaborating with a foundation has allowed the encounter with undocumented migrants to disturb and thus also transform their worship and ecclesiology.[40]

Ethnographically oriented research in ecclesiology in the Scandinavian context, then, has primarily attended to the specific dynamics between folk church and faith community, including congregational development; to what it entails being church in multi-cultural and multi-ethnic as well as rural parishes; what it means being church in the context of migration and the refugee situation in Europe; and Pentecostal and charismatic church identity and spirituality. Moreover, some studies have also specifically addressed methodological questions and issues of reflexivity and normativity (see also below).

The Study of Worship Services and Christian Practice —Empirical Field

Over the last decade a number of reforms and changes have taken place in Church of Norway. These include the separation between church and state and thus a new church constitution (kirkelov), a liturgical Reform, a Christian Education Reform, a new Hymnal and a new translation of the Bible. Several studies have addressed these reforms, especially the liturgical reform and the Christian Education Reform. Moreover, empirical studies of spirituality and Christian practice have also been carried out in the Scandinavian context. It can be discussed whether or not this kind of research should be considered a contribution to the conversation of ecclesiology and ethnography. My own position would be to argue for an inclusive approach as these studies of Christian practice are sometimes being undertaken in unexpected places, and in surprising ways they can offer significant perspectives to a conversation on what it entails to be church in the Scandinavian

---

39. Helgesson Kjellin, *En bra plats.* See also Helgesson Kjellin's chapter in this volume.

40. Nahnfeldt, "Motstånd," 15; Wyller, "Undocumented Embodied"; "Becoming Human."

context. There is often an implicit ecclesiology and spirituality inherent in such practices, which might be disclosed by empirical studies even if the researcher does not explicitly engage in this ecclesiology and ethnography conversation herself.

Empirical Studies of Worship and Preaching

In Norway, then, there has been an emphasis on empirically oriented studies on Christian practices and ecclesiology related to worship and congregational and professional practices. One contribution is the edited volume *Gudstjeneste på ny* [Worship Anew], which discusses the liturgical reform from various theoretical angles.[41] The book includes a few empirical studies on church architecture, the Christian education reform, and model participants in worship (Øierud, Johnsen, Sandal respectively). The volume as a whole foregrounds the worship service as embodied action, and thus worship as practice and participation. *Gudstjeneste Á la Carte* [Worship Á la Carte] is another contribution on the liturgical reform based on an empirical study employing a mixed methods design.[42] The authors of this edited volume argue that the reform has opened up for a large variety of worship patterns and expressions, and that the congregations now pick and choose and put together their own "worship menu."

In a Swedish empirical study, religious educator Caroline Gustavsson explores how young adult (between the ages of nineteen and forty) choral singers experience worship services in CofS, and how these experiences relate to worship participation.[43] Her sample consists of church members who have a paradoxical insider-outsider perspective as they sing and participate in worship, yet do not necessarily experience the feeling of belonging or partaking (delaktighet) in the worship practice or community of practice. This piece of research also specifically addresses the particular folk church context of the Scandinavian countries as well as the focus on how worship is experienced.

Danish homiletician Marianne Gaarden's doctoral work on how church participants experience preaching is another empirical study related to worship in the Scandinavian folk church context. Gaarden's theorizing on these empirical findings has partly been conducted collaboratively with Marlene

---

41. Hellemo, *Gudstjeneste*. The authors are scholars that used to be located at the Practical Theological Seminary (PTS) in Oslo, which is now part of the Theological Faculty at the University of Oslo.

42. Balsnes, *Gudstjeneste*.

43. Gustavsson, *Delaktighetens kris*.

Ringgaard Lorensen.[44] Gaarden makes the case that when the preacher succeeds, what she terms a "third room" is facilitated in the encounter between preacher, listener, and the preached word in the situated worship service. In this "third room" a new sermon emerges, and meaning is created for the listener. Hence, preaching is not a transfer of a substance or a message from a sender to a receiver but rather a dialogical interaction that cannot be fully controlled by the preacher (see Gaarden's chapter in this volume). Further, Danish practical theologian Kirstine Helboe Johansen has contributed to this field with work in ritual and liturgical studies that focuses on worship and the wedding ritual in the specific folk church context where a number of church members would like to be married in the church yet seldom attend regular Sunday worship.

Practical theologians located at the Theological Faculty at the University of Oslo have recently published an edited volume on worship services during the year of confirmation training. They observed three services in three different locations in Norway where confirmands participate in various roles. Their focus was on what characterizes ordinary Sunday services that confirmands are required to attend and participate in as ministrants.[45] Building on Gaarden's work in Denmark, a research group at MF Norwegian School of Theology (which I direct) is currently working on an empirical study called *Mer enn ord: Forkynnelse for Små og Store*, abbreviated FoSS [More than Words: Preaching to Young and Old]. This study explores how preaching is enacted and how it is experienced by adult and children as listeners in worship services where children of a given age are invited.

Empirical Studies of Spirituality and Christian Practice

The turn to what I have previously termed "new old" spiritual practices—that is, classic spiritual practices undertaken in new ways and in new (and sometimes unlikely) places—might be another characteristic of the Scandinavian context.[46] Drawing on in-depth interviews with Norwegian parish pastors, I make the case that the spirituality of the research participants can be described as a new old spirituality, and that the clergy can be considered spiritual *and* religious.[47] Moreover, I contend that every day spirituality mat-

44. Gaarden and Ringgaard Lorensen, "Listeners"; Gaarden, "Den emergente"; *Prædikenen*.

45. See Johnsen, *Gudstjenester med konfirmanter*.

46. This term is borrowed from the title of my dissertation. See Kaufman, *New Old Spirituality*.

47. Kaufman, *New Old Spirituality*.

ters not only for lay people but also for pastors and that mundane practices embedded in everyday life should be acknowledged as "the real thing."[48] However, sources of spiritual nurture found in the ministry itself and in spiritual practices that must be intentionally approached are also significant to the interviewed clergy.

The latter category above is partly characterized by various retrieved spiritual practices rooted in the Ignatian tradition.[49] Furthermore, the practice of facilitating the Ignatian Exercises in the prisons of Kumla in Sweden and Halden in Norway has sparked some research in this regard.[50] In a recent article I argue that offering the Ignatian Exercises in a maximum-security prison in the secularized society of Sweden can be considered a life-transforming resource to long-term incarcerated persons. Thus, ecclesial practices might be undertaken in unlikely places in new-old ways.[51] Several other empirical studies of pilgrimage and spiritual practices in the context of incarceration have been carried out in the Scandinavian context during the last decade. One example is Leif Gunnar Engedal's study of Norwegian inmates participating in a pilgrimage to the pilgrim site of Nidaros.[52] Two questions come to mind: What does it entail to be church in the context of incarceration and what implicit ecclesiology does research of such cases disclose? These cases could be further explored from the perspective of practical ecclesiology.

Thus, various aspects of worship and Christian practice have comprised a number of recent empirical studies, especially in the Norwegian context. This includes studies situated in the curricular subdisciplines of liturgy, homiletics, religious education, and ecclesiology. Moreover, empirical research from this context also explores ecclesial practices undertaken in unlikely places and outside of the specific religious sphere. Additionally, there has been a renewed interest in spirituality, broadly understood, but not least within a Christian framework, yet approached from a more subjective angle. However, not many of these studies engage in conversation with

---

48. Kaufman, "Real Thing?"; "Plea for Ethnographic Methods."

49. Kaufman, "Pastoral Spirituality"; "Ignatiansk spiritualitet."

50. However, most of these smaller studies have been situated in the academic contexts of psychology, sociology, and law, and not in spirituality, practical theology, or practical ecclesiology. For some student theses reporting on the Kumla case, see Bernling, "Att gå genom muren"; Johansson, "Spirituality"; Nordström, "Bakom dubbla murar." For a few reports from the more recent Halden case, see Engedal, "Retreat"; Finn and Lunde, "Rapport om retreat." Moreover, Vegard Holm has recently embarked on an empirical study of this case as part of his PhD degree in practical theology.

51. Kaufman, "Ignatian Exercises."

52. Engedal, "Fra fengselscelle."

extant theological literature. Hence, they might still be an untapped source for constructing novel theological knowledge.

A Specific Emphasis on Children and Adolescents— Research Subjects

As previously mentioned, there has, for more than ten years, been an ongoing government-funded Christian education reform in CofN.[53] According to the curriculum of this reform, Christian education should be provided for every child and adolescent up to the age of eighteen who has been baptized in CofN. The reform has resulted in numerous new positions for Christian educators and in the development of new activities and measures aimed at various age groups. These activities, measures, and programs usually culminate in a worship service. A number of research projects have been funded by this reform, and thus empirical research on various aspects and measures of this reform has significantly marked ethnographically oriented research in practical theology and ecclesiology in the Norwegian context.

The first wave of research reporting on the initial pilot stage of this reform took the shape of rather evaluative studies.[54] However, several recent PhD theses and other studies have investigated various areas of this reform, not least the learning processes among children, adolescents, and volunteers working in congregations where the reform has been implemented[55] as well as experiences of community.[56] Moreover, a few research projects have focused on aspects of Christian social practice (diaconia) related to the reform.[57] Additional recently completed and ongoing projects relevant to the field of ecclesiology and ethnography focus on spirituality, preaching, and worship in the context of this reform.[58]

---

53. On the following website a link to the English version of the Plan for Christian Education Reform, see Church of Norway, "Resources." https://kirken.no/nb-NO/church-of-norway/resources/plan-for-christian-education/.

54. One example is Hegstad et al., *Når tro skal læres*.

55. Holmqvist, *Learning Religion*; Nygaard, "Caring to Know"; Johnsen, "Religiøs læring"; Holtedahl, "'Community'"; Fretheim, *Ansatte og frivillige*; Leganger-Krogstad, "Trosopplæringen."

56. See Lorentzen, Fretheim, and Mogstad, *Fellesskap og organisering*.

57. See, for example, Kaufman and Sandsmark, "Vilje til læring?"; "Landsby eller forstad?"

58. See Johnsen, *Gudstjenster med konfirmanter*. Two further examples are the projects "Bricolage og byggeklosser" [Bricolage and building blocks] directed by Kristin Graff-Kallevåg and "Forkynnelse for Små og Store" [Preaching to Young and Old], directed by me.

There has also been a significant interest in youth ministry studies in the Scandinavian context, and some of these studies are both ethnographically oriented and relevant to ecclesiology. One example is Norwegian practical theologian Knut Tveitereid's doctoral dissertation on the understanding of discipleship in Norwegian youth ministry organizations and movements.[59] Furthermore, a few years ago Tveitreid and his colleague Norwegian practical theologian Bård Norheim undertook a small-scale study on adolescents and worship services, which is another example of empirically oriented studies in the wider field of ecclesiology.[60] They describe how adolescents shape the worship space according to their own ideas, "overwriting" the given structure of the sanctuary or church building. Norheim has published considerably in the field of youth ministry studies and has been involved in the conversation around ecclesiology and ethnography, yet most of his work has not engaged fieldwork.[61]

However, the degree to which these contributions explicitly address theological aspects and ecclesiological conversations vary, and a tendency is that their main emphasis is not on ecclesiological issues. Yet, as part of a larger empirical project evaluating this reform, one sub project will specifically attend to theology and ecclesiology.[62] Nevertheless, the particular Norwegian empirical focus on children and adolescents is worth mentioning as a feature of recent research on ecclesial practices in the Scandinavian context. Moreover, this is a specific contribution to the wider international conversation of ecclesiology and ethnography and seeks to represent the experiences of children and adolescents related to studies in practical ecclesiology.

Sociomaterial and Sociocultural Approaches—Theoretical Lenses

The LETRA project at MF Norwegian School of Theology directed by Geir Afdal has produced significant empirical research on ecclesial practices by studying learning trajectories among young people, professionals, and volunteers in three congregations.[63] Perhaps more importantly, this research group has contributed to a theoretical renewal at MF and among other researchers in Norway and Sweden, as this overall research project has

59. See Tveitereid, "Pragmatics."

60. See Norheim and Tveitereid, "Stemning."

61. See, for example, Norheim, *Practicing Baptism*; "Ministry as Womb"; "Cultivating a Vision"; "Christian Story."

62. The overall project is directed by Morten Holmqvist, and the sub-project has been conducted by Tron Fagermoen and Solvor Lauritzen.

63. LETRA is short for Learning and Knowledge Trajectories in Congregations.

introduced sociocultural and sociomaterial paradigms and demonstrated the relevance of such approaches to empirical studies of practical ecclesiology and practical theology.

In their article-based PhD dissertations, Morten Holmqvist, Ingrid Reite, Marianne Rodriguez Nygaard, and Elisabeth Tveito Johnsen studied the learning processes of confirmands, pastors, deacons, and six-year-olds employing various sociocultural and sociomaterial lenses as analytical frameworks.[64] While Holmqvist employed practice theory and James Wertsch in his research on learning processes among confirmands, Reite situated her work within a sociomaterial paradigm and utilized Actor-Network Theory more specifically as a sensitizing device when studying the learning processes of parish pastors.[65] Nygaard researched knowledge production and the significance of care in the professional practice of deacons drawing on various sociocultural perspectives.[66] Similarly, Johnsen also used various sociocultural perspectives when studying learning processes in the Christian education reform with an emphasis on six-year-olds.[67] Moreover, drawing on Actor-Network Theory, Øivind Holtedahl studied modes of learning for adolescents in the CofN for his PhD thesis, whereas in his dissertation, Fredrik Saxegaard looked at pastors as leaders through the analytical framework of Cultural Historical Activity Theory (CHAT).[68]

I suggest that this specific theoretical approach has opened up the empirical field, allowing them to see things that they would have otherwise missed. These sociocultural and sociomaterial lenses have served as sensitizing devices that have created an analytical distance to a field in which many of us are deeply embedded.[69] Hence, this sociomaterial and sociocultural sensibility also adds to issues of researcher reflexivity and representation, attended to in this volume. By focusing neither solely on the individual nor on the cognitive or verbal dimension, then, this particular lens has enabled scholars to see more of how numerous human and non-human actors are

---

64. Reite, "Between Settling"; Holmqvist, *Learning Religion*; Reite, "Between Blackboxing"; Johnsen, "Religiøs læring"; Nygaard, "Caring to Know." Johnsen, "Religiøs læring."

65. See Holmqvist, "Learning Religion."

66. See Nygaard, "Caring to Know."

67. See Johnsen, "Religiøs læring." See also Johnsen, "Teologi."

68. See Holtedahl, "Community"; Saxegaard, *Realizing Church*.

69. See Kaufman and Sandsmark, "Spaces." In this piece, a sociomaterial sensibility allowed material objects to be part of our analytical radar, which also led my colleague Astrid Sandsmark and myself to discover the significance of non-human actors in a study on how Christian education was facilitated for children and adolescents residing in childcare institutions.

interwoven in networks that are dependent on each other. Hence, the exploration of such networks and connecting actors might enable us to better understand the phenomena and practices under investigation.

Moreover, this approach also offers a specific understanding of more overarching themes such as normativity, ontology, and epistemology, which are addressed in part II of this volume. Here, researchers in the LETRA project and others draw heavily on scholars such as Bruno Latour, John Law, and Kristin Asdal.[70] These authors can be situated in the Actor-Network Theory (ANT) paradigm (Latour) or Science, Technology, Society (STS) (Law and Asdal). They argue for a post-constructivist approach to ontology and epistemology, making the case that there is not only one reality but rather multiple realities, and that these are created as a number of actors relate to one another in ongoing and ever-changing networks.[71]

All of these studies demonstrate the potential of taking a sociocultural and sociomaterial approach to ethnographic studies of ecclesial practice. Theory is not used in a deductive manner to be tested but as a sensitizing device, enabling us to see new dimensions of well-known phenomena and practices. Moreover, by not only focusing on the individual or the cognitive dimension of learning, but rather on practice, action, and artifacts, these studies open up the field, which expands our understanding in a horizontal way, as "a movement within below," to quote Afdal.[72]

QUESTIONS OF NORMATIVITY, REFLEXIVITY, AND REPRESENTATION FROM THE SCANDINAVIAN CONTEXT

How does recent Scandinavian research in practical ecclesiology relate to the three themes of this volume: being a researcher (reflexivity), making decisions (normativity), and creating stuff (representation)? In the previous extended literature review I have at times mentioned these themes but not to any extensive degree. In the following, my aim is to address these questions a bit more in depth. Still, this should be seen as more of a sketch than as a thorough discussion.

---

70. Latour, *Reassembling*; Law, *Organizing*; *After Method*; Asdal, "Returning."

71. See also Kaufman and Ideström, "Why Matter Matters." In this article Ideström and I make the case that materiality (or matter) does matter in understanding theological action research and when negotiating various normative theological voices, both in the practice field as well as part of the research practice itself. Furthermore, we argue for the potential of the epistemological position proposed by Latour, Law, and Asdal for practical ecclesiology.

72. Afdal, *Researching*.

Reflexivity—The Insider/Outsider Role of the Researcher in
Practical Ecclesiology

Theologians who study ecclesial practices and congregational life are usually practitioners in the field of study as well, and Scandinavian scholars are
no exceptions. Hence, the researcher often shares the *habitus* of the field, to
borrow a term from Pierre Bourdieu. This gives her a paradoxical insider/
outsider position in terms of being embedded in the field, yet also allows her
the outsider perspectives and resources of the researcher. Several Scandinavian researchers have reflected on such issues arguing for the possibilities of
studying one's own profession or a field, in which the researcher is herself
embedded.[73] Yet, there is still a certain anxiety of not having a sufficient
distance to the field. Hence, autoethnography and similar approaches are
still rare in Scandinavian practical ecclesiology, and it might be time to call
for some creative and daring approaches.

Among Scandinavian scholars, then, there has been an awareness that
it is necessary to create a certain analytical distance to the field and to reflect extensively on researcher reflexivity. The latter emphasis is probably
an influence from the social sciences. Thus, such studies have made use of
various theoretical lenses as sensitizing devices that help the researcher to
see possible blind spots also in terms of representation. Examples are the
sociocultural and sociomaterial sensibilities and practice theory in much
recent research from MF scholars and others related to the LETRA project
as well as Bourdieu's theoretical framework in the work of Felter.[74]

The Danish scholars who conducted the study on what happens to a
traditional Danish folk church congregation when a number of migrants
worship and participate in congregational life discovered that they also had
to include themselves as research objects as they needed to have their own
habitus disturbed. This was made clear to them when they discovered the
discrepancy between their observations and subsequent interpretations of
certain situations on the one hand, and, what the research subjects reported
about these situations during the interviews on the other. This discovery
made them agonizingly aware of their own particular identify as female,
ethnic white, middle-class Danes. Drawing on Bourdieu and Franklin D.
Pilario, they engaged in the practice of scholarly reflexivity, where they had
to objectify their own pre-conceptions by dialoguing with theologians of
different positions. Moreover, such practice requires interdisciplinarity and
an engagement in the field of practice. Thus, the research subjects were

---

73. Kaufman, "Normativity"; Wadel, *Feltarbeid*; Leer-Salvesen, *Moderne prester*;
Kaufman, "From the Outside."

74. See Felter, "Mellem kald og profession."

made co-researchers not unlike what is common in action research approaches, and their voices were heard and paid attention to in a way that did not "overwrite" them with the voices of the researchers.[75] In this case we also see how closely related the two themes of reflexivity and representation are.

As a crucial part of practicing validity in qualitative research is related to good craftsmanship and enabling the reader to follow the decision trail of the researcher, transparency is of utmost importance. This is intimately connected with researcher reflexivity, as the reader should be able to make sense of the interpretations offered and also to identify possible alternative understandings or interpretations. Based on my own doctoral work, I further argue that practicing researcher reflexivity might turn out to be a significant analytical resource.[76]

Normativity—Various Normative Dimensions in Interdisciplinary Work

Theologians who set out to study ecclesiology by taking an ethnographic approach necessarily have to work in an interdisciplinary manner. The empirical turn in theology has sparked a number of more overarching questions regarding normativity that have been frequently discussed in the conversation of ecclesiology and ethnography.[77] This theme will also be further elaborated in this volume's response chapter to the section on normativity.

In the essays featured in the edited volume *Perspectives in Ecclesiology and Ethnography*, the authors have to fight a war on two fronts, or put in a less aggressive way, justify their position in two different directions—to those who are critical to theologians drawing on ethnographic research and to those who are about to lose their identity as theologians altogether. While John Webster might serve as an example of the former,[78] some of the Norwegian contributions to the field, including my own work, might possibly be accused of the latter.

In a sense, those of us who are situated in systematic or practical theology and who acknowledge the significance of drawing on fieldwork face the challenge (and sometimes conundrum) of how to relate to both the social

---

75. Buch-Hansen, Lorensen, and Felter, "Ethnographic Ecclesiology," 222, 227, 239ff. Similarly, Ideström and I argue for the possibilities of action research in practical ecclesiology by drawing on the systemic action research framework of first, second, and third person positionality of the researcher and research team Ideström and Kaufman, "Whose Voice?"

76. Kaufman, "Normativity."

77. Ward, *Perspectives.*

78. Webster, "Society of God."

sciences as well as to traditional text-based theological research. Scandinavian theologians drawing on ethnographic methods have paid much attention to such questions as the relationships to the social sciences have been extensive. In the following I briefly present two different trajectories.

An Empirically Oriented and Social Science Trajectory

Both Johannes van der Ven's empirical theology approach and Don Browning's practice-theory-practice model have been predominant in our context and have shaped the work of Scandinavian practical theologians.[79] Drawing on van der Ven, Hegstad has opted for theology as *intradisciplinary*; that is, theology itself must become empirical.[80] Although a significant interlocutor and inspiration also in the Scandinavian context, Browning's position has nevertheless more recently been nuanced and critiqued.[81]

Moreover, neighboring disciplines such as psychology of religion, sociology of religion and anthropology of religion have played a major role in practical theological and practical ecclesiological research in the Scandinavian context, not least in Norway. Practical theology and ecclesiology draw on all of these disciplines. Yet, theological tradition and doctrinal theology might not play a very significant role in a number of these interdisciplinary studies, and practical theologians working across disciplines might be encouraged to make more use of extant theological resources and also possibly to contribute the production of theological knowledge.[82]

A Theologically Oriented Trajectory

As mentioned above, significant ecclesiological work has taken place in Sweden, both text-based and ethnographically oriented. Especially the latter trajectory of these contributions has aimed at combining an ecclesiological and an ethnographic approach but while seeking to participate in a theological conversation. A few examples can be found in the work of Ideström and Sune Fahlgren (although he uses historical material), which is partly situated within the ecclesiology and ethnography conversation.

79. Browning, *Fundamental*; van der Ven, *Practical Theology*.

80. van der Ven, *Practical Theology*. Hegstad, "Praktisk teologi." Yet, for van der Ven (more than for Hegstad), this has often implied larger quantitative studies. Similar approaches have also been undertaken by the department of analysis in CofS and by KIFO in Norway.

81. Afdal, "Teologi"; Kaufman, "From the Outside."

82. See Ward's chapter in this volume.

Ideström, for example, chooses theologians such as Nicholas Healy, Paul Fiddes, William Cavanaugh, Mary McClintock Fulkerson, Gordon Lathrop, and Rowan Williams as conversation partners, and explicitly engages in a theological discourse.[83]

Moreover, in Denmark scholars such as Gaarden and Felter have situated their work in the vein of homiletics and practical and systematic theology, respectively, yet are drawing on qualitative studies.[84] Gaarden, for example, addresses the gap between theologically-held doctrine and the empirical experiences of pastors related to how preaching is experienced by listeners. Thus, her work adds to the ongoing conversation of how to understand normativity in practical ecclesiology, as she refuses the binaries between transcendence and immanence, divine and human action.[85]

Representation—Whose Voices are Represented and How?

One crucial issue in ethnographically oriented ecclesiology and theology is how our texts can represent the thick and complex realities we participate in when doing research. This question is of course closely related to issues of both reflexivity and normativity.

Making the case that religion is not a fixed entity but is rather always in motion and that research itself (for example in religious education or practical theology) should be considered a practice, Afdal questions Browning's understanding of the descriptive phase, arguing that theology itself is both a theoretical and practical activity.[86] Drawing on various practice theorists from the social sciences and activity theorists, Afdal and other researchers at MF Norwegian School of Theology have given attention to practice theory.[87] Their approach also understands practice as an activity with an underlying teleological dimension; that is, a practice is always directed toward an object or an aim.[88] Afdal's understanding of research as a practice is

---

83. See various publications of Ideström referred to in this chapter as well as Fahlgren and Ideström, *Ecclesiology*.

84. See Felter and Gaarden in this volume.

85. Gaarden, "Den empiriske fordring"; *Prædikenen*. See Gaarden's chapter in this volume.

86. Afdal, "Teologi"; *Researching*.

87. See, for example, Schatzki, Knorr Cetina, and von Savigny, *Practice Turn*; Reckwitz, "Toward a Theory."

88. See, for example, Afdal, *Researching*. It should be noted that this is a different understanding of practice than the one that has been prevalent in North American practical theology, drawing on Bass and Dykstra's appropriation of MacIntyre's virtue ethics. See Dykstra, "Reconceiving Practice"; Dykstra, *Growing*; Bass and Dykstra, *For Life*; Volf and Bass, *Practicing Theology*. This trajectory of practice has also been

a way of attending to both the various voices of this practice and how they are represented when the research process is turned into a text.

The focus on children and adolescents in recent Scandinavian (and especially Norwegian) practical ecclesiological research is an expression of the significance given to the voices of young people as research subjects in this context. This is corresponds with the Scandinavian culture, which encourages children to have their own voice and opinion, as opposed to more authoritative cultures, where children are told to obey adults. There is furthermore an awareness when it comes to listening to voices outside of the particular religious realm or sphere as the Scandinavian folk churches are so interwoven with society as a whole and also with local communities. Thus, ethnographically-oriented ecclesiological research in the Scandinavian context will most likely represent a broad spectrum of the population in terms of religious practice.

However, being societies with relatively minor class difference compared to other countries, issues of class have not often been raised in such research. One exception is Gyrid Gunnes's doctoral work. Drawing on ethnographic fieldwork in the Church of our Lady (Vår Frues kirke) in Trondheim, Norway, she explicitly attends to class and gender in her analysis of who is part of the body of the folk church. She challenges existing folk church ecclesiology by offering a power-critical perspective: "Does the folk church only have people or also poor people?"[89]

Similarly, neither issues such as ethnicity and gender nor more comprehensive theories of intersectionality and approaches drawing on postcolonial work have been significantly attended to in Scandinavian research in ecclesiology and ethnography. Yet, there is one important exception. Ninna Edgardh has introduced the term "feminist ecclesiology" to this context, making the case that the church and ecclesial practices need to be both degendered and regendered.[90] Hence, not all voices have been equally attended to, and it would serve Scandinavian practical ecclesiology well to pay attention to the question: whose voices are automatically given dominant positions and whose voices are not being heard?

While social justice and climate change are significant social and political issues in the Scandinavian context and also of deep import to churches and other Christian movements and organizations, these areas have not been subject to much practical theological research in the Scandinavian countries. Furthermore, how are various voices of the marginalized represented in the

---

discussed by Norheim. See Norheim, *Practicing Baptism.*

89. Gunnes, "Folkekirkens folk."

90. See Edgardh, "(De)gendering"; "Social Agent."

actual texts emerging from the research mentioned above? As scholars we need to critically ask if vulnerable or marginalized research subjects, such as undocumented refugees, the long-term incarcerated, homeless people, and migrants—to name but a few—are represented in a way that objectifies them to serve the career of middle-class researchers. Are they primarily used as examples for us to make our case, or are their voices represented in a way that might challenge the researcher as well as the practice of both the academy and the research field in which the research subject is embedded. In my view, there is an existing lacuna in explicitly addressing such issues in practical ecclesiology from the Scandinavian context.

CONCLUSION—SCANDINAVIAN CONTRIBUTIONS AND CHALLENGES

To sum up, ethnographically oriented ecclesiological work from the Scandinavian context might contribute to the international field by offering perspectives raised by its distinct context, where people have a heterogeneous and ambiguous relationship to church and ecclesial practices. However, the Scandinavian approach to this ecclesiology and ethnography conversation is not uniform. Although situated in a similar Scandinavian folk church setting, scholars take different approaches to the study of practical ecclesiology. Some of the Swedish and Danish contributors might be more explicitly theologically-oriented than are their Norwegian colleagues. Yet, scholars located in the Norwegian context have also produced a large number of empirical studies of ecclesial practices, not least research on children and adolescents related to the Norwegian Christian education reform. As this particular perspective has not been significantly attended to in previous research in the conversation of ecclesiology and ethnography, these works constitute an important contribution to this field. Thus, they emphasize the significance of listening to the experiences and voices of children and young people and seek to represent them in an adequate way.

Moreover, the sociomaterial sensibility that has marked part of this research is worth noting, as it has enabled the disclosure of dimensions and perspectives that have previously gone unnoticed. These are also strongly related to issues of normativity, reflexivity, and representation as well as epistemology. This also supports the practice of researcher reflexivity. Furthermore, while seeking to attend to various dimensions of normativity, recent Scandinavian publications opt for a non-prescriptive normativity.

Quite a few Scandinavian scholars in practical ecclesiology contribute to the international conversation of ecclesiology and ethnography by raising questions and offering novel perspectives relevant to practical ecclesiology.

Still, some of these scholars might be encouraged to draw more extensively on theological resources and participate in a theological and ecclesiological conversation in order to challenge the way theological knowledge has traditionally been produced. Hence, engagement with such theological works might be an untapped source for theological reflection in practical ecclesiology in the Scandinavian context.[91]

91. One possibility would be to facilitate a conversation between some of these works and those of scholars such as Natalie Wigg-Stevenson, Mary McClintock Fulkerson, Eileen Campbell-Reed/Christian Scharen, Pete Ward, Paul Fiddes, or others who have opted more boldly for an integration of ecclesiology and ethnography.

PART 1

Reflexivity

The contributions in Part I take as their point of departure the experience of being a researcher in the messy practice of doing theology empirically or ethnographically. The three chapters engage in different perspectives of reflexivity.

Knut Tveitereid argues that theology must engage in empirical reality. Yet, he also identifies a recurring difficulty that appears when theologians reach the particular phase of data analysis. Namely, there seems to be a shortage of or a lack of confidence in finding helpful theological theories that can make the data speak.

In his chapter Jonas Ideström raises the question: what does it mean to faithfully participate when doing ethnographic ecclesiological research? His contribution challenges a position of fixed boundaries between the research practice and the ecclesial practices of the field studied by arguing that the research practice might in fact also become an ecclesial practice.

Eileen Campbell-Reed addresses the relational character of reflexivity by exploring some of the "foibles and missteps" that she made as a researcher. In her honest and personal text, she reflects on "the messy relational pathway that researchers must traverse." Her experience of reflexivity challenges a one-dimensional understanding of reflexivity as only a question of the location of the researcher.

In her response, Natalie Wigg-Stevenson notes that "the three chapters together . . . demonstrate . . . the need for producing fresh strategies of reflexivity as we as theologians embrace ethnography's transdisciplinary migration to our shores."

4

Making Data Speak—The Shortage of Theory for the Analysis of Qualitative Data in Practical Theology

Knut Tveitereid

THEORY FOR ANALYSIS AFTER THE EMPIRICAL TURN

The ecclesiology and ethnography network is but one example of how the "empirical turn" in theology has created exciting and enriching ways forward for research. Elements from the lived and practiced, the ordinary and operant, and experienced and everyday, is again connected to the discourses of academic theology.[1] Consequently, theology and the social sciences are touching bases. Methods and modes for establishing and analyzing empirical material (often qualitative data, it seems) are no longer strangers to theological research.

This chapter addresses one of the central elements in empirical research: the phase of analysis. In most projects, analytical perspectives are found at several stages throughout the research process. Still, analysis could be regarded as a specific phase in the research process—the period in which concentrated attention is given to actual data analysis. In qualitative research, this phase tends to be a rather long and enduring one, possibly a

1. The many names highlights slightly different aspects and approaches in what I see as a mutual renewal of interest regarding empirical reality in theological inference.

period of frustration and chaos, before eventually reaching clarity as the data "opens up" and "starts to speak."

Furthermore, this chapter focuses on the use of theory in the phase of analysis. From the social sciences, theologians learn that *theories* are the primary tools that enable researchers to *see* more clearly what is already there and what is at stake in the data. Theories make data speak. A successful use of theory is one that provides the researcher with perspective and analytical clarity—in a way that is transparent to others. In this respect, theories make the researcher see, but equally important, make the reader see how the researcher saw what he or she saw.

This brings us to the heart of this chapter: As theologians reach the phase of qualitative data analysis, many of us face recurring problems regarding the use of theory. First of all, we are confronted with a shortage of useful theory for this purpose. Theologians are acquainted, of course, with notions of theory, but this is often theory in a broad sense. Generally, we speak about theory as the antonym of practice, but we seldom use the term "theory" to describe theological insights (i.e., Luther's theory of justification by faith). We have other names for this. Secondly, reaching the phase of data analysis, theologians are also confronted with our lack of experience in using theory as a means for data analysis. In comparison to the social scientists, most theologians are novices at this practice. Simply put, a deliberate use of theory as analytical tool is not always a prerequisite in theological inferences. This chapter, however, does not refer to a general lack of overview among theologians about analytical theories (even though this might be the case) or a general lack of skill among theologians in using this theory (although this might be the case at times). The problem is more fundamental: the acknowledgement that there is a real shortage of a kind of theory suited for qualitative data analysis within a context of practical theological research.

The aim of this chapter, then, is to *identify and reflect on underlying problems and possibilities in the use of various kinds of theories for analyzing qualitative data in practical theological research.*

Analytical Theory in Practical Theology

In the following, as a background for a discussion of this topic, I will use experiences in my own doctoral work: *Pragmatics of Discipleship: A study of ambiguity on a strategic level in Norwegian Christian youth organizations.*[2] The study is situated within the field of practical theology *and* has a qualitative research design. The focus of the study was on *the use of discipleship*

2. Tveitereid, "Pragmatics."

vocabulary as a phenomenon. More specifically, I was interested in how *language* and *theology* were connected and intertwined on a strategic level in a sample of ten very different Christian youth organizations. The material consisted of official documents (such as by-laws, annual reports, strategy documents, etc.) and interview transcripts with organizational executives. The driving research question in the thesis was: *How is the use of discipleship vocabulary understood on a strategic level in Norwegian Christian youth organizations—with a special focus on ambiguity?* (See Figure 1)

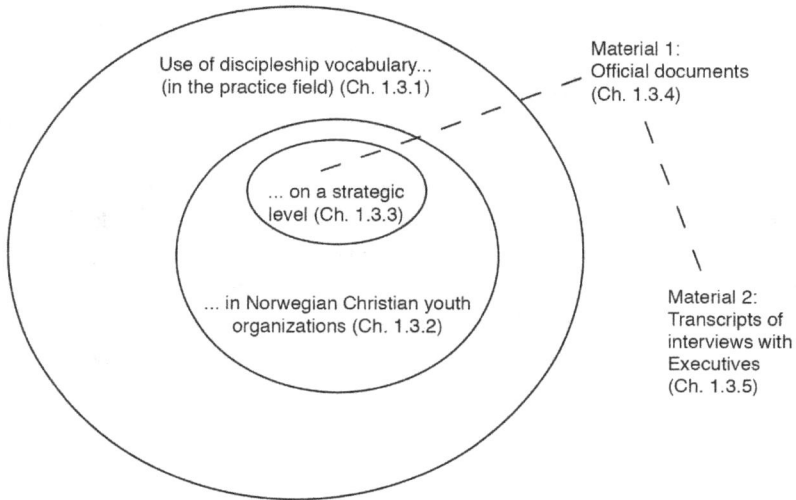

Figure 1: Unit of analysis, its context, and data sources[3]

The coding of the material resulted in three analytical chapters: A first chapter on *pragmatics* highlighted social and strategic implications of discipleship vocabulary in different organizations. To accommodate this, various *social science theories* were brought to the table. A second chapter on *ministry* highlighted ecclesial and educational implications for youth ministry. For this, I drew on selected *theological typologies* as analytical theory. A third chapter analyzed *theological implications* of discipleship vocabulary for organizations, with analytical language and categories borrowed from systematic theology. The following discussion focuses in on the use of these three kinds of theories (social science theories, theological typologies, and systematic theology) for analyzing qualitative data in practical theological research.

---

3. Ibid., 31.

The Data-Theory Relation in Practical Theology—Abduction

Before turning to the various theories in more detail, some general considerations on the data-theory relation in practical theology, and particularly *abduction*, should be mentioned. Without undermining the role of any other analytical mode, abductive modes of inference find their way into many qualitative research projects within practical theology. The reasons for this are many and diverse. One is certainly the similarity between abduction and hermeneutics *and* of abduction and contextualization. The very process of abduction—which often is understood as a back-and-forth motion between data and theory—evokes association to the fusion of horizons or the spiral motion between dialectic relationships in a hermeneutical circle, etc. As most theologians are familiar with various forms of interpretation, the way to abduction is short. Furthermore, working abductively is at times compared to working contextually, which also is something many theologians are accustomed to do. The Swedish sociologist Berth Danermark, for one, has concisely described abduction as a *redescription* or as a *recontextualization*: to see something (the data) in light of something else (the theory).[4]

The roots of abduction go back (at least) to the nineteenth century American logician, philosopher, and mathematician Charles S. Peirce.[5] As for his works in philosophical pragmatism and analytical semiotics, abduction was developed in order to mediate and bridge dualisms of ultimate reality and empirically observable reality, knowledge, and action, and practice and theory. The notion of abduction being a working process of moving back and forth between data and theory is rooted here. Unlike *deduction*, which could be seen as deriving knowledge of individual phenomena from universal laws, and *induction*, which could be seen as drawing valid conclusions from a number of observations, Peirce saw *abduction* as the understanding of something (a phenomenon, etc.) in a new way by observing and interpreting it within a new conceptual framework. Following the lead of Peirce, a wide variety of theories, rules, and frameworks could be applied to a phenomenon in abduction.

Italian semiotician Umberto Eco has provided a further distinction between a threefold of abductions. He discerns *overcoded-*, *creative-*, and *undercoded* abduction by various uses of "rule"—or what could be called various uses of an interpretive theoretical framework.[6] In *overcoded* abduction,

---

4. Berth Danermark and others have elaborated this perspective, describing abduction as *redescription* or *recontextualization*, seeing it as giving already-known phenomena a new meaning. Danermark, *Explaining*, 80–91.

5. Ibid., 80.

6. Eco and Sebeok, *Sign of Three*, 206.

the rule is a given theorem, consciously or unconsciously applied—often resulting in spontaneous interpretations. In *creative* abduction, the aim is to create a new theory, for instance, when a researcher observes something from a frame of interpretation that nobody has used before or that at least opposes conventional interpretations. *Undercoded* abduction is to let several different rules/theories, in turn, cast light on the phenomenon or event observed. This happens, Eco claims, whenever there are multiple general rules or theories to be selected from. The researcher is interested in the differences that each rule or theory creates, and the one(s) that best explains the phenomenon of interest. The researcher can also compare, combine, and integrate abductions of different rules. Eco compares undercoded abduction to the work of a detective on a crime-site. To make sense of all observable pieces of information gathered, the detective activates every thinkable theory that could relate the various observations, put them in relation, and offer a comprehensive and viable explanation to the crime/event/phenomenon itself. This way, the detective needs to be equipped not only with a large number of theories, but also with a creative imagination to make plausible theories and a critical ability to make an informed assessment about the validity and relevance of these theories. The data at hand becomes the ultimate decider of relevant theory.

The appropriate theory in relation to analysis will vary according to the chosen research design (deductive, inductive, or abductive)—and in cases of abduction, which kind of abduction is in use (overcoded, undercoded, or creative). The very use of abduction, however, does warrant some use of theory.

EXPERIENCES WITH VARIOUS TYPES OF ANALYTICAL THEORY IN UNDERCODED ABDUCTION

The following discussion draws on experiences using undercoded abduction in a study where I tried to understand *discipleship vocabulary* as a code for something and as a sign for something. The study resulted, as said, in three analytical chapters, using various theoretical lenses for every chapter.

On the Use of Social Scientific Theories in Analysis

In the first analytical chapter of the study, I was interested in the social implications in the use of discipleship vocabulary, i.e., how the organizations in the sampled organizations experienced this in their situation. Beforehand, I was convinced that discipleship vocabulary functioned as a code word with social implications especially relevant to the processes found on a strategic level in organizations.

In order to operationalize this piece of research I framed it as a study relying on pragmatics, the branch of semiotics[7] interested in the understanding of signs that emerges in and through practice, or more commonly, "the study of how utterances have meaning in situations."[8] In doing so, I recontextualized the various uses of discipleship vocabulary as signs of something else and something more in light of their contexts. Modern pragmatics defines its task either too wide or too narrow for my use, but in Charles Morris's classic notion of pragmatics, I found a way forward. In his definition, the pragmatic task is to understand the *origins*, *uses*, and *effects* of signs in particular situations.[9]

In the actual analysis, I switched back and forth between working from below, by listening to the interviews, reading the transcripts and documents, coding, re-coding, and building code-hierarchies *and* by working from above, by heuristically trying out ever-new theoretical perspectives on the data. For this, I brought along a fairly large number of theories borrowed from the social sciences—some of which proved to be of little help, while others really paid off.

One such theory, Hatch and Schultz' theory of top management vision and leadership, were among the more rewarding ones.[10] This theory made me aware how informants described the use of discipleship vocabulary as a negotiation between organizational culture and external context. While discipleship vocabulary could be considered useful for internal use, it could be considered deficient for communication purposes. Organizational identity and organizational image were often opponents in an ongoing negotiation in many of the sampled organizations, producing some rather peculiar linguistic practices.

---

7. Semiotics = the study of signs.

8. Leech, *Principles*, x.

9. Nöth, *Handbook*, 48ff. Morris, *Foundations*.

10. Hatch and Schultz, "Relations."

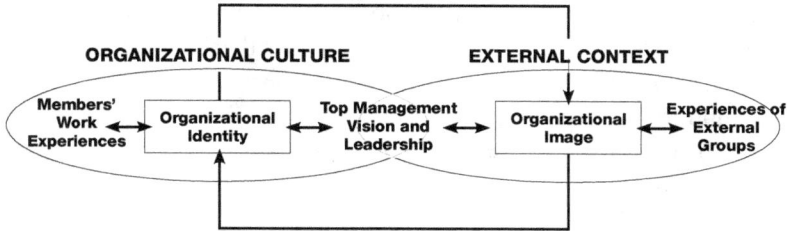

Figure 2: Hatch and Schultz' model of top management vision and leadership (facsimile)[11]

The user-friendly social science theories enthused me. For a theologian this was a whole new, exciting, and rewarding world of perspectives. There seemed to be a theory, drawn from empirical research, on just about any topic. And for every new social science theory I presented to the data, new findings seemed to emerge from it.[12] At some point, however, I did choose to abort this process. This was done out of a basic conviction that the very study object should be understood as a phenomenon with implications beyond the pragmatic and social. If I had continued this process, I would have missed important aspects of the phenomenon itself. The statements of the informants guided me to (also) consider other implications of the use of discipleship vocabulary in the data—for ministry and for theology.

Social science theories are generally generated from empirical research and are of a dimension that gives them the ability to make data speak. They are often presented as the best possible account of a phenomenon available at a given time, but are also open to further improvement. It is expected that future research will contribute to further expansion, adjustment, and refinement. This makes much of social science theory very easy to use. The theories make data speak fluently, but, in my opinion, have a blind spot for

---

11. Ibid., 361.

12. For those interested in the actual findings: By Morris's concept of *origins*, I found (inspired by discourse analysis) that the various uses of discipleship vocabulary on a strategic level in Norwegian Christian youth organizations could be understood as compositions or remixes. The organizations in the sample had combined bits and pieces of a potentially countless number of theological accounts in a creative process of composing a specific understanding of discipleship in their context.

In relation to Morris's concept of *uses*, I was able to point out five unique uses of discipleship vocabulary in the material: i) a *reference to the twelve*, ii) a *model of ideals*, iii) a *mode of spirituality*, iv) a *method of influencing*, and v) as a *marker of modification*. The latter entrusted to the linguistic instinct of each informant and context. Those in favor of discipleship vocabulary used it often for branding purposes. For others, with negative connotations regarding discipleship vocabulary, it was a vocabulary that could easily be put aside or used only with specific qualification.

theological language and perspective. Social science theory will most likely not help bring to the forefront the bits and pieces of theology there might be in the data—nor help understand their implications.

Contrary to the metatheories, which we will look at later, many social science theories enable the researcher to see dynamics, relations, patterns, and nuances in the data. One should, however, note that all theories, not only theology, are ontologically, epistemologically, ideologically, and ethically charged. Taking time to reflect on these issues would be helpful, but would not fully make up for theological disinterest in social scientific method and logic. The social science theories should, therefore, not only be a lens to see through, they are also in need of being the object of critical assessment—if the goal of the researcher is to remain a practical theologian, that is.

The basic problem with social science theories is not that they do not work, because they do. The problem is that they are not the best tool to become aware of the theology that is there in the data. However, the wonderful quality of operationalizing qualitative research and generating new theory is nothing less than exceptional.

On the Use of Theological Typologies in Analysis

Following the leads in the informants' utterances, I turned to *implications for ministry* as a focus of a second analytical chapter. It soon became clear I needed a different kind of theory to see the ministerial implications in the data, and tried out *theological typologies* for this.

A typology I regard as any theory that predominantly seeks to identify categories and types within a set. Typologies could be understood as a theory that orders an issue or a field according to their internal indifferences. In ecclesiology and practical theology, there are several classic typologies: Dulles' *Models of the church*,[13] Richard Niebuhr's typology of *Christ and culture*,[14] and Bevans' *Models of contextual theology*,[15] just to mention a few.

Equipped with numerous typologies related to ministry (ecclesiology, organization, education, mentoring, etc.), I approached the data again. The number of typologies was narrowed down, as a small handful soon stood out as especially interesting:

13. Dulles, *Models*.
14. Niebuhr, *Christ*.
15. Bevans, *Models*.

- Ralph Winter's two-structure theory of God's redemptive mission—and his concepts of sodality vs. modality.[16]

- Ivan Kaufman's distinction between intentionality vs. institutionality.[17]

- Max Weber's (and later, Ernst Troeltsch's) church–sect typology.[18]

- The classic Norwegian ellipse model with two focuses: portraying the traditional division of labor between prayer-house mission movements and local congregation in majority-church dioceses.[19]

Through an analytical process of undercoded abduction, it was possible to identify the affiliation to sodality, intentionality, sectarianism, and mission in organizations with a frequent use of discipleship vocabulary. The organizations that for some reason used discipleship vocabulary less were marked by a seemingly opposite loyalty—toward modality, institution, and local church.

	Sect	Church
Weber	Sect	Church
Winter	Sodality	Modality
Kauffman	Intentionality	Institutionality
Double economy	Fresh expr.	Parochial
The Norwegian ellipse		

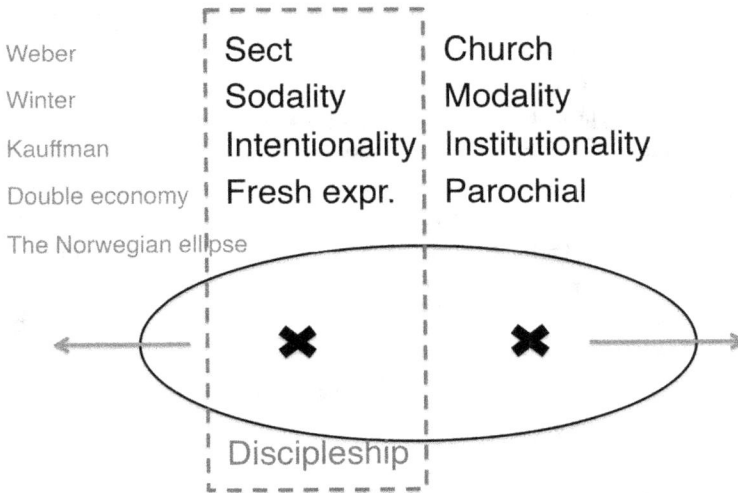

Figure 3: Illustration: Typologies positioning the use of discipleship-vocabulary in ministry

With the use of typologies, I was able to identify relations between the specific use of language (discipleship vocabulary) and specific understandings of church, in a very distinct way. Over time, however, this clear conclusion bothered me to an increasing degree. After having spent more time with

16. Winter, "Two Structures." Winter and Beaver, *Warp.*

17. Kauffman, *Follow.*

18. Heelas and Woodhead, *Religion*, 40f.

19. Haanes, "I Jesu navn." Lerheim, "Lekmannsforsamlingar." Kjøde, "Fra ellispe."

the data, the informants started to reveal a kind of dynamic complexity that the typologies simply did not account for. It became clear, for instance, that organizations that used discipleship vocabulary frequently on a strategic level, were not necessarily already affiliated with a sodal-, intentional-, and missional form of church, but had an attraction and inclination toward this form of ecclesiology in their use of discipleship vocabulary. Likewise, with organizations using little or no discipleship vocabulary: they were not necessarily already representatives of a kind of modal, institutional, and local church setting, but had affiliations pulling them in this direction, in some cases, expressed as strategy, even. With this finding, discipleship vocabulary, then, became more of a vision longed for, more than a position or identity already present.

The typologies were helpful in the sense that they offered categories for interpretation, but simultaneously misleading as they made the dynamics in the data obscure. The typologies indicated tidy and static differences, whereas there were actually complex processes of ongoing strategizing. Firstly, categories in a typology tend to be rather broad and integrating. This is a necessity to order reality in types. Their analytical strengths lie in naming overarching positions, not identifying exception, variation, and messiness within or between types. Secondly, categories in a typology tend to favor marks of property over dynamics in the data. Findings generated by using typologies would often tend to present lived religion as tidier than it is. The goal of ethnography and qualitative research, on the other side, is generally not to merge the many layers of reality but to understand the many dimensions and their relations in deeper ways, and, therefore, in truer ways.

As with the social science theories, we are faced with a type of theories that has clear advantages, but also limitations. If *theological language* is a blind spot for the social science theories, *dynamics* and *layers* are blind spots of typologies. Their clear categories offer a powerful analytical language, but they also conceal inclinations, motions, and dynamics present in a data set—and thereby in practice.

On the Use of Systematic Theology in Analysis

In the mentioned study on discipleship vocabulary, I found, through a process of coding, a total of 641 unique excerpts containing theological statements. I ordered these thematically (instinctively as a systematic theologian), and distributed the statements according to the organizations' use of discipleship vocabulary (in categories of high-, moderate-, and low-frequency organizations). This resulted in something that resembled a small-scale quantitative study within the larger qualitative study.

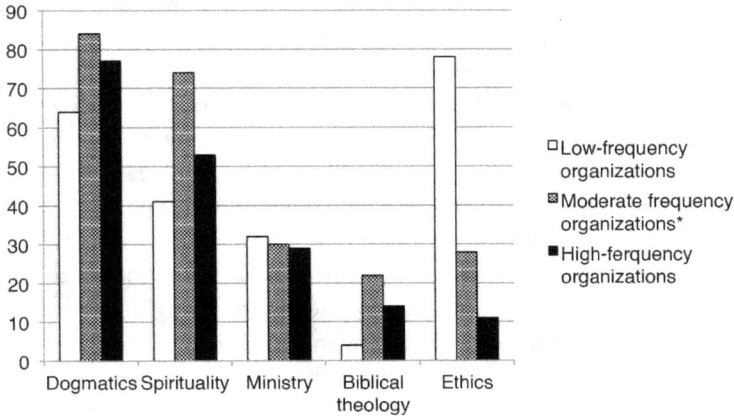

Figure 4: Overview excerpts coded as "theological assumptions" in interview[20]

It was, of course, interesting to see various correlations in the material between the use of discipleship vocabulary on one hand and the occurrence of theological topics on the other: I found for instance (as expected) that high-frequency organizations seem more engaged with evangelization and mission compared to organizations in the mid- and low-frequency organizations. But more interestingly: low-frequency organizations speak far more about Jesus than their counterparts. Low-frequency organizations, the organizations not accustomed to using discipleship vocabulary, also represented almost all the interview excerpts focusing on ethical issues (both social ethics and individual/personal ethics).

I treated these preliminary findings as indications. These and similar findings aroused my curiosity, and prompted me to revisit the interview transcripts with ever new questions: Why are the discipleship-talking organizations so interested in mission and evangelization? Why are they so seemingly little interested in ethics and Jesus, etc.? This process resulted in an in-depth bottom-up study of the lived Christology and lived soteriology of high-frequency organizations.[21]

20. Tveitereid, "Pragmatics," 208.

21. For those interested in the findings: This second analysis made clear that the use of discipleship vocabulary on a strategic level in Norwegian Christian youth organizations marks a constructive attempt to reformulate soteriology. I was able to identify three different uses of discipleship vocabulary that had the purpose of expanding the space for a spirituality that embraces more of life, while at the same time staying loyal to a Protestant understanding of God's redemptive work of Christ. I summarized the three attempts as: centered set theology, anti-antinomist theology, and Kingdom of God theology. In this way, I argued, discipleship vocabulary could be seen as a code word for

As I tried to bring the data into conversation with systematic theology, a gap became evident—a gap between worlds. Much of what we call theology is formulated in the University, accustomed to the world of ideas and equally remote from empirical reality. Theology, especially the systematizing disciplines, has inherited its logic from the humanities, not the social sciences. A typical theological candidate, in Norway at least, would very seldom be introduced to empirical research methods during his or her 5–6 years of study. Theological theory to a typical Nordic theologian would be a theory of grand proportions, comparable to what in the social sciences is referred to as a *metatheory*, a theory of the highest level. These are broad-brush theories, large in scope, and fundamentally relating to the world of ideas. They are derived from ideas, and seek to contribute back to the world of ideas with new even more coherent ideas. Their relation to the empirical world of experience is more indirect.

The problems of adapting theories of too grand proportion to qualitative data, is not exclusively a problem for theologians. Researchers from other branches in the humanities could easily have similar experiences if trying to introduce social sciences methods to their field. If a researcher in psychology, for instance, were to use the Oedipus complex to analyze qualitative data on, say, the therapy-situation, a comparable situation could occur. Although the famous Oedipus complex has offered patients and therapists meaning and framework for generations and is among the most established theories in the psychodynamic strand of psychology, in dealing with qualitative data it would offer the researcher limited help.[22] The theory, originating from Greek mythology, simply lacks sufficient empirical backing and grounding. It is a theory of too grand proportions, a universal metatheory not drawn from empirical data and not intended to explain particular phenomena on an empirical level.

The example of the Oedipus complex has, at least to some degree, transferability to theology. For instance, if theologians in analysis wanted to use systematic theological insights as theories, he or she would, for the same reasons, find this "theory" of limited use for analytical purposes. Systematic

---

affiliation to, but not full affirmation of, classical evangelical soteriology.

Similarly, the analysis showed how the person of Christ is understood and used differently in different understandings of discipleship: A Christocentric discipleship draws its understanding from Christology. A Christ-encountering discipleship understands discipleship as the practice of encountering Christ. A Christo-secluded discipleship has problems transposing their image of Christ as savior to the life of the disciple. A Christo-oblivious discipleship has conceptualized discipleship to such a degree that it appears rather disconnected from Christology.

22. Thanks to Dr. Erik Stänicke for sharing this example from his own research experience.

theology has brought existential meaning to individuals, institutions and communities for centuries, but only partly in extension of human everyday experience. Its explanatory power may even to some extent depend on this distance.

The divide between the world of ideas and the empirical world is not easily overcome. Theology is developed as systematic grand theories well-distanced from the lived, it is, as a consequence, only partially accessible to empirical research methods—and in our case: the large-meshed theories of theology are only partially commensurable to delicate empirical data.

Systematic theology, similarly to theological typologies, offers analytical language and categories, but because it also represents an idealized form of theory the transfer value is limited. At some level, however, systematic theology did work as a discussion partner in analysis: In some instances, the small and less reflected bits and pieces of theological statements in the data could be connected and filled out by established systematic theological reflection. In my study, established Christologies and soteriologies offered this kind of help. Still, the problems of compatibility were obvious, and maybe more evident.

CONSIDERATIONS REGARDING FUTURE USE OF ANALYTICAL THEORY IN PRACTICAL THEOLOGY

To summarize the argument: Various types of theory represent unique qualities when used in the analytical phase of qualitative research. I have identified some strengths, but also some weaknesses connected to the usability of three kinds of theory in this very phase: Social science theories are unrivalled in making data speak as social data, but are equally disadvantageous when it comes to bringing theological potential or theological implication in the data to the forefront. Theological typologies offer analytical language and tidy categories, yet at the same time, they overlook too easily the relational dynamics between categories, agents, artifacts, values, practices, etc. in the lived. They do, however, show some potential for analysis, which I will return to in a moment. Systematic theology, which I have called theological metatheories, manages at its very best to bring theological fragments in the data into conversation with grand theological ideas. Yet, more often, the same systematic theologies tend to overlook and underplay the significance of theology in the data. This last section seeks to clarify the problem of analytical theory through suggesting a threefold distinction fundamental for theologizing after the empirical turn.

Firstly, future research should acknowledge a distinction between the world of ideas and the empirical world; this includes a distinction between theories coming from the two worlds. Kant's famous distinction between *phenomena* (what belongs to empirical reality) as opposed to *noumena* (what belongs to the world of ideas) is still valid. Phenomena are tangible and open to empirical investigation. Noumena, on the other hand, are not. This again relates to the classic rationalist-empiricist debate in philosophy.[23] Theology, as an academic tradition, has traditionally been an activity drawing more from the world of ideas than its counterpart. With the empirical turn in theology, this is about to change. Future theology will probably be informed to a greater degree by experiences in the lived.

More than half a century ago, American sociologist Robert King Merton developed the notion of *theories of the middle range.*[24] In my view, this is exactly the kind of theory that theology is lacking: theory on a level not too remote from the empirical reality. According to Merton, his theories of middle range are a type of intermediate theories, between the minor and mega, between daily assumptions on the go and the grander general systematic descriptions:

> We focus on what I have called theories of the middle range: theories that lie between the minor but necessary working hypotheses that evolve in abundance during day-to-day research and the all-inclusive systematic efforts to develop a unified theory that will explain all the observed uniformities of social behavior, social organization and social change. Middle-range theory is principally used in sociology to guide empirical inquiry. It is intermediate to general theories of social systems, which are too remote from particular classes of social behavior, organization, and change to account for what is observed and to those detailed orderly descriptions of particulars that are not generalized at all. Middle-range theory involves abstractions, of course, but they are close enough to observed data to be incorporated in propositions that permit empirical testing.[25]

Part of what makes social science theories intriguing to empirically informed theology relates to Merton's (and others') concept of middle-range theory. What we today refer to as social science theories are often abstracted *from* empirical data, and due to the efforts of multiple researchers, been improved, contested, adjusted, and expanded over and over again. They do not pretend to represent *the* truth, but simply the best possible piece of insight or knowledge available about a specific and limited piece of empirical

23. Markie, "Rationalism vs. Empiricism."
24. Merton, *Social Theory.*
25. Ibid., 39ff.

reality at this moment in time. The level of abstraction is modest, but more importantly: observed data can still be incorporated. The very nature of the middle range theory is to be tested and contested, improved and adjusted, and through an ongoing and cumulative process, research advances. The practice of doing research with the help of middle range theories stands far apart from the practice of many theologians. In theology, the tendency is to either accept or reject someone's theory, not adjust the parts that need improvement.

A second distinction is as little controversial as the first: Although the two are connected, even in the very name "Theology": God is beyond the world of ideas. It is generally accepted that theology is limited to the ideas, the reflection, and the discussion about God—not God himself. Theology will never exceed being our mere words about God. God, even after the incarnation, is for the better part, inaccessible to us. The Kantian distinction between *Ding an sich* and *Ding für mich* is as valid in theology as in any other discipline. In this, university-theology as a reflective practice relates to the humanities, and especially philosophy.

Having said this, it should be uncontroversial to suggest a third distinction: between empirical reality on one hand and God on the other. Even though God has become flesh, and is revealed to us in Scripture and Sacraments, God is not a fully integrated part of lived reality. The Christian hope is that this will one day happen, but till then, our experience of God is as a poor reflection in an unfocused mirror—at its very best.

Given the above, it is now possible to outline three distinctively different, yet in a limited sense, overlapping spheres.[26]

---

26. It is fundamental for theology to insist on some overlap between God and the other two spheres. Creation, incarnation, etc. warrants this. God is the creator of the empirical world, and it was in this world he left human beings in his image to fill it. Through incarnation, God became flesh, took on human nature, and in so doing, expresses the full presence of the human and divine. Other important theological ideas supporting the same are, for instance, the descent of the Holy Spirit, God's work in history, the priesthood of all believers, and the sacraments, etc., through which God is in touch with empirical reality and part of human reflection. The creator's identification with creation is, however, never of a kind that empirical method would be able to read off in a scientific way, and human reflection would never manage to account for it fully.

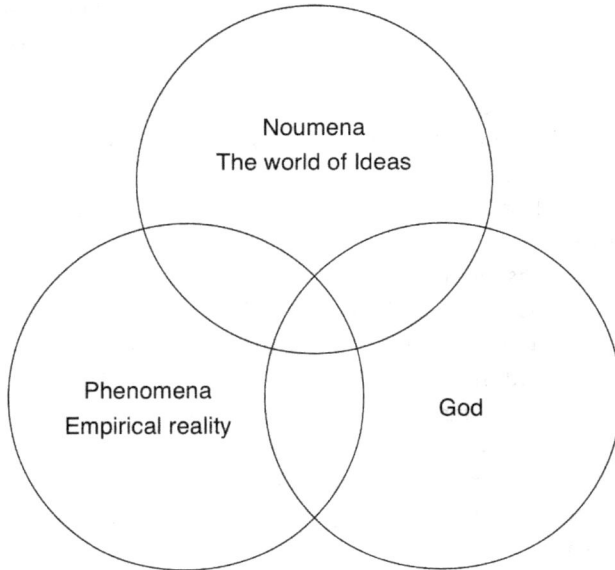

Figure 5: Illustration: Spheres of reality

This is the problem: when a social scientist conducts empirical research, he or she deals with two spheres of reality: a) phenomena in empirical reality and b) theories/noumena in the world of ideas relating to this phenomenon. The middle-range theories are found in the overlapping sector between empirical reality and the world of ideas.

Likewise, in traditional theologizing only two spheres of reality are in play: a) the world of ideas and b) God. Good practice for both the social scientist and the theologian relies heavily on the exercise of humbleness and reverence. The theologian knows that no ideas could ever grasp God and no words could ever express God fully—still he or she is dedicated to trying. Similarly, a social scientist knows that social-empirical realities always represent more than any theory could ever account for—still he or she is dedicated to do so.

Interestingly, when a practical theologian sets out to do empirical research, he or she does not only deal with two, but three, spheres of reality: a) God, b) the world of ideas, and c) empirical reality. Like any social scientist, we are determined to relate phenomena in empirical reality with noumena in the world of ideas. And as practical theologians, we are determined to relate to the theological tradition. This is in many respects challenging, not only methodologically, but at least also here.

At least two conclusions could be drawn from this. Firstly, and most importantly, as practical theologians working with empirical data we should seek to understand the underlying challenges in what we claim to do. Alongside working on actual empirical research projects, we should encourage and take part in discussions concerning our methodological foundations. Questions concerning the ontological status of our objects of study should be a part of that. In practice, this attitude should also be expressed in methodological diligence and humility. Our challenges are far greater than that of traditional social scientific research *and* that of traditional theological research, as we claim to "do the impossible," either this is to introduce theology to empirical reality or this is to introduce God to social scientific methodology. As empirically informed practical theologians, we are bound to theory and data that far from fully encapsulates our unit of analysis. The obvious conclusion is a need for practical theologians to exercise modesty in our use of theory and in theorizing. Consciousness about what our methods can and cannot do is vital, and awareness about the limitations in our theories is key.

Secondly, a possible way forward is to reconsider the use of *typologies* in analysis. These are in many cases already attempts to bridge the world of ideas and the world of empirical phenomena, at times even including God. But because they are fundamentally generated deductively—from above—they tend to overlook the dynamics of the lived and are inclined to order empirical reality too tidily. One way forward is to stop treating typologies the way we treat doctrines, and start approaching them as intermediate propositions, as starting points for further critical research. This is the very modus operandi of social scientific research. The way a theory here is treated as the best available expression of what is known now, and only that, is exemplary. This attitude invites further empirical investigation, building on the achievements of others. There really is no need for another journal article suggesting that for, instance, Niebuhr's typology on Christ and culture has weak points and thereby should be rejected altogether. The identification of a weakness in a typology should instead be regarded as a starting point for further improvement of that very theory. A better way forward, therefore, would be to expand, combine, and adjust already existing typologies with both the measures of theological reasoning and empirical research.

In this chapter, I set out to identify and clarify the shortage of useful theory. Ironically, I have ended up with suggesting two improvements, not to theory, but to research practice—which underlines how intertwined these things are. Keeping theology at a distance from empirical reality, or keeping social scientific method apart from theology, is simply no alternative in the future. An empirically informed form of practical theology is not the easy way forward; it is just a necessary one.

5

Faithful Participation—Engagement and Transformation in Ethnographic Ecclesiology

Jonas Ideström

INTRODUCTION

We are sitting on the floor in the basement of a small hotel in a Saami village close to the mountains in the west of Sweden. The basement has been arranged into a room for prayer, with candles and an altar. At the altar rests pieces of bread and a cup crafted by a Saami artist out of horn. We had been eating a dinner in the dining hall, a way of ending a research project that I have conducted in two northern rural parishes in the Church of Sweden (CofS). The report from the project had been published and presented at a conference the previous day. After finishing the dessert they took us downstairs, where, without my knowledge, two of them have arranged the basement for celebrating the Eucharist. Now I'm sitting with most of the participants from the two reference groups that have played important roles in the research process. One of the participants asks me to lead the celebration of the Eucharist. I am surprised and moved. I'm a researcher and an ordained minister in CofS. I quickly decide to accept the invitation, and we share the bread and wine. After the short and somewhat improvised liturgy, one of them, we can call her Mary, tells me that the cup is a gift to me. "When you look at it you will remember us." Today the cup, the inside of which has been stained red by the wine, is standing next to an icon with the face of Christ in my family's living room.

The Aim of This Chapter

My experiences of ecclesiological field studies in northern Sweden is my point of departure for reflections on the relationship between researcher and research field—between research practices and the practices of the field. How do we in ethnographic theology or ecclesiology understand these relationships? How can we in, fruitful ways, perceive the creation of knowledge in relation to ecclesiological aspects of the research process? Trying to give a response to these questions I argue for a relationship shaped by *faithful participation* and a research process characterized by *participation, engagement,* and *transformation.*

CHURCH OF SWEDEN IN NORTHERN RURAL SWEDEN— A CASE

Between 2012 and 2014 I conducted a research project on CofS in rural areas in Northern Sweden.[1] The purpose of the project was to explore, from a theological perspective, how CofS appears in rural areas. The project involved field studies in two parishes in the provinces of Lapland and Jämtland. The research approach could be characterized as ethnographic ecclesiology with components of action research. The aim was not only to deepen and broaden the understanding of the identity and role of the Church in Sweden in rural areas but also to contribute to the pastoral theological reflections in these particular parishes. In each parish a reference group was put together, and these groups played important roles in the research process and the overall conversational approach.

The groups consisted of the vicars, one more church employee, two chairpersons from the parish board, and two persons somehow involved in the life of the parish. I met with each group at three occasions. At our first meeting I asked them to reflect on what had shaped the life of the community and the parish, from both a long and short historical perspective. Based on what came out of the conversation we also formulated potential challenges for the church and questions they would like the project to examine. At our second meeting we had a conversation based on a dialogue with a Gospel narrative—focusing on questions of how the local context and its

---

1. The project and its results are presented in Ideström, *Spåren.*

history relates to the narrative. At our final meeting we read and interpreted data from the field studies that I had compiled.[2]

One of the reference groups contained Mary, mentioned above, who had clearly spent time thinking about her role and participating in the life of the local parish. In one of our conversations, she has described herself as a person in the borderlands. She is a member of CofS and previously, during a brief period, worked part time with children for the parish. Today she's not very active in the organized life of the parish. Yet she is both engaged and involved in issues concerning the local community.

During the time of the project I had several conversations with Mary. She made it clear that the meetings with the reference group created an important space for her to deal with issues of faith and relations to the church. Because of this, she conveyed that participating in the research project affected her faith and relationship to the church.

CHALLENGES AND QUESTIONS

Already this initial snapshot points to a conclusion that can be drawn both from my experiences in the field and from something that I will elaborate on further in this chapter. Looking back at the research process I see that the research practices clearly are mixed up and entangled in social and personal processes affecting faith and ecclesial imaginations in the local parish life. The academic process of generating knowledge is intertwined with ecclesial processes in the lives of the churches and communities where research is conducted.

In this particular case the meetings with the reference group have also resulted in deepened relations between all who participated. That, in turn, created a space where it was possible, through our conversations, to interpret and articulate reflections on the life of the church, which has contributed to a better understanding of the identity and mission of the parish. This has generated important knowledge for the academic research *and* affected the ecclesial imaginaries of all the participants (including myself,

2. After the project was finished and the results published, we arranged conferences in the two parishes. The conference in the diocese of Luleå was arranged as a video conference where about 100 people from eighteen different parishes participated. Representatives from the two reference groups also visited each other's parishes during the conferences. It was after the second conference, in the diocese of Härnösand, that we ate the dinner at the hotel and celebrated the Eucharist in the basement. The two reference groups are interesting examples of dynamics of a research process shaped by participation, engagement, and transformation. They will, therefore, work as a sort of case in this chapter. I focus on one of the participants in the reference group in the diocese of Härnösand, the woman referred to as Mary who had taken the initiative to celebrate the Eucharist together.

the researcher). These intertwined processes have then also involved expansions and transformations in the roles we play as researcher and informants. For instance, a transformation was manifested in the invitation to me to celebrate the Eucharist with them.

These experiences have challenged me to reflect on how I understand my relationship, as researcher, with the field and those subjects with whom I interact. That in turn raises questions on what the explicit or implicit academic ideals are that has shaped my understanding. *How should researchers doing ethnographic research relate to the field? How should the academic practices relate to the practices of the field?* It is generally accepted within the social sciences, that the researcher should try to uphold neutrality and a certain distance in relation to the object of study. That is: the academic research practices should not be mixed up with the practices of the field. Within academic disciplines using ethnographic methods there are of course deep and well-documented understandings and reflections concerning the interaction of the researcher with the field questioning various forms of positivistic approaches. But, as the argument below will show, even within these disciplines there are strong and widespread ideals that the researcher, though using participation as a method, should be able to return to a neutral position unchanged by the participation. It is by holding the research practices distinct from the practices of the field that the researcher can gain knowledge that the informants cannot. In this chapter I want to challenge and problematize such an understanding by engaging in a conversation with theologians and sociologists that can help me interpret my experiences from the field studies in northern rural Sweden. But before I do that, let me turn to another meal, the one celebrated on the way to Emmaus with the risen Lord and two disciples, as told by Luke.

FAITHFUL PARTICIPATION—VOICES FROM SCRIPTURE

As I have argued elsewhere, based on the work of Gordon Lathrop, the Gospel can (and often should) work as a constructive conversation partner in ecclesiological research.[3] Luke's witness of the disciples on their way to Emmaus can contribute with important theological motives to the argument I make here. By introducing these theological voices at such an early stage, I want to make the point that theology is not a perspective or a normative voice that can be added to a practical ecclesiological research process at a certain point. Rather, the whole process is theological in all its stages and dimensions. But saying that I am not claiming that theology can offer a privileged perspective or that theology should be understood as a singu-

---

3. Ideström, "In Dialogue."

lar a unified voice. As Tone Stangeland Kaufman convincingly argues, it is necessary in ethnographic theological research to uphold ongoing reflections on *which* theological voices are allowed into the process and *what* roles they are allowed to play.[4] In her argument she makes a distinction between *normativity from within* and *normativity from the outside*. When I allow the gospel narrative to contribute with theological motives I understand it as a normativity from within, since the understanding of Gospel narratives as normative texts is undisputed in the field that I study.[5] There are three perspectives I focus on in Luke's narrative: the disciples do not recognize Jesus and they need to get to know him anew; it is through participation and engagement that they recognize him; the narrative is one of several examples in the Gospels of Jesus' faithful participation.

In two of his well-known paintings Caravaggio (1571–1610) captures the very moment when the two disciples suddenly recognize the risen Lord in the man who they have walked and talked with on their way to Emmaus. When he breaks the bread they recognize him. A striking feature in the few narratives in the Gospels set between Jesus' resurrection and ascension is that people do not recognize him. And as Rowan Williams puts it: "he is not what they have thought Him to be, and thus they must 'learn to know' Him afresh, from the beginning."[6] The disciples who knew Jesus well now need to get to know him anew: through talking about what has happened, interpreting it in relation to scripture, and breaking the bread together.

With Williams I would argue that these narratives of disciples having to get to know Jesus anew are ecclesiologically crucial. They say something fundamental about the relationship between Christ and his church and therefore about the very ontology of that which we name church. Church is not a stable and well-defined community or space where Jesus Christ is contained. Nor does the church own its own body. Rather, Jesus Christ needs to be known anew by those who are limbs in the body of Christ.

Caravaggio helps us to see the relationality, performativity, materiality, and situatedness of the encounter with the risen Lord. He also illuminates how a central element of surprise is woven into the very life of the church— an element that, as Paul Fiddes reminds us, should also shape theological and ecclesiological research. Since all is done within the life of God we should expect to be surprised.[7]

4. Kaufman, "From the Outside."

5. See ibid.

6. Williams, *Resurrection*, 75.

7. "The biblical notion of God's promise is not a tight, enclosed sequence of prediction and outcome, but has scope for divine and human freedom in bringing about something genuinely new in fulfillment, something surprising." Fiddes, "Ecclesiology," 33.

The second perspective in the narrative that has relevance in a conversation on ethnographic theological research is the fact that it is through conversation, participation, and engagement that the disciples get to know Jesus anew.

Finally, the Gospel narratives, as a whole, tell us of Jesus' faithful participation in the life of this world and in God. This nuanced and thick understanding of participation is an important influence when reflecting on the work of doing ecclesiology in various forms. Jesus performs miracles "but never as a substitute for the hard material work of changing how people see God—never as a substitute for the bodily cost of love, which reaches its climax on the cross."[8]

With my experiences from field studies in CofS and the theological motives from the Gospel narrative, I now engage in a conversation with other scholars on participation, engagement, and transformation in ethnographic ecclesiological research.

PARTICIPATION

Arguing that participation is necessary for a researcher in order to understand a social setting or phenomenon is of course nothing particular for ethnographic ecclesiology. Rather it is common sense within disciplines such as ethnography and anthropology. In order to understand social realities, the argument goes, it is necessary to observe and experience them from within. Therefore, ethnomethodologies emphasize the importance of digging deep over a longer period of time using methods such as participatory observations and open-ended interviews. Approaches where participation is key also challenge a separation between the processes of discovery and the process of justification in research. They are rather seen as "part of a single process."[9]

Anthropologist Michael Burawoy has written on how participation is necessary in a process of improving theory through case studies. He argues for a constructive understanding of the relationship between a single case and generalizing theories of the phenomenon being studied. In what he defines as an extended case study, "the social situation is viewed as an anomaly."[10] The single case makes it possible to develop and improve a theory by pointing to anomalies in relation to the theory. Such an improvement is only possible through participation in the life-world under investigation. "It is not a matter of applying the knowledge of the expert but of

8. Williams, *Silence*, 90.

9. Burawoy, *Ethnography*, 8.

10. Ibid., 9.

the observer joining the participants in a joint movement of analysis and action."[11] Burawoy also makes clear that when he talks about theories it is not restricted to those developed through academic research.

> [A]ll of us have social theories that inform the way we orga-
> nize and pursue our lives. Participant observers are particularly
> aware of lay theories, or commonsense knowledge, and this can
> always provide a point of departure for reconstruction.[12]

Using Burawoy's reflections it is possible to view the participatory element in ethnographic ecclesiology as a way of engaging in a process of challenging and developing a wide range of theories concerning church and theology, within both the life of church and that of the academy. In my own research, I have used concepts such as *ecclesial imagination* (Taylor, Bass, and Dykstra) and *expressive ecclesiology* (Afdal) to define various forms of theories being used and communicated in the field.[13] The conversations I led with the reference groups can be understood as occasions aimed at both discerning such theories and engaging in a process of challenging and reconstructing them. Elsewhere I have shown how the actual situation of a conversation with the reference group, with all its components (actors) in time and space, contribute to the particular expressive ecclesiologies that come out of the conversation.[14] In all of this, participation is key.

To these initial epistemological dimensions of participation I now want to add one that draws us into questions of ontology.

A Relational Ontology

French sociologist and philosopher Bruno Latour has, within what is often defined as Actor-Network Theory, suggested an understanding of "the social" that is fundamentally relational. According to Latour, the task of empirical sociology is not to explain the empirical world by referring to various theories of the social. Rather it is to trace and analyze what this phenomenon, known as the social, is actually made of.[15]

According to Latour the actor is not a stable entity whose intentions can be used as an explanatory cause for an action. The task of the researcher, then, is to trace how the actions of the actor are connected with other actors and their actions. It is a relational ontology. Every actor or action

---

11. Ibid., 283.
12. Ibid., 26.
13. Ideström, "Implicit Ecclesiology."
14. Ideström, "It is That Loving Gaze."
15. Latour, *Reassembling*, 11–12.

presupposes a thick fabric of connections and relations. According to Latour this makes participation necessary in empirical sociology. He argues that only by following the actors and participating in the situations and settings where they communicate and where connections are made is it possible to gain knowledge of what makes up the social.[16] He encourages the researcher to stay on the ground and not to be too quick to step back and add a third dimension by imposing a theory from the outside: the work of adding this third dimension of understanding to the complex webs of interactions is already being done by the participants themselves.

Latour's relational ontology adds important dimensions to understanding the role of participation in ethnographic ecclesiological research. But it also points beyond participation to questions of engagement, to which I now turn.

ENGAGEMENT

As Natalie Wigg-Stevenson points out, in a discussion on the reflexive character of ethnographic theology, it is common to separate a scientific habitus from that of the life world of the field in sociological ethnography. She quotes Pierre Bourdieu who argues that the sociological ethnographer needs to "prioritize their scientific or academic habitus over any bodily wisdom they may gain in and of their field."[17] The academic practice needs to be distinct from the practices of the field. This also goes for Burawoy who, on the one hand, argues for participation, as we have seen above, but on the other underscores that the researcher should participate by *observing*. The researcher needs to remain an observer to be able to see and understand things that the participants themselves cannot see.[18]

Wigg-Stevenson argues that here is an important difference between sociological and theological ethnographic work. The theologian doing fieldwork "cannot understand their subject position as being external to the practices they engage . . . the theologian already embodies, to varying degrees at least, aspects of the wisdom that her field of study bears."[19] In Wigg-

16. Latour, *Reassembling*, 132. An important point in ANT is that actors can be humans as well as nonhumans.

17. Wigg-Stevenson, "Reflexive," 12.

18. Burawoy, *Ethnography*, 284. Burawoy writes, "As observers [the scientist] who also stand outside the lifeworlds they study, scientists can gain insight into the properties of the system world, which integrates the intended and unintended consequences of instrumental action into relatively autonomous institutions. Indeed, these can be understood only from the standpoint of the observer."

19. Wigg-Stevenson "Reflexive," 4. In her argument she is referring to Kathryn Tanner.

Stevenson's argument the focus is on the multiple roles of the researcher; in her case that of a researcher, a minister, and a friend. And it is in dealing with these roles that the reflexive character of the theologian conducting fieldwork becomes so central.[20]

To add further nuances and depth to the understanding of participation and engagement in ethnographic ecclesiological research I now turn to English theologian Paul Fiddes. He has, from a trinitarian and sacramental understanding of reality, engaged in conversations on the themes of participation, observation, and engagement in ethnographic theological research.

According to Fiddes a Trinitarian understanding of reality seems to suggest an ontology where "[w]e need to get beyond subject-object thinking to a kind of thinking characterized by engagement and participation."[21]

Paul Fiddes challenges the vocabulary used by Bourdieu and Burawoy when he proposes a somewhat modified model for theological empirical research in relation to traditional models for academic research. In the latter *observation* is used as a term to distinguish what the researcher does when he or she tests theories or concepts in relation to concrete expressions of a social phenomenon. In Fiddes's modified model the term "observation" is substituted with "engagement." His change of vocabulary and model presupposes belief in divine revelation.

> God is not an object like other objects in the world and so cannot be observed, but this does not mean that all we have to go on is the data of human religious experience. Theology, I suggest, presumes that we live in the presence of a self-revealing God.[22]

So we cannot observe God, but we can, according to Fiddes, engage ourselves in God—participate in the relations we can describe as Father, Son, and Spirit. "This is the greatest challenge to the assumption of the Enlightenment that human beings are the great subjects of the world, and that

---

20. There are parallels between what Wigg-Stevenson describes and what I faced in the current example—but there are also important differences. In her case she, in an explicit way, uses her role as a minister in her research process. It is by being a minister who teaches theology in a congregation that she does her fieldwork. She takes on a role given by the congregation. She is a representative of the congregation who upholds and facilitates an ecclesial practice. In my case I am there as a researcher. I have informed people I meet that I am also an ordained minister in CofS. I do participate in ecclesial practices of the parish but not as a representative of the parish. But, as I will expand on later in the paper, it also became clear during the research process that the research practices also, to some extent, became ecclesial practices. They affected the social life of the parish and the life of the participants.

21. Fiddes, "Ecclesiology," 26.

22. Ibid., 25.

the remainder of nature is an object to be mastered and controlled."[23] And this then means that we need to move beyond this dichotomic thinking to a thinking characterized by engagement and participation.

Taking the theological rationale of Christian tradition seriously involves, according to Fiddes, seeing the participatory character of theological language. Theological talk of God is not primarily an observational language but one that draws humans into the relations of the triune God—and therefore a language that has its roots in pastoral settings. Therefore, involving theological dimensions in ethnographic research on churches necessarily also involves aspects of engagement. And from that it follows that it is not possible to uphold a separation between the scientific habitus and that of the field—which, of course, is not the same thing as saying that no distinctions can be made. But the important point is that the process of creating knowledge is shaped by engagement in a way that makes it impossible for the researcher to retreat back to a position outside of and unaffected by the process of engagement.

Before moving on I want to make one more reflection concerning the relationship between sociological and ethnographic ethnography. At this point it might seem natural to settle for an argument that explains the differences between a theological and a sociological approach by pointing to the particular character of theology as a field where academics and practitioners are engaged in the same conversation. But both Fiddes and Latour seem to resist making such a settlement too easily.

As Wigg-Stevenson argues, the theological dimensions of an ethnographic study of a church clearly have effects on the role of the researcher and how he or she relates to the two habitus. But with that being said it is important to highlight that there are other factors that shape the understanding of the role of the researcher. Both Fiddes's and Latour's arguments can be read as a challenge of, what they describe as, a modern dualistic separation between a scientific habitus and that of the life worlds studied. They both question an understanding of subject-object relations that goes beyond that of a theologian doing ecclesiological research. Fiddes' argument, though theological, is not limited to a theological sphere or field. He makes the rather significant point, based on the sacramental understanding of reality, that such spheres cannot be upheld. In a similar way, Latour's relational ontology and materially heterogeneous understanding of the social challenges clear separations between theology and sociology. This point will be emphasized further below.

---

23. Ibid., 26.

With this said I now want to go further in exploring what engagement, from an ecclesiological perspective, might entail in relation to transformation.

TRANSFORMATION

This focus on engagement as a significant aspect of a faithful participation points to questions of transformation. How can one understand the role of the researcher and the research practices in relation to a process of generating knowledge, which at the same time contributes to social transformation? First of all I want to make clear that a blurring of the differences between the two habitus does not per definition lead to a position where the researcher and the research practices lose their identities and roles—their possibilities of contributing with something particular and important to the process of creating new knowledge. Engaging in a conversation in a common space does not mean that you have to give up your own voice. But, in my case, the researcher also contributes with more than being just one voice among many. Through the research practices, led by the researcher, possible spaces for conversations and interpretations are created in the ecclesial life world where new knowledge can be articulated.

And as various forms of action research can show, new ways of articulating and theoretically describing the reality one is engaged in can lead to transformation of practices.[24] In that sense, the spaces created by the research process can contribute with transformation at both a reflective and a practical level.

Processes of Ordering

In making sense of these processes of transformation, English sociologist John Law is helpful. In regards to theory, he is moving in landscapes similar to the those of Latour. In his book *Organizing Modernity* he shares the complex process of doing fieldwork in a research laboratory studying social ordering. Law rejects any attempt by the researcher to step outside of the various modes of ordering in the field.

> We [the researchers] are caught up in ordering too. When we write about ordering there is no question of standing apart and observing from a distance. We're participating in ordering too. We're unavoidably involved in the modern reflexive and self-reflexive project of monitoring, sensemaking and control. But since we participate in this project, we're also, and necessarily,

24. See eg., Cameron et al., *Talking About God.*

caught up in its uncertainty, its incompleteness, its plurality, a sense of fragmentation.[25]

From a sociological perspective Law here clearly rejects the possibilities of upholding the separations between a scientific habitus and that of the field. The researcher is, to a large extent, part of the same project of making sense and creating order as the practitioners. Echoing ANT he argues that the social is:

> a set of processes, of transformations. These are moving, acting, interacting. They are generating themselves. Perhaps we can impute patterns in these movements. But here's the trick, the crucial and most difficult move that we need to make. We need to say that the patterns, the channels down which they flow, are not different in kind from whatever it is that is channeled by them. So the image that we have to discard is that of a social oil refinery. Society is not a lot of social products moving round in structural pipes and containers that were put in place beforehand. Instead, the social world is this remarkable emergent phenomenon: in its processes it shapes its own flows. Movement and the organization of movement are not different.[26]

This way of understanding "the social" is also relevant in ecclesiology, and as mentioned, it communicates rather well with theological models that draw on a fundamentally relational and participatory understanding of revelation and Christian tradition. The researcher engaged in field work, whether she is a sociologist or a theologian, participates and is engaged in a process of ordering that cannot, in any distinct way, be separated from the processes of social ordering going on in the field. Thus, it seems logical that the research practices in ethnographic ecclesiology also, to some extent, should be understood as ecclesial practices—spaces where processes of social and ecclesial ordering take place.

Social Ordering and Church as the Body of Christ

Ecclesial and theological imaginations, or expressive ecclesiologies, are reflective processes of ordering. In an ecclesiological landscape they, in one way or another, involve reflections on the relationship between the embodiment of church and Christ. The identity of the church cannot be understood in a relevant manner without relating it to the identity of Christ. The Body of Christ metaphor reminds us of this analogy between the church and

25. Law, *Organizing*, 2.
26. Ibid., 16.

Christ. But just as there is a plurality of processes generating meaning out of data in a laboratory, so it is in a church concerning self-understandings on its identity in relation to Christ. There's not one common and shared understanding of the relationship between Christ and the church. This is an important point made by Fiddes, grounded in a Trinitarian understanding of reality in which all that is exists within the divine life of God.

> If God makes room in the divine life for all created things, then ecclesiology will need to reflect on living in tension between several expressions of the body of Christ. In the New Testament the phrase "body of Christ" has a threefold reference—to the glorious resurrection body of Christ (who is to be identified with the earthly Jesus of Nazareth), to the church, and to the Eucharistic bread in which the community shares. But developing the witness of Scripture, in line with our Trinitarian vision, we will want to speak of the embodiment of Christ in the world beyond the walls of the church. . . . Different spatial dimensions of the body of Christ—incarnate, Eucharistic, ecclesial, and secular—are thus related but not simply identical. We may say that the human Jesus, in his body, offered an obedient response to God his Father that was exactly the same as the movement of responsive love within God's life that we call the eternal Son.[27]

As Fiddes shows, there is not a simple or given identity between the concrete church and Christ's body. This is a similar point to the one made by Williams in relation to the resurrection narratives in the Gospels. The church does not own Christ. Christ and the knowledge of Christ are not contained within the church. Rather church is here imagined as a place, space, or situation where people, by participating and engaging, are drawn into the relationships of the Triune God and thereby also, over and over again, into getting to know Christ in new ways. In that sense, transformation is a fundamental aspect of the eschatological identity of the church, and doing theological and ecclesiological fieldwork in churches means participating in the processes of such transformation.

> Different bodies in the world—the individual bodily form of Jesus Christ; the sacraments of bread, wine, and water; the Eucharistic community; groups in society; and all the variety of matter in nature—are then all related to a common space. The space they occupy in God is not a kind of container, but a reality characterized by relationships, and in this way Christ can be

---

27. Fiddes, "Ethnography," 31.

embodied in all of them; his form can be recognized in them and in all of them he can take flesh.[28]

In line with how Law understands the social, Fiddes concludes that the ontology of the social we name church should be understood as relational. Social spaces and organizations are not containers filled with people and relations that exist on their own. Space is created through relations and therefore the relations generated through the researcher doing fieldwork necessarily participate in the making of social spaces and imaginations that shape and transform the church being studied.

Transformation and the Framing of the Field

These perspectives open up for yet more significant ecclesiological questions concerning the framing of the research field. The plurality and relational character of a particular embodiment of church is not only a matter of internal processes. As Fiddes's reflections on the various expressions of the Body of Christ indicates, it also opens up for processes external to what might be defined as church, congregation, or parish. The processes of ordering are also processes ordering the very understanding of who, what, and where the church is. The relational ontologies suggested by Fiddes, Latour, and Law offer a great challenge to ethnographic approaches where there is a strong call to particularity. It is, of course, an important task of ecclesiological research to study and make sense of ecclesial imaginaries that frame the church in space and time: even when such imaginaries are shaped by what could be defined as various forms of identity politics—making the very issue of defining an identity central. In relation to such tendencies, an ethnographic research approach shaped by, for instance, the theological perspectives of Fiddes, can contribute with important perspectives and data into the processes of theological social ordering in local churches. And such contribution can of course in turn lead to transformation in different ways.

In the research project I conducted I found the work of Latour and Law inspiring and creative. The relational and materially heterogeneous relational understanding of what the social actually is made of led me to follow some of the traces left by interactions between actors in a certain activity or situation. And they led me to other actors, other places, and other times. By going there I gained perspectives and knowledge about the initial activity or situation that I could bring back to the conversations in

---

28. Ibid., 32.

the reference groups—and by doing so influence conversations on the very self-understanding of the community.[29]

To focus on how self-understandings and identity-shaping imagery and experiences are mediated and translated through various objects adds a dimension to the understanding and mapping of the community that is theologically significant. What is actually participating in the events that shape our experiences? Adding these dimensions can assist in the mapping of how the community is intertwined with other actors. But this mapping and analyzing is not a way of distancing myself from the life of the community. I am not retreating back to a neutral position in order to contribute with these perspectives. Such distance adds nothing of importance to my possibilities of studying and understanding a community. The only distance that really matters is that between the understanding of the study object before and after the study.[30]

FAITHFUL PARTICIPATION—RETURNING TO THE REFERENCE GROUP AND MARY

Let us now return to the reference group in the diocese of Härnösand and Mary. As I look back at the research process with a particular focus on the group and Mary, I see that the above reflections lend important perspectives that shed light on what transpired. In my transcriptions and in the final version of the book presenting the results from the project, I see examples of how Mary contributes with important theological and ecclesiological reflections to the research process. Reflections that, as she confirms, are examples of an expansion and transformation of her own ecclesial imaginary.

In the third and final meeting with the reference group, the participants had read a document in which I had put together pieces of data that I had collected during the field studies. One topic that came up was the low attendance at Sunday worship and a common focus on numbers when judging whether the parish is successful or not. In the ensuing conversation, Mary said, with a clear aim at employees in the parish, that they must not be reproachful.

> It's not that worship is yet another activity. For me, who is a bit more "privately-churchy" (privatkyrklig), the fact that people

---

29. Another aspect has to do with the body, the subjectivity of the researcher, and the research process. Looking at this from an ANT perspective one could raise questions of what other artifacts and components participate in the act of interpreting the situations that the researcher also participates in (pens, notebooks, glasses, language, etc.). See Latour, "How to Talk."

30. Ibid., 219.

meet is sacred. It is important for me to know that they meet.
I believe that there are things that we cannot grasp or measure
and to me those things are important. And I believe it is important to others as well, even though they don't show up.

She says that she doesn't want to put any more burdens on the employees but make them realize that the time and energy they put on worship is
important, even if only a handful turn up.

At another occasion in the conversations she tells us how actions of the
vicar can be important to her and her faith.

I don't think I could survive if I did not believe that there was a
sense of magic in life, the magic of life—that things can change,
that things can happen and that you can be amazed. When do I
get amazed in relation to church? Maybe it's not necessary with
exceptional things to happen. It could be that NN [the vicar]
comes on his bike to visit someone in the village who I did not
think of as anyone who needed a visit.

From the conversations with the reference group I know that this is
not a way for Mary to idealize the vicar or to say that she is impressed by his
competence. It is his action in relation to the fact that he is the vicar that is
important to her. Maybe one could describe it as if the actions of the vicar
have a sacramental dimension. They embody and point to something that
goes beyond the action itself.[31]

A similar perspective was articulated by another participant in the reference group. At our last meeting, Arne [as I call him here] said that he felt
a need to tell us about the situation of the Saami people. According to him,
he and others often experienced a derogatory attitude from government
authorities. "They treat us as if we have less value than others." He told us of
younger Saami men committing suicide due to feelings of great frustration.
In his reflections he was also very clear on what he saw as a responsibility of the church to side with those oppressed. Eventually his reflections
ended up in perspectives emphasizing that Christian faith should focus on

---

31. See Fiddes, *Participating*, 294–95. He argues for the sacramental character of
the ministry of pastors and priests. He writes, "Like other professional careers—doctors, nurses, social workers—in the Christian ministry there is a blurring of the line
between person and function, between being and doing. The sort of person that any
pastor seems to be will affect the way that she or he will be able to help others. . . . They
point beyond themselves to some value, such as concern for health and welfare, or
the benefits of education, and they are expected to embody these values in their lives.
Christian pastors (of all kind) are therefore sacraments of the transcendent grace of
love and forgiveness, and the kind of persons they are will be bound up with the things
they do. They are 'living symbols' of the sacrificial and persuasive love of Christ."

possibilities of reconciliation, and he told us of a time when the vicar in the parish had participated in work with reindeer in the Saami village. "He was the first vicar ever to come to us and participated in that work. We really appreciate that and people asked me who he was. And I told them that 'he is *mijjen hearra*—it's our priest!'"

The pride is clearly embodied in the way Arne articulates these words. The experiences shared by Arne became important components in the conversations with the reference group and contributed to the ecclesial imaginaries taking shape. For some of the participants in the reference group it also meant that they, to a larger extent than earlier, got involved in the life worlds of the Saami people in the parish. It also became clear to me that the experiences shared by Arne resonated with experiences that Mary had. She told us, with a clear tone of anger, of a lecture given by a college teacher. According to Mary, he had told them about a young and talented girl living in a village who "threw her talent away by staying in the village and not moving to a town or a city." Mary was offended. In her eyes the man gave voice to, and confirmed, a derogatory attitude toward people living in rural areas.

These experiences of rural areas and the life of Saami people as somehow peripheral to urban life—a strong norm in Swedish society—clearly shaped the ecclesial imaginaries in our conversations. The church and its presence through buildings, social practices, and people were understood as signs of faithfulness.

And as I return to the Eucharistic celebration in the basement in the hotel I see how these imaginaries are embodied both in the liturgy and the way the room was decorated by Mary and Arne. A long blue cloth incorporated the altar with the rest of the room, like a stream of water pouring from the altar down on the floor. On the altar, the two had set branches, candles, reindeer horn, and the cup made by a Saami artist.

Altogether the liturgy embodied important dimensions of the ecclesial imaginaries of our conversations in the reference group. In that sense it was a form of illustration. But it was also a performative practice that transformed the reference group into an ecclesial body, limbs in the body of Christ, at this particular place. And by asking me to take the role as celebrant they also engaged me in a way that expanded and transformed my role as a researcher.

At the same time the celebration of the Eucharistic liturgy also worked as a ritualization of ending the project and leaving my engagement with the parish and the reference group. And this is a fundamental and crucial aspect of a researcher's engagement with the practices of the field—it is limited in time. My engagement is based on an agreement that I only participate in the life of the parish during a limited period of time. And such an agreement also makes it clear that there is a fundamental difference between me and the participants in the local church. I am there, participating and engaging in the life of the parish, but trying to participate faithfully also means being true to the role I have and have been given in relation to the field.

FAITHFUL PARTICIPATION—AS A WALK TO EMMAUS

It is time to sum up my argument for an ecclesiological research approach shaped by faithful participation and engagement, which deliberately aims at transformation. I do that by returning to Luke's witness of the disciples on their way to Emmaus.

Doing ethnographic ecclesiology, in the manner I am suggesting here, means participating and being engaged in a movement. Like the disciples in the narrative, I (as a researcher) come from somewhere and am on my way somewhere. My participation and engagement in the field is shaped by motion. Through the research process I am also relating to others, listening, participating in conversations, and visiting new places and spaces. To a significant degree this movement is open ended; it has no premature closure or unification. The process involves transformation in relation to all dimensions of the research process, and therefore it cannot offer an unchanged place or position outside of the practices of the field to which the researcher can retreat. That, of course, does not mean that the movement of the researcher is simply by chance. There are plenty of important decisions and choices to be made by the researcher on the way that presupposes an ongoing scholarly and spiritual reflection. Fostering an attitude toward the field by engaging in an ongoing dialogue with other scholars and narratives of Scripture and Christian tradition might make us dare to be surprised or walk in ways that might make us feel lost. The narratives of Scripture can remind us that we are not always in control of where life and research takes us, but we are never outside the reach of God. And actually, it is by moving into what might even feel like alien territory that we can be surprised and contribute with important insights and perspectives to the churches that we study and with which we interact.

Such an attitude embodies something of God's faithfulness made visible in Jesus from Nazareth. And such faithfulness not only allows us to be surprised. It also makes us, as researchers, and the research practices, signs of the inherent value of the communities where we do research. Where we listen, engage in conversation, and participate in social practices, we become living symbols who testify that those places are not peripheral in God's eyes. So being faithful also literally means *faith*ful. It is an act and embodiment of faith in the life-giving and liberating movements of the triune God in the world. Or to borrow the words of Rowan Williams:

> [T]here is the way in which a Christian church can be a sign of fidelity, of a pledged body, in a community from which so much has fled or drained away . . . without much to show in the way of religion or morals or culture to interest the person looking for stimulus . . . the church remains pledged; its pastors and people and building speaking of a God who is not bored or disillusioned by that he has made—and so they speak of the personal possibilities for everyone in such a situation.[32]

And in this task the researcher has an important vocation to explore the richness of the empirical world in which the church is embodied and in and through that vocation to also be a sign of God's faithfulness.

32. Williams, *Silence*, 93.

6

Reflexivity—A Relational and Prophetic Practice

Eileen R. Campbell-Reed

AN UNEXPECTED EMAIL

One autumn day a few years ago, I was preparing the final manuscript for my first academic book when I received an email from one of the main participants in my study of Baptist clergywomen.[1] She was responding to a prompt from me, but her message really pulled me up short and gave me a sinking feeling in my gut.[2] I had written her in the summer, and then I failed to send a timely follow-up amid all the other follow-up calls and emails to other women in my study. Here is what Corey's email said:

> When you sent the email in June I started reading the chapter but found it very out of place to my present life. I thought you would email me again (as you indicated) but you did not, so I assumed, since the July deadline had come and gone, that you would simply leave this chapter out of the book. I had not said yes to publication.

---

1. Campbell-Reed, *Anatomy*. The study had oversight from Institutional Review Boards at Vanderbilt University and Luther Seminary.

2. Kerdeman, "Self-Understanding," 154. Kerdeman observes that being "pulled up short" is a "deep recognition [which] confronts the fundamental limits of what human beings know and can do."

When I read the email there was a lot of internal cursing and disbelief and berating myself for dropping the ball. Yet I also continued to regulate my emotions because I knew I needed to remain steady and positive if I was to avoid pushing Corey into a defensive place or losing her partnership in the book project. Over the next several weeks, I had to work to keep putting my best foot forward, to respond in timely but non-anxious ways, and to make a strong case for her story remaining in the book. At each step I had to listen carefully to her concerns and respond to them promptly and thoroughly. I needed and wanted her chapter in the book, but more importantly I wanted to honor her experience and tell the story in a way she could fully recognize her experience without giving away her identity.[3] The task was further complicated by the fact she was undergoing a family crisis in the weeks when we were exchanging emails and phone calls. One of the reasons I wanted and needed to include her overall story, besides having done the hard work of putting it together, was that several features of her story were uniquely compelling for the arguments of the book. Yet my discussion of those aspects of her story was creating feelings of discomfort for Corey.[4]

A number of conversations, negotiations, and relational energy went into the weeks that followed the email above. The result was that the chapter was revised in small but important ways to help Corey reach a comfort level, and the chapter was published as part of the book. This essay explores some of the foibles and missteps I made as a researcher, and how I worked to recover, so that together with study participants I could move the book forward. The difficulties I encountered are common and yet rarely addressed in a forthright and transparent way in the literature about ethnographic writing or practical theology. What is usually available is a finished project in cleanly edited and smoothed out form. Sometimes a "methodological essay" comes in an appendix, but it rarely addresses the messy relational pathway that researchers must traverse.[5]

---

3. Balancing transparency and confidentiality in writing up qualitative research remains a challenge. One key to the dilemma is to aim for "thick description," a method credited to Clifford Geertz. See Geertz, *Interpretation*. Qualitative researchers and practical theologians alike advocate for "thick description." See, for example, Browning, *Fundamental*, 107; Miller-McLemore, "Living Human Web," 24; Rubin and Rubin, *Qualitative Interviewing*, chapter 11; Mason, *Qualitative Researching*, chapter 9.

4. The exact character of those discomforting feelings will remain unstated here, so as not to transgress the boundaries of confidentiality.

5. Some examples of methodological essays: Browning et al., *From Culture Wars*, 335–41; Luhrman, *When God*, xix–xxv.

THREE TYPES OF REFLEXIVITY

This essay takes time to bring into the open some of the challenges at various steps of the research and writing process that gather around the ethnographic concept of reflexivity, or what practical theologians might call humility and prophetic critique. In this essay, I will be concerned with three types of reflexivity in the work of theological ethnography: 1) the social location or position of the researcher, 2) the range of possible alternatives a researcher may offer in relation to changing or revising the situation under critique, and 3) the combination of a researcher's position and a thick description of the complex situation. This third instance of reflexivity is the basis for ethnography as cultural critique, or in theological terms, prophetic critique.[6]

When it comes to reflexivity—the self-awareness, social location, and cultural critique required for qualitative research—there are other related problems: must I *show* my work in everything I write? And what about the problems of remembering and wanting not to remember parts of one's life? How do I respond when participants want to pretty up their past or gloss over something difficult? Sometimes the reluctance to tell a story is quite complicated. For instance, some individuals in another study I conducted desired not to harm important ongoing relationships in their lives by taking the risk of allowing a powerful story in one of our publications.[7] What do we do? And other times study partners like Corey feel a distance from the stories or words they have shared in an interview. How do we close that gap? We can write sooner and while it is fresher for everyone, yet as researchers and writers we need critical distance. How do we balance the need for immediacy and the need for greater time and reflection for our writing?

When I enter a research task I am navigating how to be in relationship and conversation with participants in my various studies. I do the work as a person of faithful convictions, as a practical theologian, and simultaneously as a pastor. I'm never *not* in one role or another, because I am habituated to all of these roles (and others), which always linger with me in embodied and relational ways.[8] Thus the relational tensions are internal to my experience and not simply situational with study participants. In what follows, I want to

6. Marcus and Fischer, *Anthropology*, 113–16 [2nd ed.].

7. This relational concern from study participants has arisen several times with participants in the Learning Pastoral Imagination Project, an ecumenical and longitudinal study of ministry in the United States directed by Christian Scharen and me.

8. One contemporary iteration of the study of practical wisdom in its embodied and embedded forms can be found in the field of situated cognition. See Gallagher, "Philosophical," 35–51. For more about ethnography focused on sensory knowing, see Pink, *Doing Sensory Ethnography*, 23–26.

show the relational struggles and insights of qualitative research, and I want to use my own experiences as a launching point for a conversation with new (and more experienced) researcher-writers who face similar circumstances. This essay takes the leap and dives into these important conversations.

Reflexivity is not simply me proclaiming: "I'm a European descended, middle class, heterosexual, cis-gendered female, raised as a Baptist in the Southern U.S., trained as a pastor and researcher, working as a theological educator, mother of one, wife and daughter, extroverted, chocolate lover." I mean, what? It starts to be ridiculous. And in the age of Google you could have figured most of this out without me spending an entire paragraph on it every time I write something. The more important consideration, how-ever, is that naming one's social location is but a beginning point, and the critical features of that location should be apparent to the researcher from the outset of designing the project and not merely part of an introductory paragraph in a dissertation or journal article. Admittedly, seeing the impact and significance of one's social location at the start of a research career, or even at the start of a new research project, is enormously challenging.

Once I see my location in relation to the situation I'm going to study, the real significance of reflexivity is that I act responsibly with the knowl-edge of where I'm situated and complexities of how I am related to the people in my study. Further down the road of the project another set of relationships to you, the readers, emerges as I write, and in my writing I am facilitating yet another relationship between to the people I learned about in my study and those who will meet them in my writing. Our shared learning is more significant than anything I toss out as my "social location." And most significantly, how shall I critique the social and theological worlds that have shaped me (both past and present) as well as those I am seeking to un-derstand? And is it my work to offer alternative possibilities for comparison and perhaps even inspiration for the sake of change? In other words I must decide whether a constructive proposal is in order when I write up my find-ings and to whom that proposal might be directed.

When it comes to reflexivity about my self-understanding, there re-mains an enormous amount of hiddenness in who I am, which cannot be reduced to essence or captured in words. I cannot introduce myself fully to you even as we begin a learning conversation. On the other hand I am ethi-cally and morally compelled to act and work responsibly to acknowledge my place in the situation, to attend consciously to the power I wield, and to acknowledge the power I do not have or that with which I may be indelicate. So an introduction is useful. Yet if I spend too much time making these things explicit in a piece of ethnographic writing, my self pre-occupations may become a distraction from my ability to introduce you to the people

I've been learning from. If writing is something like hosting a conversation, then it needs honesty and transparency but also manners and grace, which were designed to make space for people, and put people at relative ease so that social interaction is possible within a frame of understanding. However, manners are also products of social class and work to keep some people ill-at-ease if they don't comprehend the rules or find the customs pretentious. Manners and social customs—including writing styles and publication formats—also work to keep those with power *in power* like a secret handshake or passcode that allows them entry to privilege while keeping others out.

How then shall I go about introducing you to each other? Like other kinds of social hosting, my work is to make space for the parties I want to introduce to come face to face, in the medium of the written (or spoken) language. When I write I am working with words to bring us together: you the reader, you the study participant, and me the researcher-writer. On one hand I need to create conditions of confidence for a study participant to engage me about his or her life, allow me to observe when she or he is in the flow of work and to clarify in various ways what I am noticing.[9] On the other hand, when I give shape to the insights I've reached out of my relationship with these participants, they need a say in what I've written. Here is the first very real and very big rub of reflexivity in the writing. This was the point at which the discomfort Corey felt became evident. This rub, and how I navigated it with Corey, is the focus of the first section of this essay.

I think in practice the second big rub of reflexivity comes at the point of noticing how my social location as a researcher is working in the situation I am studying. How our personal social locations as researchers impacts the research design and data gathering, is challenging at any stage, and especially for beginners. The familiar in our worlds is hard to make strange and the strange is hard to make familiar.[10] Instead, beginning researchers and writers often worry along these lines: what if I get things wrong or miss something obvious? What if they don't like what I write? What if I see something that I should not tell or that would make the participants look bad? What if people in my study refuse to participate any longer? Will my project (my career, my future) be ruined? Such self-preoccupations are to be expected in learning a new practice like qualitative research or ethnography. In this section of the essay, I'll offer some learning from my time as a minister and suggest how those learnings supported me on my pathway to becoming a theological ethnographer of the practice of ministry.

9. "Triangulation" is the common term for using a "combination of methods to explore one set of research questions." Mason, *Qualitative Researching*, 148.

10. This adage is common among ethnographers and anthropologists.

The final big relational rub that I will address in this essay is the relationship with one's own cultural setting and its many shaping influences, which can be the most complex to decipher. Sometimes the cultural relationship is the last one to rub truly against our understanding. How can this be? Primarily because we are products of our culture, and seeing cultural influence can be like asking a fish to notice water. Culture is simply the world in which we live, and its surrounding values and practices and power dynamics are notoriously difficult to see much less to sort out and bring prophetic critique. This moment of making the familiar strange enough to see it and engage it in fresh ways (we can never escape it or speak outside of it) is the focus of the final section of this essay.

RELATING WITH PARTICIPANTS

When I began my training as a researcher it did not occur to me that I would be forming lasting relationships with those I studied. Based on stereotypes, my vision of human subject research was like the sociological and anthropological studies I read about in high school and college. Sociological experiments were conducted dispassionately like a laboratory scientist pouring liquids in a beaker. Anthropologists worked far away in remote villages or hidden countries stuck in a distant and mysterious past. Any relationships that emerged between social scientists and those they studied were, in my mind, temporary, detached, and limited by the work of the research itself, driven by the fact that the researcher would soon depart. My unreflective and uncritical vision was a product of both the idealization of the natural sciences by the social sciences and the colonializing impulse of twentieth century ethnographies.[11]

Until 1978 when Barbara Myerhoff published *Number Our Days*, anthropology had largely stayed behind its own gaze at the "exotic other," considering cultures outside the U.S. and European contexts.[12] The goal was to make the strange familiar and share the findings. Any aim to critique the anthropologist's home culture remained a "marginal or hidden agenda."[13] But Myerhoff's study of a community of elderly Jews in Venice Beach, California, signaled a dramatic shift, which returned the ethnographic gaze

11. Bent Flyvbjerg, *Making Social Science Matter*, 1–3. The Western colonizing impulse embedded in nineteenth- and much of twentieth-century anthropology participated extensively in constructing gender, sexuality, class, and race in the modern understanding of these terms. The problems of "othering" in anthropology—like other social sciences of the last 150 years—run deep and need further deconstruction. See Gunaratnam, *Researching*, 9–14.

12. Myerhoff, *Number Our Days*.

13. Marcus and Fischer, *Anthropology*, 111 [2nd ed.].

back onto the researchers' own places and cultures.[14] In the new moment, ethnographers began to see with fresh vision how the "familiar has become exoticized."[15] In his introduction to Myerhoff's book anthropologist and ritual theorist, Victor Turner, says of her writing that an anthropological perspective is present always, but it is offered in service of presenting the people and events of the study. Turner concludes that Myerhoff's work makes important theoretical contributions, chiefly that identity and meaning are captured in the stories that humans tell about their lives, and that her findings embody a kind of "compassionate objectivity" and "realistic humankindness."[16]

Emerging around the same time of Myerhoff's study, and other "experiments" in form and approach, anthropology took its gaze and analysis one step further still, arguing for the fullness of the purpose of anthropology as cultural critique, a purpose intended but unmet from its beginnings.[17] In their landmark book *Anthropology as Cultural Critique*, George Marcus and Michael Fischer surfaced a nagging concern about the problem of "representation" of "others" in ethnographic writing, even as anthropologists explored human cultures in new and experimental ways. Marcus and Fischer distinguished two separate and overlapping types of reflexivity: 1) the social location of the researcher and his or her impact on the situations under study through lived engagement and through writing, and 2) a more potent form of reflexivity that turns its critique onto the very paradigms and structures of culture and knowledge.[18]

By the time theologians began to borrow and adopt ethnographic means of understanding the world(s) they cared about, anthropologists had already debated these points and shifted their research practices to account for the postmodern problems they encountered. Some theologians, especially those trained in practical and pastoral theology, are able to draw on nearly a century of research methods in their own fields that engage

14. Ibid., xxiii. Marcus and Fischer describe how anthropologists had not previously put in the foreground studies of American or European contexts, neither had they asked particular questions that tended to the domain of sociology, nor had they engaged explicitly in critique of the West, although that impulse was with the discipline of anthropology from its inception.

15. Turner, "Foreword," xiii–xvii.

16. Ibid., xvii.

17. See Marcus and Fischer, *Anthropology*, 21–25 [2nd ed.]. Most anthropologists until the 1980s (and still in many circles) were expected to do their first project in a culture and circumstance far from their home situation. Postmodern sensibilities increasingly confirmed that no "exotic" places or people exist free of the influence of modernity, and that era of the discipline came to a close.

18. Ibid., 111–17.

the social sciences. Yet they also bring theological and spiritual concerns into the research and writing. Theologians focusing on care, proclamation, education, and ritual practice continue to draw on established approaches for investigating human situations, even while they expand understandings of how theology operates in practice. For the last century in the U.S. these socially oriented theologians focused on suffering and other problems of contemporary human situations, and along the way they adopted practices like verbatim-writing and case-study-based learning. They also borrowed from medical professionals, psychologists, and social workers the qualitative techniques of data gathering.[19]

More recently, especially since the 1990s, a growing number of practical and pastoral theologians in the U.S. and Europe have been intentionally training in sociology, psychology, and anthropology for the sake of using a wider range of tools for better theological understanding. These new "theological ethnographers" are also interested in making what we can call constructive proposals or prophetic critique related to the very situations they study. With a definitive multi-disciplinary turn to "practice" in the 1990s, a growing number of systematic or doctrinal theologians and ethicists have also joined the ranks of theologians doing qualitative research or ethnography more intentionally borrowing tools from anthropology and sociology.[20]

Various streams of qualitative study, for the sake of theological understanding, continue to influence my own research approach and writing direction. I explore my relationship to the research more fully in section two of this essay (below). The important point to make here is this: Doing the work of theological ethnography today, or employing any qualitative means for the study of theology and practice, is unavoidably a relational task. While more theologians were borrowing qualitative research tools from anthropologists and sociologists, the issues of *identity* and *relationality* themselves became more of a focus of ethnography in the 1980s and '90s.[21] My own training in both theology and psychology has prepared me to think relationally about the enterprise of qualitative research. My goal here is to reflect on the relational dynamics of the complex relationship be-

---

19. Thornton, "Clinical Pastoral Education," 178. As "clinical training" established itself in the U.S. and joined forces with seminaries, in the 1920s and '30s, the use of "case studies" from physician and nurse training and the development of "verbatim" for theological reflection became standard.

20. A few examples include: Browning, *Fundamental*; van der Ven, *Practical Theology*; Swinton and Mowat, *Practical Theology*; McClintock Fulkerson, *Places of Redemption*; Moschella, *Living Devotions*; *Ethnography*.

21. Marcus and Fischer, *Anthropology*, 40–44 [2nd ed.].

tween researcher and study participant with its power dynamics, relational challenges, and collaborative efforts to bring what is mostly hidden in the life of ministry to be part of public reflection.[22] Like Meyerhoff, I chose to study my own religious group and a situation of conflict and change that had not been looked at closely from the viewpoint of a marginalized sub-group. I was going to have to make the "familiar strange" in order to understand more and then make it newly strange to my readers, so they might learn more about the situation as well.

I interviewed Corey for the first time in 2004 just after I passed my comprehensive doctoral exams. She invited me to her home for the interview and we spent the typical amount of time (between two and three hours) that I spent with women in my initial study. We are both part of a progressive wing of (mostly white) Baptists with several acquaintances in common. Like many research relationships ours was asymmetrical with regard to power and interest. I was the one asking most of the questions and recording the conversation and hoping to learn something for the sake of completing my dissertation, but I also invited her as I did each woman in my study, to share in the learning and partnership in the project. I would give her opportunities to give me feedback about how I interpreted her story. After completing my dissertation in 2008, I began a total re-write of the material from my study into a book for a larger audience.[23] In the following assessment of email exchanges, I will share salient points of my interactions with Corey to demonstrate some of the contours of what it is like to attend to reflexivity as a researcher in an ongoing relationship with participants in a study.[24]

When I wrote to my study participants in early June of 2014, I told them about my new publisher, and I said,

> This is exciting and confirming of the work we've been laboring over for several years now. This summer I'm making a few revisions (most of them quite minor) and I want to offer you one final opportunity to see the chapter that features your story and send me feedback before the book goes to press in September.

22. Miller-McLemore makes a parallel argument about the hiddenness of parenting practices and the wisdom and coherence of embodied knowledge arising from the labors of mothering. She argues for pushing through the dilemmas of work and family in order to make the maternal knowledge more public and available for reflection. Miller-McLemore, *Also a Mother*, 37–38, 129, passim.

23. Changes to the writing that I attempted in that transition are numerous. Among the more important was a choice to place five women's stories as centerpieces in the twentieth century Baptist narrative.

24. Many issues could be explored, and I hope readers will take the issues as fodder for additional reflection.

> I tried to incorporate your concerns from earlier conversations [in late 2012] into the chapter, and it is also more abbreviated than the last version you read. . . . I'm deeply grateful for your partnership in this project and look forward to getting these stories and insights out to the world.

I think my message both invites and assumes partnership with study participants. It offers some reassurance from me about the timetable and earlier changes to the chapter, resulting from a previous conversation. Once I located Corey's correct email address, I sent the chapter and two main questions: "Are you ready to say yes to the publication of this story? Is there anything that needs attention or change?" I requested a reply within five weeks from my message, and I said I might send a reminder prompt. In the subsequent weeks I was verifying information from others in my study and writing responses to the academic peer reviewers and the press. I realized in late October I had heard nothing from Corey, so I contacted her again thanking her and working with an assumption that her lack of response was ascent, and still inviting any final feedback. Her reply came as a surprise:

> When you sent the email in June I started reading the chapter but found it very out of place to my present life. I thought you would email me again (as you indicated) but you did not, so I assumed, since the July deadline had come and gone, that you would simply leave this chapter out of the book. I had not said yes to publication.

To my chagrin, the intervening four months revealed my inattention to important details, namely following up as promised in a more timely fashion. In my June message I was depending on the fact that I worked hard to include her feedback to an earlier version of the chapter. She closed her email by saying, "I will try to look at it again. It is very hard to look at something describing events greater than 15 years ago . . . when I am in such a different place at this time in my life." I sensed either one or both of us could become defensive at this point, and I wanted to go very slowly forward. In my next reply (after a long weekend to think about my words) I tried to express empathy with her feelings of distance from the earlier part of her life, and I invited a phone conversation.

I didn't hear anything from Corey for two weeks, so I decided to write again. I felt a little more desperate by then, knowing email is rarely effective in getting through relational exchanges. In the intervening time, I mentioned the situation (anonymously, of course) to a couple of academic colleagues—others who do ethnographic work. They were aghast: "How can she do this to you!? Didn't she sign a consent form?" The reactions captured my own feelings, and yet they also missed the point entirely that it is *her story*. This precise fact helped me keep the empathic door open and reach out with all I could muster to keep her talking to me and honor her feelings and experience.

I said in my email, "I've considered mounting my case to you about why I need your story in the book, Corey. However, I'm very sensitive to not being pushy—ever, with anyone who participates in any of my studies." I asked again for a phone conversation, and then I listed all the things I could send to her to help with the discernment:

- a review of her chapter by a colleague at a prestigious school;
- a full "blind" review of the book by a historian;[25]
- a full "blind" review of the book by a practical theologian (I explain "blind" review as necessary for a contract from the press; and signal they are each very positive, asking for minimal revisions);
- a list of ways I think her story contributes to the overall project;
- the book's introduction describing how chapters fit into the whole book;
- a timeline recounting our contacts and revisions over the previous 10 years
- the whole book manuscript (noting she would be among the first besides the publisher to see it).

I offered a lot here (perhaps some would say, too much), but I wanted to err on the side of grace and generosity. I wanted her story in my book. I did not want to delay its publication any further.[26] Corey took me up on the offer. She asked to see the review of her chapter by my colleague and my "list of contributions" I think her story makes. I sent both things on the day she asked. Many items on my list are too revealing to quote fully, but here are some of the things I said. I described positive feedback given about the chapter featuring her. I addressed the specific questions and concerns she raised about being included in the book. I suggested that the feelings of

25. "Blind reviews" are designed to give formal feedback about books or articles by scholars who don't know who the writers are, and writers should also not be privy to who the reviewers are, making the review "blind" on both sides. The idea is to avoid bias. That purpose is useful to a point for making evaluative judgments, but is also limited in other ways because contextualized knowledge is complex and value laden. See Flyvbjerg, *Making Social Science Matter*, 38–40.

26. Previous delays were not related to Corey in any fashion, but I was at the point of wrapping up and wanted to avoid any other delays.

disconnection from past events were quite normal. I reminded her that both her unique story and my book as a whole are part of larger narratives and changes for church life and women in ministry in America. I confessed my hope for doing no harm, and I also acknowledged that I could do so, unwittingly. I asked Corey's forgiveness—for not following up in a timely way. I described my timeline with the press and all the hurry-up-and-wait typical of publishing processes. I closed with the following plea:

> And I want the world to learn from your life. That's what it comes down to. I'm a "middle-person." I present the stories of these amazing lives. I do it as faithfully as I can. And show how they hold so much more depth and wisdom than anyone assumes. They (you) offer insight, imagination, character, and strength, and no matter how I weave your story into the larger Baptist story for an academic book, your story stands on its own. I want it to stand with the others in this book.

The items on my "list of contributions" are specifically about the content and process of my book and Corey's story. Yet the list is also about the relationship that Corey and I have been participating in over many years. Somehow we kept the shared space open enough that she could reply to me a few days later. This time she shared concerns about four things: 1) a personal/family crisis had arisen, 2) she found "significant awkwardness" in some of my writing or retelling of her story and wanted it clearer, 3) she continued to feel distance from the time in her life, and 4) she expressed concern about being recognized.

When I wrote back, I addressed each concern. Writing a story in an ethnographic project, I say, takes, "serious balancing" of the several tensions, which can be in conflict. I must balance getting the story *right* and *fair* and *anonymous* by holding together the following:

- staying faithful to the text of the original [interview] transcript;
- keeping identities (names, places, etc.) anonymous;
- incorporating participant feedback;
- preventing speakers from sounding impetuous or less intelligent because *spoken* stories are not the same as *written* stories;[27]
- working within the constraints of space and word count;
- telling a tight story, which can result in awkward summaries.

27. Luhrman, *When God*, ix. Luhrman does a nice job of explaining why quotes must be adapted for written stories because they do not translate directly from spoken language.

At that point I remained willing to make additional changes with Corey's guidance, although the time crunch was on. She also suggested that she talk to a mutual friend to get another perspective on her story and its place in my book. This was a huge relief for me. I had imagined the possibility, but for the sake of keeping her anonymous, I didn't want to recommend it. In the end we revised the chapter in several ways. Some recommendations were mine and others were Corey's. She gave her approval, and the book included a chapter about her.

You will find many reasons to judge my choices in this extended exchange with Corey. You would have done it differently. I should hope so, because people navigate relationships in many ways. My goal, and obligation as a researcher and pastor, was to make every effort to remain faithful and engaged in my relationship to Corey, and simultaneously hold fast to the goal of sharing the stories and analysis of the book. My intention and hope to share the stories of others put me in a position of interested power, so treading lightly and with respect and humility was my particular burden. I attempted to approach my work with a kind of deference to my research partners. Yet partnership in research is a complex and ever-changing reality. In the process I failed at several points (delaying follow-up, explaining the process fully, telling the story "awkwardly," etc.), yet by sticking with the situation my failures eventually led to greater empathy and better understanding on my part through receiving Corey's feedback. Ultimately, I think that feedback made for a better book. The founder of self-psychology, Heinz Kohut, explored at length how failures to understand and grasp another's experience are a basis for a process of greater empathy and understanding.[28] He describes "optimal failures," as the human failures of understanding that happen but do not sever relationships. Rather by working through the missed understanding, as well as the attending feelings like anger and disappointment, one can reach a more empathic understanding. For myself I can say I learned more, expressed Corey's story in a way that resonated (at least minimally) more for her, and learned some valuable lessons about how to be a better researcher.

RELATING WITH MYSELF

In the same autumn of 2004, when I interviewed Corey, I also was invited to speak on a graduate student panel for Wabash Center for Teaching and

---

28. Kohut, *How Does Analysis Cure?*, 564–72. Kohut argues that "optimal failures" between parent and child or therapist and client, or we can assume any two humans, are frustrations of understanding, which allow one to retreat and explain. When the exchange is complete these "failures" help to establish resilience, empathy, and self-esteem.

Learning.[29] The organizers asked me "to reflect about what has, and has not, prepared me for teaching religion or theology."[30] The exercise coming at the midpoint of my doctoral education became a significant reflexive transition between pastoral work and scholarly work, providing me with a synthesizing moment. At the consultation I shared a list of pastoral skills I learned beginning in seminary and continuing through five-plus years of ministry experience. Putting together my presentation made me aware of how I depended on pastoral wisdom and translated it intuitively into the academic classroom, which was the focus of the consultation. My list included the following skills:

- taking initiative without taking over;

- thinking theologically about situations and decisions;

- facilitating small groups—task and process oriented;

- responding to people in crisis with appropriate care, and ritualizing such needs through both personal and corporate worship;

- mobilizing people to action in response to needs of individuals, local communities, and the wider world;

- negotiating the politics of church and denomination;

- making connections between people, resources, and vision that are both empowering and sustaining;

- and caring for my own vocational well-being by attending to my spiritual, psychological, and physical health.

These pastoral skills did not stop helping me at the classroom door. My experience in ministry also laid significant groundwork for my practical theological *study of ministry*. This reflexive look back showed how various aspects of my pastoral learning came together and formed a kind of practical wisdom that was transportable to other related domains.[31] The skills and insights of ministry settled into my embodied and relational knowing, and they carried me through my doctoral program and early forays into research. When I entered the world of ministry—what was familiar to me—to study it, I brought new tools and perspectives. As a researcher I began to

29. At the time I had a role as one of four principle investigators in the "Teaching for Ministry" pilot study conducted at Vanderbilt University Divinity School (2003–04).

30. "Wabash Conference of PhD/ThD Granting Institutions, Graduate Student Panel (Indianapolis, Indiana) October 1, 2004." Unpublished remarks.

31. Not all the skills translated neatly, and the rub between the academic worldview and the pastoral worldview also caused some angst. One stark example was the difference in search committee protocol.

make it strange again. But my immediate familiarity with the practice of ministry made the qualitative study of ministry that much richer.

As I was interviewing Corey and the other Baptist ministers in my study in 2004–05, I was beginning a foray into a "bicultural identity" as pastor and researcher. Just such a "bicultural identity" is what philosopher Charles Taylor noted in the work of nursing scholar, Patricia Benner. He commended how she developed expertise in both nursing as a practice and nursing as a field of study in the overlap between ethics and medical care.[32] In my own transition, I did not immediately understand the interconnections between my two roles to be fluid. Rather I saw each role—pastor and scholar—as separate and somewhat distinct, hats to wear, if you will. In fact as a beginning researcher I was trying on many titles and roles to describe my work and identity, as evidenced by my CVs and brief biographical sketches written in that time.

Looking back at my interview notes with clergywomen in my first qualitative study, the information I took down is sketchy. I was more concerned with capturing all of their words (recorded and transcribed) rather than making other observations about the setting and person before me. Yet all the pastoral skills in the list above were with me. My embodied knowing of how to approach the situation as a minister made me comfortable, and it activated a kind of intuitive and practical wisdom in my interview with Corey and each other woman in my study. For example, as I conversed with Corey about her story, I was concerned about persuading her without undue pressure. I called this "taking initiative without taking over" when describing my pastoral work. I tried at each step to leave the door open for her to make choices, rather than forcing the outcome. At the interview stage of research and later, I experienced a deep and abiding recognition of each woman who sat before me as she shared her life stories. Hearing each woman's story of call, seminary, first employment, sexism, family dynamics, Baptist politics, and conflicts resonated with my own story, although of course in the particularities each story was unique.

The pastoral knowing I accumulated in the ministry years laid other groundwork for my encounters with the Baptist women as well. First, working in the parish cultivated my intuition through the daily practices of ministry, which gave me a sense of recognition about the demands of their work and lives. Secondly, I also learned about how to respond pastorally when critical and crisis moments presented themselves, which helped me to be a calm presence as interviewees shared difficult stories. Additionally, some of my foibles and failures along the way even became fodder for better

32. Charles Taylor, "Reply," 246.

understanding ministry on a broader scale as a focus of my research.[33] As a more seasoned researcher I now have more expansive language for articulating the practical wisdom that I brought with me from my time as a minister.[34] In the Learning Pastoral Imagination Project we call this knowing-what-to-do-in-a-situation, *phronesis* (practical wisdom) or in the case of ministry, pastoral imagination.[35]

In hindsight I had two blind spots (at least) as I began my work in qualitative research. First, for all my hard won pastoral knowledge, I still was preoccupied as any beginner is with some of the necessary—but not salient—aspects of research when I started interviewing for my study: what if I get things wrong or miss something obvious in the interview? Is my equipment working? What if Baptists or the women I interview don't like what I conclude? What if I witness something that I should not tell or that would make the participants look bad? What if people in my study refuse to participate any longer? Will my project (my career, my future) be ruined by some misstep I make along the way? Although these self-preoccupations can be expected in learning a new practice, I think it is helpful to name them. I admit to making them the source of freewriting and journaling as well. This is the very point at which the textbook recommendations to keep a reflexivity journal are just the right advice.[36]

Secondly, I brought with me from ministry a thin and single-faceted self-knowledge about my social location. I was highly aware of the ways gender marked me as different and as an outsider to church leadership. Never was it more obvious than the two years I searched for my first ministry job. Ordained women were rare in Baptist life in the 1990s. And finding a church that would hire me took time. Despite my extreme awareness of how my gender marginalized me in ministry, I was far less aware, verging on oblivious, about the ways that the privileges of being white, middle class, and heterosexual benefitted me and my congregation(s).[37] It would take going to graduate school again to open up my understanding of intersectionality, or

33. Campbell-Reed, "Wisdom."

34. Miller-McLemore, "Practical Theology," 171–73. Miller-McLemore is writing about *phronesis*, in terms of the practical wisdom that embodies theological know-how for seminary teaching.

35. Aristotle, *Nicomachean Ethics* 1142a–12. See also Campbell-Reed and Scharen, "'Holy Cow!'" 327–28.

36. Erlandson et al., *Doing Naturalistic Inquiry*, 114–15, 143–45.

37. I made attempts to expand my understanding of race and sexual identity while I was a seminarian and pastor, through reading and conversation. But I had very little sense of how gender and race worked with and against each other as identity markers. Nor did I comprehend the kind of privilege that being "white" afforded me.

the complex ways the race, class, gender, sexual identity, and other identities interact, support and depend on each other for meaning and power.[38] My experience of gendered marginalization fueled my research questions and helped me dig deeper with follow-up questions while I was interviewing. Gender became one of the main themes for analysis and interpretation when I wrote both dissertation and book about Baptist clergywomen. As I worked through analysis in dialogue with theorists and theologians, I found my own intuitive experiences became a sounding board or testing ground for thinking through certain conundrums of the gender knot. Increasingly as I came near the end of the book, footnotes began to fill up with references to the ways race or sexuality were implicated in the arguments. These are themes I will continue addressing in subsequent projects.

This personal recollection of my experience of learning a new practice as a qualitative researcher, on my way to becoming a theological ethnographer, highlights how my pastoral experiences shaped my research interests and prepared me to see the women in my study in particular ways. My self-understanding framed my early study and motivated my questions, and it was a crucial source of knowing as I constructed my arguments. What I did not know fully (i.e., social location) also shaped the findings and gave limits to the critiques I could offer. It is the work of relating to culture and constructing critiques to which we turn now.

RELATING WITH CULTURE

Stepping back to take the broadest view of the research that has been holding my interest for many years now, I want to make some connections between what I am attempting to do, a theologically oriented ethnography, and the strands of cultural critique that run through the field of anthropology in the last century and a half. The cultural-relational moment of making the familiar strange enough to see it and engage it in fresh ways, as I noted above, is not a matter of stepping outside one's culture, which cannot be achieved. Rather it is bringing a newly improvised set of observations and potential suggestions and relating them to each other in a way not previously understood. Here I cannot develop themes of the cultural-relational moment fully, but rather I will make some suggestions. In this essay, I have been describing "relational rubs" that I have felt as a researcher and how each one is a significant aspect of the reflexivity required for doing ethnographic research and writing adequately. I want to make three connections and offer two caveats at the intersection between theological ethnography and cultural critique, giving examples from my own work.

38. Crenshaw, "Demarginalizing," 40–45.

First attending to the relationship with culture, a theologically oriented ethnographer will bring to the foreground much that has been hidden. Although we do indeed each have relationships with our surrounding cultures, those relationships for many people remain deep in the background of their awareness. As I suggested earlier, showing people culture, or the situation in which they operate, can be like showing fish water. When I set out to do a theologically sensitive ethnographic study, I frame it as practical theological work, what theologian Edward Farley calls, "the interpretation of situations." Farley sums up the component tasks of practical theology thus: "The tasks of a hermeneutic of situations are to uncover the distinctive contents of the situation, probe its repressed past, explore its relation to other situations with which it is intertwined, and confront the situation's challenge through consideration of corruption and redemption."[39] This theological work of uncovering and articulation resonate with the work of the culture critic.

Founders of the modern social sciences were culture critics who looked for the hidden aspects of human lives and tried to make them more visible, more conscious, and more available for critique. Largely they were opposing in some fashion the Enlightenment obsession with rationalized reason and the story of social progress that went along with it.[40] Critical analysis among these early figures often took an ideological or philosophical cast, yet the critics were also using direct observation and cases studies. For example Freud offered psychoanalysis and uncovered the hidden features of the mind, emotions, and culture. Friedrich Nietzsche offered analysis of the ills of mass culture. Max Weber and Karl Marx wrote social and economic analyses. Marcus and Fischer argue, "Cultural critique is always one possible justification for social research," yet it is embraced in particular times and places particularly as the primary purpose for such research.[41]

Later culture critics, argue Marcus and Fischer, are more direct in their analysis and even more empirically based in their assessments of social institutions and day to day lives of humans. These studies they say came in the form of "economics, politics, and religion" and "fostered a pervasive romantic style of cultural critique." Those critics were concerned with "the fullness and authenticity of modern life and . . . the satisfactions of

---

39. Farley, *Practicing Gospel*, 31–33, 43. Farley is working to reimagine the purpose of practical theology after two "narrowing" moments in its history. The first uncoupled it from the ethics (or normative decision making tasks of the church), and the second limited it to narrowly understood ministerial tasks (i.e., care, preaching, liturgy, education, administration, etc.).

40. Marcus and Fischer, *Anthropology*, 114 [2nd ed.].

41. Ibid.

communal experience."[42] Such studies concerned themselves with the loss of communal features of modern society and the growth of individualism and isolation emphasized in a mass culture. This connects to the second point about theologically-focused ethnography, which like romantic culture critique, is likely to be concerned with posing theological alternatives to the cultural narratives which support contemporary life— consumerism, war, mass-incarceration, poverty, ecological crisis, etc. The alternatives are the stuff of practical and theological constructive recommendations with which many theologians of the church are concerned.

In the later twentieth century, Marcus and Fischer argue that the earlier ideological and later romantic forms of cultural critique increasingly merged.[43] Projects taking on both ideological and lived concerns require two careful steps of reflexivity. The researchers must first be able both to show their own social location in relationship to the situation and how that location shaped the frameworks and insights they are using. And secondly, the researcher must be able to locate alternative social conditions or beliefs or practices to the ones that are being criticized.[44] On this final point, offering alternatives for what is being criticized, common paths have included appeals to utopian visions (everything will find peace in heaven) or idealized values (if we would only embrace justice) or cross-cultural aspirations (we must act as the early church did). However, in the time in which we live presently, most appeals to the past or distant cultures or idealized notions are suspect in a host of ways. Thus we face the more complex challenge to offer alternatives, "within the bounds of the situations and life-styles that are the objects of cultural criticism."[45]

To sum it up Marcus and Fischer say, "ethnography as cultural criticism locates alternatives by unearthing those multiple possibilities as they exist in reality."[46] In a similar vein Farley argues that the final and most complex task that practical theology tries to understand is the "challenge" or "demand" of the situation on individuals or communities which one studies. This final task assumes a normative aspect of the theological investigation, which calls for a response. Farley says about the variety of possible demands, "One kind of demand occurs when the situation endangers the participants. Another kind occurs when promise and possibility are offered;

---

42. Ibid.
43. Ibid.
44. Ibid., 115.
45. Ibid.
46. Ibid., 116.

another, when obligation is required."[47] He also argues that in every situation one can imagine there is a possibility of both corruption (idolatry or evil) and redemption.[48] This brings us to a third connecting point about theologically focused ethnography: the relationship between one's own social location and the constructive proposals one makes is key to making a truly prophetic critique of a situation.

As a theologically oriented ethnographer, I, too, place myself in the stream of critique that is concerned to show otherwise hidden aspects of culture and to demystify, where possible, the hidden functions, especially where they are doing harm to the people living in the flow of embedded beliefs and potentially harmful traditions. Stories I received from Corey and other women in the study of Baptists provided deeper insights into the everyday demands of Baptist life. I am concerned with both ideas and lived religion. And in that regard I am in the stream with the group of late twentieth century culture critics and theologians who are looking for ways to offer new alternatives *within* the situation under consideration. For example in *Anatomy of a Schism*, I was writing to show the power of gender to shape people's lives and the entire Baptist life world, even as Baptists resist *and* reproduce a culture of complementarity.[49] To do gender analysis I was using insights and tools from psychoanalytic thinkers and practitioners.[50] Yet I am also theologically inclined so I drew on more than might be considered "contained" in the situations to which I turned my researcher's eye. I was looking for the "more" of the situation, the intangible realities by which many people live, and the wisdom that cannot be contained in rational ideas or logical arguments. Thus I was concerned both how Baptists in my study reproduced the sins of sexism and also how they participated in undoing its harms in redemptive moments of grace and sacred recognition.

Finally I want to offer two relational caveats to consider when undertaking a theologically oriented ethnographic study. One of the yielding points comes in adopting the tools of ethnography without being properly critical of the values that they import to your project. Reflexivity is necessary at the point of choosing research tools that are the best suited, and available, and taking time to reflect on them theologically before, during,

47. Farley, *Practicing Gospel*, 40.

48. Ibid. See also Farley, *Good and Evil*, in which he develops a theological anthropology where corruption and redemption are the ever-present possibilities of any situation.

49. Campbell-Reed, *Anatomy*, 57–61.

50. In particular I make use of work by analysts D. W. Winnicott, Heinz Kohut, and Jessica Benjamin, and pastoral theologians Christie Cozad Neuger and Pamela Cooper-White.

and after using them.[51] Such risk-taking (there are no perfect tools) and responsibility are a never-ending cycle in the work of an ethnographer, a theologian, and any person of Christian faith.

When Western theological ethnographers and practical theologians in the last twenty-five years increasingly borrowed the tools of qualitative research, they frequently turned those tools toward seeking understanding and offering critique of the religious societies to whom they owe their very existence. My own research, one slice of which is displayed in this essay, does precisely that. Such religious communities and groups—churches, synagogues, nonprofits, intentional or monastic communities, and the like—are never able to escape or live entirely beyond the totalizing capitalist society in which they are situated.[52] None of these communities live a unified existence, but rather by competing values, rituals, and relational patterns, which may seek to contest and criticize the powers and principalities of the postmodern world, yet they cannot escape the consumer driven post-industrial world. Having the reflexivity to see how the competing Western values and retrieved Christian values for living co-exist, co-opt one another, and struggle for power—even in the tools of research which we take up and use—is a significant contribution to both sociological and anthropological knowledge and understanding.

Early on in my interviews with women in my study, I was less aware of non-theologically reflective borrowing I was doing as I took up tools for qualitative research. I read all the qualitative research and ethnography books assigned to me. However, at the writing stage, I did evaluate the tools I used for their implicit values and embraced the ones that fit best. Listening and attention are core practices for both prayer and research. Using these pastoral research tools put me on familiar ground. Inquiry and critical questions are drawn on the pastoral skills of "thinking theologically about situations and decisions." Many times in my life I have shaken a fist at God and found the presence of the holy always returning to me with compassion

51. Campbell-Reed and Scharen, *Ethnography*, 254. We offer this theological note about the service to which the tools of data gathering should give way: "If God attends to all human lives, and calls us to participate in that caring attention, then the work of interviewing is a work of sacred attention. It is work that we share with each gathered group, together making space, yielding to one another, listening in silence, and building trust and confidence. It is not the individuals who embody God's presence, but the process itself, the relationality and shared practices that allow God's creative and graceful presence to be discovered."

52. McClintock Fulkerson, *Places of Redemption*, 35. As McClintock Fulkerson points out "places," even and especially religious places, are shaped by a whole variety of practices and habitus-forming forces, including global capitalism that resist simple descriptive reductions.

and peace. No questions of research or faith could be too much. And I was in familiar territory. These practices of listening, finding a way forward with questioning, and faithfully returning served me well in my relationship with Corey. At the point of wrapping up the book, I found help in the practices of seeking forgiveness and making amends. These are crucial for managing my missteps and miscommunications, allowing the failures to be optimal rather than foreclosing crucial relationships.

Another danger of any ethnographic project comes at the point of relational responsibility: How can we speak on behalf of another person or community?[53] In the first place it is impossible to speak truly for another, and doing so is politically and morally harmful, and we might say or write things that are theologically sinful.[54] Yet there are instances that warrant, even while they remain fraught, speaking on behalf of another who needs representation or in theological terms *witness*. Linda Martin Alcoff argues that speaking on behalf of others, even in our research-based writing, must be considered an event, with speakers, hearers, material culture, and impact.[55] The speaking does not end with the speech but rather with its effects. Here again is the relational aspect of reflexivity, even at the point of presenting findings and offering theological alternatives or prophetic critiques. It is into a relational context that we speak. The full weight of that context drives an undeniable need for humility on the part of the researcher.

Ethnography as a research practice remains particularly appealing to theology and other social sciences that explore the human condition in all its historic and postmodern tensions. Ethnography offers the possibility of pairing close and careful readings of a situation with a self-reflexive positioning of researchers themselves. This matrix of relationships—between the researcher, the researcher's situated historic reality and social location, and the relationships already present in the situation under consideration—make space for cultural critique. Theologically oriented ethnographers could say this approach allows for humility, careful—even prayerful—attention to the situation, and prophetic critique rooted in the ongoing interpretation of meanings about the sacred and the human. The challenge remains for theological researchers to make use of both kinds of reflexivity. We are obligated to position ourselves as critics with humility that is both honest and bold in posing multiple alternatives in order to make arguments that are theologically sound and prophetically provocative.

53. Alcoff, "Problem," 5–6.
54. Ibid.
55. Ibid., 25–27.

8

"To Walk in Ways that Might Make Us Feel Lost"—Response

NATALIE WIGG-STEVENSON

I always love that moment that happens at academic conferences when I bump into another theologian who is experimenting with ethnographic research methods. We'll buzz together about the joys and challenges of getting lost "in the field," as all those colleagues who spend their time lost only in texts fade for a moment into the background. I chose for my title the line from Jonas Ideström's chapter in this book—about losing one's way in the midst of negotiating all the ideas, traditions, practices, and people that contribute to constructing an ethnographic theology—to highlight not only the vulnerabilities, but also the possibilities of doing theology in *an ethnographic way*. As anthropologists Fabian and deRooij and others have argued, when ethnography makes its transdisciplinary migration, the new disciplines in which it takes up residence should not seek to *apply* this research method to their usual modes of knowledge production, but should, instead, reinvent it anew.[1] As ethnography has migrated into theology, then, we have to craft new maps, new ways of moving through our terrains. Otherwise ethnography will remain hovering at the fringes of the places we already know well, never reaching its way into the hinterlands. Indeed, by migrating into theology, not only will ethnography be changed: theology will be changed too. So it's no wonder those of us charting these new paths

---

1. Fabian and de Rooij, "Ethnography," 613.

feel la ittle lost. Getting lost is just a part of exploring something new. As I've bumped into new and old friends at these conferences again and again, and we've discussed this sense of getting wondrously lost with each other, a common theme for dealing with that feeling of displacement keeps resurfacing: the practice of reflexivity is what helps us all find our bearings.

Reflexivity functions, therefore, like something of a compass: it really only shows us enough about where we are in any terrain we're trying to map to help us figure out which way we should be heading. Reflexivity asks us to understand and interrogate ourselves, but not as a practice of solipsistic fixation. Instead, what matters about reflexivity in ethnography is that it asks us to understand and interrogate our selves specifically in relation to our fields of practice. We do so in order to ensure ethical practices in working with human subjects for research, of course. At the most basic level, reflexivity helps us endeavor to *do no harm*. But increasingly so, ethnographers and ethnographic theologians are using reflexivity in more creative ways. Pierre Bourdieu and Loïc Wacquant's approaches to reflexive sociology have been particularly influential among theologians who use ethnography for their research, for example. Here reflexivity takes on a specifically methodological hue, as the researcher's own embodiment becomes a vector for knowledge production. Likewise, theologians have been using reflexivity as a frame for dealing with the issues at the heart of contemporary theology— ethnographic or otherwise. For example, they have tackled the normative pitfalls and possibilities of ethnographic theology through the framework of reflexive practice.[2] It makes sense, therefore, that as ethnographic theologians try to find their bearings in a new terrain, that the very practice of figuring out one's location in relation to one's surroundings should be the practice that helps us take our next steps.

The three chapters in this section either highlight or tackle issues of reflexivity from the particular contexts of their own research—because truly, a topic so situated as reflexive practice cannot be considered in distinction from the sites where it is exercised. Indeed, as is evident in these three chapters reflexivity cannot even be disentangled from other ethnographic values. In particular, reflection and representation here are tangled up in the questions these authors raise. Reflexivity is not a naval-gazing endeavor. Rather, reflexivity, beyond ethics, has everything to do with how knowledge is produced, who gets to contribute to its production, how we move from field to text, and what even constitutes knowledge itself. Each of the authors in this section takes a different approach to these questions, each taking similar and different paths to similar and different conclusions. And each

2. See, in particular, Kaufman, "Normativity."

invites us into that vulnerable space of allowing ourselves to get lost for a moment—lost in the field, lost in our thinking, lost in our writing, lost in our relations—in order to let something new emerge. In essence, they invite us to get lost for a moment so that we can find ourselves being found.

Ideström's piece truly blurs the boundaries that surround an ecclesiological research field—not only between the fields of church and academic writing, but also between church, academia, one's home, and own internal life of faith. The Eucharistic cup in his essay, for example, appears across the locales of his life—first in the ritual he is invited to oversee, then "colored red inside by the wine . . . standing next to an icon with the face of Christ in our living room," throughout as a symbol in the text of his writing, and finally as the work of a Saami artist's hands. As Ideström reminds us throughout his essay, there is no place to which the researcher can retreat that is neutral. Christ's overflowing cup of life—perhaps especially when that cup is molded by hands typically relegated to the margins of life—will reach us anywhere we go. In response to this emerging realization, Ideström proposes "faithful participation" as an appropriately reflexive practice for ethnographic theology or ecclesiology. Faithful participation, for him, outlines a research approach of participation and engagement with the relational life—including the divine relational life—that composes the research field. And it does so with a deliberate intention to foster transformation. This transformation is of self, but also of the field itself (and I found myself wondering, then, if of the Divine herself, too?).

As a creative take on the forms of knowledge production typified by academic practice, it is this transformation itself that Ideström claims for his ecclesiological epistemology. Knowledge is not created as a stage of reflection subsequent to practice that can then be re-applied to practice in order to transform it; knowledge is instead created through and by transformative practice. Academic and ecclesial practices remain somehow distinct while becoming indistinguishable in this scheme, as they converge in the embodied, spiritual practice of the researcher holding it all together. Asked to provide the hands to raise the cup and pass it round, Ideström reveals the importance of reflexivity for ethical oversight, certainly, but also for the ways in which ethnography as a type of liturgical performance can produce faith-filled insight that is not available through interview data or even participant observation alone. Ideström's chapter, therefore, presses ethnographic theologians into some new methodological terrain in albeit nascent ways. I want to ask him, then, what would happen if such liturgical flourishes at the end of a research project were moved to its centre? What would the methodology of an ecclesiological ethnography be that didn't end with liturgical performativity, but that began with it? Ideström's creative use of group bible studies as a research method begins to carve out such an approach. And perhaps establishing the Word before the Table speaks as much to his Lutheran roots as it does to anything else. But I'd be curious to see what types of knowledge could be produced out of a fuller, more complete liturgical experience with his research partners from the beginning of the project. What would the final, beautiful image of acceptance, love and hope be at the end of that research? What might be found as a potent symbol of healing beyond the cup of Christ?

If Ideström's chapter offers us a beautiful image of all the pieces of a project coming together in delightful, even divine, coherence, Tveitereid's essay takes us in completely the opposite direction. Here the research process is slowed down to focus on one particularly anxiety producing moment: the movement from field to text. How, Tveitereid asks, can we make our data speak? As Tveitereid rightly points out, there is a shortage of the types of theories that are appropriate for distinctly practical theological reflection. At times, then, Tveitereid would recognize the failure of a particular theoretical frame not by its inability to produce knowledge out of the data but, instead, by it producing *too much* knowledge. And here is where reflexivity plays a particularly curious role in his chapter. He describes his own visceral reaction to applying such "user-friendly social science theories" to his data; they made him feel "enthusiastic," as "whole new, exciting, and rewarding worlds were opened up." The foreignness of this alternate "world" is important here. In seeking to make his data "speak," Tveitereid inadvertently makes it babble fluently and fervently, just in a dialect that doesn't quite make sense in the context.

Social science theory, he concludes, turns the theological into the social. Theological typologies can organize data into helpful categories, but it cannot account for the relationships between those "categories, agents, artifacts, values, practices etc. in the lived." Finally, his creative use of Christian doctrine to interpret the data yields interesting insights while nevertheless creating an unbridgeable gulf between more idealized academic approaches and lived practice. At each turn Tveitereid describes emotional responses of confidence waxing and waning, while his agitation does the same. While his conclusions about *theories in the middle range* is certainly an interesting and fruitful one, what matters here for our reflection on reflexivity is the extent to which this ethnographic value matters for him not only in the field, but also from the desk from which he interprets data to write it up. Tveitereid does not blindly trust things that seem to work and that feel good for his academic prowess in the moment. He carefully analyzes his own emotional reactions to academic knowledge production, using reflexivity not just as a tool for ethical engagement with research informants, but also as a tool for testing the goods and limits of theological interpretation.

My hunch is that Tveitereid would be at least mildly suspicious of Ideström's turn to doctrine in his own ecclesiological ethnography. Is it the application of a doctrinal metatheory—through the invocation of Fiddes, in particular—that facilitates the rich Eucharistic images that tie the piece together so beautifully? I wonder also, however, if Ideström would want to push Tveitereid to keep refining those doctrinal approaches that he finds so problematic. In my own work I have suggested that we can frame our research questions and, I would add, our research design such that they include the precise shape of the theoretical and theological inquiries animating our projects.[3] By incorporating both into the whole process of research, and not just at the stage of data interpretation, I think we open more possibilities for that nuanced middle ground theory that Tveitereid is seeking. But then I should acknowledge that my work is unlikely to pass muster with the more rigorously scientific approach that Tveitereid is seeming to pursue. Nevertheless, the question I am left with for him is, does it make any difference to what we do if instead of using theory to try to make the data speak, we instead used it to tune our ears to hear?

Finally, Campbell-Reed's essay takes us deep into the type of mess where reflexivity really matters—at that place where our own failures meet our sense that others might be failing us. She narrates the knot of emotional responses that arise when she forgets to follow up with a research partner who is experiencing anxiety at her story being included in Campbell-Reed's book, *Anatomy of a Schism*. When the woman begins entertaining the possibility of withdrawing her support for her story's inclusion, Campbell-Reed realizes that both she and the woman are on the verge of becoming defensive with each other—a relational move that will serve neither well. As Campbell-Reed puts it, no amount of "spewing out" one's "social location— i.e., that type of shallow reflexivity that marks the first few lines of too many ethnographic publications—can meet the difficulties of a moment of competing interests, anxieties, needs and hopes. Reflexivity, instead, she argues, requires critiquing the social and theological worlds that have shaped the researcher. And it requires doing this critique not only in relation to the social and theological worlds that the researcher is trying to understand, but also in relation to those to whom she wants to communicate her findings. Reflexivity, therefore, happens at every stage in the research process, from

---

3. I make this argument in my article, "From Proclamation to Conversation." I am indebted to Tone Stangeland Kaufman, one of the editors of this volume, for suggesting this revision to my original argument, stretching the significance of research questions into the realm of research design.

the research design to the field to the writing to the final edits on the final manuscript . . . and likely beyond. It entails negotiating one's relationship to a whole realm of cultural practices with humility that is relational in character "in order to make arguments that are theologically sound and prophetically provocative." I am particularly struck in Campbell-Reed's chapter by the fact that reflexivity never stops. We will always keep questioning our selves in relation to our projects, even long after those projects have closed.

Indeed, perhaps this is a part of the type of transformative, spiritual work to which Idestrom's model calls us. I admit I don't know what it feels like to do a purely ethnographic project. I only know what it feels like to do an ethnographic theological one. And I know I was transformed by it. Whether in the liturgical high moments that are nevertheless tinged with a sense of loss and pain as Jonas narrates, or sitting at my desk trying to make my ears hear what the data is trying to say like Knut unpacks, or fearing that I've made a mistake and trying to delicately fix it in accordance with my own ethical practice without at the same time losing all my work and feeling a bit sick about it all like Eileen so poignantly shares: in each of those moments that I too know so well, I have been transformed too. And that transformation has been, as far as I can tell, a permanent one. I have experienced it in a way that I now carry in my bones beyond the research field, beyond the research writing, beyond my academic self, into the me that's me in my living room too with my icons on the wall. The use of ethnography for theological research takes us so close to what really matters, so close to the life that God animates into the places where we find faith in that God, that how can we not be changed by it?

That these three authors tell stories of deploying reflexivity at such different phases of their research processes, and that they deploy it in such different ways, reveals how crucial a practice it is in ethnography. As Idestrom and Campbell-Reed in particular name, theologians play and embody multiple roles in their research sites, as we also carry those roles with us in the ways they have habituated us when we move from the field to the writing, speaking and communication of our research findings to wider audiences. Indeed, we carry them and the ways in which the field has habituated us too into our homes, our living rooms and every place grace meets us—which is, of course, everywhere. As Tveitereid reminds us, however, in a much more localized reflexive practice, even the act of moving from data to analysis—a move that non-theological ethnographers also must make—is fraught with theological as well as theoretical issues too. These three chapters together therefore demonstrate not only the need for reflexivity in ethnography, but also the need for producing fresh strategies of reflexivity as we as theologians embrace ethnography's transdisciplinary migration to our shores.

There is no one way to be reflexive for ethnographic theology. Each of us will have to negotiate the roles we play in relation to our research in the context of our lives. Indeed, each of us might need to risk being lost for a moment; because it's only from a place of being lost that we can then find our way . . . or, perhaps, that we can then be surprised that we've been found.

PART 2

Normativity

The chapters in Part II are concerned with the relationship between theologies that appear in the empirical field and traditional theological and ecclesial traditions. When and how are theologies operant in the empirical data allowed to make normative claims? This is particularly delicate when such theologies clearly challenge existing norms and traditions.

Taking her point of departure in an empirical study on the understanding of pastoral ministry Kirsten Donskov Felter asks: "In which ways are empirical studies able to disrupt the explicit normativity of ecclesial traditions," and how can such studies contribute with normative values in the process of producing theological knowledge?

In the same vein as Felter, Marianne Gaarden employs insights emerging from her empirical study on how worshipers listen to sermons as she recounts "how the old paradigmatic box of mainstream theology crashed when confronted with these insights." She also reflects on how ethnography can offer significant perspectives to a new paradigm for theological normativity.

In her chapter, Ninna Edgardh discusses "how ordinary people see their relation to the church in view of how they live their daily lives . . . and how the ideals of the Swedish folk church tradition are re-negotiated." Reflecting on "family as an overlooked interspace," Edgardh argues that the way the broad majority of church members look at their relation to the church is of ecclesiological and normative importance.

Pete Ward makes the case that theology is what really matters in the conversation in ecclesiology and ethnography: "the real heat and creativity in the conversation comes when there is a genuine attempt to hold the empirical and the doctrinal voices together and work with the tensions and problems that this gives rise to." He also offers reflections on how we might think of theology in constructive ways.

In the response to the texts in this section, Ideström and Kaufman introduce the metaphor of the researcher as a gamemaker shaping the research process through her decisions and choices. By making distinctions between various forms of normativity they reflect on how normativity has been considered and dealt with in the four chapters.

9

Office and/or Calling?—Negotiating Normativity in the Field of Ministry

KIRSTEN DONSKOV FELTER

> Well, I've read plenty of theology about the office, but I don't
> think it was the first thing on my mind. If I were to choose, I'd
> rather speak of calling than of office, which I think is a bit more
> like state official. I remember those old parish clerks who were
> so proud of being *officials*.[1] There is some kind of solemnity
> about that term that isn't there when you speak of calling.

T his was the reaction of a Danish parish pastor, a woman in her forties, when I asked her whether she would use the theological idea of ministry as an office, or whether she would rather use the term calling to express her understanding of pastoral ministry. Her statement was somehow surprising, as in the official theological discourse of the Evangelical Lutheran Church of Denmark (ELCD), office is a key term to describe the pastoral role. However, as I continued my study of interpretations of ordained ministry among ELCD clergy, it turned out that she was not the only one to prefer the connotations of personal involvement expressed in the idea of calling. Rather, it seemed that the de-personalizing terminology of office used in church documents and academic theological discourse—a terminology that we had in the research team adopted rather uncritically—was perceived as

---

1. Said with stiff upper lip and oratorical effect.

less attractive by some of the pastors in the field when they were to describe theologically what they were doing.

Apart from the concrete tension that appeared between different interpretations of ministry at an official level and in the views of rank-and-file parish pastors and chaplains in the ELCD, the study raises the question how to assess findings from empirical studies in practical theology. In which ways are empirical studies allowed to disrupt the explicit normativity of ecclesial traditions, as well as the implicit or tacit normativity inherent in the approach of the research team? How can empirical findings be considered to convey normative values with regard to theological thinking? And how does the background of the scholar affect the normativity that he or she brings into the research design?

In this chapter I am going to deal with these questions at two different, but interrelated, levels. Taking my point of departure in the findings of my study, in the first part of the chapter I will argue that the pastors' understandings seem to reflect changing conditions for ministry in the ELCD, as compared to the state church context underlying the traditional theology of the office and the implicit theological preunderstandings of the research team. The described tension between the voices of church documents, academic theology and voices of lived, pastoral experience lays out the ground for the following discussion, as in the second part of the chapter I will present some more principled reflections on how one can deal with the tension theologically. This becomes particularly acute, as the study demonstrated how subtly we, as theological scholars, were ourselves part of the game, adopting the traditional theological idea of the office and letting it influence the way that we defined the scope of study.

However, as our findings nudged us to reconsider our own position in the research process, the complex and messy nature of the pastors' statements indicated that the path from empirical findings to theological normativity is not a straight one. It is not a matter of shifting from one universalist model of interpretation to the other, replacing the normativity of the office with that of the person. The complex material of the interviews reminds us that reality does not come pre-packed, nor does it fit into the neat categories of the classic academically trained theologian. Instead, I suggest that we see doing theology as a hybrid process of meaning-making across different fields, as elements from different traditions are negotiated in order to make theological sense of concrete, and sometimes painful, forms of lived experience. Also, I suggest that this means that we need to pay more attention to the fact that doing theology is always socially and culturally situated, whether in the Academy or in a local church context. Or in terms of this volume: that *matters matter* in doing theology. And that attending to concrete situations and locations can enhance our sensitivity to *how* matters matter to normative decisions within theological studies.

The chapter proceeds as follows: Describing the study and its findings, I will argue that the ways that the pastors negotiate ideas of calling and office can be seen to reflect the changing conditions for the legitimacy of pastoral ministry in the ELCD, whereas the approach of the research team seem to reflect a more traditional state church backdrop. On this background, I will discuss whether the heuristic framework *Four voices of theology*, coined by the Action Research in Church and Society (ARCS) team and Clare Watkins in particular, can provide a fruitful frame for dealing theologically with the discovered tension. In spite of its valuable contribution to differentiate between theological fields of practice, I would still question whether the framework is sufficiently sensitive to the ways that any theological voice— including the formal and normative ones—is fundamentally situated, and thus reflects the messy realities in which it is rooted. Inspired by American theologian Mary McClintock Fulkerson and Filipino theologian Daniel Franklin Pilario, I suggest that in order to enhance sensitivity to the ways that theological voices tend to reflect their particular contexts, it might be helpful to work with deliberate strategies for de-centering. And, that this might allow for a more genuinely dialogical approach to the questions of normativity.

BACKGROUND AND DESIGN OF THE STUDY

In 2015, the Danish Pastors' Association initiated an empirical study of the practices and interpretations of ordained ministry among their members. The immediate background of the study was an increasing number of positions in the ELCD[2] different from that of the traditional parish pastor, and a pluralization of pastoral duties in general. Since 1971, the numbers of chaplains employed in educational and health institutions, and pastors with specialized functions, e.g., youth, street, pilgrim, or night-church pastors, have increased from 37 to 345 out of about 2100 pastors. This means that today about 1/6 of ELCD pastors have some kind of specialized function, either full-time or parallel with their position in a parish.[3] At the same time, teamwork among parish pastors is increasingly encouraged in official documents,[4] and some deaneries have gone far in organizing pastoral teams

2. In the chapter, I generally use the formal abbreviation. However, a more common term would be the (Danish) folk church. See also the context chapter for a general presentation of the Danish context.

3. Kühle, *Funktionspræster*, 90–91.

4. The organization of pastoral work at the levels of parishes, deaneries, and

that collectively serve a group of parishes. The changes within the organization of pastoral work mirror the ways that the actual activities of the ELCD have also changed since the 1990s. Apart from the ordinary Sunday service and biographical life rites such as baptism, confirmation, weddings and funerals, today most churches offer a broad range of alternative services and activities, e.g., night church, baby singing, pilgrimages, meditation services, weekday services, youth services using popular or rock music, family services followed by serving of short, child-friendly meals, and so on. Formally, as opposed to the Sunday service and the rituals of baptism, confirmation, weddings and funerals, that are mandatory parts of the pastoral duties as well as confirmation training and pastoral care, parish pastors are not obliged to enter into these new activities.[5] However, a brief look at the job descriptions in the Pastors' Association's journal indicates that the willingness to enter into—and even initiate—a broad range of new church activities directed toward specific groups of members seems to be an integrated part of the expectations from the parochial church councils when announcing for a new parish pastor. Although not formally codified, there seems to be a general recognition that to enjoy folk church status implies an obligation for the ELCD not only to continue its traditional activities, but also to be responsive toward the more individualized, or sub-cultural, religious practices of its members.[6]

On this background, the Danish Pastors' Association wished to examine how contemporary pastors themselves see their work, and how they interpret their role and functions theologically. Having mapped the field, the wider aim of the study was to discuss "the implications of the findings for a contemporary, empirically grounded theology of the pastoral office that would be able to meet the actual plurality of duties, methods and frames within pastoral work."[7] Based on qualitative interviews with 25 pastors, the study set out to examine what contemporary pastors see as their core tasks, and how they go about interpreting what they are doing in theological

---

dioceses have been a repeated theme in reports from the Ministry for Ecclesiastical Affairs since 2006. Kirkeministeriet, *Betænkning 1477*; *Betænkning 1491*; *Betænkning 1503*; *Betænkning 1527*; *Betænkning 1544*.

5. Christiansen et al., *Præst*, 216.

6. An example of the way that new initiatives become part of the generalized expectations toward the pastor are the so-called preconfirmation classes that became very popular with the parochial church councils in the 1990s and 2000s. Although formally not being part of the pastor's duties, the willingness to engage in the classes in many places became a part of the informal requirements to the applicants for positions as a parish pastor.

7. Quote from the project description.

terms.[8] Toward the end of the interviews, the pastors were encouraged to share their thoughts on the theological terms of calling and office, which are traditionally engaged to describe ordained ministry in a Danish context, as we asked them which of these terms they would prefer in order to express how they themselves perceived their ministry. The timing of the introduction of the theological terms was deliberate, as our initial expectations within the research team were that if we opened the interviews by asking these questions, the interviewees would too easily jump to traditional "Lutheran" stipulations of ministry in terms of office, swifting the mode of the interviews from the empirical to the normative.

However, when engaging the ideas of office or calling, the pastors generally seemed quite uninterested in dogmatics. Apart from an elderly pastor, who introduced the interview by sharing how he had prepared for the session by brushing up his knowledge about the official view of ordained ministry in material from the Ministry for Ecclesiastical Affairs, the interviewees in general showed little interest in the ways that ministry is described in church documents or in systematic-theological accounts. Rather, to the extent that they used the terms office and/or calling to reflect theologically on their ministry, they obviously made a point of relating them to their day-to-day experiences, rather than attempting to conform to "official" interpretations.

NEGOTIATIONS OF MINISTRY— CALLING AND/OR OFFICE?

In the opening of this chapter I quoted a pastor in her 40s, sharing how she would prefer to speak of calling in order to describe her view on ministry, whereas the term of office in her opinion seemingly represented a distancing attitude that she was not able to identify with. During the interview she described to us what it meant to her being called by concrete members of the congregation to be with them during the service, in pastoral care and in

8. The study was conducted from September 2015 to May 2016 in a cooperation between the Pastors' Association and Centre for Pastoral Education and Research. As the pluralization of the pastoral profession was a main theme at the outset of the study, the research group considered it vital to have the variations within the group of pastors represented. This meant that the interviewees were chosen according to gender, age, types of parish, types of ministry, and dioceses, so that the size of different groups matched the actual distribution in the population of pastors as a whole. Taken together, we wanted the distribution along these objective criteria to secure that the sample was not in the outset biased, as we were ourselves part of the field that we wanted to study and therefore in the risk of letting the study be shaped by our emic conceptions. Also, we were careful to have different congregational traditions and theological groups represented.

youth education. To her, being a pastor meant embodying the gospel, and being there whenever someone needed her, no matter what time of the day. Another pastor, a man in his 40s frankly stated, "I don't go about thinking a lot theologically about the office, I really don't." During the interview he described his work in terms of life style, concentrating on the traditional functions of ministry in a rural parish and the ways he had learned to balance the expectations from the parishioners and from the family respectively. To both of the interviewees, it seemed that they were actively distancing themselves from the official view of ministry in terms of office, as it did apparently not resonate with the ways that they saw their work. Rather, as theological framing it appeared counterproductive by evoking associations of pompous clerks, or irrelevant to describe their day-to-day engagement in the congregation. Another pastor, a man in his fifties, said, "No, I don't use the word office. It conveys something different to me. It reminds me of the state official. I'd rather speak of calling."

Some of the interviewees evaluated the idea of office more positively, even if they did not attach explicit theological meaning to it. The metaphor of being a link in a chain recurred in several interviews, expressing a way to deal with too heavy expectations on the part of the congregation to their personal engagement. A parish pastor in her fifties described how intensely she hated living in the vicarage, feeling invaded by members of the congregation, who didn't pay any regard to her family's need for privacy. When asked whether she preferred to think of herself in terms of ministry or in terms of office, she clearly opted for the office which would enable her to step a bit back as person:

> Office means that I step in somewhere where there has been someone before I came, and there will be someone after me. That makes sense to me. It is less personal. Being a link in a chain makes more sense to me than being called, which would be me personally. I think that's how I distinguish.

Asked to describe his theological view of ministry, a pastor in his fifties began by distancing himself from a formal theology of office:

> I do not have some fine theology with references and all that stuff. But I have a theological thought of being called by the congregation to preach and administer the sacraments. And it means that when the phone calls, I have to go. It pushes other tasks aside because this is my duty. And also that when I go to celebrate the Eucharist at someone's deathbed or whatever, I come as NN [mentions his name], but more than that, it's the

parish pastor coming. You play your role, and I think that it's extremely important to take that seriously.

During the interview he uttered some critical remarks about the younger pastors, who, in his opinion, were not sufficiently aware of the all-encompassing character of ministry. However, the younger generation of pastors represented in the study seemed to share his values of personal engagement. One of them, a woman in her thirties said: "To me, ministry is a kind of calling. Which means that in many ways it is a way of life. It is certainly not an 8–16 job. I'm certainly not afraid of speaking of calling." She continued to speak of how, as a mother of young children, she had to restrict herself from answering the phone during meals, as a means of protecting both her family and herself against never-ending demands and her own engagement in the different tasks.

In the analysis of the material it was striking, that to some of the pastors, when presented to the terms calling and office, the idea of calling—whether outer or inner—seemed to resonate far more positively with their self-perception than the idea of the office. Contrary to the distancing term office, calling seemed to capture their personal engagement in ministry. The idea of calling as an all-encompassing identity also occurred in the understanding of a parish pastor in her forties:

> I usually say that pastor, that's not something I do, but something I am. And I see it as a way of living. I mean, it's something that I've been called to, and that's why it's difficult to speak of working hours. Because if you're called to something, it isn't a job 8–16, it's exactly a thing that you are all the time.

A pastor in his forties, working part-time, said:

> It's 24/7 or at least 24/6, because I have been taught that I must keep my weekly day off. But of course, if somebody stand at my door, I will let him in. . . . It's a kind of calling the old-fashioned way. It's not a job, and it's not 7–16, and it's not just that we are on duty at Sundays, but it's kind of underlying all of one's life.

A pastor in her fifties made a point of interpreting her work in terms of office, by which she meant that she was not indispensable, which she saw as a great relief. That being said, she ended up concluding, "But I think calling is a bloody good term because it says that it's 24/7, it's a passion."

Way of living, 24/7, passion. As opposed to the idea of office, to many of the interviewees the idea of being called appears better in order to capture the heart of what ministry is about; the engagement, passion and the difficulty to cut out one's person when called for by the members of the congregation. On the other hand, employing the term of office seems to relieve some of the pressures by stressing the impersonal dimensions of pastoral work: being a link in a chain, wearing the cassock and performing traditional duties. When referring to the office, the interviewees thus express themselves within an institutional discourse: it is the parochial system and the ministerial regulations that define the rights as well as the limits of pastoral responsibility and provides them with the formal legitimacy to be there. For better, as experienced by some, when they feel invaded by demands from the church members, or for worse, as experienced by others when they feel reduced to state officials following rules and spending their time making bureaucratic decisions in front of a pc.

INTERPRETING MINISTRY IN THE LIGHT OF CHANGING CONDITIONS FOR LEGITIMACY

In Danish academic theological discourse, the idea of ministry as an office—in Danish *embede* or German *Amt*—as the expression of a formalized, objective calling by a congregation, the *vocatio externa*, has been almost exclusively dominant in twentieth century. This can partly be seen as a result of strong Barthian influence skepticism toward any kind of religious subjectivism, and partly due to the work of Danish Theologian Regin Prenter in his dogmatics on ministry seen through the lens of the office in a Lutheran context.[9] The strong ideological demarcation of the pastoral office as a function of the formal calling of the congregation meant that another understanding of calling, meaning the subjective experience of being called by God, the *vocatio interna*, which had its prime time in the nineteenth Century Danish revival movements, was made theologically suspect.

From a sociological point of view, the theological controversy between internal and external calling, between subjective experience and the institution of office, can be described as a discussion about what constitutes legitimacy. German/American sociologist Max Weber identifies three basic forms of legitimacy. An early form of legitimacy is that of *tradition*, which is characterized by being beyond critique as it is taken for granted. Another form of legitimacy is that of the *charismatic* leader, whose leadership is grounded in his outstanding personality.[10] According to Weber, both the legitimacy of tradition and that of the charismatic leader are typical of pre-modern societies where they are represented by the hegemonic leadership of the priests and the subversive power of the prophet, respectively. However, also according to Weber, what distinguishes modern societies is

9. Prenter, *Kirkens*.
10. Weber, *Wirtschaft*.

exactly its *rational* delegation of power, which he finds incarnate in the idea of the office. As opposed to its earlier forms, the office is to be respected because it is rationally instituted, and the commitment to bureaucratic procedures helps maintain its public legitimacy.

Against Weber's idea that legitimacy in modern societies must be guaranteed by the rationality of the institution, Canadian philosopher Charles Taylor has argued that what characterizes modernity is exactly the tendency of rationalism to undermine itself. According to Taylor, the subjective turn is a consequence of the inherent logic of modernity, as individuals can no longer base their moral and religious conviction on any authorities outside themselves. The subjective turn thus implies a claim, not to institution but to authenticity, that is: the moral obligation to realize the values that are experienced as true to the individual person.[11] By shifting the authority to the individual, Taylor challenges the premise of Weber, that legitimacy comes with the institution, whether it draws on the power of tradition, on the charismatic personality of the leader, or with the rational delegation of power to state officials. As described in the chapter on ecclesial context, in Denmark the institution of the parish pastor has historically been closely connected with that of the state official, undertaking a broad range of tasks that were both clerical and secular, which seems to mirror the normative weight of the term of office in the traditional discourse on ministry.

As for the references in the material to the subjective experience of being called, one might see this as an incidence of the charismatic legitimacy in Weber. However, there is little evidence that the pastors see legitimacy as founded in their outstanding personalities. Several of them are careful in stressing that they find the interest in the pastor's person problematic. On the other hand, from the ways that the pastors describe their priorities, it is also apparent that they do not see the legitimacy of their work as exclusively determined by the institution of the office. Rather, the experienced importance of personal encounters and relations, and the passion that they put into their work, seem to indicate that the quest for authenticity described by Taylor is part of the way that the pastors see themselves. Despite stories of the fundamental confidence from the members of the church that seems to come with the cassock, the pastors seem to enact their functions on terms of individualization where the institution at best provides the frames that he or she is to fill out in person. On this background I suggest that the personalized interpretation of ministry, that makes up an important finding in the study, can be interpreted meaningfully in the light of changing conditions for legitimacy. Interpreting ministry in terms of personal calling rather than

11. Taylor, *Malaise*.

in terms of office seems to mirror the situation of the Danish folk church in a secularized and highly individualized society, where the call for authentic presence has replaced the rationalized authority of the institution that Weber saw as a main characteristic of modernity. However, the personalized ethos expressed in the ways that the pastors' interpretation of their work in terms of dedication and passion challenges the dominant theology of ministry in a traditional state church context, where the legitimacy of pastoral work is guaranteed by the institution of the office, rather than by the person-based, experienced quality of the situation.

EMPIRICAL STUDIES AND THE QUESTION OF NORMATIVITY

Apart from the concrete tension between different views of ministry, the findings of the study raise the question of how to assess the empirical findings compared to the weight of theological tradition. Or, what is the relationship between a classic view of normativity as inherent in theological text and tradition, and the norms to be read from the practices and interpretations of individuals? Building on the project Action Research in Church and Society (ARCS), British theologians Helen Cameron, Deborah Bhatti, Catherine Duce, James Sweeney and Clare Watkins propose that when doing empirical theological studies, one must attend to the different theological dimensions that are at work in the interplay between researchers and practitioners in the field studied.[12] In order to distinguish between these different dimensions and to discuss the ways that different theological perspectives are at work, they suggest a heuristic framework called *Theology in four voices*. As for the empirical perspective, they distinguish between what they call the *espoused* voice, that is, what is expressed explicitly by the agents, in contrast to what they call the *operant* voice, which means the inherent or implicit theologies that are enacted in the practices of the agents. On the part of the researchers, the model distinguishes between the *formal* voice of academic theology as represented by the scholar, and the *normative* voice that arise from the tradition of the church.[13] Cameron and her colleagues have fully demonstrated the fruitfulness in applying the terms espoused and operant theologies to describe the complex interaction between the explicit and the implicit values inherent in the theological practices in the church, as what the practitioners say they are doing is often at odds with the things they actually do. Also, the framework fruitfully addresses the inherent tension

---

12. Camerson et al., *Talking*, 49ff.

13. Watkins, "Practical," 177ff.

between a scholarly perspective on church practices and the perspective of the church practitioners themselves.

However, the relations between the empirical and the normative voices in the ARCS-model do not appear to be quite resolved.[14] Even though Cameron and her colleagues are careful in claiming the theological relevance of the voices from the empirical field, it seems at best ambiguous whether they ascribe normative quality to the espoused and operant voices of the field. Or, whether the normative and formal voices of tradition and academy are granted *a priori* privilege when deciding what voices should be judged as theologically relevant. In a critical assessment of the *Four voices*-framework, British theologian Elaine Graham has argued that the ARCS team seems to "resolutely write themselves off the page," failing to reflect critically on the part of the theological scholar in empirical field work, and thereby adding to the asymmetrical relations between the different voices.[15] In a recent article, Scandinavian practical theologians Tone Stangeland Kaufman and Jonas Ideström note that Clare Watkins has in her later works adopted a more self-reflective take on the role of the scholar, making her own position more transparent. However, they find that even if Watkins has modified the privilege of the normative voice, stressing the very encounters of the voices as the place where truth is located, as *moments of disclosure*, the relationship between the empirical and the normative voices still seems somewhat unresolved.[16]

Agreeing with Graham, Kaufman, and Ideström, I would add that despite its qualities in discerning different perspectives within theological fieldwork, the *Four voices* framework seems less sensitive to the ways that the different voices borrow from and build on one another. In my reading of the interviews from my study, again and again I noticed how the pastors used the terms of calling and office to negotiate their own day-to-day experiences theologically. However, it also seemed characteristic that whether calling and/or office were accepted as adequate terms in order to describe ministry, depended on whether they made sense to the way that the pastors viewed themselves. Far from being unison, the voices of the pastors resounded in different keys, reflecting their hybrid experiences with the struggles and joys of ministry. In other words, listening to the voices of the field pushes for a more nuanced understanding of theologizing as a process

14. Kaufman, "Normativity," 95ff.

15. Graham, "Research," 149. The criticism raised by Graham especially addresses the question of whether the work of the ARCS team complies with the methodological demands on action research.

16. Kaufman and Ideström, "Why Matter," 7.

rather than a piece of cut-and-dried content that can be transferred from one context to the other.

Taking the hybrid voices of the field seriously as sources of theological knowledge would mean that they cannot a *priori* be lumped into the pre-packed categories of the scholar. Rather, their negotiated nature should call for a more sensitive approach, demonstrating how theological processes of meaning-making are situated in specific contexts. As American theologian Mary McClintock Fulkerson proposes, instead of asking the question whether empirical findings are "biblical"—or, in this case, "Lutheran"—which are already normative labels, the fact that the voices from the field are different from the voices of tradition and academic theology should be taken seriously as expressions of different situations of faith.[17] Also, according to McClintock Fulkerson, it is exactly the gap or the discrepancy between what is usually acknowledged as normative, and the attentiveness to actual practices that can generate new knowledge. To McClintock Fulkerson, theology is not so much a product as it is a process that can be described as a kind of creative reflection generated by a wound. By that she means that "(a) dilemma is perceived (or felt) that generates new thinking, takes on the tradition, and develops new configurations and convergences of insight and reality."[18] The wound that might generate creative theological reflection in this study could be the divergence between what is officially coined Lutheran—the idea of the office—and what is perceived meaningful by Lutheran pastors in their day-to-day practices. A hint of how this wound is felt can be seen in the ways that some of the pastors struggle to combine the theological normativity of their academic training, having *read plenty of theology about the office*, with their daily experiences in the field of the church. In this respect, acknowledging the voices of the field to be genuine expressions of theology on equal terms with those of the academy or with that of normative texts, is a step toward the *de-centering* of theology called for by McClintock Fulkerson. This means that the production of theological knowledge is not seen as the privilege of the academic scholar, but as a joint endeavor between academics and practitioners.[19] Or, in this case, bearing in mind that Danish pastors are academically trained, between theologians situated in the Academy, and in the messy realities of ministry. However, the study also turned out to raise issues of normativity within theology in an even more subtle way.

17. McClintock Fulkerson, "Interpreting," 126.

18. Ibid., 138.

19. McClintock Fulkerson, "Foreword," xiii.

TOWARD A DIALOGICAL METHOD IN EMPIRICAL
THEOLOGICAL RESEARCH

Within computer terminology, the abbreviation WISIWYG—*What You See Is What You Get*—has been used to coin how an image on a screen that is exactly the same when printed. However, one might also use it as an illustration of how the taken-for-granted premises of the theological scholar tend to slip into the research process, and, once they have got in, tend to reproduce themselves in the results of the study. As pointed out by Kaufman, the normativity of the scholar can function both as a pitfall and as an ally in theological research. Whether it is one or the other depends on whether the scholar is critically aware of the norms and values that he or she brings into the study and is able to make them explicit.[20] However, as also indicated by another Danish study, the very nature of the scholarly field may be an obstacle to this critical insight.[21]

As we designed the study, we were very careful to avoid biases in our sampling of the research population.[22] However, we were not aware to what extend our scope reflected our own location within the Academy and within the dogmatic discourse of the ELCD. Neither were we aware that we seemed to assume that the pastors would share our scholarly perspective. When formulating the overall research aim of the study in term, we said that we wished to "discuss its implications for a contemporary, empirically grounded theology of the *pastoral office* that would be able to meet the actual plurality of duties, methods and frames within pastoral work." On the surface this may seem quite straight, as in a Danish context *theology of the pastoral office* is the way that theological thinking about the pastor's role and functions is normally expressed. However, the very translation into English might have made us aware whether the framing is as neutral as it seemed, as in most contexts, especially those that are ecumenically inspired, one would not speak of theology of office, but rather theology of ministry. This means that already in its outset the project proved to be deeply immersed in a quite specific context. And, also, that by entering into the discourse of the theological norms and values of this context, it turned out how profoundly they were inscribed in our approach, even if they were invisible to ourselves. Still, it was not until we confronted the pastors' far more nuanced and creative negotiations of meaning that we realized this. It is worth noting that in our initial description of our expected theological outcome, the term office

---

20. Kaufman, "Normativity," 91.

21. Buch-Hansen, Felter, and Lorensen, "Ethnographic," 238.

22. See also footnote number 8.

seemed to be the only concept at hand if we were to argue for the relevance of our expected findings.

The idea that the scholar is so to speak able to "step back" from his or her inscribed norms to some value-free refuge has been fundamentally questioned during most of the twentieth century. In his seminal study of how personal dispositions mirror the social structures within a given field, French sociologist and anthropologist Pierre Bourdieu has convincingly argued that knowledge is not only historically, but also always socially situated, and that individuals always carry the weight of the world,[23] as the shared values of a group enter into the individual's dispositions as *habitus*.[24] As someone trained within the academic field, dominated by the logics of systematics and structural analyses, the theological scholar tends to take for granted that practitioners in the field will be acting according to the same kind of logic. But as knowledge is always situated, Bourdieu warns that as a researcher in the field of practice, the scholar risks committing what he calls the scholastic fallacy: the liability to interpret his findings according to theoretical structures valued in the Academy.[25] Inspired by Bourdieu, Pilario has argued that the same reflexivity should also be performed by theologians doing empirical studies. However, to counteract the normative bias that tends to privilege established theological traditions, Pilario argues that it is necessary to establish reflexive spaces, where the taken-for-granted understandings of the theological field as a whole can be tested.[26]

Learning from the study it seems especially urgent to create spaces for reflexivity that can bring out tacit assumptions underlying the formal and normative voices in the theological field. Being not only an academic theologian but also a pastor myself in the ELCD, raised in a conservative revival tradition but migrating through a moderately activist position to a more open or liberal stance, I proved to be deeply embedded in the field. What I was able to see—or not to see—depended initially on my habitual predispositions. But, also, as the study proceded, the encounters with pastors in different contexts and from various traditions, and the creative ways that they negotiated their ministry by activating and combining different elements of the tradition, disturbed the pre-packed categories that I brought into the field.

The privileging of the academic and official voices of theology over the voices of the practitioners seems to rest on the assumption that the

23. Bourdieu, *Weight*.
24. Bourdieu and Wacquant, *Invitation*, 117.
25. Ibid., 249.
26. Pilario, *Back*, 457ff.

theologian—whether academic or clerical—is able to write him- or herself off the page. But, as aptly demonstrated here, this is not an option, as we as academic theologians find ourselves in the middle of the fuzzy practices that, according to Pilario, characterizes *the World of Where and When*.[27] Rather than trying to guard the formal and normative voices of theology against being disturbed by the, unauthorized, espoused, and operant voices of the practitioners in the field of the church, the findings of the study could be seen as incentives for breaking with the idea of *a priori* privileged positions. American-Canadian ethnographic theologian Natalie Wigg-Stevenson suggests that ethnographic studies should be acknowledged as productive *disruptions* to theological normativity, both in shifting the focus from textual to practical methods and by shifting the mode of theological speech from proclamation to conversation.[28] In a similar vein, McClintock Fulkerson's idea of theological *de-centering* described above proposes a more equal distribution of power as it incorporates the insight that the theological scholar is no less than others situated in deeply normative and value-laden contexts that shape her interests and insights. Shifting the mode of theological speech from proclamation to conversation thus implies a more equal or modest role for the formal and normative voices. To learn from practice means that academic theology "relinquish its 'final word'" in the judgment about reality to enter into dialogue with differently situated theological voices.[29] Inviting the experiences and the reflections of the pastors themselves into this conversation might be the start of a mutual learning process, describing what a theology of pastoral ministry and pastoral being could be like on the conditions of contemporary society.

27. Ibid., 449.
28. Wigg-Stevenson, "From Proclamation," 6.
29. Pilario, *Back*, 464.

10

How Do We Break Out of
"the Old Paradigmatic Box"?

MARIANNE GAARDEN

INTRODUCTION

One of the major challenges in working with ecclesiology and ethnography is that theology already has an integrated world view. It points to the crucial question of how we can get behind our own preconceptions in our theological research. In my experience, one of the answers is the method—derived from the Greek words μετά (metá) "after" and ὁδός (hodós) "way or journey." A new method is like a way that can take us into foreign landscapes offering new insights from new perspectives. Thus, new methods can lead to new perspectives, which has been the case in my research. Without being aware of the consequences I chose a methodology which paved the way for new perspectives challenging the normative dimension in mainstream theology.

The point of departure in my research was in *ethnography*, understood more generally as qualitative research.[1] The point of arrival when I had to finish my dissertation was unintentionally in *ecclesiology*, understood as

---

1. I here use Scharen's definition of ethnography and ecclesiology, and I am indebted to him for the precise description of this urgent movement from empirical research to normative theology in his introduction to *Explorations*, 3.

normative theological research.[2] The inductive empirical research process brought me into a new landscape of ecclesiology, which I realized after finishing my research is of growing interest. It has been a new experience for me to encounter the work of other researchers in the process of cultivating the same landscape of *ethnography and ecclesiology*.

In this chapter I offer my contribution to the cultivation of this "newfoundland" in a meta-reflection on my own research process which led to a breakdown in the old paradigm and the emergence of a new. I shall describe the methodological decisions that influenced the research project in normative ways, and explain why I made them. Additionally, I shall account for the epistemological premise which challenges traditional theological dogma, and how these dogma were at the same time important in inter- and counter-action with the empirical results and ethnographic theological insights. Finally, I shall describe how the old paradigmatic box of mainstream theology crashed when confronted with these insights, but also how ethnography can offer empirical perspectives to a new paradigm for theological normativity.

HOW THE NORMATIVE DIMENSION ENTERED INTO MY RESEARCH PROCESS

Originally I only aimed to give a descriptive analysis of the congregations' experience of the preaching event. The results, however, were not consistent with the traditional Evangelical-Lutheran concept of preaching. During the process of analyzing the interview material with the churchgoers and preachers, it became clear to me that mainstream theology of preaching builds on certain assumptions that conflicted with my empirical findings. Of course, I could have rejected the way people actually *listen* to sermons and told them that they were wrong! In the best case, nothing would have changed; in the worst case, such a response could push people away from the church by my disrespect for their experiences. I was therefore challenged to analyze these assumptions, compare them with the empirical findings, and suggest another way to understand the preaching event. So the normative dimension grew out of the discrepancy between theological conviction and human experience, so to speak.

My project was an empirical research into five different congregations' experience of the preaching event by means of qualitative interviews with churchgoers and preachers and processed through the use of (constructing)

2. See Gaarden, "Den emergente." It was defended at Aarhus University, Faculty of Arts, June 2014.

Grounded Theory.[3] It was inspired by the listener-centered approach to preaching in contemporary homiletical literature with its implicit assumptions about the listening process.[4] These assumptions are typically based on understanding articulated in the theory and then applied to interpreting the listener's experience. The traffic thus travels one way on the bridge of interpretation—the theory is used to explain what happens when people listen. But the researcher seldom attends to what actually happens in the act of listening from the perspective of the *listener*. If "faith comes from hearing,"[5] however, why not listen to those who listen? And so I did.

From interviewing churchgoers, the empirical research demonstrated that theological conviction and practical experience are in conflict. From the perspective of the pew, the preacher's ethos is important for the listeners, who relate positively or negatively to the preacher when responding to the sermon according to whether they perceive the preacher as authentic, open-minded, and respectful toward the congregation. This is a challenge to the traditional interpretation of Protestant theological conviction which emphasizes the divine agency in preaching, based on the *Confession Augustana*: "through the word, as means bestowed, the Holy Spirit works faith where and when it pleases God."[6]

Traditional Protestant conviction ascribes an inherent religious function to the listening process, as "faith comes from hearing" (Rom 10:17). For dialectical theology including an anthropology perceiving humans as sinners alienated from God—which is prevalent in many Danish preachers' theology—the empirical results are challenging. So how are we to understand this theological conviction together with the empirical findings emphasizing the preacher's importance for the congregation's experience of the sermon? This drew me toward the task of defining the assumptions of those convictions in order to investigate whether they can be consistent with the empirical experience of preaching.

3. I shall explain Grounded Theory later in the chapter.

4. At that time I was teaching homiletics at the Pastoral Institute in Arhus and was using these contemporary homiletical theories primarily inspired from the North American movement the New Homiletic and Other-wise Preaching.

5. Rom 10:17. In the original Greek text, the verb "come" is not explicit, but it has nevertheless been understood as "comes" in the third person singular. The sentence "faith comes from hearing" is an indirect passive construction that masks the primary agency of faith, and the passive construction is open to interpretation. Of course, it is implied that God is behind the mask, as only God himself can inspire faith. For a more detailed explanation of the masked agency in preaching see Gaarden and Lorensen, "Listeners."

6. Augsburg Confession, article V.

HOW TO OVERCOME THE DICHOTOMY BETWEEN
EMPIRICAL RESEARCH AND THEOLOGICAL CONVICTION

If the dichotomy between human and divine agency had to be repealed, then it should be possible to articulate a communication theology of preaching where both the divine and the human agency remain intact. This led me to the conclusion that it is fruitful and relevant to interpret the "Word of God" as an embodied interactive event situated in time and place in which both preacher and listeners participate. In the search to overcome the dichotomy between empirical findings and theological convictions, I entered into a normative approach to theology—a normativity that was both rescriptive and hermeneutical.

Furthermore, the research revealed the same incongruence between the interviewed preachers' actual experiences and their theologies. The preachers agreed with the churchgoers that their authenticity and faith are very important for the congregation's experience and reception of the sermon—they know this from experience, but theologically they found it problematic. The normative interpretation of Evangelical Lutheran confession gave rise to a theological distinction between divine and human agency in preaching. The sermon and the entire worship are carried out by God, and if the sermon inspires faith, it is not due to the preacher, but to the Holy Spirit, even though this is not consistent with the experience. There was therefore a tendency to consider the importance of the preacher's ethos as theologically problematic. The preachers operated with both an ideological homiletic—it is God alone who inspires faith, deriving from their normative understanding of the confessions, and a practical homiletic—the preacher plays a crucial role in the listeners' experience of preaching, deriving from their own practical preaching experiences.[7] The dichotomy is rooted in two different paradigms: an anthropocentric and a theocentric.

This dichotomy between the empirical findings and the theological ideals encouraged me to rethink the normative dimension of the theological paradigm. I argued that what at first glance seems to be a dichotomy between empirical finding and theological understanding can be overcome by redefining the premises of the theological thinking. So even though my starting-point was ethnographic, aiming to generate data to obtain the perspective of the listeners about the preaching event, I ended in ecclesiology, understood as normative theological research. What I assumed was a too reductionist understanding of the communication process in preaching led me into far more complex theological questions. Thus I was moved during the research process from actual lived experience in church to core

7. This theme is outlined in Gaarden, "Den empiriske."

systematic theological questions about how we are to understand the relation between human and divine agency, which includes both subjectivity and the image of God.

THE EPISTEMOLOGICAL PREMISE FOR ETHNOGRAPHY— THEOLOGY IS BOUND TO HUMAN REASONING[8]

The premise of ethnography in ecclesiological research is that faith can be studied empirically, as theology is bound to human perceptions and reasoning. Traditional Christian theology distinguishes between the object of faith—what one believes in—and the practice of faith—the subject who believes. Two Latin terms are traditionally used to express this distinction: *fides quae*, what one believes in defined as the objective faith, and *fides qua*, faith as a human activity, defined as the subjective faith. Obviously faith as human activity, *fides qua*, can be studied empirically. From a sociological or phenomenological point of view an argumentation for this premise seems superfluous, since the starting-point for empirical research is of course the human who believes, and thus theology is not perceived as unique and incomparable with other subjects. Nevertheless the distinction between faith as human activity and the object of faith (God) involves a subject-object dichotomy which often affects the discussion about the use of ethnography in ecclesiological research.

In an Evangelical-Lutheran context, which for decades has been influenced by a dialectical theological way of thinking (as is the case in a Scandinavian country like Denmark) it is necessary to argue why and how ethnography is useful to gain new knowledge and theological insight. Empirical theological research often encounters suspicion and objections, as theology is assumed to be a unique subject incomparable with other subjects: "The more intensively empirical methods of modern social science are adopted by theology, the more urgent are the critical questions about the theological 'proprium' of this research."[9] So in the rapprochement between empirical research and theological understanding I shall here briefly outline the epistemological starting-point for the ethnographic methods.

It is argued that "the main problem is that the social scientific analysis and theological reflection are governed by entirely different paradigms."[10] There seems to be a discrepancy or dichotomy between ecclesiology as normative theology and ethnography as empirical research. The theological re-

8. This is a summary of the epistemological account of my research presented in Gaarden, *Prædiken*; *Third Room*.

9. Heimbrock, "Praktisk teologi," 28 [my translation].

10. Ganzevoort, "Van der Ven's," 53–74.

jection of empirical research assumes that the reality of God is independent of our limited human perception of God and our discourse about God. The action of the Trinity in the world can never be captured by our limited human understanding and analysis. Therefore, it is not empirically possible to say *anything* about God's agency in the world, which will always exceed human experience. Only in faith, which is a divine gift from God, can we engage with the reality of God. There is a general theological distrust of human experience as a source for theology. The role of the human being is presumed to be as an objective interpreter of the divine revelation.[11] The premise of this theological argument presupposes a transcendent reality independent of our immanent reality—but what then is the role of the researcher or theologian?

THE ROLE OF THE RESEARCHER OR THEOLOGIAN PARTICIPATING IN THE RESEARCH PROCESS

The fallacy in this line of argument is that the researcher or the theologian should have direct access to this transcendent and objective theological reality independent of their own personality. This has been contradicted by the last two hundred years of epistemological understanding of human reasoning.[12] It is impossible to think, understand, or talk about God independent of our own thought and understanding. There is only the *immanent* access to the transcendent reality. The Danish philosopher, Dorthe Jørgensen, defines transcendence as a concept of *experience*: "transcendence is, indeed, identical to the experience of transcendence."[13] Thus she operates with the concept of the *immanent experience of transcendence*, allowing people to have experiences of transcendence, and these are by nature immanent and thereby possible to study empirically.

Doing theology is an interpretative enterprise within which divine revelation is interpreted by human beings, who are contextually bound and subject to their own personal and theological agenda with different life experiences and backgrounds.[14] The researcher or the theologian is always a part of the research or the proposed theology. The distinction between an anthropocentric and a theocentric starting-point easily leads to the assumption that the theologian or the believer has privileged access to an objective truth about God, disregarding their own pre-understandings and

11. Hegstad accounts for this theological thinking in *Ecclesiology*, 34.

12. A tradition beginning with Emanuel Kant's epistemology and further extended in the phenomenology (Husserl) and the hermeneutics (Weber).

13. Jørgensen, "Experience" 39.

14. As argued by Swinton and Mowat in *Practical Theology*, 89.

participation in the process of recognizing. I argue that this is not possible. The Danish Professor of Anthropology, Kirsten Hastrup, expresses this precisely:

> By acknowledging that our own *participation* in the world under study is a distinct (anthropological) avenue towards understanding, the search for independent or external evidence breaks down. This again locates "rightness" in an epistemological awareness rather than in ontological certainty. It also shifts the objective of generalization from being (primarily) an identification of shared systems of meaning to the processes by which meanings are established, challenged and altered.[15]

If we accept that theology is bound to human reason and human thereby participate in the research process, there is no difference between the epistemological starting-point for ethnography and ecclesiology. The immanent human is always participating in the reality under study even though this reality is transcendent reality. This must be the epistemological starting-point for ecclesiology too.

THE INTER-SUBJECTIVE PREMISES FOR ETHNOGRAPHY

Qualitative research is not to be considered as a method to obtain objective knowledge about the perceived world in the positivistic way of understanding knowledge. Yet the entire idea of objectivity in knowledge about human activity is highly questionable. As I have argued above, human interpretation and experience is always dependent on the situated subject. As such, the qualitative interview is neither an objective nor a subjective method—it is by nature an inter-subjective interaction aiming to generate new and situated knowledge. The quest for objective knowledge, on the other hand, is related to the widespread dichotomy between objectivity and subjectivity in Western thinking. This thinking is based upon the fundamental belief "that there exists a permanent, ahistorical matrix to which we ultimately can appeal when we need to determine what knowledge, truth, reality or goodness is."[16]

---

15. Hastrup, "Getting It Right," 466 [emphasis mine].

16. Kvale, *Det kvalitative*, 74. It is often claimed that qualitative research interviews lack objectivity, writes Kvale, especially because of human interaction in the interview situation. He disproves the objection by pointing to the very notion of "objectivity" as a subjectively defined concept: "According to the definition of objectivity, objectivity is inter-subjective consensus. But the lack of inter-subjective consensus witnesses to objectivity being a rather subjective concept." Ibid., 72.

The Bible and God are for many theologians exactly such "a permanent, ahistorical matrix." So rejecting a matrix of a static and eternal truth is challenging for the theologian.

A way for the theologian both to give up the idea of being able to reach this objective eternal truth and to accept the inter-subjective premises for ethnography, is to accept the participation in the reality under study—which is for me perfectly consistent with Pauline theology: "For our knowledge is only in part, and the prophet's word gives only a part of what is true."[17]

This awareness of one's own participation in the research process includes a focus not only on the obtained knowledge of a perspective, but upon the process in which this knowledge is generated, interpreted, and makes sense. Or as Hastrup states, "rightness" is in an epistemological awareness rather than an ontological certainty. This awareness demands transparency in the role of the researcher and in the entire research process and has the keyword: *participation*. Using empirical methods, I also implemented an epistemology consistent with the social sciences, but unfamiliar to traditional theological thinking. Implementing these methods in my theological thinking opened the door for new perspectives.

"WHAT'S GOING ON"
SEEN FROM DIFFERENT PERSPECTIVES

Often we assume that we know "what's going on," as we already have an experience and an understanding of the phenomena we wish to investigate, in my case the preaching event. However, our understanding and experience are seen from our own perspective, and we may have blind angles and spots for other and different perspectives. Without letting our own preconceptions block the view of the others, the main question in *Grounded Theory* is "What's going on?" When applying the Grounded Theory method the researcher does not formulate hypotheses in advance. The hypotheses come as a *result* and constitute a theory that is grounded in the data—not the other way round.[18]

The logic of the method is called the abductive way of reasoning.

> Inductive reasoning develops general principles from specific observations, and the conclusion is probable, based upon the evidence given. In contrast, deductive reasoning moves from one or more premises to a logically certain conclusion. Deductive

17. 1 Cor 13:9.

18. In many ways, Grounded Theory method resembles what researchers do when retrospectively formulating new hypotheses to fit recorded data. The methodology operates almost in a reverse way from research in the positivist tradition.

reasoning thus links premises with conclusions, whereby the conclusion is a direct result of the facts presented. However, creative ideas emerge neither from deduction nor from induction but from abduction. A handy way to think of abduction is as inference to the best or the most likely explanation.[19]

The method does not aim to tell "the truth," but to conceptualize what is going on by using empirical research. For this purpose, Grounded Theory offers a systematic methodology to collect, codify, and analyze the empirical data obtained from qualitative interviews in order to generate a suggestion for new theory. Thus, the goal is to formulate new theory (or hypotheses for new theory), based on conceptual ideas developed through the analysis of empirical data. The empirical perspectives can thus challenge built-in assumptions, as was the case in my own research.

NEW PERSPECTIVES CHALLENGING THE OLD PARADIGM

Together with many other academically-trained theologians I straightforwardly assumed that the core of the action in preaching is that the congregation must come to an adequate *understanding of the Gospel*—and that the preacher can use words as an instrument to create this understanding. Built into this assumption are several cognitive premises, such as that the preacher has the power to control the listener's production of meaning, and words themselves contain a meaning. However, Grounded Theory provided a way for me by which I got *behind* my own preconception. The empirical methods opened the possibility for me to penetrate into what happens in the sermon *interaction* and hence paved the way for a theory of a new communication theology that is more adequate to what empirically seems to happen in the interaction between pulpit and pew. It required a tolerance of the feeling of being out of control from the beginning of the research process, until the relevant topics were identified, categories were built up, and a new theory was formulated on the basis of the hypothesis—in my case The Third Room of Preaching.

Previous empirical research within sermon listening has elaborated and expanded the understanding of the listening process by using predetermined theory. Yet one of the challenges in sticking to already formulated theory is that the research tends to stay within the familiar paradigm and perceive the investigated phenomena through predictable glasses. It is a challenge to allow for unpredictable results which do not accord with the familiar paradigm. I wanted to let the empirical data propel my research,

19. Gaarden, *Third Room*, 86.

which proved to be successful for new perspectives that forced me to see the world with different eyes. Thus I did not have a theoretical point of departure: instead I used the methodology of Grounded Theory, involving the construction of theory through the analysis of empirically-based data.[20]

THE EMPIRICAL SOURCES CANNOT BE CONTROLLED BY THE RESEARCHER

Empirical sources are often mistakenly perceived as more colored and influenced by the researcher, who participates in the generation of data, unlike one working with written sources only. Nevertheless, experience shows the opposite.[21] One of the reasons is that the sources are *alive* and can contradict the interviewer, can act or pull the interview in a direction the interviewer did not expect. So the sources can be rather difficult to control. In this kind of fieldwork one needs to accept that the sources are indeed alive, so one is actually participating in the generation of data without knowing where the research process will lead. Often the researcher is so involved in the data generating process that previous hypotheses prove to be inadequate and therefore the call is for more nuanced theories. Thus empirical research has a greater tendency to falsification of pre-assumptions than "dead" sources. However, this demands an ability to navigate in what can be experienced as chaos and confusion, since the sources one is using are out of one's control.

According to my experience with the qualitative interviews it was difficult to stay focused during the interview process as the interaction of the interview demanded that I should be present and follow the informant's thoughts. During the process of analyzing at my desk helped to create a constructive distance which was fruitful for the interpreting of data. The process of analyzing involved large amounts of unstructured data which had to be systematized into non-predefined categories as required by Grounded Theory. Obviously it would have been easier and less time-consuming to analyze the empirical data if the interviews had been more controlled and structured by a detailed and predetermined set of questions. However, the sources generated for the research project were more nuanced and my assumptions and ideas were corrected and nuanced.

In ecclesiology studies based on traditional written sources—such as biblical exegesis, language philosophy, works of systematic theologians or other important historical thinkers—the sources can be found and selected

20. The intention is to have an inductive approach, with no theoretical frame of references, but it is almost impossible to approach data without some kind of prior understanding—therefore, I argue for the abductive approach.

21. Flyvbjerg, *Kvalitative Metoder*, 481.

in a library, or even in front of a computer screen. Normally researchers have time to read and choose which sources to use, as the sources already exist; they do not go away, if the researchers are not present. Nor do they argue against them, if they do not agree with them. The sources will not question the researchers' assumptions, if they do not understand. It is easy for researchers in archive studies to stay at their desks defining, selecting, and delimiting the sources written in books. There is an element of being in control— quite the opposite to ethnography research—and thus it is easier in archive studies to operate within the assumed paradigm without being contradicted by living sources.

The original purpose of my research project was threefold: 1) to explore *what* churchgoers had heard in the sermon, 2) to compare the results with the preachers' own intention and theological understanding of their sermons, 3) and to analyze the results using contemporary homiletical theory. After a few pilot projects this research design quickly revealed that the first question, regarding the way the listeners had listened to the sermon, was not productive. The variation in what the churchgoers had heard was equal to the numbers of interviewees. However, by focusing on *how* the churchgoers had listened, I saw a pattern emerging. In consequence my first research design was adjusted, and I no longer focused on *what* the churchgoers had heard, but on *how* they had listened to and interacted with the sermon.

THE BREAKDOWN OF THE OLD PARADIGM AND THE EMERGENCE OF A NEW

However, looking back I realize that adjusting the research design caused the breakdown of the assumed paradigm. I was not aware of the consequences of leaving the concept of preaching as a cognitive enterprise, but the empirical results highlighted how the "Word of God" is less a semantic concept and more an interactive event in time and place in which the listeners and the preachers are participating. As a logical consequence, normative theological questions emerged. For example the core question of *who* God is, should rather be *how* we can *experience* God. These were my first reflections and struggles to adjust theological conviction to empirical findings. It was a slowly growing realization throughout the entire research process.

My first draft of the research design was formulated within the existing homiletical paradigm, assuming that preaching primarily is about *understanding the Gospel*. As an academically trained theologian I assumed that the preacher's role is to provide an understanding of the Gospel for the congregation at a semantic and cognitive level in order to make the churchgoers come to an adequate understanding of who God is, what God offers and requires of us, or how God operates in this world. But the research results based on the encounter with real churchgoers challenged one of the most taken-for-granted homiletical/rhetorical axioms in preaching—that the preacher primarily uses words as a tool in order to create understanding. This result put me on the normative theological track and forced me "out of the paradigmatic box," and I was compelled to rethink the assumptions interwoven within both my own pre-understanding and within theology in much historical and contemporary homiletical thinking.

As a child of the linguistic turn and I was of course aware of the language philosophical understanding of words as not having isolated meaning in themselves, but primarily a use in a context. I had participated in the deconstruction of the traditional understanding of communication as a one-way transfer from an active speaker to passive listeners. The so-called transfer model was theoretically inadequate and I understood preaching as an interactive event. Yet I was trained in rhetoric and assumed that communication is intentional orality to create an understanding of one point of view by the other—assuming that it actually *is* possible for the other to adopt one's point of view. However, I was corrected by my research.

THE THIRD ROOM OF PREACHING

The brief conclusion to my research is that the encounter between the listener's experience and the preacher's words facilitates what I call *The Third Room of Preaching*,[22] in which the listener, in internal dialogue, creates a surplus of meaning that was previously not present in either the preacher's intent or the listener's frame of reference. This inter-subjective surplus of meaning is more than the words of the preacher and more than the listener's experience: it emerges in the *situation of preaching*. The preacher cannot control the production of meaning but must surrender to the preaching event. Thus the preacher is not the carpenter of the Third Room, while the Third Room is dependent on the preacher's willingness to serve as an instrument. So what happens in the listening process is *not primarily about understanding* the Gospel or the sermon at a cognitive level but about *the creating of new meaning* or experiencing a meaningful and contemplative state of being in dialogue with the listener's personal life and the Gospel, incarnated through the voice of the preacher. Thus the preacher participates in the incarnation of the Gospel in the listener's universe.

The ethnographic theological insights of my research offer new perspectives on the normativity of mainstream theology in the united

22. The results of the dissertation are rewritten and published in Gaarden, *Prædikenen*; *Third Room*.

human-divine agency in preaching. They point toward an *incomplete* assumption embedded in the traditional paradigm. Embedded in my new proposal for understanding the "Word of God" as an emergent event situated in the service of worship in which both the listeners and the preacher participate are a number of normative theological questions. For instance, how are we to understand the "Word of God" written in the Gospel? The ethnographic insights from my research offer a new perspective for understanding the "Word of God" and new paradigm for a communication theology of preaching. The questions raised by the interaction between the traditional and the ethnographic theological claims have sent me on the track to look for the answers. And to be honest—I'm still *on* that track, although I do have some tentative answers.

PARTICIPATING IN GOD

Throughout history, Christianity has continuously borrowed its paradigms and world views from its surroundings. By redefining the paradigm of theological thinking it is possible to overcome what looks like a dichotomy. If the antithesis of divine and human action is false, it calls for a theology of transcendence-in-immanence to be elaborated.

Instead of seeing human beings as alienated *from* God I suggest a theology of incarnation as human participation *in* God. Participating in Christ is a gift of divine grace. If God in Christ is to be seen as humanity's deepest ground, then the preacher is in Christ and Christ is in the preacher, as Pauline and Johannine theology claim. This implies theological thinking in which humans are in Christ, and Christ is in God. Incarnation is to be understood as a double movement in which, by entering the world, God incorporates the world into himself.[23] When God became human, he united himself both with humanity as a whole and with the human as an individual. God resides in each person, not as a stranger but as the most personal in that person. Human beings cannot speak about God without already being or participating in God. This suggests that the contradiction between divine and human agency is false. The believer's participation in Christ is not a new theological thought; it penetrates both Pauline and Johannine theology.[24]

Thus the empirical research brought about more normative theological issues than I had anticipated. I realized that empirical research is useful

23. This understanding resonates with the perspective of process theology.

24. The theology of participation has gained renewed interest during the twentieth century. Over the past decade an exegetical and systematic theological interest has been increasing, while focus on the Word in Protestant theology has decreased.

not only for data generation in order to gain *descriptive* insight into how the congregation acts and experiences the lived life in church, but also in order to propose *normative* theological statements. It is my experience that empirical research can be transformative when we can go beyond the presupposed paradigm and think out of the theological box in which our thoughts normally move. Different ethnography methodologies can be constructive tools in adjusting our assumptions, but this can also happen by our working together in inter-disciplinary research projects where our ideas and thoughts will be altered and challenged by others persons' ideas and thoughts in a fruitful way to help us break out of the old paradigmatic box.

11

Where We Belong—Family as an Overlooked Interspace in the Passing On of Christian Tradition in Twenty-First Century Sweden

Ninna Edgardh

The family kneels around the grave. The two year old places the candleholder on the grave of his grandad, with just a little help. Vapor is coming out of his mouth, in the cold Swedish November night, but the atmosphere around the little family is warm. Several hundred of candles shine in the dark and people come and go all the time.

To visit a cemetery at this time of the year, in order to decorate the family grave and light a candle, has become a popular tradition in Sweden over the past hundred years. The tradition may be recent, but it has deep roots. The Church of Sweden (CofS) celebrates All Saints' Day on the Saturday that occurs between 31 October and 6 November. The following Sunday, All Souls' Day is celebrated. In special services of worship in commemoration of the dead, candles are lit for those who have died within the past year.

The younger generation, fostered by media and commercials, increasingly mix the popular feast with the more recent import of Anglo-Saxon celebrations of Halloween. Still, the vitality of the tradition around All Saints' is a surprising and somewhat disturbing facet of an alleged example of secularity. The image of Sweden as a typical—or even *the* typical—case of

138

secularization, fits badly with people lining up, hoping for a parking lot by the graveyard, or queuing at the entrance of the church.

If the queues on All Saints Day blur the secular image, on the first Sunday of Advent, the full churches could give the impression of a highly religious culture. The people attending might not regard themselves as Christian and might never appear on a regular Sunday, but going to church on the first of Advent is still part of what you do as a Swede, at least if you belong to the Lutheran folk church.

AIM AND THEORY

The paradoxical and rapidly changing contemporary religious situation in the Scandinavian countries, described in the introduction to the book, and exemplified by the little boy lighting a candle, is the starting point for this chapter. The ideals of the Swedish folk church tradition are being re-negotiated in Sweden today, between national church, individuals and families. The focus of this chapter is on how ordinary people in Sweden see their relationship to the church, in view of how they live their daily lives. Examples from an empirical study on how values are passed on in families with small children will be related to observations made in other studies.

The theoretical question concerns how empirical studies of this kind may inform a discussion on ecclesiology. Of importance for the argument will be the concepts, coined by Grace Davie and introduced in the first chapter of this book, of "belonging without believing" and "vicarious religion." Both notions catch important aspects of Swedish religious life, including the statement that "what the Scandinavians believe in is, in fact belonging."[1]

Grace Davie is one of many sociologists who have struggled to understand the particularities of the Swedish and Scandinavian context. The current role of Christianity among a majority of Swedes has been described as "cultural." Religious belonging is according to this line of thought reduced to providing "a sense of personal identity and continuity with the past."[2] This seems to fit well together with the idea of "believing in belonging." Ann af Burén in her doctoral thesis suggests that the majority of the Swedes are better described as "semi-secular," in that they are neither non-believers nor believers in any straightforward sense. Their approach to religion is according to her observations characterized by simultaneity—"both and" rather than "either or"—and a certain "fuzziness" with regard to the contours of

1. Davie, *Religion in Modern Europe*, 3.
2. Demerath, "Rise of 'Cultural Religion,'" 127.

both unbelief and belief.[3] This argument seems to give more credit to the faith of majority Swedes.

Burén's study falls into the strand of research called "lived religion."[4] Nancy Ammerman in an assessment of these kinds of studies observes that they have paid "attention to laity, not clergy or elites; to practices outside religious institutions rather than inside; and to individual agency and autonomy rather than collectivities or traditions."[5] Approaching "lived religion" has been a way to counter a dominant tendency to equal religion with dogmatic belief and formal relations.

"Lived religion" has developed as a sociological concept, in a way similar to how ethnographic methods have increasingly been used to discuss ecclesiology, as exemplified in this book. Ammerman underlines in her article the need for sociologists to take a step further, and re-connect observations of lived religion with institutionalized religion. In ecclesiological studies, the focus on traditions, collectivities and ordained ministries is essential, but less attention has been paid to the daily lives and practices of the majority of a population. What I want to suggest is not a shift, but a way of keeping the two aspects of ecclesial life together.

I will not, in what follows, focus on blue-prints of how the church *should* be or develop, deduced from a specific theological starting point.[6] Rather my aim is to focus ecclesial life "in such a way that the actual life of the church is attended to, thought through theologically, and thereby strengthened."[7] In my understanding those who belong to CofS are, in some way or another, part of "the actual life of the church," even if they hesitate to call themselves religious or Christian. Their voices are thus worth listening to in a reflection on ecclesiology.

A CASE IN POINT OF EXTREME SECULARIZATION

Sweden has for a longer period of time distinguished itself as "a different country" in the waves of data collected by the World Values Survey (WVS).[8] A new "cultural map of the world" was published by WVS in January 2015. The map offers an easily accessible presentation of the results from the sixth wave of data from 61 countries on people's views on areas such as family, work, religion, politics, science, safety, violence, and the future.

3. Burén, *Living Simultaneity*.

4. McGuire, *Lived Religion*.

5. Ammerman, "Lived Religion," 83.

6. Healy, *Church*.

7. Scharen, *Explorations*, 2.

8. Pettersson and Esmer, *Vilka är annorlunda?*

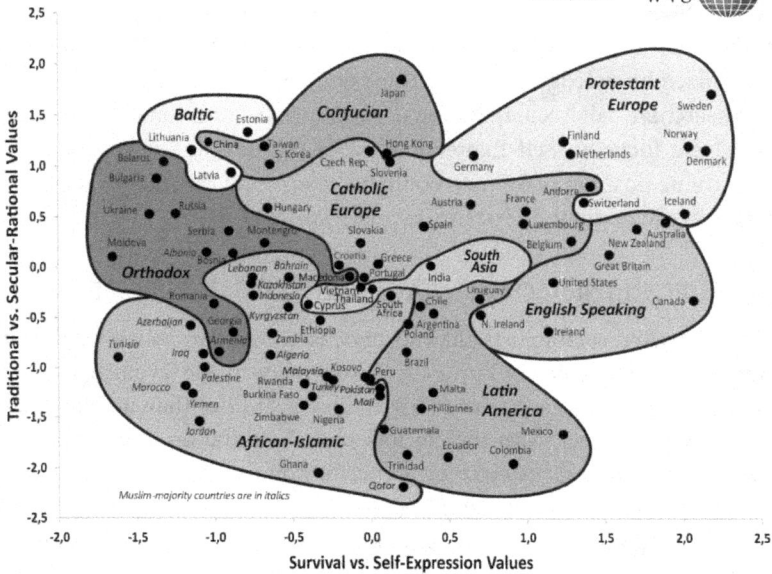

Figure 6: World Values Survey: Ronald Inglehart, "cultural evolution" (2015)

The position of the countries on the map emerges out of a combination of results from the WVS. A move upward reflects a shift from *Traditional values* to *Secular-rational* and a move rightward reflects a shift from values related to *Survival* to values of *Self-expression*. According to the terminology *traditional values* implies seeing religion as important, as well as valuing parent-child ties, deference to authority and traditional family values. People who embrace these values also tend to reject divorce, abortion, euthanasia, and suicide. Societies where these values are embraced, typically have high levels of national pride and a nationalistic outlook. *Secular-rational values* represent the opposite to the traditional. Less emphasis is laid on religion, traditional family values and authority. Divorce, abortion, euthanasia and suicide are seen as relatively acceptable.

With regard to the second parameter those who embrace *Survival values* place emphasis on economic and physical security. These are linked to a relatively ethnocentric outlook and low levels of trust and tolerance. *Self-expression values* at the other end means high priority to environmental protection, growing tolerance of foreigners, positive attitudes toward gays and lesbians and gender equality, and rising demands for participation in decision-making in economic and political life.[9]

9. World Values Survey.

In the 2015 version of the map, Sweden is once again to be found in the upper right corner, as the most extreme in a group of countries gathered under the label "Protestant Europe." These countries are all wealthy and highly modernized knowledge-societies. Their populations tend to embrace what the researchers call Secular-Rational, rather than Traditional values. They also have a focus on Self-Expression values rather than Survival values.[10] The extreme position of Sweden could be taken as an argument for Sweden being *the* case in point of extreme secularization.

ECCLESIOLOGY IN A CHANGING CONTEXT

Theologians and sociologists alike struggle to come to grips with diverging tendencies of religiosity, in Europe and worldwide.[11] The Swedish situation has been described as a case of religious change, rather than an exemplary case of secularization, with the old folk church taking on a new role, as a personal and cultural resource or arena for communication.[12] The Swedish situation has also been described as Post-Christian, indicating a stage where the role of historic Christianity is left behind.[13] It is also described as Post-Secular, hinting primarily at a return of religious voices in the public sphere.[14]

It is worth stressing that ongoing religious changes relate to a deeper change affecting the whole of Swedish society. In a rather short time, Sweden has moved from being a sparsely populated, poor and rather homogenous country, to being one of the richest in the world, with a wide cultural heterogeneity.[15] Concepts that decades ago had the political power to gather the population, have as a consequence lost much of their attractiveness. That is true not least of the idea of the country as a *folkhem* (home of the people), as the basis for the welfare system, with the state as a good parent, taking care of the population "from cradle to grave."[16]

10. The pre-understanding held by the researchers, which is nevertheless seldom made explicit, is that a movement from left to right, and from the bottom and up, represents a path toward democracy and liberation, closely connected to modernization and a loss of religious values. For the theoretical basis of this analysis, see Welzel, *Freedom Rising*, 37–56.

11. A good overview of the sociological questioning of secularization theories is given in Berger et al., *Religious America*.

12. Bäckström, Edgardh, and Pettersson, *Religious Change*, 25.

13. Martinson, *Postkristen teologi*; Hagman, *Efter folkkyrkan*; Thurfjell, *Det gudlösa folket*.

14. Sigurdson, *Det postsekulära tillståndet*.

15. Gregson, "Richest Countries"; MigrationsInfo, "Forskning och statistik."

16. Pettersson and Edgardh, "Church of Sweden."

The changes affecting ecclesial life are related to these changes, just as the ideas of the folk church were related to the idea of the *folkhem*. The number of studies published on the theology of the folk church in recent years suggest a crisis for ecclesial identity.[17] Pastors and decision makers have to live with the paradox of a still high degree of belonging, combined with a low degree of belief, but the paradox causes increased debate. I here want to sketch two tendencies in the debate in order to show the different roles they imply for the members and the population at large.[18] For the sake of the argument, I will present them as two opposite poles, one exclusive and the other seemingly inclusive. The inclusive tendency accepts the rules set by social change, arguing that the role of the church cannot be but one producer of services among many in a free market. The exclusive tendency underlines the otherness of the ecclesial community, and argues for the building of more tight worshipping communities from below.

The alternative of the church as producer of services is inclusive in that it minimizes the difference between member and non-member, believer and seeker. They all appear as customers in relation to what the church has to offer. In a way, this is a re-formulated folk church theology, building on the old ideas formulated by Einar Billing in the 1930s of the Swedish church offering the forgiveness of sins to the people inhabiting the geographical area called Sweden.[19] The church serves individuals in a similar way today, but authority has shifted. What the church has to offer becomes more negotiable, when the power to choose is in the hands of the consumers. If people do not ask for the forgiveness of sin, it might not be offered, at least not in an explicit way.

When the otherness of the ecclesial community is stressed, the authority of the organization is preserved within the worshipping community, gathered around the means of grace. The community may be open to anyone, but the offer is not subject to negotiation. There is no reason for a non-believing member or a Swedish citizen who does not belong to the church to relate to what is going on.

EMPIRICAL BASIS

The empirical basis for what will follow is the study *Family and Values in Sweden*, performed within in *The Impact of Religion program* at Uppsala

---

17. For an overview of recent literature on the subject, see Ideström, *Folkkyrkotanken*.

18. Cf. Vikström, *Folkkyrka*.

19. For a more thorough analysis, see Ekstrand, *Folkkyrkans*.

University.[20] The study is based on in-depth interviews with parents of small children.[21] While taking the results from the WVS as its starting point, the project tried to reach beyond the type of answers typically covered by questionnaires.

Parents of small children are a key group, as the experience of raising a child necessitates taking stands and making choices related to values. Parents are in this way prone to reflect both over their own childhood and the choices made by their parents, *and* over their own new role. The interview guide consisted of key question posed in the WVS study concerning values, religion, and family. For each immediate response, the interview person was encouraged to elaborate on the reasons behind. Concrete examples of what the response could mean in daily life were encouraged.

The interviewees were parents of young children, who attended open day care centers. The municipality runs one of the centers. CofS runs the other, on behalf of the municipality, which is a quite common arrangement. The center is open to anyone, but it is located close to the church building for "Livets ord" [Word of Life], an evangelical-charismatic Free Church congregation with roots in the Word of Faith-movement in the US.[22] Three interview persons were active in this congregation, while still taking their children to CofS pre-school. One person was a regular visitor to the Word of Life meetings, but also to other Free Church congregations, while another interview person was a passive and non-believing member of another Free Church. One person was fostered in the folk church in another Nordic country, but had chosen not to enter CofS when immigrating. One person had actively left CofS. Eight were more traditional members of CofS, one of them an active member. All in all the interview persons were rather typical of the Swedish majority population with regard to religious belonging, except for the persons involved in the Word of Life, who represent a small minority.

Also with regard to family patterns, the interviewees represent a wide breadth. Twelve of fifteen were married, one of them to a person of the same sex. Three were co-habiting without being married, one of them engaged. Six of the interview persons had one small child, five had two children, two had three children, one five children and one had an adult daughter and a

20. Centrum för studiet av religion och samhälle, "Impact of Religion."

21. The study is made in collaboration with the sociologist of religion, TD Martha Middlemiss Lé Mon, and is based on fifteen interviews, eleven with women and four with men, conducted 2013–15.

22. According to their annual report 01.07.14–30.06.15 the congregation had 3,200 members all in all. Livest Ord, *Årsredovisning 2014/2015.*

grandchild, but had started anew with two kids and two "bonus-kids" of her husband.

RESULTS FROM THE INTERVIEWS

Belonging as a Key Concept

With few exceptions, all Swedes belonged to the national church up until the 1950s, when religious freedom received protection in the law. Members of the free churches were for example, also often members of CofS. This is one factor behind the tendency for Swedes to "believe in belonging." Even if the situation is different, still today membership in CofS is often taken for granted. This is illustrated by the surprise shown by our interviewee Lena. Confronted with the question as to whether she belongs to any religious community she first says no, then corrects herself:

> I: Do you belong to a church or religious denomination?
> Lena: No . . .
> I: Did you grow up in any religious tradition?
> Lena: . . . or, rather, I belong to, am a member of the church, one does belong . . .
> I: One does belong to the church?
> Lena: Yes, I guess I am a member of the Church of Sweden, but I am not active and go there.
> I: No, exactly. But you do pay a church fee?
> Lena: Yes, I do, and I guess that is the only thing . . .

Lena does belong, as one does, including paying the fee for being a member. That is the only thing membership entails for her.

The decline in formal belonging to CofS has to do, at least partially, with immigration. To be a Swede is no longer equated with having grown up in Sweden and thus not with being a member of the folk church. Many immigrants are however Christian and represent a new type of Christian plurality in Swedish society. Immigrants included, about 70 percent of the Swedish population has a formal relation to a Christian community. What that entails with regard to beliefs and practices is more difficult to say. Data from the most recent wave of results from the World Values Survey (2010–2014) show that 41 percent of the Swedes said they believed in God, 30 percent said they took part in worship at least once a year, 35 percent said they prayed once a year. Our interviewee Maria illustrates how this fits together:

> I think churches are nice and very peaceful . . . so sometimes when I pass a church I go in. . . . But . . . I do not go to any

services—the church is there for people in need . . . and it is open for everyone . . . and I think a lot of people find comfort by going to church and feel some kind of belonging. In this way, I think the church fills an important function.

Maria is baptized and confirmed, but not particularly religious, she says. Still she and her husband have had their son baptized:

Baptism is for me to celebrate that he has come into existence. Then baptism is that he becomes a member of Church of Sweden . . . and then also, that it is what you do—Then he will choose when he is older what he wants to do or not.

God as Free Choice

The dominating story told by the sociologists of religion, with regard to the development in Sweden over the last century, is of a move from strong institutional authority of the church, to a situation where authority belongs to the individuals, who choose their life views.[23] Our interviewees confirm this story. Irrespective of religious belonging and personal belief, they embrace the idea that their children will choose by themselves when they are old enough. Robert, a non-believing member of a Free Church congregation, says they do not feel comfortable talking about faith with their daughter, as they are not believers themselves. One day he and his wife will explain that there are people who believe in God, but then they will present it as "a possible theory, or one view of things." Lisa, who belongs to CofS, says it is important that her son will decide on his own:

If he wishes to believe in God that is very ok, and if he does not that is very ok too. To me the most important is, as I said, respecting other people, that you should treat everyone equally.

Another interviewee, Ruth, who has left CofS, is ambivalent toward letting her daughter take part in a voluntary short time of worship as practiced in CofS pre-school. She accepts it, because her daughter will choose on her own when she is big enough and then it is good for her to know about it. Still she finds it a bit problematic, as she cannot offer her the same experience of a mosque.

This stress of individual choice goes hand in hand with a strong appreciation of the institutional church, in a way that fits well with Grace Davie's theory of religion as "vicarious" in modern Europe. Members and former members of the national church alike, appreciate the church for defending

23. Bäckström, Edgardh, and Pettersson, *Religious Change*, 57–61.

basic values that fit with the values of Swedish society at large, for doing good deeds and for being on hand, when people are in need. This appreciation does however not necessarily entail a more personal involvement, belief or identification as Christian, as for our interviewee Edith:

> The Church of Sweden is like something positive for me still, although I do not believe I think they fill an important function in society . . . and then I would not leave because I think it is important that they exist—in general it is something positive for many . . . and gives good answers on questions that fits with . . . the values of society.

Member, but Not Religious

Only about thirty percent of Swedes see themselves as religious, according to WVS, compared to the seventy percent mentioned above, who have some sort of formal belonging to a Christian community. The figures indicate a conflict around the interpretation of what it means to be a Christian and the role of the church.

This conflict has been analyzed by the historian of religion David Thurfjell in his book *Det gudlösa folket* [The people without god].[24] Thurfjell takes his starting point in the strange Swedish combination of vague beliefs, low practice and high degree of belonging. In Thurfjell's view the high figures of belonging reflect a mentality, a way of being Christian, which is not new, but quite traditional in a country where being a good person and a good Christian was for a long time one and the same thing and did not necessarily entail much of individual religious practice.

What has happened the last century is that the national church has lost its monopoly to define what it means to be Christian. People may stay as members, but they do not necessarily identify as Christians. Thurfjell traces the background to this in the early twentieth century Christian revival moments, which had a much more demanding understanding of Christian faith than the state church with regard to personal involvement. These movements managed to take over the very definition of being Christian, and religious, he argues. The process was fueled by the public schools taking over the basic teaching of Christian faith, placing Christianity alongside the other world religions as one possible option for the autonomous individual.[25]

24. Thurfjell, *Det gudlösa folket*.

25. Karin Kittelmann Flensner shows in her dissertation on the teaching of religion in Swedish schools, how a secularist discourse is hegemonic in the classroom practice

Later this more narrow understanding of Christian faith became a welcome target for secular humanists. The debates they initiated confirmed negative images of Christian faith. It is this understanding, Thurfjell argues, that in part lives on, and motivates people to stay connected to the church, but disassociate themselves from what they perceive as a negative interpretation of Christianity. Thurfjell concludes that CofS today faces a rather hopeless task, as it has lost, through the processes described, the interpretative power over the faith that is its own native tongue.[26]

Something of this ambiguity seems to be reflected in the WVS data, as respondents seem to have quite clear and positive ideas about religion, while still not themselves being willing to see themselves as religious.

Let me illustrate. When asked which of two alternatives would best express their understanding of religion, 6 percent of the WVS-respondents ticked the box for "following religious norms/practices," while 89 percent ticked "to do good to other people," which seems to represent a "golden rule"-type of religiosity. This religiosity seems concentrated on this world, rather than some "other-worldly" reality, as the respondents, when asked if the basic meaning of religion would be to make sense of life after death or to make sense of life in this world, 13 percent would choose life after death, and 78 percent life in this world.

Other results from the WVS show that 89 percent of Swedes see it as important to help people around them. Why then do they not want to identify as religious, if that is what they think religion is about? My hypothesis is that the responses reflect what people think religion *should be*, but not really what they expect to meet in church. Our interviewee Elisabeth illustrates this, by not identifying as religious, but still recognizing that her values are traditional Christian values:

> This thing with tolerance and fellowship . . . what Jesus stood for in a way. That is what I see as important too, even if I do not call myself Christian.

Elisabeth hesitates to say that she believes in God. That becomes too abstract. Her faith is about what is close to her, to live according to the values she has chosen to embrace:

> And then I end up close to the Christian, those Christian values . . . that I think the church and Christianity should be about,

---

today. Religion is treated as outdated and belonging to history. Swedishness is, however, still connected to Christianity, although without any personal spiritual involvement. Flensner, *Religious Education*.

26. Thurfjell, *Det gudlösa folket*, 65.

but that they do not achieve all the time, unfortunately. It is too intolerant, too traditional, too narrow, so . . .

As an example of the too narrow understanding, Elisabeth tells me the story about one of her children, who is not baptized, but sings in a children's church choir. Elisabeth recalls how upset the child was, when a priest explained during their rehearsal, that those who are not baptized are not children of God.

A similar ambiguity toward authoritarian interpretations of faith is expressed by Lisa:

> Ambiguous is a good word. Ambiguous feelings in relation to church and religion and all that. I don't think you can sit and say, but this is how you should live and that there is a God who sits and decides what is right and wrong and who is going to live and who is going to die—But the fellowship and that . . . that I can embrace.

Swedes as a Special Kind

So if not in a church that is perceived as too authoritarian and normative, where do Swedes shape their faith and their values? How are all these individual choices made? Henrik Berggren and Lars Trägårdh, in their book *Is the Swede a Human Being* identify some typical traits of what they see as Swedish mentality.[27] Swedes turn out to be human, after all, in their interpretation, but of quite a peculiar sort, combining an unusually high degree of individual autonomy with a strong sense of social solidarity. This moral logic, they argue, has been institutionalized in Sweden through a radical alliance between the individual and the state, which they call "statist individualism."

The idea is important for the argument in this chapter, because it says something about a typical Swedish relationship between the individual, the family and the larger community. Statist individualism typically liberates the individual from the ties of dependency in relation to family and charities. Instead of relying on family, Swedes (in the spirit of the *folkhem*) have trusted in the public authorities to guarantee the security of the individual. This social contract differs dramatically from those of other modern, Western democracies.

The first edition of the book does not attribute any role to religion in the development of this statist individualism. When a second edition of the book was published in 2015, an additional chapter was however included,

27. Berggren and Trägårdh, *Är svensken människa?*

filling what the authors now saw as a serious lacuna, concerning the role of the church. In the preface they write: "With our cheeks turning red in embarrassment we have come to realize that we are guilty of one of the most common errors of the majority culture in this country: to believe that Swedish political culture is unaffected by faith convictions."[28]

The additional chapter deals with the close alliance between state and church, which was still at work during most of the twentieth century and which in fact, the authors now admit, had great impact on the creation of the Swedish welfare state, the *folkhem*. By the inclusion of the new chapter the authors try to show how church and society in Sweden have in fact developed in parallel, so that the development of the one cannot be explained while excluding the other. The idea of the *folkkkyrka* was constructed in parallel with the development of what Berggren and Trägårdh now call its "secular twin" the *folkhem*. The folk church in this process became a "laid back and wide fellowship, with room for almost everyone and with few and small demands on the individual."[29]

CofS is presently in law described as "an open folk church"[30] and the church board decided in 2004 that the central values communicated by the church should be "presence, openness, hope."[31] This open character is much appreciated by our interviewees and is probably a basis for the fact that trust in CofS is relatively high (41 percent) in Sweden and has increased since twenty years back.[32]

A Renewed Role of the Family

While Berggren and Trägårdh catch important aspects of Swedish mentality, involving religious aspects, the continuing importance of family remains hidden in their depiction. Within the sphere of welfare research, a feminist critique articulated since the beginning of the 1990s, concerns a negligence of the role of the family in welfare provision.[33] This negligence has its background in that mostly women, outside of the formal economy, provide welfare services in the family. These are then more difficult to measure in numbers. The role of the family in welfare thus fell outside the floodlight of

---

28. Ibid., 9.

29. Ibid., 415.

30. Sveriges Riksdag, "1998:1591," §2.

31. Svenska kyrkan, *Svenska kyrkans kommunikationsplattform.*

32. Medieakademien, *Förtroendebarometern 2016.* Church of Sweden is in this web-based survey included among societal institutions, and ranked on the same level as the royal house, but higher than the parliament and the government.

33. Sainsbury, *Gendering*; Daly and Rake, *Gender.*

research, until feminist researchers observed the problem. Something of the same phenomenon might be true for the role of the family in relation to the passing down of Christian values and traditions in modern Sweden.

Religious adherence has primarily been measured in terms of individual membership, participation in worship and personal convictions about God. Meanwhile, the role of families have not gained similar attention. The "statist individualism" discussed above has moved responsibility from families to public authorities. This role of families is however not lost. Swedes do not any longer depend as before on their family for material survival, but for their well-being, the family is of utmost value.

This is visible in the latest WVS survey, where 89 percent of the Swedes in fact valued family as very important and an additional 9 percent saw the family as rather important. The comparable figures for religion are 7,9 (very) and 18,3 (rather). The figures fit well with the responses from our interviewees, who unanimously saw the family as very important or the most important thing in life, more important than work, money, career, religion etc.

These figures seem however more problematic to fit into the overall image painted by the WVS researchers, of Sweden as a country where traditional values related to both religion and the family are left behind. The explanation seems to be the transformed role of the family, including the very definition of family. In the wake of the old family patterns the myth of the lone Swede has developed.

That this is more of myth, than reality, is argued by the Swedish economist Agneta Stark.[34] Only 16 percent of the adult population live alone, she observes, which means that eight out of ten adult Swedes share their daily life with another person. For women the most common period of living alone is in old age. 5 percent of the adults live alone with a child. Parenthood rather than loneliness is characteristic for Sweden at present, Stark argues. Swedish birthrates are high in European comparison and by the age of 45, 86 percent of Swedish women have become mothers.[35]

In international comparison Sweden still has a relatively high percentage of people living alone. But that doesn't automatically mean they are

34. Stark, "Nej, svenskarna."

35. The data Stark refers to shows that out of a population of 9.9 million Swedes, 2.5 million are children; 4.5 million of the adults are married, live in registered partnership or cohabit; 355,000 are lone parents, living with infants; 1.6 million live alone, that is 17 percent. For women, the typical period of living alone is after the age of sixty five. For men, living alone is most common from twenty to fifty, but more infrequent after retirement. Older women living alone are mostly widows with close contacts with their children and grandchildren. For more data, see SCB, *Personer*.

lonely or that they do not have people whom they count as "family." As we see in our interviews "family" includes a wide range of people, from old parents, to children, siblings and other relatives and sometimes even very close friends, or in the words of Ruth:

> I do not think of family as a family in constellation of . . . of maybe parents and children . . . but maybe more of how you . . . what you define as family. I myself have . . . two of my brothers whom I grew up with are not my full siblings, but we are half-siblings but it feels exactly as . . . we don't have another kind of relation than my full siblings. And the same with my child, whom I have not carried myself and am not the biological mother of, I have such a strong relation to him, happiness as much as the son I gave birth to myself. So I think a lot of . . . that I like to know a number of persons that are closest to me. Sure could have maybe a good friend whom I felt to be part of the family.

As openness is constitutive of CofS, as argued above, the same seems to be the case for the Swedish family. Families are mainly constituted by couples living together, sometimes with children. The WVS enquiries raise phenomena that people are asked to judge as justifiable or not, on a scale from 1 to 10. Among the issues raised is homosexuality. Swedes score high on seeing homosexuality as always justified (65 percent), which is reflected in the Swedish gender-neutral marriage law. In fact, among our interviewees some even saw the idea of homosexuality having to be justified as provocative. Robert said that "if you are homosexual you are, that is how it is" and Lena found it "a bit provoking that it is something to be argued for as justifiable or not." The family thus may be constituted by various gender combinations. It may include those other than biological parents and children and it may be extended and include parents, siblings, and sometimes even close friends.

Irrespective of who counts as family, our interviewees stress its emotional and existential importance. The family is their platform in life. That is where they spend time, what they give priority. The family gives them identity and security, as illustrated by our interviewee Eve:

> It is like my stability, where I seek support . . . it is my whole life I can say that my family . . . then I do not think only of [husband and child] but of my own parents and his. . . . It is like a security.

An interesting ecclesiological aspect of the role of the family is that many of the interviewees stress the importance of shared meals, even if these are difficult to uphold in large families with many activities going on. The family is where you spend your Sunday mornings and they are the people with whom you celebrate the great feasts, like Christmas, Easter and the for Swedes very important occasion of Midsummer.

The interviewees were confronted with the question from the WVS questionnaire of whether the church provided them with answers to their basic questions in life. As most of the interviewees were not personally related to a parish, this was generally not the case. Interestingly this was also true for the most religiously active interviewees, who belong to the Word of Life congregation. They would rather turn to the Bible, as they read it themselves, than give the authority of interpretation to the congregation or the pastor, or with the words of Emma:

> I think faith itself always has to do with yourself and your personal relation to God and so on . . . the church can never replace your own relation to God.

The response seems typical for a twenty-first century Swede, rather than for a traditional member of a Christian congregation. This individualistic approach underlines the role of the family, in that interpretation of faith is referred to the private sphere, where all the issues of life are to be put into practice.

When asked about the values they want to transmit to their children, among the alternatives presented in the WVS-study, the values given highest priority among our interviewees were tolerance and respect for others, mentioned by out of fifteen (87 percent in WVS). Independence was mentioned by eight persons (71 percent in WVS).

Several interviewees stress in their comments that they want their children to know what Christian faith, as well as other faith traditions, are about. They see it as important for their kids to have knowledge about religion, "otherwise you are a bit handicapped" as our interviewee Sonya says. Her kids get to hear about God and Jesus through the neighbors, who belong to the Word of Life congregation:

> So, [the kid] says all the time that he believes in the God of our neighbour. So I have read the children's Bible so that they will understand what the neighbor is talking about. They were very interested in crucifixions. They found that really exciting.

DISCUSSION

The starting point for this chapter is the paradoxical and rapidly changing social and religious situation in Sweden. The national church has lost much of its former interpretative authority. Together with a whole range of other social institutions, CofS struggles to find a new role in a rapidly changing society. A majority of the population stays on as members and makes use of rituals according to their own choice, but hesitate to call themselves Christian and seldom take part in regular worship.

The cultural map from WVS seems to indicate that both religion and ties between parents and children are relatively unimportant for Swedes. Our interviews, along with other interview studies, modify this image. It seems rather to be specific models of institutional religion that are rejected. Families are obviously of central importance for Swedes, however in a much more open and non-traditional form than how WVS tend to use the concept when results are summarized. This is problematic, as the image of Swedes as the most secular people is widely circulated in media and this image hides important aspects of how people in Sweden actually think.

Against this background it is important for theologians not to accept simplified interpretations of secularization. I have, quite roughly, sketched two alternative ecclesiological ways forward, one more exclusive, the other seemingly inclusive. The exclusive concentrates on building tight communities around regular worship. A major problem with this tendency is that it provides little connection between the worshipping community and people who rather than calling themselves Christian seem to "believe in belonging." Whether we call them "cultural Christians," "semi-secular" or something else, exclusive ecclesiology does not count on them as partners in a dialogue. It is of course possible to argue that people who do not identify as Christians would do better not to belong to a Christian church.

Having looked at the WVS data and listened to our interviewees I would however hesitate to draw that conclusion. As shown by Thurfjell, among others, there may be several more or less well founded reasons for people to uphold an ambiguous attitude toward the church. To stay on as a member because you feel that the church safeguards important values, which somehow reflects a shared mentality, seems to me to be worth respect, even if the contours of one's individual belief are somewhat "fuzzy." A certain "fuzziness" at a time when trust in institutional authorities is weak and each and everyone has to find their own belief system, seems to me more sound than problematic.

The other and more inclusive alternative, of the church as provider of services in a market also inhabited by other actors, has other problems. While the more exclusive alternative seems to safeguard important confessional aspects of the church, these will much more easily be lost in a situation when the church becomes an actor in a market regulated by supply and demand. A quick glance at some parish websites in Sweden today shows a supply side that has expanded far beyond what anyone would have thought possible some decades ago. It is not necessarily negative. The gospel may take on many faces. But it may be quite difficult to distinguish a specific Christian identity that keeps the many offers provided together.

Moreover, even the inclusive alternative runs the risk of reducing the role of the "semi-secular" church members. Their faith may have fuzzy contours, but a vague faith is not necessarily shallow or trivial. The "semi-secular" struggle with their lives and may have a deep need to be included, not as consumers of activities, but as part of the people of God, members of the body of Christ, in need of healing, teaching and transformation.

Quite apart from what the cultural map of the world seems to suggest, our interviews have shown transformed families to be a key arena for ordinary Swedes in their meaning-making and passing down of basic values. This is a reminder in a situation when privatized and individualized images of faith dominate. Then tendency to build tighter worshipping communities from below in this way catches important needs, having to do with the corporate nature of Christian faith that the consumerist tendency does not manage to accommodate.

These worshipping communities has an important vicarious role, as Grace Davie has well argued. This role may be sociologically possible to register. It fits well with the argument from some of our interviewees that they are willing to pay for the church to be there, even if they do not engage themselves more than that. The vicarious role is also theologically viable. The word liturgy has its root in the idea of a group of people doing something in public on behalf of a wider community.[36] This important "on behalf"-aspect tends to be lost in both the exclusive and the inclusive tendency discussed above. Rather than raising higher demands for right belief, or reducing people to consumers, I would like to argue for "vicarious religion" as a serious model of belief, connected to both risks and possibilities. Furthermore, the various kinds of families that exist in Sweden, are important communities in-between the individual and the wider community. It remains to be studied what roles families may have in the Swedish practices of "vicarious religion."

Running pre-schools is widespread in Church of Sweden parishes today. These may have an unacknowledged ecclesiological importance, offering a meeting point for parents with small children, where they may encounter aspects of the church that they are not able to provide at home. It may be in something as simple as the reading of a text from a children's Bible. The same may be true for parish activities directed toward schoolchildren.

---

36. Edgardh, *Gudstjänst*, 223.

An Easter drama enacted for schoolchildren may offer their only connection to the Christian Easter narrative. When families celebrate Easter and Christmas, the focus is normally on shared meals, gifts to the children and encounters with relatives, rather than the Biblical stories. The pre-schools and the activities for school children have an important role in keeping the connections to Christian faith traditions alive. In this way they may serve as meeting-points between family traditions and the wider and theologically founded Christian tradition.

With my empirical study on the "actual life" of young parents in Sweden, relating in various ways to the ideas and practices of Christian churches in Sweden, I have tried to give an example of how ethnography can inform a discussion on ecclesiology. In line with the thought of Grace Davie, parishes in CofS serve as important vicarious upholders of a culture of shared beliefs, related to fellowship, sharing and tolerance. Families serve as an important interspace, between individuals and the wider church tradition, in the passing on of these traditions.

The chapter started with the story of the little boy who lit a candle for grandad in the graveyard, surrounded by his family, but also by hundreds of other families and individuals doing the same thing. What they actually do is to remind themselves that there is light in the deepest darkness. In doing this, they "do church." What I have wished to contribute is a heightened awareness of the importance and wider implications of their actions in the shaping of a community called church in a time and place that is ambiguously called both post-Christian and post-secular.

12

Is Theology What Really Matters?

PETE WARD

The conversations around ecclesiology and ethnography have been on going now for around ten years.[1] At its inception the concern was to explore what it would mean for theology and for theologians to explore fieldwork and qualitative methods.[2] As the conversation has progressed this discussion has become more sophisticated and nuanced.[3] The essays in this volume illustrate very well the deep commitment to methodology and reflexive integrity that characterizes much of the work that is being done in this field. Theologians in the Scandinavian countries and elsewhere are clearly imbibing the rigor and the demands of qualitative empirical methods with considerable enthusiasm and expertise. What is also evident is that these methods are wonderfully productive as a means to highlight and draw

1. The first meeting of the network was held at Yale in 2007. Papers from the early meetings were published in the twin volumes Ward, *Perspectives*, and Scharen, *Explorations*.

2. Foundational texts to the conversation came from systematic theologians who called for a turn toward ethnography in ecclesiology. These included Healy, *Church*. The contribution of theological action research has also been decisive for the project, see Cameron et al., *Talking About God*. Adams and Elliott, "Ethnography"; Scharen, "Judicious Narratives."

3. The first three volumes of the journal of the ecclesiology and ethnography network, *Ecclesial Practices*, chart the developing conversation around the use of qualitative empirical methods.

attention to aspects of the life of the church and of the wider society that might not have held the interest of theologians, or at least these areas might not have been given the close attention that they truly deserve. Qualitative method then, has brought a new precision and focus to theological discussion. All of this means that it is hard not conclude that these are exciting times for this new field of research.

The essays in this volume framed our conversations held in Uppsala in 2016 and as the discussion developed I found myself continually voicing the question "What do we mean by theology?" In this chapter I want to explore that question in more depth than I was able to in our interchanges around the papers. I want to argue that it is theology that really matters in this conversation. It has been something of a refrain in the ecclesiology and ethnography network that qualitative empirical methods allow a return to the Concrete Church.[4] Concrete is an unfortunate metaphor, particularly if like myself you want to imagine the church in more fluid ways, but it has generally been used as a way to express a move away from ideal or abstract forms of theological expression.[5] There is then a growing sensibility, that is shared by many within the ecclesiology and ethnography conversation, that close attention to the lived forms and expression of the church has priority over, or is preferred to, more traditional doctrinal formulations. These developments are in my view unfortunate. Unfortunate because it was never the intention of those of us that started the ecclesiology and ethnography conversation that empirical methods should replace doctrinal forms of theology. Ironically it was systematic theologians who were the first to call for a turn toward ethnography so it is worth noting that it was not really our plan to abandon doctrine, rather to set up a conversation around the lived and the doctrinal where qualitative forms of enquiry would always be in dialogue with these forms of theology. It is I think also important to point out that the real heat and creativity in the conversation comes when there is a genuine attempt to hold the empirical and the doctrinal voices together and work with the tensions and problems that this gives rise to. So my sense is that while I celebrate the detailed attention to empirical method and the vivid and complex forms of data generated through qualitative research I am also more than a little concerned that we should work hard to ensure the place of theology in the on going conversation and that the conditions that will help this to happen require a clarity about what we mean by theology.

4. See Healy, *Church*.

5. I first explored this metaphor in Ward, *Liquid Church*. I further developed the ideas in Ward, *Participation*. Ward, *Liquid Ecclesiology*, sets out a more detailed theology of culture for this fluid understanding of church.

THINGS TO BEAR IN MIND WHEN MENTIONING
THE "T" WORD

Before trying to clarify what might be meant by theology there are some cautionary notes to make. Over the years as the conversations within the ecclesiology and ethnography network have taken place it has become more clear, at least in my mind, that there are number of habits and academic conventions that act to reduce the tension between doctrine and empirical research. They do this by effectively silencing or marginalizing systematic or doctrinal forms of theology. These ways of operating then develop a congenial space for empirical work but they have done so largely by excising systematic theology/doctrine from the conversation. There are historical and indeed some theological reasons to avoid including traditional forms of theologizing from the conversation. I understand why this is the case. I would accept that it is really awkward to pursue qualitative empirical forms of enquiry and to try to include within a single project systematic or doctrinal theology. These are different language games that do not easily over lap. But there are other factors at play in strategies that close down the theological voice or that seek to reposition it. It is worth touching on these before exploring an argument that says that it is theology that really matters.

One of the chief ways that theology is excluded from the conversation is through a particular convention around what is meant by the term practical theology.[6] It is usual to regard any project that falls within the areas of Christian education, church organization, liturgical study, pastoral care, or church leadership as being practical theology. In recent years it has largely become the case that these areas have been researched through empirical methods, either qualitative or quantitative. Doctrinal concerns as a result have often receded into the background, or they have in many cases been substantially replaced by theories drawn from sociology or anthropology. These theories are seen as being more appropriate to the study of social reality and practice. They also produce a synchronicity in a research project without the disruption and disjuncture that a doctrinal or systematic theological voice generally brings. Theology is then seen as a different kind of enterprise, one that is somewhat disconnected from practice. Doctrine, it is implied, is dealt with by systematic theologians and they have their conversations that are all very well and have their place but those of us who are engaged in empirical research have our particular conversation and when it

---

6. This approach to practical theology is particularly common in a Norwegian context. It is, however, important to note that the particular understanding of practical theology is often not shared by those coming from a systematic theology background. Here, doctrine still remains a key dialogue partner.

comes to practice we have a better way of looking at things. The fact that this kind of social scientific enquiry is generally regarded as practical theology because of it substantive area of study serves to disguise what is effectively a move away from theology or at least it is a redefinition of what we mean by theology.

This approach to practical theology is often set alongside a tradition within German influenced academic research that makes a strong distinction between faith and theology. Theology, it is argued, is a rational scientific enterprise. As such it is located within the academy and is not to be confused with the ongoing life and communication of the church. The proper role for theology that is conceived in this way is to critically examine the expression of the church. This exercise takes place in a way that is properly distinct from faith perspectives or commitments. Here systematic and doctrinal forms of theologizing are very much part of the conversation but they are often pursued in ways that are effectively dislocated from the commitments and the concerns of the church. This approach to theology is congenial to the empirical move in practical theology because it effectually polices a space, in which an exclusively social scientific approach can thrive. It also dislocates the theological task from the life of the church and hence there is no real urgency to address the turn toward ethnography and the concrete as it has been expressed and felt in the US and in the UK. In effect the split between a social scientific approach that deals with the lived reality of the church and abstract theological conversation around the church is institutionalized such that projects that intentionally seek to cross this boundary become problematized by worries such as is this practical theology or is it ecclesiology? The result of this institutional and disciplinary boundary is that the conversation that is common within the ecclesiology and ethnography network is hard to sustain.

In the US the academic field of practical theology has generally orientated itself toward human experience as the locus for theology. Practical theology, it is asserted, does not seek to apply doctrinal or theological perspectives rather it starts with the lived practice of the church. Human experience is a web of meaning that is to be interpreted as a theologically generative and significant location. This perspective is often very closely allied to a range of interrelated liberationist perspectives that see context and issues of power as fundamentally determinative for the generation of theological perspectives. These traditions and voices within American practical theology, it must be stressed, see themselves as being deeply and authentically theological. What they are advocating is seen as a corrective or a replacement for more traditional and historic theological voices. Doctrinal or systematic theology is largely regarded as being in some way part of the problem, i.e., the product of power and privilege variously articulated. In this current discussion the significant insight here is that the move toward experience and context is much more hospitable to qualitative empirical enquiry than more systematic approaches. They spring from the same theoretical and philosophical sources and hence they are sympathetic to each other in ways that the conversation with theology is almost inevitably more problematic. Doctrinal or systematic theological perspectives are excluded albeit for different reasons but it is still the case that they are left outside the conversation.

It is precisely the inconvenient nature of the relationship between theology and qualitative methods that has been the creative spark for ecclesiology and ethnography.[7] Of course none of us is in the conversation simply because this enterprise is intellectually challenging rather it is because we have felt that there is something important that is at stake. It is worth saying that importance stretches both ways in the conversation, i.e., from theology to qualitative empirical methods and from the practices and findings that arise from fieldwork toward theology. The crucial thing here is to realize that the conversation is not simply about the detail or complexities of ethnography or qualitative ways of conducting research just as it is not solely about ecclesiology that progresses through abstract reasoning alone however important or helpful or legitimate these might be. The conversation properly is about what it means to hold these two together and to wrestle with the issues. The reason for this is the intuition that something is lost when the problems are resolved by isolating, redefining, or excluding one or the other.

WHAT IS MEANT BY THEOLOGY?

I have already used four terms in these opening paragraphs: doctrine, systematic theology, practical theology and theology. This illustrates the problem in exploring the relationship between qualitative empirical methods and theology. Theology is quite simply a slippery term that means different things to different people. In fact it is also worth pointing out that it is very often used in different ways within the same piece of work—as I have done here. Part of this slipperiness comes from power, or at least from the contested and continually negotiated nature of theology in the church, in the academy and increasingly in a wider popular discourse. This means that a question like, "is this research actually theological?" is never an innocent question. There is no point trying to avoid the fact that in the question there is positioning going on. Just as in the approaches I have highlighted above

7. For example, see Fulkerson, "Interpreting," and Bretherton, "Generating."

there are also interests and positions at play. In acknowledging the issue of power I want to set out my stall for a way of understanding theology because it is this understanding that prompted my response to the papers in Uppsala and it is this perspective that shapes my contribution in this essay. The starting point for this I think requires some mapping of the contemporary theological terrain, or at least the part of that terrain where I think I come from.

Within the theological world in the US and in the UK it has become common-place to speak about theology within the modern era as being shaped around two polarities.[8] The one polarity is generally described as a cognitive or propositional approach to theology.[9] The other is spoken of as an experiential or expressivist form of theology. These two, it is argued, characterize alternative and opposing frameworks for theological work. Both are to some extent seen as being the product of modernity, i.e., they seek an accommodation with a modern mind-set. The one presents itself as a theoretical form of describing reality through rational processes, the other seeks to re-express doctrinal forms in terms that are universal and readily understood. Over the last thirty years or so these polarities have been seen as problematic by many theologians and as a result there has been much debate around what might constitute a post-modern or as some have described it a post-liberal alternative. This debate is on going and it has various different articulations but it is worth saying that in its origins the conversation around ecclesiology and ethnography arose from within and to a large extent was shaped by these perspectives.[10] So it is worth sketching them out in this chapter because I think they give an important background to the reasons why it is felt that there is something important at stake in the question "What do we mean by theology here?"

The post-liberal move in contemporary theology has three important markers for the ecclesiology and ethnography project. The first is the concern to move away from theology that is structured around the assumptions of modernity and a move toward forms of theologizing that arise from within the discourses that are habituated and natural to the lived practices of the church.[11] There is then a desire to see the practice and social reality of

8. This typology is found in Lindbeck, *Nature of Doctrine*, and it is repeated in Frei, *Types of Christian Theology*. It is picked up and used to describe the pattern of theology in modernity by Ford, "Introduction."

9. Lindbeck, *Nature of Doctrine*.

10. In this context it is worth indicating that there is some significance in the fact that the first ecclesiology and ethnography symposium took place at Yale where one of the founders of the network, Chris Scharen, was at the time a member of staff.

11. This discussion is worked out in some detail in Hauerwas, *With the Grain*, but it is also the key backdrop to the arguments of Lindbeck and Frei. Kathryn Tanner

the church as constituting a perspective or a culture. Secondly it is argued that this perspective is nurtured through a particular doctrinally structured biblical narrative. Contemporary theologians have prioritized the church and the practices of the Christian community as a key focus for theology.[12] This operates in different ways but the common theme is that the embodied, cultural, and social expression of church are brought to the very centre of systematic theological work. It is important however to grasp the extent to which this a move that is a reaction to modernity. In other words the turn to the church is a turn away from a perceived accommodation of Christian theology to discourses and conventions that lie outside of its habitual and inherent ways of speaking and understanding itself. So the task of theology becomes one where reality is to be seen in and through a Christian narrative that is scriptural in orientation and structured doctrinally through the key themes of Trinity, Christology and Soteriology.[13] And thirdly it is suggested that this narrative should form the basis not only for how the church is spoken about but also how the church both acts and speaks.[14] This reorientation of the theological enterprise, while it is not without its critics intersects in number of ways with the ecclesiology and ethnography project.

There is a triple inflection in the relationship between the contemporary attempt to reconstruct the theological enterprise and the conversation within ecclesiology and ethnography. The first inflection is a renewed focus on the church as the locus for theology. In particular the sense that abstract ecclesiological descriptions in doctrinal terms do not in themselves capture the real significance of church. In fact this is not what doctrine is meant to be.[15] Church is theologically significant because it forms and shapes a community through its practices. The habitual and embodied aspects of

---

develops an acute critique of postliberal theology in Tanner, *Theories of Culture*, but she does so by advocating a turn toward postmodern understandings and so she can be taken as another theological voice making this kind of move. A further critical intervention in these debates has been made by Nicholas Healy's discussion of the work of Stanley Hauerwas: Healy, *Hauerwas*, although he is, as the book says, very critical he does not fundamentally draw apart from the direction of travel that is there in Hauerwas and much of contemporary theology.

12. Another example of this might be Coakley, *God, Sexuality and the Self*.

13. Lindbeck calls this a grammar that structures the cultural linguistic expression of the church, see Lindbeck, *Nature*, 79–84. The idea of grammar is, I think, not terribly helpful simply because doctrine operates not so much in a regulative way in relation to the lived expression of the church; rather it exists, for instance, in the liturgy and in preaching as the very content of that expression.

14. See Hauerwas, *Community of Character*, 9–35.

15. This is Healy's point about blueprint ecclesiology, see Healy, *Church*, 25–51. See also Ward, "Blueprint Ecclesiology."

the lived community therefore become a central concern. The irony here is that most theologians who have advocated this position have not paid any attention to actual churches or indeed to the practices and ways of operating that characterize lived communities. Never-the-less these perspectives have played directly into the ecclesiology and ethnography conversation. This gives rise to what I am calling the second inflection.

The turn to qualitative methods of enquiry by theologians that I have been describing has been generated out of the renewed significance of the church in contemporary theology. The sensibility that is inhabited by ecclesiology and ethnography might be seen therefore as arising from a desire to take these theological perspectives on the church at their word. So if the practices, worship, and communal life of the church are important and in deed central then qualitative methods are the means to study actual churches. Paying attention to the local and lived is a way to explore the contours and the contradictions that the move toward church in contemporary theology has opened up. There is however something rather perilous about this project. The direction of travel in contemporary theology, as I have pointed out, has been generated out of a powerful and enduring sense that modern forms of theology have accommodated themselves to forms of thought that are not endemic or habitual within church. The emphasis on the practice and the distinctive theological narrative of the Christian community is therefore seen as an alternative starting place to the reductionist tendency of theology as it has been shaped by modernity. The peril in ecclesiology and ethnography comes from the possibility that by adopting qualitative empirical methods and in particular when using theories from social science in research on the church the reductionist tendencies of modernity are effectively re-introduced. These worries are not misplaced in my view. It is really easy to reach for theoretical frameworks and perspectives that shape research design and analysis because they promise to open up the lived practice of communities without entirely grasping that these same theories preclude the kind of theology that gave rise to the project in the first instance.

The ecclesiology and ethnography project then carries within it a perilous possibility of subverting the theological source from which it springs. This is therefore the third inflection in the complex relationships with contemporary trends in theology that exists in our conversation. Fundamentally the issue is epistemological. Qualitative methods and theories and perspectives from the social sciences are clearly part of what is required in successfully paying close attention to the lived expression of ecclesial communities. The question is how should these relate to theology? The perspectives that have been generated within contemporary theology would caution that these should be located within an epistemology that is shaped by the Christian narrative. Such a framing is not at all straightforward. Some theoretical frameworks are antithetical to theology or at least unsympathetic. There is work then to be done in any project to make clear how it is theological and how that theology is understood and operative within the project. These epistemological issues I want to argue should not be assumed or left implicit. Rather it is imperative that epistemological considerations concerning theology are at the forefront of the methodological task.

GENERATING A THEOLOGICAL EPISTEMOLOGY

The shift away from modernity in contemporary theology is predicated on the central importance of the Christian narrative for knowledge. At its worst this assertion has led to a tendency toward a kind of theological triumphalism. In a celebratory return to medieval forms of thought Theology it is argued is the queen of the sciences.[16] Such a move in my view closes down the options for the ecclesiology and ethnography project. Having said this it is fundamentally important to generate a theologically framed understanding of both qualitative empirical methodology and the limits and possibilities of theories that arise from outside of the theological tradition. In this section I want to explore my own take on a theological epistemology. In doing this I recognize that this will not be acceptable to everyone in the ecclesiology and ethnography conversation. I am therefore not presenting it as *the* right approach. Rather I want to say this is how I approach these issues. But in saying this I think I am also concerned to put down some markers to encourage others to make more explicit their own take on theological epistemology. I believe this is important simply because there is a danger that in failing to pay attention to these sorts of questions the theological aspects of the conversation may become more marginal or less significant.

I have shaped my take on theological epistemology around three statements: Knowledge of God is not like other Knowledge, Knowledge of God is shaped by the Being of God, and Knowledge of God is Communal. This will be a prelude to the final section where I will explore how theology conceived as I have framed it intersects with qualitative methods.

---

16. These ways of thinking, while something of a caricature are evident in the early days of the radical orthodoxy project see Ward, Milbank, and Pickstock, *Radical Orthodoxy*.

Knowledge of God is Not Like Other Knowledge

Theology I want to suggest is about God and about how all things relate to God.[17] Knowledge of God then is not like other knowledge. This is part of the reason why it sits uncomfortably in the ecclesiology and ethnography conversation.[18] God is not the object of study in the way that any other kind of reality might be.[19] Knowledge of God is given as an act of grace or illumination that comes in and through Jesus Christ.[20] Once given this knowledge

17. This is to echo Thomas Aquinas, "Now all things are dealt with in holy teaching in terms of God, either because they are God himself or because they are relative to him as their origin and end." Aquinas, *Summa Theologiae*, 1a.1.7. See also how Paul Murray draws on Aquinas in Murray, "Searching the Living Truth." The opening sentences of Calvin's *Institutes* represent a similar starting point: "Our wisdom, in so far as it ought to be deemed true and solid Wisdom, consists almost entirely of two parts: the knowledge of God and of ourselves. But as these are connected together by many ties, it is not easy to determine which of the two precedes and gives birth to the other." Calvin, *Institutes*, Book 1.1. For Calvin, this relationship is determined by his understanding of the Gospel and it is this framework that determines how he approaches human experience. So this quotation should not be read correlationally; rather, human experience is interpreted in and through Calvin's particular understanding of the Gospel. The point here is not so much that it is necessary to accept Calvin's anthropology, which is admittedly problematic; rather, that a theological anthropology is central to the challenge and possibilities of ecclesiology and ethnography.

18. The argument that theology is about God is a crucial move. Some would prefer a position where theology is understood as the examination of the church's expression about God. This moves the task onto territory that can be seen as being wholly cultural level. If, however, theology is about God then the dynamics that I start to set out here come into play. It is worth saying, however, that even as I would argue that theology is about God it is always and everywhere expression. It is therefore cultural and it is an examination of varied cultural expressions. The argument that it is about God does not avoid this cultural dimension. The point is that theology is about God in and as it engages in these conversations. How and to what extent it is about God is a project that is without guarantees and therefore needs to be undertaken with humility.

19. Here I am drawing on T. F. Torrance: "It is God who has given and revealed Himself in Israel and in the Incarnation to be understood but he remains the Lord God transcendent in His eternal and infinite Being who cannot be comprehended even when we apprehend Him." Torrance, *Theological Science*, 344.

20. See Barth in his discussion of Anselm's Proslogion in Barth, *Anselm*. The idea of divine illumination as the basis for knowledge is found in a number of places in Patristic thought. Maximus the Confessor interprets the divine light at the Transfiguration as a revealing and clothing. The robes of Christ that shine with the divine glory revealed in the transfigured Word speak by analogy of the scriptures and of the natural world as places of contemplation where the same Word may be encountered even as the light is veiled. Maximus the Confessor Difficulty 10.17D in Louth, *Maximus the Confessor*, 108–10. The contours of the issues at stake concerning divine illumination and epistemology, I would suggest, are traced in interesting ways in the hesychast dispute between Barlaam and Gregory Palamas in the fourteenth century, see Palamas, *Triads*. See also Meyendorf, *Study of Gregory Palamas*. For more on divine illumination

does not then become the object for rational discourse in the same way that other knowledge can be (this is contrary to the cognitive and propositional polarity in modern theology). Knowledge of God takes place through participation in the Divine Being. It is a work of the Holy Spirit leading the church into truth. Knowledge of God then is relational.[21] Having said all of this however theology as knowledge is also cultural and proceeds rationally. So it looks and acts in many ways like any other kind of knowledge. In other words it is possible to proceed as if theology is like any other area of study but this is to miss the fundamental nature of what it means to know God. Knowing God is a spiritual practice.[22] The act of doing theology is not distinct from knowing God or indeed being known by God. This means that the cultural and rational processes that theology shares with any other academic discipline are simultaneously an act of participation in the divine being.[23]

This understanding of theology has become more commonplace in the ecclesiology and ethnography conversation. In discussing fieldwork researchers are often conscious of a sense that as they share in the lives and experiences of others they are somehow on Holy Ground. There is then a spiritual perception of participation found in the processes of research that reflexivity is bringing to the fore. There has for instance been debate around the appropriateness of prayer as part of fieldwork and the research process. These concerns generally focus on the researcher and the relationships that are undertaken with participants during data gathering.[24] They also form

---

as epistemology in the Western tradition, see Schumacher, *Divine Illumination*. An important insight that Schumacher brings to the conversation is the crucial link between epistemology and soteriology that divine illumination assumes. This perspective, I want to suggest, orientates the discussion around theological ethnography in ways that preclude, for instance, the assumption that theology is a rational science distinct from faith. A parallel insight comes from the maxim of Evagrius of Pontus: "If you are a theologian you truly pray. If you truly pray you are a theologian." Chapters on Prayer 60 in Ponticus, *Praktikos*, 65.

21. This participative approach to the knowledge of God and epistemology is explored at length in Fiddes, *Seeing the World*.

22. This approach to theology might be critiqued as *fideist*. My response to that would be yes it is, because faith is the basis for the knowledge of God. This does not mean that methodologically theology is set apart from rationality, but rather that it carries certain understandings about how reason operates with humility in relation to the divine. I have explored this drawing on a critical realist epistemology in Ward "Blueprint Ecclesiology."

23. I have talked about this relationship as paradox in Ward, *Liquid Ecclesiology*, 56–67.

24. A good example of this is the Learning Pastoral Imagination Project where the research is spoken of in these terms. "We intentionally inhabit the hybrid roles of

part of reflexivity on projects where the faith commitments of researcher are made explicit and consideration is given to how these might or might not form part of or influence the research. So for instance if the research involves attending worship services questions are commonly asked about the level of participation such as to what extent should the research share in the act of worship.

There is however another and perhaps more significant implication of the understanding of theology as the knowledge of God that relates to qualitative research. If theology is about God and how all things relate to God then if a project is to be theological this relationship needs somehow to be made explicit. In other words there needs to be consideration given to how and in what way the project is discernable as theology, i.e., how do the findings generate knowledge of God. I would argue that this concern is as important as any other methodological concern such as sample size, or what critical theory we engage, or how reflexivity is exercised.

Knowledge of God is Shaped by the Being of God

There is a contentious and yet essential question that needs to be at the heart of any kind of theological ethnography: What exactly do we mean by God? The turn away from modernity in contemporary theology has directly addressed this issue in terms of biblical narrative and doctrinal formulation. God, it is argued, is the God revealed in the bible. The Christian community is shaped by its understanding the story of God found in the scripture and this understanding is organized or ordered through doctrinal formulation. The creedal formulations of the Trinity and Christology therefore act as an interpretative framework for the Christian understanding of what it means to be situated in the biblical narrative. The point here is that the question of God is addressed in and through the ways of speaking and habituated forms of practice that are the everyday and ordinary fare of the church. Narrative and doctrine should therefore not be dismissed as the imposition of frameworks upon lived reality from the outside by theologians rather that these are already carried in the everyday practices, particularly in the worship, of the whole community.

---

theologians and researchers, for instance, beginning group interviews with prayer, and making explicit to our participants that we, too, are pastors who have heard a call to ministry and served congregations as well as other church-related roles. Among other things, this has heightened our respect for listening deeply, and allowed a crucial place for silence in the midst of our work as the space in which God holds us in love, and out of which God hears us into speech." Scharen and Campbell Reed, *Learning Pastoral Imagination*, 11.

These perspectives are obviously contentious. Communities differ on how they read the story and how they understand themselves. Doctrinal perspectives in communities are variously understood or even in some cases not acknowledged at all. In addition to this many theologians have been, and continue to be, uncomfortable with doctrinal formulation as it is expressed in the creeds. Such reservations are understandable but I want to suggest that they do not preclude an explicit engagement with the underlying question of what is meant by God. So the question I have asked about how theology as part of particular projects I want to argue needs to go through these debates. What is meant by theology and by God cannot simply be assumed neither should it be asserted without a consideration of the framing of theology that has become common in contemporary theological debate. This means that for a project to be theological there should be reference to these conversations and others like them to establish how the particular understanding of divine that frames the research and indeed the researcher sits in relation to the wider theological conversations. It is this kind of explicit discussion that I would argue makes a project theological.

Knowledge of God is Communal

A perspective that is closely related to what has been argued so far is the sense that theology is communal. Qualitative methods highlight how there are particular perspectives and ways of operating that are shared by communities of faith.[25] This sharing however extends across time. Communities are part of on going traditions of thinking and interpretation. This communal sensibility can be read back into what it means to speak of the knowledge of God because such knowing is never individual it is shared. This means that the practice of theology as the knowledge of God should always be concerned to develop in dialogue not simply with lived communities in the present but also with the residue of reflection and thought that are passed down to us from the past. Theology then is an on going conversation with those who have sought the knowledge of God in different times and in different places.

If qualitative empirical work is to be theological then it should situate itself in a flow of conversation from Christian communities across time. It is therefore in my view a mistake to valorize the voices of lived communities such that there is no need to locate these in a wider tradition. No community or individual practices faith in a vacuum and indeed no researcher operates in a vacuum. That said the purpose of research is to generate knowledge. The

25. This is something of an extension of the notion of participation as it is found in the work of Paul Fiddes, see Fiddes, *Participating*.

project that is seen in the ecclesiology and ethnography conversation arises from the belief that there are new things to be seen through this methodology and new perspectives that should be taken into account. The point here however is that this knowledge should be discussed in relation to the tradition. The reason for this is that the knowledge of God is communal across time. This is a lot more than name checking a few systematic theologians or making reference to some doctrinal perspectives. There needs to be a much deeper engagement with the tradition in order to demonstrate how and to what extent knowledge of God is being generated through our research and more to the point why this knowledge is innovative and significant.

THEOLOGY AND THE RESEARCH PROCESS— EMIC AND ETIC PERSPECTIVES

Having sketched certain ground rules for how theology might be conceived I want in this final section to explore briefly how this way of thinking about theology, as the knowledge of God intersects with the research process. Theology I want to argue can exist in two different ways in relation to qualitative empirical research: *emic* and *etic*. Emic and etic are terms that have been used for some time in anthropology.[26] Emic refers to those perspectives that are present in the context and communities where the fieldwork is taking place. Etic perspectives are those that might be introduced by the researcher. Etic perspectives are therefore always from outside the fieldwork context. There are then both emic and etic forms of theology that are rightly at play in theological qualitative research at every stage of the research process from project design to data gathering and presentation, to data analysis and the overall argument and conclusions.

Theology I want to suggest should be fundamental to research design. There should be an explicit consciousness of how and to what extent the qualitative empirical work forms part of a wider theological conversation. This consciousness is etic, i.e., it exists outside the fieldwork context. It might for instance be a discussion about the nature and significance of infant baptism or the theological ethics involved in the politics of immigration policy. However it is framed the point is that as knowledge and as knowledge of God this wider theological conversation should form part of the way the research is framed. Closely related to this kind of etic theological considerations, there will also be emic theology. Emic here relates to the lived theology that is carried within the researcher them selves. These emic theological convictions are almost always part of the reason why a project

26. Etic and Emic originates in the linguistic work of the linguist Kenneth Pike. See Pike, *Language*.

feels to be urgent at a particular time. Again through reflexivity emic theological perspectives should be foregrounded in how research is presented.

Both etic and emic theological perspectives are also present in fieldwork. Theologically orientated qualitative empirical methods have generally focused on the theological perspectives and voices that are present in communities. Sometimes the theological content of these voices is more implicit than explicit but never-the-less the turn to ethnography has served to highlight a range of examples of the way that theology is woven into and throughout the Christian community and I would want to argue that it is evident outside of the church in wider society. Some of these perspectives are inhabited as convictions. They are affective and hence they shape how people live their lives. These I would argue are what should be regarded properly as emic in nature. At the same time there are a myriad of other voices that are part of a fieldwork context but that are not habitual. They form part of what is going on and they have a place in the data gathering and presentation but they might or might not be closely attended to or invested in by individuals or communities. I want to suggest that these could be thought of as being etic in nature. They are present in a context but they can also be read as coming from outside. These etic theological perspectives form apart of the data collection and presentation.

Both etic and emic theological perspectives should form a part of the data analysis. Theologically orientated qualitative research is distinctive in that it is attuned to the ways that theology is present in the lived context of communities and for individuals. Empirical research has not always been so attuned and some theoretical perspectives from the social sciences may serve to marginalize the presence or the significance of emic theology. The ecclesiology and ethnography conversation is an attempt to redress the balance in the reductive forms of interpretation and theorizing that I have discussed above. Emic theology then has a central place in how projects analysis and discuss data. Analysis however will also involve the inclusion of theoretical and theological perspectives from outside the fieldwork context. This kind of discussion forms part of how a research methodology both interprets the material that is generated and presented in the data but it also becomes a way that the significance of the fieldwork is brought to bear on wider academic conversation. Etic theology is therefore both a hermeneutical tool and it is also a conversation where the findings are brought to bear to generate new insights.

WHAT REALLY MATTERS?

My contribution to this volume has come out of the experience of our discussions at the meeting in Uppsala. My recurring question as we talked together was as I have explained what do we mean by theology? I have tried to explore in this chapter in more depth what I mean by that question firstly by painting a picture of the context in which theology might be quite easily overlooked or by passed in the discussions. These observations are brief and consequently a little too sweeping but I want to argue that they carry some truth. From there I have tried to set a framework for reinstating theology as part of ethnographic research by setting it within the on going conversations within contemporary theology associated with a shift away from the polarities of modernity and toward a more ecclesial focus. This setting of my question is important because without it the call for theology can be read as an aspect of the conflicts and debates within modern pattern of theological work. I have wanted to try and show how this is a mistake that the turn to theology arises from the collapse of the conflict between liberal and conservative theological positions and it is precisely the collapse of these positions that has been the generative force for the ecclesiology and ethnography conversation. Exploring these dynamics however means the ability to trace the way that there is a complex series of moves that forms a triple inflection in relation to contemporary theology. With this as a starting point it is possible to start to flesh out what is meant by theology. I have done this in three main ways firstly be exploring how Knowledge of God is not like other knowledge, then by discussing how Knowledge of God is shaped by the being of God and finally by arguing that Knowledge of God is Communal. These three ways of situating what it means to speak of theology I have explicitly linked to the research process through the idea of emic and etic forms of theology. This framing of conversation I want to suggest explains to some extent why in my view it is theology that really matters.

13

The Researcher as Gamemaker—Response

JONAS IDESTRÖM AND TONE STANGELAND KAUFMAN

I n this response chapter we address questions of normativity in relation to the four chapters in this part of the book. We frame our response by suggesting that the researcher can be considered a Gamemaker, in the sense of a Gamemaker in the Hunger Games, such as Seneca Crane.[1] By this we mean that the researcher in many ways makes decisions and choices that shape the entire research process. The researcher has the power to decide which voices to bring into the research process and at the same time to decide which roles they are allowed to play.

THE GAME BOARD—THEOLOGICAL VOICES AND NORMATIVE DIMENSIONS AT PLAY IN THE RESEARCH GAME

One heuristic tool that identifies various theological voices is *The Four Voices of Theology* model developed by the British research group Action Research—Church and Society (the ARCS team).[2] This model distinguishes between the following four theological voices:

---

1. The concept of the researcher as Gamemaker draws on Kaufman, "Researcher." See also Collins, *Hunger Games.*

2. Cameron et al., *Talking About God.*

- The *espoused* voice—what is expressed verbally in the empirical field.

- The *operant* voice—what is enacted in the empirical field.

- The *normative* voice—Scripture and the ecclesial traditions at work in the empirical field as well as theological voices that can be drawn in by the researcher at various stages of the research process.

- The *formal* voice—theological reflections and studies from the academy, which are usually brought into the research process by the academic scholar.[3]

Moreover, the researcher exercises great power in how these voices are represented in the actual academic text (see the following part of this volume). Thus, the researcher, as Gamemaker, is in the position to orchestrate various theological and normative voices from the empirical field, the theological tradition as well as from the academy. Hence, the normativity exercised by the Gamemaker can be understood as an overall normative dimension.

Seeking to move beyond the dichotomy of descriptive and normative, we follow Geir Afdal, who makes the case that "there is no clear-cut line between the descriptive and normative. Rather, the difference is one of degree."[4] Still there are various normative dimensions at play in ethnographically oriented ecclesiological research projects that have to do with *how* the theological voices are dealt with. Thus, as a further conceptual framework for this response chapter, we suggest four different kinds of normativity that the Gamemaker deals with and orchestrates: *evaluative* normativity, *prescriptive* normativity, *rescriptive* normativity, and *emergent* normativity.

Evaluative normativity (*normativity from-the-outside*)[5] is often what we automatically associate with the term "normativity." This entails using academic and ecclesial authorities (for instance the Bible, theological doctrines, or the theology of a certain theologian, such as Martin Luther, Dietrich Bonhoeffer, or Sarah Coakley) as the normative standard or measuring rod for the theology or spirituality enacted and expressed by the research participants in the empirical field. In certain Lutheran contexts, Luther can always be employed as a non-negotiable trump card.

Prescriptive normativity refers to the kind of normativity that is often termed "strategic" (Browning) or "revised" (Swinton and Mowat) theology; that is, the last stage or the outcome of a qualitative research process in

---

3. Watkins, "Practical Ecclesiology," 177–78.

4. Afdal, *Researching*, 73.

5. The concept "normativity from-the-outside" is borrowed from Kaufman, "From the Outside," 148.

theology or ecclesiology.[6] Prescriptive normativity often takes the shape of prescribing a good, helpful, or relevant way to conduct a certain practice. Prescriptive normativity is usually offered in the shape of concrete suggestions for concrete actions.

Rescriptive normativity (*normativity from-within*) acknowledges that an account of a research process is not simply "a mere description" of the practice field, but a re-description, a re-making, and thus a *rescription*.[7] This rescription also includes normative theological dimensions and is consequently a contribution to the production of theological knowledge. As previously argued by Kaufman, the location of such a normative process might primarily take place *in the practice of the research process* or primarily *within the empirical research field*.[8]

Emergent normativity is the normativity that emerges from the encounter between different voices in a conversation that is facilitated and directed by the researcher as Gamemaker, who is then in the position to grant various roles and priorities to these different voices.[9] Yet, the Gamemaker cannot fully control either the outcome of the conversation or the normativity that emerges from it.

THE GAMEMAKER AND THE ROLE OF THEOLOGY

The chapters in this part all address questions of normativity. At the same time, the authors of these chapters also operate as Gamemakers not only by explicitly and implicitly allowing some normative voices into the text while excluding or ignoring others but also through the role the voices are granted in their arguments and texts.

In his chapter Pete Ward makes the case that it "is theology that really matters" in the academic conversations in the field of ecclesiology and ethnography. And he is "concerned that we should work hard to ensure the place of theology in the ongoing conversation and that the conditions that will help this to happen require a clarity about what we mean by theology." This is clearly a question at stake when reflecting on normativity in qualitative theological and ecclesiological research: what do we mean by theology? And how does an answer to this question influence the actual process of a research project? The "T-question," as Ward puts it, is one that any researcher, in her position as Gamemaker, will have to deal with. And according to Ward, addressing this issue explicitly is crucial in qualitative

6. See Browning, *Fundamental*; Swinton and Mowat, *Practical Theology*.

7. Kaufman, "From the Outside," 147–49.

8. Ibid., 150–58.

9. This concept is inspired by Gaarden, "Den emergente."

theological research. Ward himself states that "[t]heology . . . is about God and about how all things relate to God."

The three other chapters in this section also add important perspectives and reflections to a conversation on the role and essence of theology. Marianne Gaarden begins her chapter by stating that "[o]ne of the major challenges in working with ecclesiology and ethnography is that theology already has an integrated world view." This is an example of an explicit reflexivity of a researcher looking back at a research project. And it is a Gamemaker well aware of the normative dimensions of theology. Gaarden's concern over how the researcher can deal responsibly with theological normativity is shared by Kirsten Donskov Felter who raises some crucial questions concerning normativity and theology in a research process:

> In which ways are empirical studies allowed to disrupt the explicit normativity of ecclesial traditions, as well as the implicit or tacit normativity inherent in the approach of the research team? How can empirical findings be considered to convey normative values with regard to theological thinking? And how does the background of the scholar affect the normativity that he or she brings into the research design?

Felter's reflexive questions can be read in light of the heuristic model of theological voices. There are the espoused and operant voices in the empirical material; the explicit normative voices of an ecclesial tradition, and the formal voice present through implicit or tacit normativity in the research approach and in the background of the researcher. Yet, her approach also addresses the importance of researcher reflexivity, and of the researcher being aware of and able to handle these various normative dimensions. Hence, her questions quite vividly illustrate the image of the researcher as Gamemaker.

All four chapters raise questions concerning the espoused or operant voices from the field and what role they can or should be allowed to play in constructive theological and ecclesiological work. In Ninna Edgardh's chapter, the espoused voices—in her case voices of families with children—play a crucial role as theological voices. This is grounded in an ecclesiological understanding where those who belong to The Church of Sweden (CofS), of which most become members at baptism even if they might not describe themselves as Christians or religious, are part of "the actual life of the church." This is, according to her, a way of attending to and theologically thinking through expressions of ecclesial life, thereby strengthening it. Edgardh thus opts for an interaction between voices from the tradition and the contemporary voices heard through the interviews—a dialogue between espoused and normative theological voices. She makes clear that she is not interested in focusing her attention on how the church *should* be (prescriptive normativity). Rather, she engages in a hermeneutical process resulting in normative claims, which can be considered an emergent form of normativity. Drawing these voices into the theological conversation and allowing them to play a significant role in the encounter with other theological voices might, in her view, be an asset to ecclesial life.

We see a similar approach in Gaarden's chapter where the method she uses brings forth a normative dimension in the interaction between espoused voices on the one hand and normative and formal voices on the other. She describes how she was "challenged to analyze these assumptions [mainstream theology on preaching], compare them with the empirical findings, and suggest *another way* to understand the preaching event" (emphasis ours). What she describes is a move from a descriptive approach, through a rescriptive one (her account of the interviews with the churchgoers, and the role she grants this normativity), ending up in an emergent form of normativity. And this move is not about replacing the normative voice of tradition with the espoused voices of interviewees as evaluative or prescriptive normativity. *It is precisely in the very interaction and juxtaposing of the different voices that a new understanding emerges.*

Ward also raises questions on the relationship between espoused and normative/formal voices of theology. One of his concerns is that the normative (doctrine and liturgy) and formal theological voices of tradition (systematic theology), for various reasons, tend to be silenced in qualitative theological research. Hence, according to him, the implicit normative voices of social theory are given priority in the process of bringing forth and interpreting the espoused and operant voices in the field.

THE GAMEMAKER AND THE PROCESS
OF DOING THEOLOGY

When looking at Edgardh, Gaarden, and Felter as Gamemakers in their projects, it is easy to agree with the Felter that "the path from empirical findings to theological normativity is not a straight one." As they all show, this is "not a matter of shifting from one universalistic model of interpretation to the other." In all three projects we see examples of an implicit normativity in the will to try to make sense of the lived experiences given voice through the methods they use. As Felter puts it, this "is a complex and hybrid process of trying to make meaning" since it involves elements from different traditions and takes place across different fields. It therefore seems fair to conclude that the projects shared by Edgardh, Gaarden, and Felter are examples of what Ward (in a clearly prescriptively normative way) defines as a proper scholarly conversation in ecclesiology and ecclesiology:

> The conversation properly is about what it means to hold these two [ecclesiology and ethnography] together and to wrestle with the issues. The reason for this is the intuition that something is lost when the problems are resolved by isolating, redefining, or excluding one or the other.

As Ward reminds us in a footnote on the nature of theology—theology is always expressions in and through various forms of culture. Looking at the ecclesial field as forms of culture also means approaching the field as a landscape of meaning-making processes. In this landscape, what we define as theology should be understood as a verb rather than as a noun. It's a matter of "*doing* theology," as Felter points out (emphasis ours). Making meaning is a process of articulation and interpretation where bits and pieces of tradition and experiences are woven together.

In Ward's reflections on the distinction between *emic* and *etic* perspectives in theology we also see examples of how the researcher can be made aware that some bits and pieces of tradition might have been integrated into the habitus of the local church (emic) while others might be present in the field but not used (etic). Related to the four voices of theology one could say that emic perspectives primarily are expressed as espoused voices in the field while the etic is brought in by the researcher (or made visible by the researcher as they might already be present in the field); both can be seen as normative or formal voices. The etic perspectives might also be used as hermeneutic tools in a process of discerning operant theological voices in the field.

THE GAMEMAKER AND THE COMMUNAL ASPECT— TIME AND SPACE

As Ward reminds us there is *a communal aspect* of the research process and theology that needs to be made explicit. This has to do with the question of who are seen as relevant actors and voices to be brought into the conversation. When reading the four chapters, it becomes clear that this communal aspect has to do with both *time* and *space*.

Ward emphasizes the *temporal* dimension of the communal aspect and argues that qualitative, theological work "should situate itself in a flow of conversation from Christian communities across time." Moreover, he argues that it is by letting voices from the Christian church in other times and places into the conversation that the researcher "can demonstrate how and to what extent knowledge of God is being generated . . . and more to the point why this knowledge is innovative and significant."

The temporal dimension is present in the other three chapters through theological voices from other times and places in the Christian tradition, yet in their projects we also see the significance of *space*. Thus, in these texts we see how actors from different locations are brought into or kept outside the conversation staged by the researcher. In Edgardh's and Gaarden's projects, the decision to include the voices of families and churchgoers is significant. Grounded in theological and ecclesiological convictions they are seen as relevant and important ecclesial voices and actors. This also shows that there is an interplay between the dimensions of space and time when discerning which voices to include and listen to.

Edgardh's chapter is a good example of this, as she makes the case for the significant, vicarious role of those who represent the church. Her work shows that some of the interviewees "are willing to pay for the church to be there, even if they do not engage themselves more than that." An important argument for her is that the vicarious role is "theologically viable," and she does so by pointing to etymology of the word liturgy as used by the church in history: "The word liturgy has its root in the idea of a group of people doing something in public on behalf of a wider community." However, she does not go further into detail about how this insight from the Christian tradition is brought to bear in her work.

For Gaarden the use of ethnographic methods was a choice she made to partly lose control over the material and to participate in "the reality under study." In this example we see two crucial steps taken by the Gamemaker that allow for a constructive process of emergent normativity. First, she made the decision to pay close attention to the voices of churchgoers listening to sermons. Second, she chose a method that helped her create a nuanced and rich material, which opened ways into new territories. And she sees this overall approach as consistent with the words of Paul: "For our knowledge is only in part, and the prophet's word gives only a part of what is true." Both Gaarden's reference to Paul and Edgardh's reference to the liturgy are examples of how the researcher engages normative voices from the Christian tradition when listening to and interpreting voices that are usually not otherwise listened to in scholarly theological conversations.

THE RESEARCHER AS A RESPONSIBLE GAMEMAKER?

The four chapters in this part of the book offer rich material when reflecting on normativity in qualitative theological research. They also give us a good idea of some of the challenges that face the researcher as Gamemaker in all the decisions and choices that have to be made during the research process. As demonstrated in this chapter, the researcher cannot step out of the role as Gamemaker. However, she can be a *responsible* Gamemaker, who is transparent about her assumptions, location, and pre-understanding, as well as giving warrants for the choices made. Hence, the responsible researcher practices *self-reflexivity*—what we would consider a *reflexive* approach to normativity. Such an approach means being aware of two crucial questions related to a qualitative research process: (1) Which voices are included and drawn into the conversation? (2) What roles and positions are these voices allowed to play?

Albeit having foregrounded rescriptive and emergent normativites in this chapter, we also acknowledge the significance of prescriptive and evaluative kinds of normativity. However, these are more commonly thought of when speaking of normativity, and we therefore appreciate how the chapters in this part of the book can help in widening our understanding of normativity and thus challenge a common narrow understanding of normativity as primarily being a normativity from-the-outside (a prescriptive and evaluative normativity). In line with Ward's concerns, we also see a risk that theological, scholarly conversations fall into a false dichotomy between description and normativity or ethnography and ecclesiology. Normative dimensions that are rescripted and emerge from within the research process itself offer constructive ways of overcoming such dichotomies.

However, this calls for the researcher to be a responsible steward of the various normative dimensions at play throughout the entire research process, and perhaps particularly of the normativity that emerges in the encounter between various theological voices in the conversation facilitated by the Gamemaker. More importantly, the researcher needs to be aware that the issue of normativity cannot simply be understood as a problem that can be resolved once and for all. Rather, questions of normativity should be considered and dealt with as part of an ongoing conundrum that is inherently part of any qualitative research project in ecclesiology and ethnography.

PART 3

Representation

How can we as ethnographers and ethnographically oriented theologians faithfully recount and represent the experiences and practices of the individuals, populations, and congregations we research? How do we create "stuff" or texts based on fieldwork, interviews, photographs, video recordings, digital materials, and other artifacts? This third part of the volume seeks to address the challenge of representation.

Offering autoethnography and performance ethnography as two methods and examples, Natalie Wigg-Stevenson considers "the so-called *crisis of representation* in anthropology as a potentially productive site for ethnographic theological fieldwork and writing." She argues that these "critical ethnographic approaches challenge simple applications of qualitative methods to theological questions, while also shaking up some of traditional academic theology's core norms and goals."

Engaging a historical material, yet taking an ethnographic approach, Sune Fahlgren explores the spirituality of a non-creedal Scandinavian denomination, namely Baptist congregations. His concern is the process of how historical data such as artifacts and photos can be represented in a descriptive, ecclesiological text. Moreover, Fahlgren includes the observations and reflections of the researcher as part of his material–and thus analysis and interpretation–not unlike an ethnographer.

In his chapter on digital ethnography Tim Hutchings offers three questions concerning representation: (1) How do ethnographers represent themselves to the groups they study? (2) Whom do they represent within the group? (3) How do they represent the group to an external audience? According to Hutchings, "technologies are integral to the practices and routines of Christian congregations and the researchers who study them."

He therefore suggests that through digital ethnography "rich, first-hand appreciation of the context and meaning of digital practices can become one of the cornerstones of digital theology."

Kristina Helgesson Kjellin grapples with the question: "How can anthropologists in a just way interpret and represent what people are doing when they are trying to 'do good'?" Reflecting on how people's actions and motives are to be understood, she also engages questions of colonialism, class, power and asks whether the researcher can and should "take a clear normative stand in favor of acts of solidarity carried out by one's informants?"

In her response to the texts in Part III Eileen Campell-Reed starts out by stating that "[r]epresentation in any production of knowledge ushers the scholar into a variety of dilemmas or *conundrums* that are not easily solved or dismissed." She engages in a conversation with the authors based on the idea that representation is "reductive *and* evocative; descriptive *and* interpretive; powerful *and* harmful; contextual *and* skilled."

14

Trying to Tell the Truth About a Life— The Problem of Representation for Ethnographic Theology

NATALIE WIGG-STEVENSON

Both in his writing and his public speaking, I have heard the theologian, Mark Jordan, grapple repeatedly with variations on a single struggle: "how do we tell the truth about a life?" The first time I heard him articulate this question, I was intrigued. The second time, it got under my skin and began to agitate me. By the third time, this question that haunted him now haunted me too. When trying to engage theologically with ethnographic fieldwork, just how do we tell the truth—what even constitutes truth?— about the familiar yet bewildering, simple and seductive lives of our research subjects and/or partners? Is truth constituted differently in ethnographic theology than it is in sociological or anthropological approaches? Can ethnographic theological writing enflesh the truth of a life? Can it incarnate it and, if so, can it crucify it? What then of resurrection? Or glorification?

The question Jordan raises (not to mention the questions his question raises for me) relates to the issue of representation—an ethnographic value with which ethnographic theologians have not yet wrestled in any particularly significant way. We have paid much attention to the ethnographic value of reflexivity, particularly the type of reflexivity required for negotiating our fieldwork relationships ethically. But we have paid less attention to the types of reflexivity required to negotiate the distinction between ethnography as fieldwork and ethnography as a craft of writing. We have worried much about the relationship between empirical description and theological normativity, but have done so in ways that presume the former is a more stable conversation partner for the latter than many anthropologists—particularly interpretive anthropologists—would understand it to be. By directing our attention to the issue of representation, then, Jordan diagnoses a deeper issue at the heart of any ethnographic theological project, an issue that undergirds questions of reflexivity, empirical description and normativity all at once. This chapter sets out to explore that issue in more detail, highlighting its methodological implications and possibilities for ethnographic theology.

In what follows, I take up the so-called *crisis of representation* in anthropology as a potentially productive site for ethnographic theological fieldwork and writing. After outlining the issues surrounding this crisis of representation, I discuss two fieldwork/writing methods inspired by it, and situate each within a framework that demonstrates its capacity to bring fresh insight to constructive theology. First, situated within the framework of feminist theology's concern with the category of "women's experience," autoethnography helps us re-imagine Christian doctrine in a way that is both methodologically robust and theologically compelling. Second, situated within the framework Kathryn Tanner articulates for theology understood more broadly, performance ethnography helps us re-interpret theology as a genuinely collaborative project. In both cases, the critical ethnographic approaches challenge simple applications of qualitative methods to theological questions, while also shaking up some of traditional academic theology's core norms and goals. The result is a challenge to the preservation of the status quo in academic theology: a challenge some might perceive as threat, while others—myself included—encounter as liberation.

THE CRISIS OF REPRESENTATION AND ITS IMPORT FOR ETHNOGRAPHIC THEOLOGIANS

After outlining what the *crisis in representation* refers to in anthropology, noting not only arguments from its proponents but also its critics, this section outlines three ways in which engaging these debates could impact ethnographic theology moving forwards. I will mostly only gesture toward the first two: the need to historicize the shared colonial complicity of anthropology and theology, and the import of recognizing a less stable foundation for empirical data for questions of theological normativity. But the third—an opening for more diverse methods of ethnographic fieldwork and writing—will be unpacked more fully in the next two sections of this essay.

The crisis in representation begins in the burgeoning awareness that ethnography is not only a particular research method (i.e., fieldwork that studies the lives of a people and culture, *ethnos-*), but that it is also a form of writing (*-graphy*). Prior to the publication of *Writing Culture* by Clifford and Marcus in 1986, little attention had been paid to the latter half of this equation, however: the writing. As Clifford puts it in the introduction to that text: "The fact that it [i.e., the writing of ethnography] has not until recently been portrayed or seriously discussed reflects the persistence of an ideology claiming transparency of representation and immediacy of experience."[1] Ethnographic texts cannot, however, be viewed as simple "reports from the field"; they are, rather, themselves also artifacts of cultural production that, if they nakedly represent anything, represent a potent, indissoluble mixture of the culture studied, the ethnographer's own culture, and the selfhood of the ethnographer himself.

The role played by *Writing Culture*, then—as well as by other key texts like Said's, *Orientalism* (1979), Marcus and Fischer's *Anthropology as Cultural Critique* (1986), and Denzin's, *Interpretative Anthropology* (1997)— was to expose how this ideology undergirding the possibility for transparent representation was.[2] Or, to put it differently, these texts succeeding in constructing a "framework that makes the direct link between experience and text problematic."[3] Questions of reflexivity, of course, came to the fore, as ethnographers were pressed to consider more carefully the implication of their selves in their projects. But anthropologists also began to acknowledge how the craft of writing requires deploying intelligible social codes and conventions to communicate the practical dynamics of identity and culture.[4] In other words, the craft of ethnographic writing necessarily utilizes conventions that are foreign to the culture being represented to represent it. As a result, the text is not a representation of a culture. Rather, the act of producing a text is the method by which ethnographers invent, create or produce a culture; it is the method by which they write a culture into being.[5]

Critics argue over just how much of a crisis was really produced by these issues of ethnographic representation. Flaherty's rhetorical strategy, for example, depicts proponents of the crisis as despairing skeptics. One consequence of this is that even more measured arguments became misinterpreted as histrionic purges of any possible objectivity from anthropological

1. Clifford and Marcus, *Writing Culture*, 2.
2. Ibid.
3. Denzin, *Interpretive Ethnography*, 3.
4. Clifford and Marcus, *Writing Culture*, 10; Jordan, "Writing the Truth."
5. Denzin, *Interpretive Ethnography*, 3; Clifford and Marcus, *Writing Culture*, 2.

methods.[6] If we have "no recourse to facts," Flaherty argues—which for him are directly equated with data—and "it's all just interpretation," then "what authority do we have to represent another?"[7] If there really is a *crisis* in representation, it seems that ethnography may as well give up now. Such polemical frames are, however, unhelpful, and only allow critics like Flaherty to double down on the assertion that ethnography must be undergirded by a purely empirical epistemology if it is to be a true science. In these views, ethnography needs to become aggressively *more objective*, rather than deal with the destabilizing—but also fruitful—possibilities that a critique of empirical objectivity might allow. Snow offers another clear example of this critique as he writes: the crisis only ensues because ethnographers "subscribe to the 'crisis frame' and thus abandon various sociological principles and methodological guidelines that, if used as the basis for conducting ethnographic research, can mitigate or mute the practices that presumably engender misrepresentation."[8] In Snow's view, then, the crisis is therefore "a kind of self-fulfilling prophecy that leads to a style or variant of ethnography that affirms the presumed crisis."[9] While this is true in some cases—there will always be better and worse ethnographies!—such critics nevertheless tend to overshoot their mark by failing to acknowledge the very careful and creative work being produced out of the crisis frame.

Far from despair and skepticism, in fact, a survey of the "crisis in representation" literature reveals its proponents as celebrating the inspiration these debates provide for a "deep epistemological, methodological, and ethical self-questioning."[10] Questioning what can authorize representations of so-called others is not intended to dismiss attempts to do so, but rather serves as the "intellectual stimulus for the contemporary vitality of experimental writing in anthropology."[11] Furthermore, those raising questions about representation do not claim we have "no recourse to the facts"; rather they want to explore the social conditions that produce the so-called facts. This point is particularly crucial for theologians who engage concrete contexts in order to challenge inherited theologies we might typically refer to as revealed, "the tradition," or normative. Raising questions about representation facilitates attention to dynamics of power and privilege and the ways in which processes of cultural production and reproduction accumulate

6. Flaherty, "Crisis in Representation," 481.

7. Ibid.

8. Snow, "On the Presumed Crisis," 499.

9. Ibid.

10. Conquergood, "Rethinking Ethnography," 179.

11. Marcus and Fischer, *Anthropology*, 8.

and distribute various forms of social capital, for example—all dynamics to which theologians with an orientation toward liberation must attend.

The conditions that produced the crisis of representation, as well as the arenas of its impact invite three areas for reflection in theological ethnography. First, as various scholars point out, an early major threat to the stability of empirical, objectivist science came from the postcolonial critique.[12] Prior to Said's publication of *Orientalism* in 1979, cultural anthropologists understood their projects—quite paternalistically—to be salvaging cultures that were threatened by annihilation from global Westernization.[13] Said's work, however, took away any pretense to such presumed noble goals. His argument demonstrated just how implicated in these projects of colonization ethnography was. At the simplest level, ethnographic data was deployed frequently in service of colonial expansion. More insidious, however, Said reveals, are the ways in which ethnographic strategies of representation reproduce colonial relations. As his convincing argument goes, the rhetoric of ethnographic texts has a tendency to reinforce Western domination through its replication of the researcher (Western) as active subject and the researched (typically colonized peoples) as passive objects. These crucial insights have led to the proliferation of multiple approaches seeking to decolonize ethnography.[14] But scant attention has been paid to these critiques as ethnography has made its more recent trans-disciplinary migration across the social sciences and humanities, and to theology in particular.

Particularly given the complicity of Christian missionaries and theologians in colonial expansion, ethnographic theologians must also begin to take seriously the epistemological, methodological and ethical dynamics inherent to the relationship between colonialism and representation. And given the arguments made by Said, Asad and others, we must do so not simply in terms of what fieldwork sites we choose (although we also do well to note that there are very few, if any, sites in the world that remain untouched in some way by colonization). Because, as postcolonial theorists demonstrate, the traditional strategies for representation were forged from colonial fieldwork crucibles, ethnographic theologians picking up these methods must also, therefore, begin to take seriously the potential colonial, epistemological implications of producing knowledge—of writing culture—out of any fieldwork site. We cannot simply instrumentalize these methods divorced from the conditions of their creation.

12. Clifford and Marcus, *Writing Culture*, 10; Conquergood, "Rethinking Ethnography," 179.

13. Asad, *Anthropology*; Marcus and Fischer, *Anthropology*, 102ff.

14. See, for example, Brown and Strega, *Research as Resistance*; Denzin, Lincoln, and Smith, *Handbook*; Smith, *Decolonizing*; Wilson, *Research as Ceremony*.

Second, as Denzin has argued, the crisis in representation is linked to a wider anthropological crisis of legitimation and praxis.[15] If, as the crisis of representation makes evident, "experience is created in the social text," Denzin argues, then traditional standards of validity, reliability and generalizability for authorizing an empirical account no longer apply. By extension, then, anthropology's praxis—that is, its capacity to effect change in society (a goal which Denzin, but not all anthropologists pursue) —is undermined.[16] Ethnographic theologians have, thus far, paid more attention to questions of legitimation and praxis than they have to the issues of representation that undergird them, however, particularly when we have tackled concerns about theological normativity. Acknowledging the limits of objectivity vis-à-vis problems of representation would, therefore, open up more complicated and nuanced possibilities for negotiating the relationship between the empirical and normatively theological in our ethnographic theological projects.[17]

Finally, as Marcus and Fischer argue—pace Denzin—the crisis in representation provides ethnography with the opportunity to reorient its core practices and "rethink its regulative ideals," not to deny dominant frameworks so much as to suspend them for a moment such that traditional "intellectual resources [can be] used in novel and eclectic ways."[18] Their insight thus echoes Kathryn Tanner's vision for contemporary theological creativity as a form of bricolage whereby theologians work "with an always potentially disordered heap of already existing materials, pulling them apart and putting them back together again, tinkering with their shapes, twisting them this way and that."[19] This is the very type of bricolage that I have argued elsewhere ethnographic theologians are or, at least, could be pursuing.[20]

Theologians have, thus far, tended to use the term "ethnography" as a stand-in for fairly traditional forms of data collection, however: primarily, participant observation and interviewing, as well as survey collection and, only recently but increasingly, more participatory action research based approaches. Our ahistoricized approach has therefore unnecessarily restricted the diversity of methods with which we have been willing and able to engage. In the next two sections I explore two approaches to ethnography that

15. Denzin, *Interpretive Ethnography* ; "Confronting."

16. Denzin, "Confronting," 482–83.

17. I have written about this in Wigg-Stevenson, "From Proclamation to Conversation."

18. Marcus and Fischer, *Anthropology*, 10.

19. Tanner, *Theories of Culture*, 166.

20. See Wigg-Stevenson, *Ethnographic Theology*; "From Proclamation to Conversation."

have arisen from engagement with the crisis in representation, and with which theologians have not yet fully experimented. The first, autoethnography, turns to a focus on the ethnographic self, and can be situated within a lineage of feminist, womanist and mujerista theologies long concerned with issues of representation. The second, performance ethnography, leads us in a different direction, taking up Denzin's call that "properly conceptualized" ethnography should become "a civic, participatory, collaborative project, a project that joins the researcher and researched in an ongoing moral dialogue."[21] In a rare moment of a non-theological discipline acknowledging its debt to—not to mention the mere existence of—theological disciplines, Denzin notes that the roots of such collaborative approaches are in, among other things, liberation theology.[22] By taking seriously the historical locations of these two methodological practices, then, we also take seriously the ways in which more liberative forms of theology were involved in the initial turn by theologians to ethnographic practice. And, in this way, I hope that a return to questions of representation will also help us to reclaim some of our more radical roots.

FROM "WOMEN'S EXPERIENCE" TO FEMINIST AUTOETHNOGRAPHY

The problem of representation is buried deep into the foundations of feminist theology, due to the field's advent in Valerie Saiving's influential article, "The Human Situation: A Feminine View."[23] The heart of Saiving's article was simple, yet profound: whenever theologians reflected on humanity—particularly on the effects of sin on humanity—they were really only talking about men. For Saiving, theology's corrective, therefore, entailed taking into account "women's experience" for understanding what it is to be a human being caught up in the drama of salvation. While it took almost twenty years for the full effects of Saiving's argument to take hold—as its re-publication in *Womanspirit Rising* re-situated it within a feminist movement that had a much more robust hold on the wider culture—when it did, it brought the category of women's experience to the center of debate for feminist approaches to theological re-imagining. If women's experience is to destabilize the masculine hegemony of human experience, then which women's experience counts? How should women's experience be represented, and who has the power to represent it?

21. Denzin, "Confronting," 485.
22. Ibid.
23. Saiving, "Human Situation."

For example, womanist, mujerista, queer and other liberation theologians quickly—and rightly—responded to the white feminist projects that Saiving's article inspired that gender, as an interpretive or analytic lens, cannot be constructed without careful attention to the raced, classed, sexual and other social dynamics that shape its meaning and power. The question of how to represent women's experience—as well as how to represent black women's experience, Latina experience, queer women's experience, and trans-women's experience, etc.—thus, always plants an essentializing fault-line into any argument within which that category is used; and that fault-line will always crack, leaving the argument crumbled in its wake. Because as debates across a few generations of feminist, womanist, mujerista and other theologians who incorporate analytics of gender into their wider theological work have now made clear, no one woman's experience can be representative of every other's. And no single group of women-identified people can define coherently or fully the concept or category, "woman."

Despite all this, the category of women's experience continues to captivate theological imagination. In a now classic article by Serene Jones, the author takes up this problem of representation, arguing that feminist theologians find themselves between a "rock" and a "hard place" (Jones 1995). In her typology, rock theologies have a "penchant for analytic measurements which are solid, foundational, comprehensive in scope, and generalizable in character."[24] Of course, like anything that is typically solid, foundational, comprehensive and generalizable, rock theologies, as Jones describes them, are held together problematically by the exclusion of those voices that just "don't fit." Nevertheless, she avers, it's this creative coherence that allows such visions of women's experience to construct theologies that are "refreshingly solid, strong, accessible, and steadily visionary."[25] While methodologically these theologies are found wanting, their theological substance and vision, notes Jones, are much more inspiring than theologies found on the "hard place" side of the equation. Hard place theologies rightly problematize issues of representation, but they do so to such a degree that they struggle to respond to the "pragmatic demand for sturdy visions and faith-filled truths" that the rock theologians provide so well.[26] Hard place theologies deploy poststructuralist critique and methods from cultural anthropology that opt

24. Jones, "Women's Experience," 171.

25. Jones, "Women's Experience," 178. On the "rock" side, Jones cites Johnson, *She Who Is*; Mowry LaCugna, *God for Us*; Nakashima Brock, *Journeys by Heart*; Keller, *From a Broken Web*; Williams, *Sisters in the Wilderness*; McFague, *Body of God*.

26. Jones, "Women's Experience," 172.

"for descriptions of experience which are historically localized and cultur-ally specific."[27] But the images they produce are often found wanting.

The gap between early feminist theology's sturdy, representational visions and the next generation's more sophisticated methodological ap-proaches is no longer as vast as when Jones initially mapped it, however.[28] Since she published her article, theologians and ethicists have, in fact, come a long way in developing compelling theological engagements with cultural anthropology. Moreover, with a number of texts taking seriously dynamics of gender in relation to ethnographic theology,[29] this seems like a good mo-ment for feminist theologians to re-imagine once again a more sophisticated vision for engagement with women's experience. Autoethnography—as one response to the crisis of representation in cultural anthropology—seems well poised methodologically to respond to what we might also label as a crisis of representation in feminist theology. Indeed, one of the more sacred texts in the feminist theology canon—*Proverbs of Ashes* by Rita Nakashima Brock and Rebecca Ann Parker (2001)—could be classified as a proto-autoethnographic work. I take up this unparalleled narrative—a theological argument about violence, redemptive suffering and soteriology—below. But first we need a definition of autoethnography.

Put simply, autoethnographers use their own personal experiences to bring wider cultural practices into view in a way that critiques that culture and seeks to transform it toward more liberative ends. Taking seriously the crisis of representation, autoethnographers deploy reflexive self-awareness not simply to neutralize their own bias in relation to their field of study, but also as a method for making themselves the subjects of their own analysis. Using their own personal narratives, then, they respond to the crisis of legit-imation by fully disrupting any pretension to objective and universal claims, opting instead to highlight the fragility of all knowledge production. Textu-ally, they also prioritize evocative over analytic writing: as Ellis and Bochner put it, "the narrative text refuses the impulse to abstract and explain, stress-ing the journey over the destination, and thus eclipses the scientific illusion of control and mastery."[30] Finally, autoethnographers take up the crisis in praxis by crafting narratives intended to compel readers to transformative response rather than merely convince them to a particular point of view.

27. Ibid., 172. Here she cites Tanner, *Theories of Culture*; Isasi-Díaz, *En La Lucha*; Chopp, *Power to Speak*.

28. Schneider and Trentaz, "Making Sense."

29. See, for example, Floyd-Thomas, *Mining the Motherlode*; McClintock Fulker-son, *Places of Redemption*; Wigg-Stevenson, *Ethnographic Theology*; Lassiter, *Recogniz-ing Other Subjects*.

30. Ellis and Bochner, "Autoethnography," 744.

"The accessibility and readability of the [autoethnographic] text repositions the reader as a participant in dialogue," argue Ellis and Bochner, thus calling her up into the process of social transformation toward which the text points by refusing "the orthodox view of the reader as passive receiver of knowledge."[31] Autoethnography thus deploys epiphanic moments of story-telling, those fissures in a constructed reality that reveal the possibility of an alternative way, an invitation to the reader to forge a new path.

All these elements are present in Brock and Parker's 2001 book. While it's unlikely that the two authors were using autoethnographic theories and methods consciously—autoethnography was itself a nascent movement at the time of *Proverbs of Ashes'* publication—it seems they were perhaps tapping into the same intellectual mood that compelled these cultural anthropological innovations. Indeed, Brock and Parker catalogue how difficult it was to realize that they needed to focus the book on their own personal experience. Seeking to critique theologies of atonement from the perspectives of violence against women, the authors initially disguised how close to home the stories they were telling actually hit. But as time went along, they realized that "the mask of objectivity, with its academic, distanced tone, hid the *lived* character of [their] theological questions and [their] theological affirmations."[32] Friends who read early drafts encouraged them to put the stories front and centre, however, calling Brock and Parker to step out from behind the anonymizing shield of academic prose. Immediately the authors came up against the problem of representation, even in trying to tell their own stories, as they struggled to "speak truthfully and respectfully of those whose lives have been closely linked with [their] own."[33] Yet, at the same time, they recognized the complex cultural dynamics at play in stories, as the differences between the ways in which their ethnic-cultural backgrounds shaped their modes of narrative surfaced.[34] Particularly in light of the way their divergent cultural backgrounds connected with their shared theological reflections on violence, Brock and Parker wondered if their "insights may be of value to others from a variety of experiences and backgrounds."[35]

Proverbs of Ashes thus deploys the personal to expose and unpack the cultural—and, by extension the theological. It does so in ways that grapple with the crisis of representation, with what it means to tell the truth about a

31. Ibid.
32. Brock and Parker, *Proverbs of Ashes*, 7.
33. Ibid.
34. Ibid., 7–8.
35. Ibid., 8.

life without pretensions toward objectivity or universality. Its legitimation, therefore, comes not in its generalizability, so much as with the hope that it might evoke transformative practice in its reader. And in these ways, Brock and Parker's creative, narrative doctrinal re-imagining of salvation sets a methodological agenda for feminist theological autoethnography that has not yet been taken up by any other scholar—despite the now fifteen year gap since the publication of their text. With this feminist theological prototype out there, and the earlier ad hoc partnerships of ethnography and theology now matured into their current status as a genuine theological movement, the time seems ripe to expand our methodological options, particularly in these places where they connect with an older issue already at play in a particular area of theology. Grounding our questions anew in the problem of representation thus invites such creative, even collaborative, possibilities. It is to this more collaborative type of work that we now turn with our exploration of performance ethnography.

PERFORMANCE ETHNOGRAPHY AS THEOLOGICAL COLLABORATION

The *performance* of performance ethnography can delineate a number of different methodological moments in a ethnographic project: it can refer to a heuristic for data analysis, an actual method of research, or/and the telos of the project's representational form. Used simply as a heuristic device (most certainly the least radical of these three), performance provides a metaphor for analyzing practice or descriptions of action that takes their narrative or temporal dimensions, for example, seriously. Indeed, ethnographers might frequently refer to the performative nature of human action without necessarily classifying their own work as performance ethnography at all. The same is true for theologians. It is the second two meanings of *performance* that, thus, interest us here.

Ethnographers who engage performance as a mode of research are among those who push the envelope a little further. Their approach might involve inviting their research partners to collaborate on creating a play or performance artwork, for example, and, in this way, they facilitate creative expression that is able to produce forms of knowledge inaccessible to standard ethnographic interviewing. Canadian anthropologist Magdalena Kazubowski-Houston's work offers a perfect example of this mode of performance ethnography, as she directs a mixed group of Roma women and non-Roma actors in Poland to write, stage and perform the Roma women's life stories. It is in the process of creating the play, more so than performing it, that Kazubowski-Houston gains access to her informants' lives in ways

that deep hanging out in their homes and even rich, conversational interviews cannot produce.[36] A particularly honest and haunting account of
the whole experience leaves Kazubowski-Houston questioning the efficacy
of her own methods in profoundly compelling ways. Theatrically trained
herself, she offers rich reflections on the use of artistic approaches in anthropological research, and the difficulty of balancing aesthetic and research
commitments. Her double vocation, in fact, has the potential to offer insight to theologians who also find ourselves straddling two worlds—church
and academy—as we navigate our research fields of study. What types of
ecclesial or other communal Christian practices might become the methods
for our study rather than merely the topics? How might we construct ethnographic theological methods that engage our research partners aesthetically,
emotionally, creatively and spiritually beyond the (albeit often significant)
interactions of an informant interview?

Finally, performance ethnography can refer to the final product—
written or actually performed—of an ethnographic project. This final mode
perhaps offers performance ethnography's most subversive potential, as it
disrupts the hegemonic status of the academic text as the telos of ethnography's representational form.[37] Drawing on the principles of Brechtian
theatre that are among its inspirations, this final version of performance
ethnography collaborates not only with its research subjects or partners in
this case but also with the audience. In so doing, it self-consciously deploys
the performance form—its obvious nature as a *constructed* rather than sup-
posedly *direct* representation of reality—to shape critical consciousness
and, by extension, social transformation. In this mode, as Denzin puts it,
"ethnography, like art, is always political."[38] This final version of performance ethnography is therefore less interested in representing the world
as it is; it wants to represent the world that can be—again, offering a type
of hope-filled, even eschatological ethnographic orientation that could be a
particularly fruitful conversation partner for ethnographic theology.

I noted above how Kathryn Tanner describes theological creativity as
a process of bricolage whereby theological forms, tropes, and even detri-
tus is reassembled again and again in an ongoing process of cultural (re)
production. In Tanner's influential view, then, theology is always, already
a creative, communal endeavor, whether we acknowledge it as such or not.
Theology thus involves a range of activity and discourse, spanning a spectrum of everyday practices of Christian life to the more rarified debates of

36. Kazubowski-Houston, *Staging Strife*.

37. Conquergood, "Rethinking Ethnography," 190.

38. Denzin, *Performance Ethnography*, 129.

academic theology. As Tanner outlines it, while each of us chooses—in ways both conscious and unconscious—to position the bulk of our labor at differ-ent points along this everyday/academic spectrum, no single point should be valued any more highly than another, and a complex, even conflictual, integration of all points is required for theological practice to endure. It is as if we are always already the collection of Roma women, non-Roma ac-tors and the play's director/anthropologist in Kazubowski-Houston's work all at once—whether or not we decide to engage that constellation of active relationships in our ethnographic fieldwork/writing.

As an always already creative communal endeavor, theology also there-fore always begins in the middle of the action—*in medias res*—preceded by and shaped by thousands of years of Christian and other intellectual and practiced traditions. Moreover, as such, it is always already oriented toward the proliferation, dismantling, recovery and re-assemblage of those same traditions. It is always a collaboration with a whole community of saints, liv-ing present and in memory. Like performance ethnography, then, theology brings together lay and professionals to create and recreate narratives that produce fresh possibilities for—in our case, Christian—thought and action.

The use of ethnography to intervene into this ongoing creative, col-laborative project can therefore help facilitate the theologian's intellectual, aesthetic, moral and political reflexivity vis-à-vis both the empirical and the theological. Using ethnography not only to witness but, also, to more transparently articulate the collaborations that undergird our writing has the potential to make us all the more responsible to those collaborators (in my work, at least, this makes it nearly impossible for me to think of the people who live, work and have their being in any given field of my study as research informants or subjects; they are always my research partners). Ethnographic interventions into these theological collaborations therefore also call us to responsibly name the precise position we take in relation not only to those collaborators, but also to the Christian traditions we (by virtue of our social position as theologians and, possibly, Christians ourselves) inherit—whether we're seeking to preserve them, re-configure or annihilate them. In other words, it asks us to state what precisely it is we're trying to do as we take up our place *in medias res*. The type of ethnography we use to stage these interventions into theology thus matters for shaping this reflexive moment and the types of knowledge it can produce. It is to this topic we now turn.

CRITICAL APPROACHES TO ETHNOGRAPHIC THEOLOGY

So how might understanding the crisis of representation in anthropology help theologians grapple more richly with some of our own contextual, methodological, ethical, and theological questions? "Traditional ethnography," as Denzin puts it (i.e., the types of ethnography most typically engaged by ethnographic theologians), "represents attempts to write and inscribe culture for the purposes of increasing knowledge and social awareness."[39] When theologians intervene in the theological project using traditional ethnography, then, they are more likely to deliver thick descriptions of concrete practice—i.e., to increase our knowledge of that practice—in ways that potentially and, sometimes, intentionally reproduce the status quo of that practice. In other words, even when traditional approaches to ethnography are used to reveal the internal messiness of the theological traditions, they still essentially preserve the integrity of those traditions. For many ethnographic theologians, this act of preservation in the face of messiness is, in fact, their goal.

Unlike traditional ethnography, Denzin argues, "critical performance autoethnography . . . works to expose ways in which power and ideology shape self, desire, and human consciousness in concrete institutional and interactional sites."[40] It interrogates the ways in which everyday culture is "embedded in the naturalized commonsense realities of capitalism, the media, and the neoliberal corporatist state."[41] Interventions into theology along the lines of critical autoethnographic and performance ethnographies, therefore, are able to question the very conditions that produced and continue to produce certain forms of theological knowledge. Such interventions could likewise dismantle our theological status quo. In so doing they would challenge both any pretension to direct empirical representation and any pretension to a stable theological representation in a way that could orient both toward social-theological transformation instead. To borrow Denzin's description of performance ethnography, this kind of theological intervention has the potential for revealing what theologians might refer to as the eschatological dimensions of life, in that it could cultivate a theo-politics of resistance and enact "a performative cultural politics of hope."[42]

Furthermore, by destabilizing the empirical as much as the theological, autoethnographic and performance ethnographic theologies could also require and make possible alternative normative criteria for their adjudication.

39. Denzin, *Performance Ethnography*, 33.
40. Ibid.
41. Ibid.
42. Ibid., 24.

As Denzin argues, once we abandon our methodological certainty and admit that all observation is theory-laden, then it becomes "impossible to fix a single standard for deciding what is good or bad, or right."[43] Traditional normative criteria is thus liberated from needing to function as a *policing device*, as he puts it, able instead to be discerned in and derived from the appropriate local context of the research and oriented toward the goals of the research/researched team. Such criteria can be shaped by moral, political and ethical purposes, by literary and aesthetic norms, by the politics of experience, and more.[44] For Denzin, the researcher must take a side in the ideological battles that shape her research context, and she must make the moral position of her side clear. If her project is framed by an orientation to ethics, what constitutes those ethics? Principles of solidarity, care, social transformation or revolution, for example? Or if the researcher's normative criteria has been framed by an orientation to literary aesthetic categories, within which framework for aesthetics should the work be judged? Is the criteria linked to postmodern narrative forms, or to representational or abstract art? What role do the sublime and surreal play in its articulation? Is the work striving for coherence or dissonance, and what is the connection of each to its socio-theo-politics? In both autoethnographic performance ethnography and ethnographic theology, this relativizing of various norming devices does not equate to their absence or even irrelevance, however. Rather, this dissemination of authority into the hands of the community requires that researchers take up the added task in their projects of articulating and defending their legitimating criteria, rather than simply relying upon or appealing to some *a priori* established standard.

Finally, and perhaps most interestingly, an intervention of critical autoethnographic or performance ethnographies into theological projects can help reorient theology to practice anew, precisely by reorienting theological fieldwork to something other than the standard academic theological text as its telos. Ethnographic fieldwork, as an intensely bodily practice, has the potential to disrupt the disembodied Cartesian orientation of most academic practice, and yet "the hegemony of inscribed texts is never challenged by fieldwork because after all is said and done, the final word is on paper . . . print publication is the telos of fieldwork."[45] Making a performance, or even a script or treatment for a play the telos of fieldwork, however, opens up not only new criteria for the fieldwork's legitimation, but also new audiences for that fieldwork's impact, and new ways in which that fieldwork can have its

43. Ibid., 109.
44. Ibid., 111.
45. Conquergood, "Rethinking Ethnography," 190.

impact. Like Conquergood, "I want to keep thinking about what gets lost and muted in [academic] texts," to imagine alternative modes for the payout of academic theological goods.[46]

I have written elsewhere about how theologians picture their written work having an impact on Christian practice.[47] We imagine, perhaps, that ministry students will read our books in class, or that pastors might pick them up and, if they can find the time, also read them. With one of the more condescending metaphors that academic theologians tend to use, we then imagine those ideas *trickling down* from us to the pastors to the people in the pews. Some of us break through into a form of so-called popular writing that is more widely accessible. But even so, all these strategies refuse to relinquish our own preferred modes of academic representation: writing.

But what if our fieldwork were oriented to other modes of representation, and not just toward performance based forms, but forms more conducive to the practical demands of the Christian social practices we seek to impact? Performance ethnography in particular invites theology to imagine what this might look like. Such representational forms could be collaboratively designed Sunday school or adult education curriculum.[48] They could be social media projects, short videos of Rob Bell's NOOMA variety.[49] They could be like the theo-dramas enacted by the IKON community in Ireland.[50] They could be sermons and liturgies and treatments for pastoral care. They could be something we haven't imagined yet. But most of all they could be directed toward dismantling the hegemony of the text in theology, such that the text could no longer stand as the be all, end all mediator of theological research to pastoral contexts. Alternative representational forms in fact invite the academic theologian into a vulnerable space by which she can serve the church from her weakness, not just her privilege.

---

46. Ibid., 191.

47. Wigg-Stevenson, *Ethnographic Theology*, 45–46.

48. My own work, *Ethnographic Theology*, textually records an ethnography that endeavored to be precisely this. At the time of writing, I didn't yet know about performance ethnography—as I even used the metaphor of performance art in the final chapter to unpack the collaborative nature of our shared work, as well as the dynamics of power and privilege that undergirded the theologies we communally constructed. In this way, *Ethnographic Theology* might be read as a type of proto-performance theology, much as I read *Proverbs of Ashes* as a proto-autoethnographic theology above.

49. "NOOMAtube," https://www.youtube.com/user/NOOMAtube.

50. See Rollins, *How (Not) to*.

CONCLUSION

In these pages I have outlined the so-called crisis of representation in anthropology, and demonstrated its potential import for ethnographic theology, particularly in terms of the relationship between empirical legitimacy and theological normativity, as well as for the intervention of more diverse ethnographic methods into constructive theological projects. My goal has been to ground these methods in their wider historical, theoretical frameworks, and not simply to instrumentalize them for theological usage in a decontextualized way. It is true that there are many more ethnographic methods developed than ethnographic theologians are currently deploying. Key for moving forward will be our capacity to engage these diverse methods in authentic ways, such that they help us to engage and overcome issues of representation in our work—or, to put it in Mark Jordan's more poetic prose: to tell the truth about people's lives in ways that refuse to be "violently simple or demonically final."[51]

---

51. Jordan, "Writing the Truth," 5.

15

The Enacted and Experienced Faith—Creating "Stuff" on Baptist Spirituality in Sweden

Sune Fahlgren

INTRODUCTION: ETHNOGRAPHICAL DATA FOR
ECCLESIOLOGICAL STUDIES OF THE REAL CHURCH

I am a practical ecclesiologist, and my research field is to a large extent free churches. Most of my studies represent the current empirical turn in theology as well as the more general turn to practices as study objects and practice-theories as hermeneutical keys.[1] The study presented here, on Baptist spirituality, highlights questions about ethnography and ecclesiology in relation to historical data. In particular, this chapter presents how materials can be created and used in a kind of field study, which has fields of various points in the past.

One of the distinctive marks of the Baptist communities is that they have no binding creeds beside the Holy Scriptures.[2] They belong to a group of Christian communities that are labelled *non-creedal*. Therefore it is impossible to do ecclesiological research on Baptists by employing the same kind of data that has traditionally been used in church history and ecclesiology such as creeds, liturgical books, canon laws, church orders, etc. Even if

---

1. See Hegstad, *Real Church*; Fahlgren and Ideström, *Ecclesiology*.
2. Fiddes, *Tracks*.

such data can be found among Baptists, it is not clear that they reflect actual congregational life and practices.

For ecclesiological studies of non-creedal churches it is necessary to find other kinds of historical and contemporary data, and this data is of the same kind as in ethnographic and anthropological studies, for example publications, songs, hymnbooks, letters, devotional books, sermons, biographies, photos, minutes, dairies, journals, and other artifacts.

To study Baptist spirituality I have dug into various archives, especially the historical archive for the former Baptist Union in Stockholm. In these archives I have searched for material used in different types of spirituality practices, and I have struggled to learn more about what kind of field material it is and how it can be used in ecclesiological studies.

My hypothesis is that such historical data can be collected and used with the same methods that an ethnographical researcher collects and deals with data from fieldwork. It must, for example, be organized into clusters; artifacts and photos must be transferred into a descriptive text; all data, including one's own observations and reflections, must be categorized, interpreted and analyzed within a theoretical framework. In sum: this is an inductive research process, which is in conversation with research questions and constantly searching for new and alternative interpretations.

What on Earth, Then, is Spirituality?

Spirituality was the object for my field study, and that work will serve as a point of departure for methodological and theoretical reflections on how I carried out the study on Baptist *spirituality*. Nevertheless, before going into these fundamental reflections, the study object as such needs attention. In several academic disciplines there is an ongoing search for the definition of spirituality and the integrative center for studies on spirituality. Several understandings can be found both within and without the academy.[3] This

---

3. Swedish readers from a Free Church background may have some doubts concerning the concept of spirituality in this study. Unfortunately, we have nothing corresponding to it in our vocabulary. Sometimes the word *andlighet* (religiosity) is used; yet, like *fromhet* (piety), it generally tends to signify something inward-looking and non-civic-minded.

The Baptist leader and historian David Lagergren (1919–2013) also had doubts in this question. Instead, he coined the term "types of Christianity" (*kristendomstyper*) and made a distinction between "intensive" and "extensive" Christianity, see Lagergren, "Intensiv," a distinction that has proven useful in the study of spirituality. Fahlgren, *Vatten*, 298–302. When Larsåke W. Persson wrote a study of the Baptist Union and its spirituality, he compiled an "inverse word list," mirroring the language within the Baptist Union by highlighting the words seldom or never used, see Persson, *Varför*. Among these words, one finds "altar," "infant baptism," "*bönebrus*" ("a buzz of prayer"),

particular case study on Baptist spirituality explored the hypothesis that spirituality can be defined as the lived and experienced ecclesiology, embodied in ecclesial practices and culture. I also assumed that spirituality includes, per se, a historical dimension.

Nowadays authenticity has become the primary virtue of our culture and duplicity the gravest sin. Perhaps this is one reason why historians and theologians have become more and more interested in how the Christian faith has been lived and carried into effect in various contexts and at various points in history. Overall, spirituality has become an international term for faith as action and culture. In this way, the outward history and theoretical aspects of a Christian communion (or any other religious tradition) can be supplemented by something essential—the religious existence and faith as something cooperatively enacted and personally experienced.

This perspective on practical life and its patterns corresponds with that of the Baptists, who have always been less interested in formulations of doctrine than in practiced doctrine. Although being described as "noncreedal," they are not without doctrines and conviction.[4] Yet these are written in practical life rather than in catechisms. This in turn means that among the Baptists, the patterns of action (*habitus*) and the social practices are the primary theology.

In my case study, I limited Baptists to Baptists in Sweden, and more precisely to the Baptist union (Svenska Baptistsamfundet).[5] The first Baptist congregation in Sweden was founded 1848, but since 2011 the Baptist Union is no longer a specific denomination. Swedish Baptists were part of a merger between the Covenant Church, the Baptist Union, and the Methodist Church in Sweden. The new church is called *Equmeniakyrkan* (Uniting Church in Sweden). Therefore, this case study took on an inescapably historical approach; the cases date from 1848–2011 and are drawn from

---

and "sacraments." Understanding why these words are seldom used among Baptists functions, according to Persson, as a key to understanding Baptist spirituality.

In spite of various objections, the concept of spirituality has become established in Sweden. See Härdelin, "Den kristna." An important advantage is that it underlines the belief of the work of the Holy Spirit in Christian communities. Enacted and experienced faith in the church (spirituality) is seen as a consequence of the life-giving Spirit and is sustained with the power and gifts of the Spirit.

4. Fahlgren, *Predikantskap*, 11.

5. There are several other denominations in Sweden with more or less Baptist theology and practices, e.g., Evangeliska Frikyrkan (internationally called Interact, a merger between the Örebro Mission, the Free Baptists, and the Holiness covenant), the Adventist Church, the Pentecostal Alliance of Independent churches in Sweden, and some new neopentecostal denominations like Hillsong Church.

more than twenty congregations in different parts of the country during this period.[6]

Although the historical aspect is decisive, it is essentially an *ecclesiological* study, and it has spirituality as the study object in the fields of various Baptists' congregations. The whole case thereby presents a concrete example of how spirituality—tentatively—can be described and analyzed as an ecclesial practice and habitus. The following presentation of the field study is revised and shortened in order to give space for some methodological and theoretical reflections and thus match the shape and approach of this volume.

Since the study of spirituality focuses on "the spiritual life and profile of a movement, an epoch or an individual," it goes beyond the establishment.[7] Applied to Baptists in Sweden, spirituality, to a large extent, is a matter of the creativity of the many who have found countless forms of expression in literature, art, music, and architecture. With great ingenuity, Baptists seems to have found ways to help people in need and change society for the better.

It is well worth the academic effort to try to describe and analyze the people behind Baptist communities and to bring out their way of living their faith and shaping a Baptist culture. By seeing church from the angle of spirituality, we are reminded that the Baptist movement in history has been moved forward not only by its leading figures but also by a great number of unknown persons and their inspiration and affection for God. In the same way, regular people have played important roles in other Christian traditions as well. The voices and experiences in a spirituality study must therefore represent the complex and thick grassroots realities in the Baptist movement. Thus, the ethnographical character of the field study has a rationale even in the study object per se.

Research Perspectives and Questions

Deliberate perspectives and some key questions organized the analysis of the material I created. That is to say, they became tools to find characteristic features and significant dimensions in the Baptist spirituality. The following is a brief presentation of my research tools.

---

6. I have experiences or/and material from Baptist congregations in Asker, Blacksta, Borekulla, Grundsunda (Dombäck), Göteborg, Helsingborg, Höör, Jönköping, Koster, Malmö, Stockholms första baptistförsamling, Norrmalm (Stockholm), Norrköping, Piteå, Stora Mellösa, Sundsvall, Uppsala, Västerås, Åsbro, Örebro, Örnsköldsvik (Elim, Betel).

7. Halldorf, *Av denna*, 18–21. Cf. Laghé, *Den evangeliska*, 12–14; Josefsson, *Liv*, 26–33.

Enacted and experienced faith has a particular dimension when seen from the ecumenical perspective, i.e., as the rich experiences of the world-wide church through two millennia. By observing one's own tradition from such an external perspective, one can discern the things that have ended up in "the shadow," to borrow a term from analytical psychology. *From an ecumenical perspective, what has been held back in Baptist spirituality by the emphasis on other things?* That question was raised in this case study, since Baptist spirituality is shaped to a great extent by contrasts and conflicts with other Christian traditions.

History in a Christian community means more than an enumeration of facts. It is also a matter of memories, collective and individual, which create identity in the community ("what we are") and turn the eyes of the community to the future ("what we shall be," cf. 1 John 3:1–2). This being the case, questions concerning memory and memory loss are essential in the study of spirituality.[8] As is the question of how Baptists told their narratives. *What memories have been most important in the shaping of identity and of perspectives on the present and the future? Which members of the movement have been omitted from memory?*

As becomes clear in books giving an outline of the history of Baptism in Sweden,[9] there is not one single expression of Baptist faith and tradition in Sweden but rather a great variety.[10] This plurality of expressions depends not least on *the emphasis on freedom*, which has been practiced and renegotiated in different epochs, geographical areas, and encounters with other Christians.

When Baptists and Baptist congregations have described themselves, *freedom* is a recurrent key concept ("a church language") for lived faith.[11] This freedom has many meanings: freedom of religion, freedom of conscience, freedom of assembly, "the freedom of every congregation," and freedom from the obligation to serve in the armed forces. *But how have these ideals of freedom from compulsion been applied in practice? What happened when the coercive power of the "state church" came to an end? What actions of freedom have actually formed the Baptists in Sweden?*

The concept of "freedom" undoubtedly is one of the characteristic features and existential dimensions of Baptist spirituality, and it is based on

8. Fahlgren, *Predikantskap*, 72–74.

9. For example, Åqvist, *Tro*; Fahlgren, *Vatten*.

10. Cf. Fahlgren and Joø, "Baptismens," 104–35.

11. I use the analysis concept of "church language" in Fahlgren, "Equmeniakyrkans." The underlying hypothesis is that a specific church language expresses and creates a specific life world, embedded in one or more ecclesial practices. See also Fahlgren, "Historieskrivningar," 70–71.

how congregations as well as individuals understand themselves in different circumstances. Thus, different ideals of freedom were an essential focus in the analysis of data from the field studies.

The variations of Baptist spirituality also depend on all those who have belonged to Baptist communities and helped to shape them according to their personalities and experiences of faith and life. Consequently, the study of spirituality also concentrated on collective as well as individual expressions of ideals and tradition. In a limited presentation of the study, this variety of expressions can only be hinted at, yet it must be emphasized.

Spirituality has a significant didactic side as well. Studies of spirituality in a Christian tradition therefore also pay attention to its introduction to Christian life, which in the international context is often called spiritual theology. Even if the Baptists never described their ideals of education in these terms, they were part of the Baptist training for the Christian life and the grounding of character according to Baptist ideals. Below, some examples of Baptist ideals of formation in the field study will be highlighted as well as some social practices used for didactic purposes, which is also important for the understanding of spirituality.

Adopting and working through the perspectives and questions presented here, I have compiled several tables in order to give concrete examples of typical expressions of certain types of spirituality. These tables have gradually emerged as a result of the working process, which began when I was describing and analyzing the ethnographic stuff I had created during the field studies. The process took the shape of an on-going conversation—one which embodied the idea of a hermeneutical circle—between moments of creating the material, of organizing all its data in categories, and of interpreting and reinterpreting, and then it was a matter of the step-by-step compilation of the major results into a matrix. During the process, experimental thinking, conversation with research colleagues, and writing drafts were very creative factors.

The first line in the table below mentions some key *Bible texts* that have had a formative influence on each type of spirituality, respectively. Historically speaking, Baptists have been studious readers of the Bible. The second line refers to *hymns* or *songs* that express the specific spirituality, songs that a "real Baptist" would probably know by heart. The third line gives examples of *keywords* ("church language") Baptists tend to use when talking about these matters. Since *freedom* is a recurrent motif when Baptists describe themselves, the fourth line describes a concrete meaning of freedom within each type of spirituality. The two last lines give examples of *common practices* and *historical persons* connected to a specific spirituality.

In the following presentation of Baptist spiritualties, I chose to elaborate six different kind of Spirituality, and each is summarized in a tablet with key expressions in the areas of biblical texts, hymns/songs, church language, freedom motifs, common practice, and historical personas. Each area gives concrete examples of the kind of material I created during the field studies. Thus, the tables can be seen as an ethnographic exhibition, related to enacted and experienced faith among Baptists.

In the presentation I will describe and analyze six different kind of spirituality (six tables) that I inductively found in the "stuff "from the fieldwork. Beside the hermeneutical process of creating the tables, I also completed a systematic theological analysis of the material, combined with more spontaneous impressions I got during the field studies. The result of these inductive analyses was summoned up in a typology. In the following, I present four main types of "ism" in Baptist Spirituality in Sweden (cf. with McClendon's Baptist visions below): 1. *Activism*; 2. *Ecumenism*; 3. *Legalism*; 4. *Cognitivism*. Two of these four spirituality types also have an opposite dimension. The antithesis to Cognitivism is Experientialism. The antithesis to Ecumenism is Confessionalism. Therefore, the number of tables is six.

A Renowned Study on Baptist Spirituality

The American theologian James W. McClendon (1924–2000) is often cited internationally in studies of Baptist spirituality. McClendon has studied the Anabaptist heritage and its offshoots in history and across the world. He has summarized the result of his studies in what he calls "Baptist visions," where he particularly brings out five historical ideals and convictions, one of which is freedom.[12]

1. The biblical story is also the story of every Christian and of every congregation (faithfulness to the Bible, strong belief in God's reality)

2. The task to preach the gospel also involves witnessing in difficult times (the faithful struggle of the Kingdom of God, social relations)

3. Freedom is to serve God without state/empire hindrance (ambivalent relations with the state)

4. Discipleship means deepened obedience to Jesus Christ (personally chosen faith, credible lifestyle)

5. The community of the baptized daily shares this vision in word and deed (believer's baptism, the faith community, faithful conversations as a means of formation).

12. McClendon, *Systematic*, 28 (here abbreviated).

In the faith confessed and practiced by Swedish Baptists, it is possible to find more or less clear expressions of all these visions and convictions. However, I have chosen not to take this ideal pattern as my starting point and instead make a deductive study. In the same way as McClendon identified patterns by studying a large number of concrete details, my starting point is the perspectives I have chosen and the questions I raised out of my own observations and experiences of the Baptists' lived faith in Sweden, at different times and in different places, as well as out of the observations and experiences of others. Added to this is the fieldwork I have done in the historical archives, mentioned above, in order to collect relevant data.

While it is possible to interpret individual details by using McClendon's thematic characteristics deductively, it might also be possible to identify his and other patterns inductively—as I did with the "ism" in this study. When reflecting on theology and history, embedded in ecclesial practices and habitus, it is important not to be caught up in ideals at the expense of empirical studies. The following section begins the presentation of my field study on Baptist spirituality.

EXPECTATION

Like all who belong to a revival movement, the Baptists in Sweden lived in the expectation that something was about to happen.[13] Their songs, prayers, witnessing, and activities were all expressions of this longing. Baptists expected, for instance, their children to be baptized when they had developed a personal faith and thereby "join the congregation." Baptists prayed for their neighbors and friends that they would come "within earshot" and "be saved." When gathering at meetings, all those present should be "blessed" not least by the sermon. They expected God to answer prayers and give healing, consolation, and help in life.

The concept of "awakening" was the common denominator of all this longing, as well as "growing in numbers." This was particularly explicit during the first hundred years of the history of the Baptist Union in Sweden. During certain periods, there was also a strong sense that Jesus would come back soon.

I personally remember the expectation that could be felt during the church meetings I participated in as a young person.[14] The basic idea of these meetings in the Baptist congregation, more or less consciously shared, was that we should "seek Christ's thought" together (cf. 1 Cor. 14:26–33,

13. Persson, "Spiritualitet," 3–4.

14. For the ecclesial practice of church meeting among Baptists, see Fahlgren, *Vatten*, 135–43.

Eph. 3:18–19). The congregation's common experience was that by seeking Christ's thought together, it was possible to understand God's will in a specific question. Perhaps for this reason, the minutes of the church meetings were exceptionally well written and were read in a solemn way with a great deal of interest. There were Baptist congregations that kept the minute book in a drawer in the communion table. Church meetings had, speaking with modern theological language, a sacramental character. Christ's presence was experienced "in, with, and through" the conversations in the community of believers. Something happened: "The Holy Spirit and we have agreed" (Acts 15:28).

An Activist Identity

This expectation created an activist spirituality within Baptism. Baptists invited friends and neighbors to the gatherings in the Baptist chapels so that the expectations of the Baptists could also become reality. Parents brought their children along to "meetings," and Baptist congregations had Sunday schools, youth clubs, Christian education, camps, music schools, and other activities for children and teenagers. New generations were brought up into Baptism by "coming along," and in the youth clubs there was a high degree of participatory culture that both shaped values and developed skills such as speaking in public, leading groups, and making common decisions—"fill brightest hours with labor, rest comes sure and soon. Give every flying minute, something to keep in store."[15]

Early on, the Baptist congregations started societies and other organizations for furthering the awakening by missionary work, both regionally and nationally. Missionary activities in Sweden were called "inward mission," while activities in other countries were called "outward mission." Expectation was not a matter of "biding one's time," waiting for God to act. Baptists made sure that it happened by dispatching colporteurs, evangelists, and missionaries.

The young English Baptist William Carey (1761–1834) served as a role model for this missionary entrepreneurship, which also meant that the memory of him had to be kept alive. Swedish Baptist congregations generally had members' libraries where one could find biographies and other literature on Carey. Around fifteen books on Carey have been published in Swedish. Carey was also often mentioned in Baptist sermons. The favorite episode was when Carey asked a pastor whether it was the duty of every

15. *Nya Pilgrimssånger*, 525 ("werka med rastlös ifwer, bruka wäl ditt pund"). This is an English hymn by Annie L. Walker-Coghill (1854)—"Work for the night is coming," translated to Swedish by the Baptist minister Teodor Trued Truvé (1876).

Christian to be a missionary. The pastor brushed Carey's question aside, saying, "Young man, sit down. If God is pleased to convert the heathen world, He will do it without your help or mine." Carey did not accept this answer. Instead, he founded a missionary society that sent him to India. Before his departure, he held a missionary sermon based on Isaiah 54:2–3, in which he coined his motto, "Expect great things from God. Attempt great things for God."

This expectation among Baptists, that something was about to happen, stands out when compared with other spiritualties, with their concentration on what had already happened and their diminished expectations on God's acting now. Lutheran, Reformed, and Catholic traditions all lay stress upon the objective facts of salvation history, the facts that faith rests upon. Particular emphasis is placed on the Christ event. These things a Christian can trust. They are valid for all and without our participation. This is also the reason why, in these traditions, it is possible to be baptized as a child and begin life carried by God's work in Jesus Christ. In Baptism, these objective facts are a reason not to baptize children, since God "has a lead" in every person's life.[16] Therefore, one has to wait for the active response of every individual.

From a Baptist perspective, the objective facts of Christian faith constituted a strong imperative to expect more from God and to act. Prayers are a particularly good reflection of this mindset. Baptists were expected to pray in their own words ("free prayer") and not to use what others had already written. "The prayer of the heart" was considered more authentic, since it expressed the freedom to receive guidance from God's Spirit and the freedom to put one's longing into words.

At times, the expectation that new things would happen overshadowed experiences of situations when expectations were not realized. The awakening did not begin. There were seldom or never any baptisms. The baptistery was unused.[17] Healing miracles occurred very rarely. More and more of the children in Baptist families chose not to join the congregation. Jesus had not come back, despite all the alleged "signs of the times" that seemed to indicate that he would. Most Baptists realized that at many gatherings there was no chance of being "blessed." And after the Second World War, Baptist ministers were no longer leaders in a growing movement. In this activist

16. The Swedish Baptist theologian, Bert Franzén, elaborates the idea of God's "lead" into a theology for the practice of infant dedication among Baptists, which was a practice inaugurated in the 1950s in Sweden. See Franzén, *Guds*. Infant dedication is not a dry baptism but a thanksgiving to the Creator for a newborn child and an expression of the belief that every human being is included in the redemptive work of Christ.

17. Persson, *Varför*, 12.

spirituality, there is also disappointment and frustration—something in the shadows—that one has to take into account. As all disappointments, these experiences gave rise to denial, explanations, and rationalizations in the Baptist congregations.[18]

The collective expectation that something would happen, passed on from one generation to the other, has—in spite of (or thanks to?) disappointments—been a contributing factor to the pronounced openness of the Baptist Union toward other Christian movements where something actually happened and people gathered. Here I am thinking of charismatic and ecumenical movements (Vineyard, Iona), the twelve step movement, the recovery movement, as well as programs for church growth that the Swedish Baptist Union has housed.

To a certain extent, the novelties that have emerged within Baptism in Sweden are a continuation of the passion for something to happen, except that the objects of longing are partly different than before. Today, a Baptist congregation wants to reach out and gather the "seekers," members are expected to attend conferences, the congregational music is expected to reach a certain standard, and a contract for social work is seen as a spiritual step forward. Activist spirituality lives on in the form of steadfast proficiency.

Key Bible texts	"We cannot help speaking about what we have seen and heard" (Acts 4:20), "the way home." (Luke 15:11–32).
Hymns and songs	"Verka, ty natten kommer" [Work, for the Night is Coming] (PoS 481). "Gå, gå, såningsman gå" [Go, Go, Sower, Go] (PoS 479). "Öppna mig för din kärlek, världen behöver mig" [Open my Life for your Love. The World needs Me] (PoS 96). "Jag vill tacka livet" [Thanks to life] (Violeta Parra).
Keywords	Missionary zeal, longing for the awakening (väckelse-längtan). *Later*: Spiritual seeking, private religion, WWJD.

18. Ulla Bardh's dissertation on "the congregation as a sacrament" is built on interviews with Free Church members. The Baptist members in these interviews express in general these kinds of disappointments and how they tackle them; Bardh, *Församlingen*, chap. 7 (Summary, 160–62).

Ideal of freedom	The freedom from fear of others, so that one dares to bear witness to one's faith and pray in one's own words.
	Later: The freedom to be a "seeker."
Common practice	Mission, evangelism.
	Later: Serenity prayer services.
Person and memory	William Carey and other missionary pioneers.
	Later: Harry Månsus and "the Bromma Dialogue."

Table 1: Activist spirituality

THE RITE OF BAPTISM

Historically, a Baptist meant someone being baptized with immersion after a personal confession of faith; this rite was a fundamental part of the identity, which also created different types of spiritualties among Baptists. Here I will tentatively describe two types—one with the dynamics of freedom and pilgrimage motifs in the rite of baptism and the other one with the statics of legalism in the teaching of baptism.

Toward Freedom and Into a Journey with Others

According to Baptists, the unique freedom for every human being is the possibility to "change lords." Using images from the biblical story of the exodus from Egypt such as the crossing of the Red Sea and the wandering through the desert to the Promised Land, the Christian life was imagined as a pilgrimage beginning with a breaking up. The Baptist author John Bunyan's *Pilgrim's Progress* brought this fundamental metaphor to life among Swedish Baptists, and the book as well as later diapositive and poster versions was frequently used in Baptist congregations until the 1960s. It was a kind of Baptist equivalent of the order of salvation (*ordo salutis*) preached in the Swedish revival movements, influenced by Pietism and Henrik Schartau's teachings.[19]

In exodus narratives, freedom is defined by the prepositions "from," "to," and "within." Christian freedom means freedom *from* "Satan, sin and the world," i.e., from the reign of sin and its imperative necessity. According to Paul, there are two powers struggling against each other: the reign of sin and the reign of righteousness. Since the Christ event defeats the reign of

19. In the Evangelical movement in Sweden in the nineteenth century the allegorical book by Paul Petter Waldenström—*Brukspatron Adamason* (Foundry proprietor Adam's son)—had a similar function as Bunyan's book.

sin, man can change life sphere. Today, this is formulated as the gift from God to become free from self-centeredness and evil structures and influences. But regardless of formulation, it is not a matter of freedom to do whatever one wants. In the same breath, it is made clear that this is freedom *to* God—Father, Son and Spirit—and the freedom to be a disciple of Jesus. When Baptists have reflected upon freedom, they have often used words like "servant" and "service."[20] Today this is often formulated as a freedom to "live for God" as a "new creation" and restore Creation.

According to Baptists, the believer's baptism is a manifestation of this freedom from evil. A person is immersed in water, "dies to sin," and is then raised up to "a new life" in Christ (Rom. 6). The unique concretion of the concept of freedom in the baptism also explains the close connection between personal conversion (metanoia in Greek) and the rite of baptism in the Baptist movement. In Bunyan's allegory, there was a spiritual theology that taught Baptists (and others) how this experience of faith comes about. When The Pilgrim ("Christian") meets Evangelist, he realizes that if he wants to survive he has to run away from everything and start searching for the holy city. That path starts with knocking on the narrow gate of conversion. Thus, everyone has to "knock on the door."

Before the breakthrough of modernity, spreading the message that "you have a choice" and "you can be a human even in a repulsive era" was radical. For the Baptists, this belief was the foundation of the democratic rule of their congregations. Personal choice was given to each and everyone, women as well as men, the young as well as the old, the poor as well as rich people. For contemporaries, this was extremely radical. The Baptist practices were a challenge to the existing hierarchies. Therefore, the Swedish magazine *Vi* was right when it described the first Baptist leader Fredrik Olaus Nilsson (1809–1881) as the foremost pioneer of democracy in Sweden, "one of the protagonists of universal suffrage."[21]

Within the Baptist movement, baptism has been preached and practiced as a personal conversion baptism, i.e., as an expression of a moral awakening and a person's commitment to a new direction in life with God's help. Consequently the rite of baptism was preceded by a church meeting, at which the baptismal candidate told the story ("witnessed") of his or her conversion and the insight of the need to be baptized. The congregation confirmed whether the testimony was "probable," and thereafter the baptism could take place. Through the rite of baptism, the candidate was received as a member of the congregation, which also was manifested by the laying on

20. Fahlgren, *Vatten*, 177–84.

21. *Vi Biografi*, 5/2010.

of hands at the subsequent communion. There the new member's status was made clear by the laying on of hands as well as a prayer for the gifts of the Spirit for the duties that come with being a Christian. Through this act, the newly baptized was no longer an object of the congregation's activities but rather a subject, an authorized participant.

The biblical stories and Bunyan's allegory constituted a spiritual theology within Baptism that gave rise to a pilgrim spirituality in which Jesus is "the way and the truth and the life" (John 14:6). At times, however, the breakup or the exodus became more important than the way. But there were also many who regarded the congregation as a band of pilgrims, whose homeland was heaven, and life in the congregation as a life journey. The pilgrim was thus less lonely than it would appear in *Pilgrim's Progress*. Being a pilgrim meant being on a journey with others, where everyone depended on the others and the formation for the pilgrim's life received through "faithful conversations."

This has been highlighted by Ulla Bardh in her dissertation on the sacrament of communion, based on semi-structured interviews with members of Baptist congregations and other free church congregations,[22] and in Mats Larsson's dissertation on a Baptist youth club (1865–1903) of Christian women who met regularly to reflect upon what it meant to live a life permeated with God's will.[23] The reflections were documented in minutes from the meetings.

Key Bible texts	"I am the way and the truth and the life." (John 14:6).
	"Our citizenship is in heaven." (Phil 3:20).
Hymns and songs	"Hur ljuvligt det är att möta på väg till Jerusalem" [How Sweet to be a Tone from Heaven] (PoS 301).
	"Sjungen, syskon, under vägen" [Sing, Brothers and Sisters, on your Way] (PoS 653).
	"Min framtidsdag är ljus och lång" [My Future is Bright and Great] (PoS 302).
Keywords	Chapels were named after biblical pilgrim destinations such as Elim, Bethel, and Bethany.
Ideal of freedom	Being saved and "a member of the congregation."
Common practice	Witnessing, congregational singing.
Person and memory	John Bunyan and his book *Pilgrim's progress*.

Table 2: Pilgrim spirituality

22. Bardh, *Församlingen*.
23. Larsson, *Vi kristna*.

Obedience and Other Legalistic Views on Baptism

Historically, the meaning of baptism for the whole life was not much expounded on by Baptists. It was a rite of passage that led to membership in the community of believers, which was a way to interpret life as a whole. Yet baptism itself was not used as a key to interpreting life. The central elements were the baptism method (immersion), the age of the candidate (conscious baptism), and a personal conversion experience. For that reason, Baptists have not talked about "living in their baptism." Rather, they have looked back on the time in life when they "came to faith" and "were baptized." Baptism was seen as an outward sign of an inward process.

The wider meaning of the rite of baptism was thus ignored, but there were more reasons for that than the Reformed interpretation of baptism as a human act of confession and obedience. Already in the 1850s, Puritan moralism and American Biblicism had begun to exert influence over Baptists in Sweden. Baptism went through a transition, from a symbolic manifestation of free choice—God's liberation of a human (specifically from the coercion of the state church)—to something legalistic. In that way, Baptist spirituality to a large extent became a question of obedience. Following Christ was perceived as obedience. As baptism was increasingly presented as an act of obedience, the freedom motif was overshadowed. This transition can be traced to the publication of the book *Det kristeliga dopet* [Christian baptism] by the Baptist leader Anders Wiberg (former priest in Lutheran Church of Sweden), a book that reached a wide audience.[24]

The first Baptists in Sweden had understood baptism in a different way. This is clear in the so-called Borekulla confession of faith from the 1840s, although its influence was short-lived. In this confession, there is a rich description of the meaning of baptism for the entire Christian life. Baptism is also understood sacramentally as an act of God and as a human action.[25] When the believer's baptism no longer had legal consequences in Sweden, its revolutionary character as a sign of freedom decreased. It remained, however, an act of confession.

The understanding of "obedience" can be found in the confession of faith that Anders Wiberg brought home from the Baptists in Philadelphia, and which was adopted at the Baptist "general assembly" in Stockholm in 1861. The seventh article on the purposes of the divine law opens for obedience as legalism. Wiberg's contacts in America were influenced by the philosopher and bishop Joseph Burtler's book *The Analogy of Religion* (1736), in which Burtler argues that there are commandments Christians have to

---

24. Wiberg, *Det christeliga*.

25. Fahlgren, *Predikantskap*, 97–104.

obey although they do not understand them. According to Wiberg, one such commandment was the baptism part of the Great Commission.[26] This view of baptism as primarily an act of obedience has put its mark on the understanding of freedom within the Baptist Union and its congregations. The joyful experience of baptism as a human act of freedom was eclipsed.

The application of freedom within the Baptist congregations and in the Baptist Union has historically been a dilemma for Swedish Baptists. The conversion and baptism as an act of freedom for the individual member did not always lead to freedom within the community of believers. At times, discipline was enforced in cases of perceived disobedience to the opinions of the leadership. The preacher Helge Åkeson, for example, was expelled in 1872 for promoting the idea of holiness rather than the idea of obedience. And the Baptist congregation that pastor Lewi Pethrus led was expelled in 1913; Pethrus had a fervent love of Jesus but did not teach nor practice the "right" doctrine of Believers' baptism and its consequent membership in a Baptist congregation. There are no statistics concerning how many members were expelled for similar doctrinal reasons or legalistic lifestyle and dress codes. But it happened frequently.[27]

Among Anders Wiberg and early Swedish Baptists, there was also a notion of a wider Christian community not based on believer's baptism but on faith personally chosen. This perspective gave rise to a more co-operative view of the congregation, since it included all those "born by God," which was a larger group than those baptized with the believer's baptism. This conviction was expressed in a wide-ranging culture of associations in the Baptist congregations, with a membership much wider than the Baptists.[28] There were choir associations, music associations, youth clubs, women associations, and so forth. All had members who did not belong to the congregation yet took part in the activities of a Baptist congregation by way of these associations.[29]

26. Wiberg, e.g., the reference to Butler's teaching, 165, and baptism as an act of obedience, 179–80.

27. Kennerberg, *Innanför*. The excommunications during the twentieth century had mostly private moral motifs, e.g., sex, consuming alcohol, smoking, and "worldly pleasures."

28. Bergsten "Svenskt," 57.

29. For example, the choirs in the Baptist congregations were organized as associations inside the community. (The Baptist congregation itself was not organized as association until 1952.) These associations were open also for others than the members of the congregation; Fahlgren, *Vatten*, 293–94. For a theological reflection in a local Baptist Church over this kind of organization for "the believers," see Wennerström, *Uppsala*, 4–8.

Later, this Baptist openness created tensions and crises in the encounter with the holiness movement in the 1890s[30] and the Pentecostal movement during the first decades of the twentieth century.[31] These new movements, each in its own way, had a different view of the congregation and its cooperation and fellowship with others. In these tensions and crises, another form of legalism took over within the Baptist Union, leading to exclusion of members and congregations and creating long-lasting tensions in the Baptist Union. The exclusion of the seventh Baptist congregation in Stockholm in 1913 had many reasons, but one of the most important was a legalistic understanding of access to the communion in a Baptist congregation. In this conflict, believer's baptism became a question of confession, a kind of counter-indicator.

For various reasons, the Baptist Union split in the 1930s. A large number of Baptist congregations left the union and began to cooperate only with the Örebro Mission Society. As Lagergren has shown, questions of spirituality played a large role.[32] "Baptism in the Spirit" was connected to a critique of inclusivity (i.e., culture, sports) and ecumenical openness. This critique created a kind of legalistic spirituality with a focus on questions of private morality, which became a characteristic of the new movement within Baptism.

Key Bible texts	"Whoever believes and is baptized will be saved, but whoever does not believe will be condemned." (Mark 16:16. Cf. Acts 2:41). "All have sinned and fall short of the glory of God." (Rom. 3:21–28).
Hymns and songs	"Har du mod att följa Jesus, vad det än må kosta dig" [Do you have courage to follow Jesus, whatever the price might be] (PoS 584).
Keywords	Following Jesus, obedience, saved.
Ideal of freedom	Converting and being baptized, being able to read and understand the Bible.
Common practice	Baptism by immersion, congregational discipline.
Person and memory	Anders Wiberg, Det kristeliga dopet [The Christian Baptism].

Table 3: Legalistic spirituality

30. Larsson, Vi kristna, 95–98.

31. For example, see David Lagergren's historiography over the crisis and the separation in the 1930s between the Baptist Union and Örebro Mission, Lagergren, Förändringstid, part one.

32. Lagergren, Förändringstid, 27–62.

ECUMENICAL IMPACT

The breakthrough of modernity in society contributed to the weakening of legalism in the Baptist congregations in favor of an even greater openness for diversity and cultural freedom. This freedom, however, was not always based on the theological reflections and reasons, but was rather a matter of adjustment to liberal cultural tendencies in society. However, the view of baptism did change for theological reasons among Baptists in Sweden until the 1960s. The driving force was the ecumenical movement, both nationally and internationally.

Eventually, striving for unity in diversity has had a strong impact on the spirituality of Baptists. The meaning and practice of the rite of baptism became the center for this striving and opened the doors for the impact of the ecumenical movement, especially on a local level.

Baptism and Holy Communion in an Ecumenical Context

Initially, the renewed study of the Bible texts concerning baptism was very important. Exegetical works by the German Baptist Johannes Schneider *Taufe und Gemeinde in der Neuen Testament* [Baptism and Community in the New Testament] (1952) and the English theologian and pastor George R. Beasley-Murray *Baptism in the New Testament* (1962) played a critical role in deepening the understanding of baptism in the Baptist Union. By publishing a shorter book by Beasley-Murray in Swedish, *Dopet idag och imorgon* [Baptism Today and Tomorrow (1967), the Baptist Union publishing house (Westerbergs) made sure that the advances in Biblical studies became accessible for a wider audience. Before that, the same publishing house had published a Swedish translation of Karl Barth's book on baptism.[33] Barth had questioned the symbolic interpretation of baptism and criticized the indiscriminate practice of infant baptism in the national churches.

If Wiberg was the most prominent figure in the current that understood baptism as an act of obedience, the church historian Torsten Bergsten (1921–2012) became the most prominent figure rethinking baptism from an ecumenical point of view in the Baptist Union. The starting point, he said, was participating in a Scandinavian Baptist conference at Stenungsön in 1956, at which Nils J. Engelsen from Norway and Kjell Kyrö-Rasmussen from Denmark were the keynote speakers.[34] Bergsten later participated in the conversations on baptism at Graninge stiftsgård in 1974, 1976, and 1979. The conversations became a national analogue to the international

33. Barth, *Det kristna.*

34. Bergsten, *Svenskt*, 41. See also Bergsten, Kyrø-Rasmussen, and Engelsen, *Dopet.*

study work pursued by the Faith and Order committee of the World Council of Churches, which resulted in the statement on *Baptism, Eucharism, and Ministry* in 1982 (often abbreviated BEM).[35]

The principle of "open communion tables" had been discussed as early as the 1850s, and had been practiced by the Baptist congregation in Asker among others. Yet it was not until the 1970s that the principle started to gain wider acceptance in the Baptist Union, and somewhat later in the Örebro Mission. In essence, it implied a renegotiation of the theology of baptism. The community around the communion table was no longer constituted by believer's baptism, but by the belief in Christ. Later, "open membership" was introduced in Baptist congregations as an ecumenical compromise, in order for persons baptized as infants to be able to become members. These changes were also important in paving the way for the local ecumenical movement in Sweden. Beginning in Höör in 1969, Baptist congregations were merged in congregations belonging to the Covenant Church in Sweden. Eventually, Baptist congregations also merged with congregations belonging to other communities. In a relatively short span of time, there were 150 different mergers.[36]

In these new local ecumenical partnerships, Baptists wanted to know what baptism meant. In retrospect, it is difficult to separate causes from effects. Was it the development of the view of baptism that created an ecumenical spirituality in the Baptist Union? Or was it an ever-stronger ecumenical spirituality that led to changes in the view of baptism? Most probably, it was a matter of reciprocal action.

Today, a sacramental view of baptism is fairly common among Swedish Baptists.[37] Yet there is at the same time a private religious view of baptism, related to the tendency toward private religion more generally in Sweden. Regarding the baptisms of others, many Baptists preferred not to take up a definitive position. But they certainly recognized the personal faith of others. In today's ecumenical dialogues, it has become common for Baptists to recognize the baptisms of others as Christian baptisms. In 1996 the Church of Sweden have made baptism to a prerequisite of membership. Since then, questions concerning baptism, faith, and membership have also gained renewed importance in other nonconformist traditions.

The local mergers between Baptist congregations and congregations belong to other denominations, as well as the 2011 formation of the Uniting Church in Sweden (Equmeniakyrkan), are the results of an ecumenical

---

35. Sveriges Kristna Råd, *Dop, nattvard.*

36. Bergsten, *Frikyrkor.*

37. Fahlgren, *Vatten,* 72–80.

spirituality that has prioritized *visible* Christian unity. For the individual Baptists and many congregations, it has meant a profound theological re-negotiation not least concerning the theology and practice of baptism. It is also possible to read the story of ecumenical endeavors as a confirmation of the Baptist Union being on the defensive.

Key Bible texts	"We were therefore buried with him through baptism into death in order that, just as Christ was raised from the dead through the glory of the Father, we too may live a new life." (Rom. 6:3–11). "One Lord, one faith, one baptism; one God and Father of all, who is over all and through all and in all." (Eph. 4:5–6).
Hymns and songs	"Store Gud, ditt namn ske pris" [Te Deum] (PoS 326, earlier number 1). "Many are the lightbeams" [Lågorna är många, ljuset är ett] (PoS 61).
Keywords	Merger, all Christians in the same place.
Ideal of freedom	Being one in Christ.
Common practice	United congregations, congregations belonging to both the Baptist. Union and Örebro Mission.
Person and memory	Torsten Bergsten, the free church assemblies 1905–1969.

Table 4: Ecumenical spirituality

RATIONALITY AND EXPERIENCE

In Baptism, there is a strong rational tendency. When Baptism came to Sweden, it was principally in the form of new ideas, new knowledge, and new understanding and not—as in the case of many spiritual currents today—new methods or offers of sublime emotional experiences. Accordingly, the Baptist congregations constituted a rational education movement of people reading books, meeting to reflect together, and carrying out different kinds of school activities.

Fundamentally, Baptist spirituality has been cognitive, based on the conviction that true faith develops out of insights into the truths of the Bible. Thus, matter-of-factness not emotions has been considered the surest sign of a personally-chosen faith. The field study I have undertaken gives a thicker description not only of that type of spirituality but also of its counterpart—an experience-based spirituality.

Knowledge in Order to Understand

The Baptist emphasis on the Bible has also contributed to the rational tendency within Baptist hermeneutics. The tool for understanding the Bible is free reason, but not on its own so much as in conversation with others. The biblical foundation of this cognitive and relational emphasis was Ephesians 3 and First Corinthians 12. Historically, this rationalism among the Baptists has also led to fundamentalism and sectarianism, for instance among the Southern Baptists in US.

At times the rational orientation has entailed a general restraint concerning emotional expressions of faith. A Baptist service can be one-sided. There is a lot of talking and appealing to the intellect. It does not mean, however, that Baptist services have been strict or rigid. Many preachers have been perceived by the grassroots as full of life and performing dynamic sermons, e.g., K. O. Broady, John Ongman, and Aron Andersson. Their sermons were considered to be characterized by "mental excitement." But even among these preachers, faith had a cognitive emphasis. It was a matter of *fides qua* rather than *fides quae*, a matter of what the Baptist believes rather than the believing, trusting, and seeking as such.

In my hometown congregation, gathering in the Elim chapel in Örnsköldsvik, it was said that those of us who grew up the congregation "should defer being baptized until we had reached a conscious age." With few exceptions, baptism rarely took place before the age of twelve. In other words, baptism demanded a cognitively based faith. The fact that baptism was called "adult baptism" also gives evidence of the Baptists' cognitive understanding of faith.

There are few symbols in Baptist chapels. They are naked. Many art forms are not represented at all. This tendency reached its most extreme manifestation in Spurgeon's preaching services and sanctuaries and among the Free Baptists in Sweden. The image-rich texts from the Bible could always be used, but artistic interpretation of this message was no ideal. The most essential elements were a pulpit and a cross symbol.

However, various forms of music played an important role in Swedish Baptist services from the very beginning. Particularly important were congregational singing and mixed choirs.[38] There were also usually green plants, often evocative of palm trees, in the Baptist chapels, thereby creating a homelike atmosphere and at the same time forming associations with the landscape of the Bible.[39]

38. Fahlgren, *Vatten*, chap. 8.
39. Ibid., chap. 4, notice especially 94–95, 101–3.

Through influences from the holiness movement and its developments in different directions, the rational emphasis was supplemented by personal experience of faith. More and more, praying implied waiting for a perceptible experience of God's presence. Those praying could also receive more concrete guidance in their daily lives, which gave joy and gratitude. In course of time, this led to a more experience-based concept of faith; yet rationality has remained fundamental in Swedish Baptist Congregations.

Key Bible texts	"Anyone who chooses to do the will of God will find out whether my teaching comes from God or whether I speak on my own." (Jesus in Joh. 7:17) "In the church I would rather speak five intelligible words to instruct others than ten thousand words in a tongue." (Paul in 1 Cor. 14:18–20, cf. Rom. 12:1–2)
Hymns and songs	"Jag har beslutat att följa Jesus" [I have decided to follow Jesus], (PoS 594).
Keywords	Conscious age, renewal of the mind, formation, truth, knowledge.
Ideal of freedom	Freedom of thought.
Common practice	Christianity school, Sunday school, bookshops, child blessings, lectures.
Person and memory	The Baptist preacher and educator Fredrik Pira (1831–1887) in Asker, The Baptist weekday schools in the nineteenth century.

Table 5: Cognitive spirituality

Experiences in Order to Understand

Perhaps it is the dominance of cognitive spirituality that has repeatedly created problems for Baptism in dealing with emotions, personal spiritual experiences, and ideas of "deeper spirituality." Only very rare spiritual movements have been capable of setting emotions free, opening up for personal experience, and using other ways of reading the Bible than the rational.

The expressions of deeper spirituality, in particular the so-called baptism of the Spirit, have resulted in painful schisms or strong inner tensions. And maybe it is in the services that this dilemma has been the most obvious, affecting questions such as what songs and songbooks to choose, when to pray, and what sermons to like as regards form and content.

This conflict among Baptists between rationality and personal experiences can be illustrated by a study of the music in the congregation.[40] Beside the mixed choir, a new kind of choir emerged in Swedish Baptism in the late nineteenth century called "string band music" (strängmusik). It was unique in that it combined several instruments with a singing group. Simple and accessible songs, consisting of verse and chorus, became an important part of the repertoire. Initially, the songs were collected from revival meeting songbooks, and the majority of these songs were from America and Britain. At this time, the mixed choirs in the Baptist congregations had become the music of the adults. String band music became the music of young people, simpler and livelier. In the emerging Pentecostal movement of the early 1900s, string band music was also seen as a sign of openness for the wind of the Spirit.

During the 1910s and the 1920s, Baptist congregations grew rapidly. String band music played an important role, both during revival meetings and as a form of socializing for new members. The mixed choir (as well as the men's and women's choirs) primarily sang in the Sunday morning services, whereas the string band sang in the revival meeting on Saturday and Sunday nights. But there were exceptions to this rule. Sometimes the mixed choir would sing in the revival meeting and the string band in the Sunday service.

The different types of choirs in Baptist congregations showed how different spiritualties could live side by side and support one another. In such contexts, there was no dichotomy between rational and emotional spirituality. But there were also congregations where the claims and conclusions of the Pentecostal movement created a conflict between mixed choir and string band, a conflict that mirrored the splitting between the Baptist Union centers in Örebro and Stockholm through the emergence of the Pentecostal awakening and the ecumenical movement. Different views of the way the Baptist Union was organized also became an issue of controversy.

At the heart of this splitting were a theology of the Spirit and the baptism of the Spirit that gave rise to a notion of a higher or deeper spiritual experience distinct from the conversion, a kind of perfection sometimes indicated by speaking in tongues.

The Baptist minister John Ongman in Örebro was a prominent exponent of this spirituality within Baptism in Sweden. His message and work were influenced by the keywords in the missionary leader A. B. Simpson's book *The Fourfold Gospel* (1883): Christ as our savior, our sanctifier, our healer, and our coming king.

---

40. For the following, see Fahlgren, *Vatten*, chap. 8.

From a theological point of view, the message as such was not particularly dramatic for Baptists. However, it also claimed that an additional
personal experience of faith was necessary over and above the personal
choice of belief that was based on rationality. And this gave rise to dispa-
rate perspectives leading to disintegration. Even if the concrete reason was
perceived to be a question of membership (the Pentecostal movement) or
a question of organization (the Örebro Mission Society), the difference
between spiritualties was a primary cause. The recurrent critique of the
movement for the baptism of the Spirit was that it apparently assigned an
independent role to emotions, one separated from reason and rational inquiry. Among Baptists, a search for a balanced interplay between emotion
and reason has been going on ever since these tragic divisions.

Key Bible texts	"Be filled with the Spirit." (Eph. 5:18–20, Acts 2)
Hymns and songs	Herre, se vi vänta alla" [Lord, we are all waiting] (PoS 52). "Ande, du som livet ger" [Holy Spirit, Giver of Life] (PoS 393).
Keywords	Being moved, coming through, baptized in the Spirit, surrender.
Ideal of freedom	Radical congregationalism, the freedom of the Spirit, the freedom to be sanctified.
Common practice	Singing groups, "aftermeetings" (eftermöte), prayer for the sick.
Person and memory	John Ongman, Simpson's book *The Fourfold Gospel*.

Table 6: Experience-based spirituality

In sum, the research results I have presented here demonstrate that the distinctive character of Baptist communities in Sweden is not to be found in
a particular way of baptizing, in a specific striving for freedom or in some
other single element, but rather in a singular combination of spiritualties. In
this combination of different types of enacted and experienced faith, several
conflicting ideas can be identified.

-   Activism <-> Pilgrimage
-   Legalism <-> Striving for unity
-   Rationalism <-> Personal experiences

Together, these and other types of spirituality have created identity, continuity, and reason for existence when many different traditions and currents
become fused in what is called "Baptists in Sweden." A Baptist culture has

been created and made it possible for people to examine, relate to, and appreciate Baptist traditions in earnest. In short—to live as Baptists!

EPILOGUE: THE RELATIONSHIP BETWEEN ECCLESIOLOGY, ETHNOGRAPHY, AND HISTORIOGRAPHY

This study became more interdisciplinary than I originally planned. Here are some tentative comments especially related to fact that reality is not structured into academic disciplines. Two aspects of communication were in particular an eye-opener for me in this spirituality study: *language* and *narrative*. Here are ecclesiology, ethnography, and historiography intertwined in use of both methods and theories.

Regarding language, my case study is based on recurrent significant keywords and metaphors in the ethnographical material used by Baptists in ecclesial practices.[41] I have also written down the keywords used by seven informants who were interviewed for this study and who had been in leadership in different types of spirituality among Baptists. I call all these words (metaphors, concepts, phrases) used in the material and by the informants "church language," that is to say the language used by those who participate in the life of a church—or, as in this case study, the language used by those who had a responsibility for a specific congregation.

Language is a major part of the identity of every culture and social group. A church language is thus an expression of a lifeworld supported by one or more ecclesial practices. These practices endow the keywords in the church language with meaning and real importance.[42] The introduction of "church language" as an ecclesiological and ethnographic analytical concept highlights the interplay between the language and specific historical, social, economic, and theological contexts in which a particular church language emerges and is used. Thus "church language" and "practice" partially overlap as analytical concepts.[43]

The analytical concept of church language is based on an assumption that there is an interaction between church language and church practices—and by extension, an interaction between church language and congregation/church. The fundamental question arising from this theoretical model is then: What kind of spirituality is formed by a particular church

41. All data used in the research is presented in an unpublished report, Fahlgren, "Equmeniakyrkans," 35–36.

42. Cf. Wittgenstein's latter view of language. Languages are in his philosophy depicting the world, and every language game has a specific context that gives words their meaning. The meaning of a word can be found in its use, see Wittgenstein, *Filosofiska*.

43. For the concept of "church language," see also Fahlgren, "Equmeniakyrkan."

language? And vice versa: What kind of church language is formed in a specific spirituality?

This theoretical model for a communicative ecclesiology/ethnography/historiography might have a potential to be developed and applied to other ecclesial studies.

Regarding *historiography*, the basic question in this historical case study is not how the Baptist tradition was established and developed in Sweden; in other words it is not about writing a narrative of Baptists, using historical methods and theories. To some extent, this is done indirectly throughout the study, but the basic question, which has emerged, is more one of what kind of spirituality has been created.

In theological language this is referred to as studying ecclesiology (from the Latin *ecclesia*: church, congregation). In order to address this, it is an actual church's enacted and embodied spirituality that has been studied and analyzed in the field study presented here. If ecclesiology is inconceivable without historical aspects, this is yet another reason to see the production of history as part of any church practice.[44]

Historiography also means analyzing ways in which history conveys the creation of identity. In this sense, historiography is a kind of ecclesiology—both as a result of the construction of history and as the object of scholarly analysis.[45] However, the reverse is also true: ecclesiology is to a large degree a kind of historiography.

Since the general purpose of historical descriptions (narratives) produced in a fundamental ecclesial practice is to articulate, legitimize, and provide direction for a congregation/church, these have tended over time to become a normative or direction-giving history and tradition. This has also led to the production, past and present, of subversive descriptions which distance themselves from what has been, or attempt to point to another historical era as a "golden age."

History, which has been written by actors in the church, has also influenced historical writing in other contexts. To take one example, the stories written by the early church have had a fundamental influence on historical writing in general as a result of their focus on the interest in world history and the realization of God's will. Chronology also became an early central element in the narrative, as did the emergence of "church history" (Eusebius) and other historical genres such as biographies of the saints. The Acts of the Apostles and the Books of the Chronicles in the Old Testament

44. A "fundamental ecclesial practice" is constructed by "sub-practices," see Fahlgren, *Predikantskap*, 40f, and Fahlgren, *Vatten*, 99–100.

45. For several meanings of ecclesiology as a research discipline, see Fahlgren and Ideström, *Ecclesiology*, 1–28.

are biblical role models of the ecclesial practice of writing history. I wonder what kind of "stuff" they created for such writing.

The congregations in the Baptist Union in Sweden have a long tradition of writing chronicles, diaries, parish registers, annual reports (annals), and jubilee publications. These narratives can be found in archives in the congregations, in regional archives for movements in the civil society in Sweden, and the Baptist Union has built up an extensive national historical archive in Bromma.

As a matter of principle, Baptists have not accorded either history or tradition with a normative importance. The explicit norm has been the Scriptures. This ideal created a "movement of readers" who read the Bible in search of the truth.[46] Therefore I have in the tables *Key Bible texts* that present distinctive passages in the Bible from each type of spirituality.

Sources from inter-confessional free church conventions and other attempts to unite the free churches show that the tradition has nonetheless been significant for Baptist in practice. History has not infrequently been used as an argument for unity, yet it has also been used to argue the opposite: that the churches' inherited unique differences (read: spiritualties) have made it impossible to realize unity.[47] The many and comprehensive jubilee publications within the congregations of Baptist Union—and for the Baptist Union—are in themselves also an expression of the fact that history and tradition have in practice had normative characteristics. Several informants in my case study quoted from their congregations or church's historical works to emphasize that their predecessors had Baptist visions. Consequently, the tables in this study have examples of *Person and memory* for each type of spirituality—representing the implicit norm of tradition.

These comments over history and historiography in ecclesiological studies on spirituality have relevance for the more general discussion about how the present relates to the past. The ethnographic dimension opens up for the dynamics of the study object, e.g., the plurality, particularity, and contradictions in the lived faith—in the past and the present.

---

46. Fahlgren, "När slutade," 128–40.

47. For history and Christian unity in dialogue between the free churches in Sweden, see Sveriges Frikyrkoråd, *Gemensam väg*, 82f; cf. *Frontförkortning i ekumeniken*, 11–14.

16

Ethnography, Representation, and Digital Media

TIM HUTCHINGS

INTRODUCTION: WHY DIGITAL ETHNOGRAPHY?

This chapter introduces some of the basic challenges of conducting ethnography in contexts constituted in whole or in part by digital communications. My primary focus will be one of my own research projects, an ethnographic study of Christian "online churches." Online churches use digital media to perform a range of ecclesial tasks, including worship, prayer, mutual support, social conversation, teaching and proselytism, but some Christian observers have argued that they are theologically invalid and pastorally unhealthy. These churches pose some interesting methodological and theoretical challenges for ecclesiologists, but Christian theologians have rarely tried to use ethnography to support arguments on either side. I will use this example to highlight some of the contributions that a digital ethnographic method could make to theological research.

As digital technologies have become embedded in the fabric of everyday life, they have become increasingly relevant for ethnographers and theologians. Attention to digital media is now a necessary component of any ethnographic study of contemporary Christian congregations. For example, the public presence of a church is likely to include a website, and perhaps also a Facebook page or another social media account. Many pastors now find digital resources essential to sermon preparation, and many congregants may turn to email and social media to ask their pastor for support and advice. The church building may itself be digitised, through the introduction of screens and sound systems that transform the use of space and the experience of worship. Outside church meetings, digital media are also part of the lived experience of congregants. Churchgoers may be smartphone users, members of Facebook, gamers, readers of blogs and news websites, or parents of children interested in these and other digital activities. Not all churches are aware of or enthusiastic about these many possibilities, but this inattention can itself become a topic of fruitful research, because disinterest in media can reveal valuable insights into church priorities.

This digitization of Christian life also has more existential implications. As Amanda Lagerkvist has recently argued, "our sense of time, memory, space, selfhood, sociality and death" is now experienced and expressed in part through our digital lives.[1] Online, we encounter new risks and moments of extreme vulnerability, and we search for security through information, connectivity and emotional support. We are not just users of digital media, but beings "*thrown* into our digital human existence, where the ambivalent and massive task awaiting us is to seize our vulnerable situatedness, while navigating through sometimes unknown waters."[2] Lagerkvist's work uses existential philosophy as a provocation for the field of media studies, but the idea that media could function as an existential terrain should be a valuable inspiration for ethnographers and theologians as well. Churches are existential spaces, where communities encounter and express their hopes and vulnerabilities. If digital media are now integral to the most important uncertainties of life, then theologians need to study them with great care and close attention. Ethnography offers a ideal methodological approach for this task, positioning the researcher alongside these communities, striving to participate in their experiences in order to understand them.

One of the key affordances of digital media is connectivity. Online, we can access resources and communicate with one another more quickly and easily than ever before. This connectivity has very significant implications for religion, encouraging processes of centralisation and decentralisation. The Pope can publish his prayers and insights through social media, forging a new kind of direct connection between a leader and their followers. Members of the Church of England can participate in live video Bible studies with the Archbishop of Canterbury via Facebook, and followers of American megachurch preachers can watch their latest sermons online. At the same time, digital connectivity also makes it much easier for individual

---

1. Lagerkvist, "Existential Media," 2.
2. Ibid., 2.

Christians to connect with like-minded others to form new communities of radical and resistant thought. Those wishing to criticise the teachings of their leaders can also find willing audiences online, whether their theology is more liberal or more conservative. Digital networks can be used to seek out difference, debate and opportunities for evangelism, or to create spaces where only certain views will be encountered.

Another key affordance of digital media is automation. If we search for a key term through Google, the search engine decides what to show us in a fraction of a second. When we log in to Facebook, the social network site decides what updates we should see based on its analysis of our previous online activity. These decisions are made by algorithms that are not accessible to the public, on behalf of companies whose interests are ultimately commercial. Similarly, a religious app or website can store data and use that information to make decisions for its users. A Bible app, for example, can track our reading activity and issue prompts calculated to change our behaviour.

In this complex and changing environment, we must find ways to incorporate attention to digital embeddedness, connectivity and automation into our ethnographic research and communication. This chapter will begin by introducing the concept of "online churches" in more detail, paying attention to the theological arguments of supporters and critics. We will then briefly summarise how digital ethnography can work, before moving on to use the example of online churches to engage with the key theme of representation. I will consider representation in three different ways. First, how do we as ethnographers represent ourselves to the groups we study? Second, who do we represent within the group? And third, how do we represent the group to an external audience?

ONLINE CHURCHES AND DIGITAL ECCLESIOLOGY

Christians have been creating "online churches" since the mid-1980s, using digital media to connect small groups of believers for online prayer services, theological debates, Bible study and friendly conversation. In the late 1990s, major Christian denominations began to get involved, including the Evangelical Lutheran Church in Bavaria and the Unitarian Universalists in the United States. In 2004, the Church of England and the Methodist Council of Great Britain both funded the creation of "online churches" based in the UK, attracting international press attention. In the same year, churches started appearing in a virtual world called "Second Life," which allowed users to build whatever fantasy environments they desired. Megachurches around the world began creating their own "online church" ministries in the mid-oos, expanding the "multi-site" model (which at that time was fairly new) to include "online campuses." Sermons had been available online for some time, but the online campus model now invited a congregation to watch live music and videos of sermons while talking to each other in chatrooms and on social media.

These different church projects were motivated by different goals and visions. For the small independent churches that flourished via email, forums, chatrooms and virtual worlds, the internet promised a chance to gather a handful of Christians for a new kind of conversation. In many cases, the people who created these churches were not ordained, so the internet also offered a new space to claim authority and try out skills of rhetoric and leadership.

For big Protestant denominations, the internet was a new opportunity to try to reconnect with lost generations, particularly young people. By going online, a staid establishment could try to rebrand itself as new, exciting, innovative and relevant. Anglican and Methodist experiments have to be understood in the context of the time: the report *Mission-shaped Church* came out in 2004, kick-starting the *Fresh Expressions* movement, and dioceses everywhere were hoping that new forms of community and experimental worship might help recapture some of their lost members and cultural significance.

The megachurch "online campus," most common among evangelical groups, is a very different creation. Instead of small-scale experimental communities, the online campus invites a vast online audience to focus on the words and image of a single preacher. The internet offers the chance to expand a tried-and-tested model of church growth to find new audiences, evangelising the world while boosting the profile of the church and its leader.

The online church is still flourishing today, but its shape has changed over time. Small experimental communities and denomination-sponsored online parishes still exist, but it is the online campus model that has grown most dramatically. One of the pioneers of the movement, Life.Church in Oklahoma, now gives away its "Church Online" platform free of charge for anyone to use, and a considerable number of large churches around the world have taken up their offer.

Despite this long and diverse history, online churches tend to appear in theological discussions only as a grim warning. From the 1990s to the present day, Christian writers have emphasised the value of embodied, face-to-face community, and have seen the internet as individualistic, superficial, deceptive and dangerously tempting. The idea of actually going to church online is usually taken to represent the worst excesses of technology, even for writers who are otherwise very positive about the opportunities offered by digital media.

We can find a good early example of this Christian anxiety in the book *Cyberchurch*, written by Protestant futurologist Patrick Dixon. Dixon hails the internet's potential for religion, but he also warns that the internet is encouraging "a superficial Christianity without any human obligations."[3] Online interaction must "never be a substitute for fellowship and Christian community," he argues, because these require commitment to face-to-face relationships.[4] From a Catholic perspective, the Vatican report *The Church and Internet* put forward a similar argument five years later: "the virtual reality of cyberspace cannot substitute for real interpersonal community," the report assures us, and "even the religious experiences possible there by the grace of God are insufficient apart from real-world interaction with other persons of faith."[5] These texts both assume that online churches must be in competition with local churches, luring believers away from face-to-face community.

These arguments continue to resonate with Christian critics of digital media. In 2008, for example, Episcopal bishop Katharine Jefferts Schori attacked the idea of online churches during a radio interview:

> Faith communities of all sorts need physical proximity of human beings in order to discover each other, in order to grow individually and as a community. . . . It is hard to build a faith community in a deep sense on the internet. We deal with caricatures; we deal with perceptions and positions rather than full human beings sitting in our presence. . . . The incarnate piece is missing.[6]

Baptist preacher John Piper has described online churches as "sick," comparing them to the anti-materialism of the Docetic heresy. "We are created in bodies, not just in minds," he claims, and losing "the entire bodily dimension of togetherness" would therefore be "spiritually defective . . . contrary to Christ's understanding of the church, and . . . hurtful to the soul."[7]

Online churches also have Christian supporters, and their arguments tend to be based on personal experience. Mark Howe, for example, has been closely involved with several online churches, and he has used his own experiences to show that online communities can be much more supportive

3. Dixon, *Cyberchurch*, 93.

4. Ibid., 156.

5. Pontifical Council, "Church," part 4.

6. Campbell, "Online Community?"

7. Piper, "Thoughts?"

than critics imagine. After the death of one church member, Howe argued that the online commemorations were actually more meaningful and personal than the physical funeral:

> the [online] meeting [to remember T] was virtual, but those involved knew and cared about T. The earlier physical service happened in a consecrated chapel, but one with which T had no connection. . . . Sometimes the words "real" and "virtual" fail to capture the way in which online church relates to real life—and death.[8]

More theological defences have also been proposed. Douglas Estes is one of many who have turned to a relational understanding of the Trinity for inspiration. Estes claims that the appeal of virtual community "originates with the innate, God-given need and desire to relate to other people. It's Trinitarian; it's genetic."[9] By offering new ways to connect, online environments "free us to follow our *imago Dei* need for greater depths of relationship."[10]

For many participants in the debate over online churches, a key issue has been the sacraments. In some theological traditions, offering the sacraments is one of the essential marks of a true church, and failure to do so online would disqualify "online churches" by definition. Some online churches and their supporters have therefore called for communion and baptism to be available online. These projects usually invite online viewers to participate physically in a ritual of eating (for communion) or washing (for baptism) while watching the pastor via a webcam. In 2013, for example, the Wall Street Journal reported that a Methodist church in the US was about to start offering online communion in this way:

> users can simply grab some grape juice and any bread or crackers they have in the house, and consume them after the pastor, in the sanctuary, blesses the juice and bread as representing the blood and body of Christ. . . . "We believe that God is not bound by space and time," said the Rev. Andy Langford, Central's senior pastor. "We believe that when we bless the bread and the cup in one place, if there are others who are worshiping with us, God will bless that bread and cup wherever they are."[11]

Critics have been unimpressed, dismissing such efforts as theologically impossible and pastorally inappropriate. As early as 2002, the Vatican

---

8. Howe, *Online Church?*, 5.

9. Estes, *SimChurch*, 59.

10. Ibid., 60.

11. Bauerlein, "Church's Online Communion."

declared that "there are no sacraments in cyberspace."[12] In response to the 2013 initiative, the Methodist Church formed an Online Communion Task Force and announced that communion "entails the actual tactile sharing of bread and wine in a service that involves people corporeally together in the same place."[13] Further experiments were forbidden.

These basic theological positions regarding "online church" have hardly shifted since the 1990s. Critics argue that online churches encourage believers to leave local congregations and encourage low-commitment isolation. They also argue that online communities cannot really be "church," because a true church must meet in a physical, face-to-face context and share the physical sacraments. Supporters, on the other hand, argue from experience that these communities are mutually supportive and reach new audiences, and call for more openness to experimentation in Christian rituals.

It is important to recognise the limitations of the contribution that ethnographic research can make to these ongoing theological arguments. Ethnography allows us to study what groups of people say and do, including how terms like "church" and "sacrament" are used and understood by particular groups of people. In my own ethnographic research, I have therefore adopted the language these groups use about themselves, accepting that "if a group calls itself a church, it is a church."[14] A theologian might wish to develop stricter and more rigorous definitions, but ethnography cannot help with that task.

However, ethnography can provide evidence to help evaluate many of the claims made by Christian supporters and critics of online churches. The theological debate over online churches is partly empirical, based not only on normative principles but also on claims about the social structures and behaviour patterns that are emerging online and their consequences for practitioners. When theology engages with empirical data, ethnography can make a contribution. For example, an ethnographer can ask if the members of online communities really are mutually supportive or isolated, if online churches are actually rivals to local congregations, or if they have any measurable success as spaces for youth outreach and evangelism. We can also use ethnography to find out how online churchgoers themselves talk about "being church," to explore how ecclesiology is taking shape in these new online contexts. If theologians want to make progress in their understanding of digital media, including the phenomenon of online churches, then ethnography is one of the tools they must use. At the end of this chapter, I

12. Pontifical Council, "Church," part 9.

13. Phillips, "Online Communion," 1.

14. Hutchings, *Creating Church*, 6.

will return to this debate to suggest some of the contributions that ethnography has already made to our understanding of digital religion.

WHAT IS DIGITAL ETHNOGRAPHY?

The internet was once imagined as a "cyberspace," a separate world that users travelled into, in which identity became fluid and everything became possible. Today, the internet has lost that romance and distinctiveness. The internet has become "embedded, embodied and everyday," as ethnographer Christine Hine has argued, and the idea of "going online" no longer makes sense in an always-connected world.[15] The internet is now "entwined in use with multiple forms of context and frames of meaning-making," becoming an integral and often unnoticed infrastructure for churches, homes, schools or workplaces.[16]

If our focus of interest is a separate, self-contained online space, like a virtual community, then the methods of ethnography can be applied with only minor adaptations. The researcher identifies an online field site that has a distinctive culture, and contacts the gatekeepers of that site to negotiate access. Then the researcher spends as much time online in that space as possible, observing, participating, and talking to community members. Informed consent is ensured by speaking to community members about the research project and addressing any concerns they may have. The researcher keeps extensive fieldnotes, including logs, transcripts, screenshots and perhaps videos. Over time, the researcher tries to come to understand the online space through the eyes of its participants, learning to appreciate the nuances and complexities of their thought and behaviour. When this goal is achieved, the researcher leaves the field site and translates the worldview of the community into a report that a wider academic audience can understand.

This approach may seem very similar to a conventional offline ethnography, but some degree of adaptation was still required. In a traditional ethnography, the reseacher seeks to live among the people to be studied, observing them directly and participating in their embodied activity. The inhabitants of online spaces are not usually present in the same geographical space, so the ethnographer interacts with their online personas, not their physical bodies. These inhabitants are not usually present at all times, either, so the ethnographer can only interact with them sporadically. There

---

15. Hine, *Ethnography*, title page.

16. Ibid., 33

will always be information that is left inaccessible, and the online ethnographer may struggle to decide if the people they meet are being truthful or deceptive.

These are significant challenges, but the ethnographer's task is not impossible. Distinctive cultures do form in online spaces, after all, and participant observation is a valuable way to make sense of them. Even if we cannot see people physically or interact with them at all times, there remains much that can be studied, including online language, shared images and patterns of interaction. Most importantly, the same limitations and uncertainties apply to everyone else in the online space. Participating in shared restrictions is part of what it means to be a participant observer in online communities.

Instead of studying an online space, an alternative is to conduct ethnography in a local, physical community. Rather than exploring a digital subculture, the ethnographer seeks to understand how digital media are used and understood within a particular context, by participating in embodied digital practice. That context could be a particular local church, a neighbourhood or social network. This kind of ethnographic work can be insightful, helping us to challenge homogenising narratives about digital culture and its impact on society. As Daniel Miller and Heather Horst have argued, "the Internet is always a local invention by its users."[17] Attitudes to digital media and ways to incorporate the digital into everyday practice can be quite different in different locations.

Of course, research projects can also combine these two approaches. Instead of selecting just one location for participant observation, the ethnographer can be more flexible, following their topic of research through multiple online and offline spaces. As the internet becomes more integral to everyday life, the "field site" of ethnography becomes increasingly hard to define, and methods must often be adapted and reimagined throughout the project as new data is discovered. This is the kind of research long called for by proponents of "multi-sited ethnography," which calls on researchers to travel with participants from place to place.[18] Through mobile ethnography, researchers can find out how ideas, things and individuals move through the often transnational systems of contemporary society. This was the approach I adopted in my own research, which included both long-term participation in online church communities and other online spaces and attendance at local meetings. Applied to digital media, multi-sited ethnography calls us to include offline as well as online spaces and activities in our research, while keeping an open mind about how "online" and "offline" matter to each other.

17. Miller and Horst, *Digital Anthropology*, 19.
18. Marcus, "Multi-sited."

Despite these different shifts and alternatives, a common core to ethnography can still be identified. For Christine Hine, for example, ethnography has always been "a boot-strapping method, which builds itself afresh in each location," adapting new approaches and strategies in pursuit of the same core goals.[19] In essence, ethnography is "a method for getting to the heart of meaning and enabling us to understand, in the round and in depth, how people make sense of their lives,"[20] and it is "distinctive in its use of the embodied experiences of the researcher as one of its primary means of discovery."[21] Online or offline, the key to ethnography is always experience: "an ethnographer, even in the Internet age, continues to develop a distinctive form of knowledge by being, doing, learning, and practicing, and by a close association with those who do so in the course of their everyday lives."[22]

Annette Markham also argues that the details of ethnographic method are less important than their goal. She proposes that ethnography must be understood "as a worldview, stance, or attitude, rather than a set of techniques or methods," so that "the sensibility of ethnography can remain while the techniques may adapt." The ultimate goals of ethnography must always be experience, understanding and representation:

> For me, ethnography is an approach that seeks to find meanings of cultural phenomena by getting close to the experience of those phenomena. I generally find myself looking at the details of localised cultural experience, through a range of techniques intended to get close and detailed understandings. I then try to represent what I think I've found in ways that resonate with readers or members of that cultural context.[23]

As these quotes suggest, it is not possible or helpful to propose a single definition of "digital ethnography," or a single method for pursuing it. Instead, it is up to the ethnographer to recognise exactly how digital media might be relevant for their own topic of study. The ethnographer must then search for the unique combination of methods that will allow them to get close to the experience of using digital media in that context.

Having introduced online churches, digital ecclesiology and digital ethnography, this chapter will now move on to discuss how digital

19. Hine, *Ethnography*, 5.

20. Ibid., 1.

21. Ibid., 19.

22. Ibid., 21.

23. Markham, "Ethnography."

ethnography can work in practice. We will consider three kinds of "representation," beginning with the ethnographer's self-presentation.

REPRESENTATION TO THE FIELD SITE

As ethnographers, we must find ways to represent ourselves to the subjects of our research. The ethnographer must decide how to enter their field site (or sites), whose permission they will need, and how much to explain to the people who live in or pass through the field. This is of course not straightforward: the presence of a researcher is likely to affect how people behave, and any ethnographer must reflect carefully on how their own actions and self-presentation are altering the data they are able to collect.

For a simple example, imagine that an ethnographer wishes to explore how women's voices are encouraged or suppressed in digital contexts. In order to conduct participant observation in an online church, the ethnographer will almost certainly need approval from community leaders and members. However, if these leaders and members know the purpose of the study, their behaviour is likely to change in ways that both hinder and help the research. Some may make extra efforts to conceal any evidence of gender bias, while others may become more eager to share their own gendered experiences with an outsider. The ethnographer must navigate this situation carefully. Providing a detailed account of the exact research question can be unhelpful, but a misleading explanation of the true focus of the research might damage the ethnographer's reputation within the group and undermine their ability to complete the research at all. The community will need to know something about the research project that is honest, convincing and invites interest, but also broad enough to allow flexibility and minimise impact.

In my own research, I encountered a different problem. I was interested in finding out what online churchgoers thought about the concept of "church," and I particularly wanted to know if they themselves considered their online groups to be "real churches." This was a question that these online communities occasionally debated amongst themselves, but in my interviews I found that a direct approach was not always helpful. For many of my interviewees, questioning if their online community was a "real" church was dismissive and insulting, and they responded with confusion and disapproval when I raised the question. For others, the question was over-familiar and no longer interesting. I had much more success exploring this question when I stopped asking it, and waited instead for communities to address the issue themselves. To attract the interest of the groups I wanted to study, I needed to present my research in a way that they could recognise as worthy of their attention.

One straightforward but ethically problematic way to avoid the dilemma of self-representation is to conduct research covertly, without telling anyone that they are under observation at all, and this is particularly easy online. The researcher can "lurk" invisibly, watching communication in a forum or on social media without participating directly. Alternatively, the researcher can disguise their identity in an online community or a virtual world, using a range of different avatar characters. This approach allows the ethnographer to try out different identities, to find out first-hand if a particular group's behaviour changes in the presence of a stranger with a different gender, age, or religious identity.

This is a controversial approach, because covert research means observing without consent. The researcher must carefully consider a number of factors, including potential harm to the people being studied, recognising that these individuals may perceive risks that the ethnographer is unaware of. Ethnographers must also follow the ethics approval processes required by their universities or funding bodies, and these may rule out some kinds of covert research altogether. Many leading academic societies (like the Association of Internet Researchers) have drawn up their own standards of ethics for ethnographic and digital research, and these can help the ethnographer to construct an ethically-sound research design.

In some cases, conventional and digital ethnographers have decided that nonparticipatory or disguised research is necessary and justified. For example, some kinds of research could become dangerous to the ethnographer if their true purposes were uncovered. In other, less dramatic cases, ethnographers have decided that the people to be studied are safe from any harm, that they are impossible to contact, or that they are already aware that they are in full public view.

I have adopted a version of this approach in some of my own online research. In one church, for example, a video stream of music and preaching is regularly watched by hundreds or even thousands of people, with the option to comment in a public chatroom. I introduced my research to church leaders, volunteers and regular attenders, and requested written consent from anyone I interviewed. However, attendance fluctuates throughout each service, so there is no way to ensure that everyone knows that a researcher is present. The only option would be to post continuous introduction messages in the chatroom, which would be extremely disruptive. Since the chatroom is already being watched by a large online audience, I decided that it would be acceptable to use some of these chat conversations in ethnographic research without contacting all the speakers—being careful, of course, to remove names and any identifying details.

If online communication is already public, then it might even seem ethically unproblematic to research such material without consent. However, this approach must be considered carefully. Nonparticipatory research—lurking—sacrifices some of the key principles of ethnography, because the researcher does not learn to participate and the inhabitants of the field site cannot correct his or her mistakes. Disguised research does involve participation, but has its own drawbacks: the ethnographer cannot easily share their insights with field site inhabitants for feedback, and inhabitants are unable to exercise their own free choice to participate or withdraw from the research. It is also important to consider the possible consequences of discovery: I decided not to try designing different avatars in virtual worlds, because I knew that at least some inhabitants would withdraw from my research if they found out. Online communities rely to a great extent on mutual trust among participants, even if some degree of role-play and disguise is accepted as part of group culture. A careless ethnographer who breaks the group's rules of self-representation could damage not just their own research but the whole foundation of the group itself.

Even disguised research cannot avoid the problem of self-representation altogether. If the ethnographer interacts with the group, then some degree of representation is inevitable. Throughout the research project, the ethnographer must make decisions about how and when to share their identity and interests with the group. This include careful consideration of dress, posture, what language to use and which ideas to express. For an ethnographer in a Christian community like an online church, "participant observation" is likely to include some form of participation in devotional activity and theological discussion, and this can create complex tensions between the ethnographer's sense of their own identity, the identity they try to present to the group, and the identity the group actually perceives.

Ethnographers commonly seek to study groups that are distant from their own experience and identity, because that distance is valuable for analysis. The ethnographer must learn the rules and patterns of a culture for the first time, entering the space as a stranger, and that newness can allow the ethnographer to see things that even the inhabitants of the space are not aware of. In a Christian community, however, it can be very difficult to participate fully as a stranger. Outsiders who do not share the core beliefs and values of the group may be treated with suspicion or subjected to attempts at conversion, and remaining silent about one's own ideas is not always an option either. This question of distance presents a challenge and an opportunity for the theological ethnographer. If the researcher is already embedded in the theology of the group, then the crucial ethnographic requirement of distance and strangeness has to some extent been sacrificed—but new insights and opportunities for participation may also become available.

One of the keys to good ethnography, online or offline, is self-reflection. There is no perfect location for ethnography, and every ethnographer will struggle with these questions of self-representation. A theologically-minded ethnographer who participates in the theological and devotional activities of the group will be able to recognise dimensions that an outsider ethnographer might not. Conversely, the theologian may fail to recognise and comment on the significance of ideas and practices with which they are too familiar. The outsider ethnographer will be much better-placed to analyse how the group reacts to strangers, but may struggle to gain the trust and access needed to study anything else. The most important point is not to achieve perfect objectivity and complete vision—which would be impossible—but to reflect carefully on how the inhabitants of the research field have adapted in response to the self-presentation of the ethnographer.

REPRESENTATION IN AND FOR THE FIELD SITE

Ethnographers do not just represent themselves *to* the groups they study. In some circumstances, research participants come to perceive the ethnographer as *a representative of* a faction or cause within the group, and this issue must also be included in our discussion. Participants often expect the ethnographer to speak for them, to share their story and argue their case in internal or external disputes. They may also perceive the ethnographer as a representative of their leaders, or of academia, or of the state. These perceptions can make a considerable difference to the researcher's relationships and observations, but they can become a significant personal challenge for the researcher, too. Ethnography requires long-term participation in the life of a community, and it can become hard to avoid the feeling that the ethnographer really does have an obligation to represent the interests of the community or of their closest informants. I have encountered this challenge on numerous occasions in my online research, and I will share two anecdotes here. In the following section, I will also discuss how I wrote about those two anecdotes for an external audience.

When I first entered an online church, I was often approached first by people who felt marginalised, poorly treated or just not quite at home within the community. These participants saw me as a resource, someone who could be relied upon to convey their point of view to a wider audience. This is a common experience for ethnographers: as newcomers and outsiders, ethnographers are on the edge of the group, and so it is easy to find common ground with others on the edge.

In Church A (a pseudonym), one of my first and most valuable informants was Agatha (also a pseudonym). Agatha was willing to spend a great deal of time introducing me to the world and her fellow inhabitants, but she also had a tense relationship with several of that world's churches and often wanted to share stories about their misdeeds and lack of character. In one of our text-chat discussions (quoted here with original spelling and line breaks), Agatha told me of a beautiful garden, "pretty and feminine," created some years earlier by a female leader. After that leader left the group, the others in the leadership team destroyed her work:

> they [deleted the] garden
>
> and placed a huge gorge there
>
> it almost felt like a rape to "excorcise" her
>
> It did the trick
>
> she no lionger comes

Unsurprisingly, others within the community (and the leadership) remembered these events completely differently. There was no exorcism, I was assured: the leader who left destroyed her own work, acting as a vandal rather than a victim. This divergence of accounts presented me with a research problem: should I include Agatha's story, or not?

In many of my projects, I also found that community leaders were keen to share their experiences with me. Just like Agatha, these leaders saw my research as an opportunity to ensure that their point of view reached a wide audience. Some leaders saw me as a kind of journalist or expert witness, someone who would attract publicity to their project, demonstrate its credibility and advocate for its significance. Other leaders seemed more interested in my perspective as a researcher, because I could tell them about other online initiatives they might not have encountered.

Church B is a good example of this kind of leadership interest. The church developed a close-knit and stable community over many years, and after long-term participant observation I was eventually invited to join the leadership group. This seemed like an excellent opportunity for my work, because I would be able to see how decisions were really made within the church. I would be giving up a degree of independence, but receiving new kinds of access in return.

This decision proved very useful for my research, until a sudden and intense dispute erupted between some of the leaders and some of the members. I found myself unexpectedly positioned on the side of the leadership in a community that teetered close to collapse, and at least some of the group began openly asking if my research had a hidden agenda.

To rescue my project, I needed to undertake extensive interpersonal work to reassure all sides that I really was going to listen to all perspectives and produce an impartial report. I was able to complete the project, but my efforts to rebuild rapport were not completely successful. I cannot be sure exactly what each community participant thought of my research, but I do believe that some members on both sides suspected me of being biased against them. For some, my closeness to the leadership meant I would always be suspect. For others, however, my attempts to be impartial were a betrayal: they had spent years talking to me, and expected me to stand up for them during their time of crisis.

The stories of Church A and Church B demonstrate the importance of the ethnographer's personal contacts within a community. The insights of marginal participants or leadership team members can both be extremely useful, but part of the ethnographer's task is to ensure that they balance these points of view against a wider diversity of voices. The most helpful and enthusiastic source is not always the one an ethnographer should rely on. The ethnographer must also be careful to reflect on their own location within a group: if community members see an ethnographer as a close confidante of marginal and rebellious voices or of their own leadership team, they may come to doubt the integrity and intentions of the research.

These anecdotes also show that an ethnographer can become a resource for community projects and struggles and a focal point for tension. The ethnographer is an outsider who plans to communicate something about the group to an external audience, and this unusual prospect brings something new into the group. The examples discussed here are unusually dramatic, but I have also been invited to speak at leadership meetings, strategy discussions and public events, using my ethnographic experience to speak for the groups I have studied and to offer advice to their supporters. In all of these situations, I have been called upon to act as a representative, to use my work on behalf of the whole group or a faction within it. These challenges will arise for theologians, too: who will you speak for in your research, and whose side will you be on?

REPRESENTATION OF THE FIELD SITE TO THE AUDIENCE

An ethnographer must decide how to represent themselves to their research site, and they must reflect carefully on who or what they might come to represent within and for the group they are studying. They must also find a way to represent their findings to others, in a way that is understandable and persuasive to audiences who have never seen that group before. Ethnography is not just cultural research but the work of producing a representation of that culture, "both process and product."[24] This representation cannot ever be complete, or entirely objective, so the ethnographer must also share reflections on their own position and perspective. Digital media can be a valuable ally for this work of reflexive production.

The two anecdotes presented in the previous section concern conflicts, and representing these events in my written report posed serious difficulties. In both cases, I decided that I had a responsibility to include reference to the conflict in some way. I needed to represent the complexity of each community fairly and thoroughly, including details and perspectives that could be embarrassing for the church. However, I also decided that I did not need to determine the "true story" or assign blame for the events described. Insensitive research can damage a community, and it would in any case have been difficult to secure consent to publish exact quotes from all parties involved. Instead, I focused in Church A on how participants perceived and talked about their online activities, and in Church B I spoke in broad terms about how the general characteristics of the church, including its leadership structure, had made the conflict difficult to resolve.

The representation I produced was relatively conventional, incorporating interview quotes and fieldwork notes alongside reflections on my research decisions. However, digital ethnography also allows new opportunities for more direct forms of representation. Ethnographic writings have long included photographs, but now they can also include screenshots of virtual environments, website layouts and online conversations. The digital ethnographer can include links to online videos, including tours of virtual spaces or recordings of events and conversations, allowing the audience to see the community and its environment in action for themselves. Videos like this can convey a sense of space, action and the passage of time, all vitally important for analysis but very difficult to explain in words alone.

Images, videos and other materials created or narrated by group members can also be included in a research report, as examples of how participants themselves wish to be represented. In my own work, I have published examples of cartoons sketched by group members, including some rather unflattering images of me, to show both that group's creative and irreverent sense of humour and its sometimes ambivalent relationship to my research.

Another approach is to share preliminary representations with research participants, to solicit their responses before constructing a final

24. Underberg and Zorn, *Ethnography*, 18.

representation for an academic audience. It is not uncommon to find that research participants are keen to access, read and critique what the ethnographer has been saying about them, and indeed that at least some of them have access to university libraries. Many participants in Christian online communities are themselves students, writers or academics, and they may already be very familiar with the kinds of arguments that theologians and ethnographers wish to make about their online activities. To encourage this process of conversation, I often exchange papers with research participants by email, and then incorporate their reactions and critiques into my future writing. This can be a valuable way to break down the hierarchical relationship between the researcher and the research participants, allowing participants to disrupt the analysis with their own perspectives and counter-arguments.

The drawback of such an approach, of course, is that only a few participants are usually interested in reading lengthy academic writings. To share ideas with a wider audience, one alternative is to maintain a research blog, using a digital medium to publish quick reflections on fieldwork in a format that participants—and other academics—are more likely to engage with. A blog post needs to be short, clear and enjoyable to read, and could be used to tell a story from fieldwork, to introduce a new concept or to publish a quick response to a current news story or media debate.

The best medium to use will of course depend on the specific habits and interests of the group being studied. Instead of writing blog posts, an ethnographer could record very short video presentations and post them to YouTube. A researcher might also be allowed to lead a discussion after a church service or to start a regular reading group, and some ethnographers have organised online discussions in virtual environments. It would also be possible to design an infographic to represent key ideas in visual form, and this kind of eye-catching presentation is easy to share through social media. Any of these approaches could be used to encourage research participants to respond to ideas as they develop, helping to identify problematic and provocative aspects of the ethnographer's representation of the group.

Natalie M. Underberg and Elayne Zorn argue for a more radical approach to collaborative representation. Instead of including digital materials as evidence, or sharing ethnographic texts with group members, they suggest that "cultural experiences and ideas can be represented by digital media through digital culture projects."[25] These digital projects can be highly ambitious, using the ethnographer's "narrative and new media skills to design creative interactive story experiences that transform facts and figures into

25. Ibid., 17.

a creative expression."[26] For Underberg and Zorn, ethnographers should be trying to produce digital representations that are interactive, immersive and multivocal, taking full advantage of all the new possibilities of digital media storytelling. Examples include ethnographic video games, virtual environments, animated films or websites that allow non-linear exploration of ethnographic materials. These projects can be created in collaboration with participants, allowing their own voices to be expressed at every level of project design and execution.

CONCLUSION—DIGITAL ETHNOGRAPHY AND ECCLESIOLOGY

Ethnographic studies like the ones outlined above have demonstrated that online churches mostly attract participants who already attend a local church, that online religious communities can be supportive, close-knit and stable, and that online worship and prayer experiences can be spiritually powerful for their participants.[27] These studies have considerable relevance for ecclesiology. As we have seen, Protestant and Catholic theologians from the 1990s to the present day have accused online churches of undermining local churches, by offering an easy, disembodied, low-commitment alternative. In response, supporters have promised powerful new opportunities for evangelism, particularly to younger generations. Participant observation has clearly and repeatedly shown that these fears and hopes are largely misplaced. For almost all practitioners, online religious activity, including online churchgoing, is combined with more conventional forms of local religious engagement. Ethnography can be used to encourage theologians to analyse digital religion as an integral part of larger, more complicated patterns of religious activity and belonging that include online and offline connections.

This shift to an embedded theology of digital media is already underway. Christian attitudes to digital media have changed over time, in response to wider social trends. When the internet was imagined as a separate cyberspace, it was easy for Christians to frame it as a "mission field," a new part of the world in which online churches should be planted. With the shift in our cultural imagination from "cyberspace" to the embedded, embodied, everyday internet, this understanding of the theological demands of digital technology has shifted.[28] The internet is now seen as part of society,

26. Ibid., 17.
27. Hutchings, *Creating Church*.
28. Hine, *Ethnography*.

an unremarkable aspect of our daily communication, and imagining it as a remote and dangerous "mission field" has ceased to be compelling. Instead, churches are increasingly using the internet, the infrastructure of social life, to connect to and expand their own congregations. Instead of funding an online church, Christian organisations are now more likely to appoint an online chaplain for social media ministry, or to share their local worship services online through video platforms and livestreaming apps.

This more embedded style of digital religion calls for new applications of digital ethnography. Studies of online Christian communities and networks are still needed, but digital ethnographers can also study the religious uses of the internet as part of everyday Christian life. Digital media have become part of academic work, too, from data analysis software to the growth of online and blended teaching courses and, for at least some researchers, the new possibilities for digital representation discussed above.

Digitalization presents all scholars of contemporary Christianity with challenges and opportunities. The digital offers access to new kinds of data requiring new research methods, supports new kinds of analysis, and allows us to share our findings in new ways. Digital ethnography provides a way to gather and communicate empirical data about how digital technologies are really used, how they connect their users, and what these behaviours and networks actually mean for their participants. Through ethnography, rich, first-hand appreciation of the context and meaning of digital practices can become one of the cornerstones of digital theology. Digital technologies are integral to the practices and routines of Christian congregations and the researchers who study them, and these uses and applications demand theological analysis supported by ethnographic methods of participant observation and reflexive representation.

17

Choice of Interpretation and Representation— Reflections on Power, Ethics, and Normativity

KRISTINA HELGESSON KJELLIN

INTRODUCTION

In this chapter I employ field studies that I have carried out in the Church of Sweden (CofS) to reflect upon interpretation and representation. These reflections focus on power, ethical acts, and normativity. The questions that I am struggling with are: How can anthropologists justly interpret and represent what people are doing when they are trying to "do good?" How can the actions and motives of people—in this case employees in CofS —be understood? Are their actions expressions of power that, regardless of intention, are upholding a neo-colonial and unequal order, in which "doing good" is usually problematic? Or can acts of solidarity and humanity be understood in other terms as well? Furthermore, is choice of interpretation affected by whom the subjects of study are, in this case white, Swedish middle-class Christians? And finally, is it acceptable as an anthropologist to take a clear normative stance in favor of acts of solidarity carried out by one's informants?

The background to these reflections lies in the reactions I received when I presented parts of my research at an anthropology seminar, where almost all questions and comments were concerned with expressions of solidarity being expressions of power. I do think it is important to take power relations into consideration, no matter what the subject of study is. However, is that really all that can and ought to be said about people wanting and trying to "do good?" Is there not more that can be said when it comes to acts of solidarity, of people's will to serve others? As a researcher I want to take my informants seriously—their faith, their concerns, their desire to act, to help others, and to work for an inclusive church and society. At the same time, in diversity work—the focus of my study—there are power dimensions that come to the fore that need to be addressed and analyzed. This is the challenge: to balance my interpretation and representation between, on the one hand, faith as a driving force that leads to ethical acts, and on the other, the dimensions of power and hierarchical relations that such work inevitably implies.

The question of representation has been, and continues to be, a methodological dilemma in ethnographic studies. How is it possible to make a fair representation of the ethnographic material gathered during field studies through various participative methods and through interviews and informal conversations? The representation made in the text is always a reduction, and there is a choice on the part of the researcher when it comes to what one chooses to emphasize and what one chooses to understate. In any situation, there is also a choice on the part of the researcher when it comes to interpretation, a choice based on one's research interests and theoretical leanings.

I begin the chapter with a description of the way I carried out my fieldwork. Thereafter I describe a situation in one of the parishes that has been part of my field study, a situation that clearly points at power dimensions but also directs attention to the question of interpretation and how to understand acts of solidarity. In the following section I present some perspectives on ethical acts, as expressed by several anthropologists. Then I briefly describe the historical tension between the disciplines of anthropology and theology and reflect upon whether the choice of anthropological interpretations of acts performed by Christians is affected by this historical tension. I conclude the chapter with reflections upon the responsibility of the researcher when it comes to choice of interpretation and representation and whether it is acceptable or not to take a clear normative stand as an anthropologist. I do not have the intention to provide a comprehensive analysis of how power, ethics, and normativity are dealt with and understood within anthropology. Instead, I offer some perspectives based on experiences from my field studies and begin a process of reflection that I intend to develop further in future work.

THE STUDY OF DIVERSITY WORK
IN THE CHURCH OF SWEDEN

During 2014 and 2015 I carried out field studies in CofS, more particularly within a network of parishes called "Framtiden bor hos oss" [The future lives with us]. The purpose of the study, published in 2016, was to describe and analyze the practical and reflective diversity work in which employees and volunteers in these parishes are involved.[1] As Sara Ahmed notes, diversity work is about turning walls into tables, tables that enable meetings and dialogue.[2] Identity and meaning-making, diversity work as processes that involve social relations as well as materiality, diversity work as processes of creating order, and dimensions of power are all perspectives that I have used in analyzing the ethnographic material. In my role as a researcher employed by CofS, I have had a clear aim with the study, not only to contribute to the academic debate, but also to contribute constructively with perspectives and reflections to all those who in different ways are involved with diversity work and daily meetings with migrants in CofS. The position I hold thus partly affects how I frame the conclusions I draw from the study.

The parishes in this study are situated in suburbs characterized by great cultural and religious diversity, as well as by great social needs. Furthermore, these parishes have a low membership rate in comparison to overall membership rates in CofS, which is not to say that they lack in activity, as one might think. Rather, they have vibrant church services with people coming from many different Christian traditions and they perform a great deal of diaconal work. The network is a grassroots movement that was started around 2000, and it grew out of a need among a number vicars to share experiences with others who are working in similar circumstances and thus facing similar issues.

As of 2016, there are 25 parishes in the network, and they are situated in Stockholm, Gothenburg, Malmö, Norrköping, Linköping, Södertälje and Trollhättan. The churches are physically open every day of the week and people come to church for various reasons, even if they are not members or see themselves as Christians. The network of parishes is committed to CofS becoming a more inclusive church, which means that the parishes also challenge CofS in various ways when it comes to norms and traditions. The employees involved in this network can be described as diversity workers; they actively work to include people from other cultural, Christian, or religious traditions in their local parishes. They are trying new ways in the church service to make it more inclusive and are in various ways involved

1. Helgesson Kjellin, *En bra plats.*
2. Ahmed, *On Being Included*, 174–75.

with helping and supporting, for instance, refugees and undocumented migrants.

In order to understand such a complex organization as CofS and such a big network that consists of so many parishes, individuals, and activities, it was necessary to study various parts of the network and to be as flexible as possible. I chose to carry out more in-depth field studies in one parish, Skärholmen in southern Stockholm. There I participated in as many activities as possible: church services, lunches, language cafés, I carried out interviews with the employees of the parish, and had informal conversations with church visitors. I also made shorter field visits to each city where the network is represented and carried out some interviews in order to get a glimpse of what is happening there. And finally, I have participated in network meetings, where vicars, priests and others from the various parishes in the network get together and discuss issues, reflect theologically upon their role in society, and plan for future activities. I have also included printed material and websites produced by the network and the parish in Skärholmen in my analysis.

As anthropologists Christina Garsten and Anette Nyqvist state, the researcher needs to be both flexible and open to the unexpected when studying complex organizations: "[A]s the sites of investigation are increasingly mobile and dispersed, the ethnographer's form of engagement must follow, which entails a heightened attentiveness to twists and turns in the field and an openness to the unexpected."[3] The voices that emerge in this study are mostly those of Church of Sweden employees who in most cases represent the majority society, though I have endeavored to include other voices as well. As it turned out, the fact that most of my informants represent the majority society became important since the study then highlights challenges as experienced by representatives of the majority population. As I note later in the text, it is possible that if my informants had not represented the majority society, the comments given at the seminar would have been of a different kind. Although Skärholmen has been the focus of my field studies, the example that I raise in this chapter is from another parish in the network that is situated in one of the suburbs of Gothenburg.

CONSULTATION FOR UNDOCUMENTED MIGRANTS

I am overwhelmed and deeply affected by what I have experienced this evening. So many people that come, get health care, food, support, and advice. Families that cannot afford diapers

3. Garsten and Nyqvist, "Momentum," 245.

and oatmeal. It comes so close, having a small child myself. I am
so privileged. A family that is about to be shattered, as one of the
deacons told me—how can that be possible?

I wrote these words in my diary after my visit at a consultation for
undocumented migrants. In this parish, situated in one of the suburbs of
Gothenburg, there are weekly consultations for undocumented migrants
taking place in the church building. More than 140 nationalities are represented in this suburb and one of the employees in the parish tells me that
it is not uncommon that more than twenty languages are spoken in the
Sunday service. Every day between 80 and 100 persons come to this church,
for various reasons. The church building enables many different kinds of
meetings—a chat over a cup of coffee, a soccer game in the basement, or
various diaconal activities. The church also runs a second hand-shop, and
when it opens at 1 p.m. there is usually a long line of mostly women waiting
outside of the church. "The church functions like a living-room," the vicar
says. It is not difficult to see that the church is an important meeting place
in this suburb, a suburb that is often written about in the media as a problematic area, with high numbers of unemployment and people living on the
outskirts of society. The parish has formulated its role to be a positive force
in the local community, to condemn injustices, and to be a driving force for
change. To create meeting places, to build bridges in the community and
with Jesus at the center help people to feel a sense of belonging. Crucial
words for the identity of the parish are "human dignity," "meetings," "root-
edness," and "change."

This four-hour consultation takes place every Wednesday evening and
is organized by a philanthropic movement and the Red Cross, and the parish has opened up its doors for the consultation to take place in the church
building. Every week, undocumented migrants, ineligible for government
support, come to this consultation where they can meet doctors, opticians,
dentists, psychologists, and get a bag with some food and hygiene articles.
The people involved in the consultation are volunteers or clinicians working
in their spare time. When I visited the consultation one evening in April,
the place filled up both with volunteers and with families who needed
help. Soon each and every corner of the church building was turned into a
consultation room. The employees of the parish were there supporting the
volunteers with whatever they could, sitting down with the undocumented
migrants over a cup of coffee and talking to them while they were waiting
for their turn. In the afternoon, a few hours before the consultation opened,
one of the employees gave me these questions to carry with me during the

evening as a way to deal with the experience: What do I see? What do I feel? What do I think?

During the evening I walked around in the church, talked to the people that were there to help with various things, and also talked to some of the families that came. As my words in the diary show, I was overwhelmed by what I saw and experienced that evening. The needs were so big and the commitment was so strong among all those people that came there to offer assistance in various ways. Several of the volunteers that I spoke to had a commitment to the undocumented migrants that was both personal and professional. Many of them come every Wednesday evening to volunteer at the consultation. One of the volunteers, a young man in his twenties, said to me: "This is the best church in Sweden! Everyone is welcome here, no matter the color of the skin. I have never heard of a church that helps people the way they do here." The parish has deliberately employed people with different national and cultural backgrounds so that the parish can meet people with various backgrounds in a professional way. However, the church is not without friction. Several of the employees tell me that they continuously need to handle conflicts and various issues that arise among the diverse group of employees and volunteers, e.g., conflicts arising from different understandings regarding the role of women and men in church and in society.

With this short description of the consultation in mind, we will now turn to how this type of situation can be interpreted and represented differently, starting with perspectives on giving and on power.

PERSPECTIVES ON GIVING AND ON POWER

Anthropological research on the significance of the gift for social relations points to the importance of reciprocity.[4] When a gift is reciprocated, there is balance in a relationship. But what happens when one party always is the giver and the other party always is the receiver? And how should one look upon such an activity as this weekly consultation? Do these kinds of activities reinforce a process of "othering," where those who are marginalized and powerless are helped by those who are included and privileged? Does a consultation such as this one even contribute to a political status quo, of maintaining a political system where the undocumented migrants remain outside of society? As an anthropologist, my role is to stay close to what happens in a particular locality and to peoples' understandings and discourses, but as I will develop later in the text, as a researcher one also has a choice to make when it comes to what perspectives one chooses to emphasize or understate.

4. Mauss, *Gift*, 13.

The theologian Trygve Wyller has studied and written about this particular consultation and he sees the church in this case as a "space that promotes acts of citizenship,"[5] and that "embodies a theology of the human."[6] According to Wyller, the church offers an alternative belonging that society cannot offer. At the same time it is not difficult to see the kind of power dimensions that such a consultation entails, where the life-situations of those that come to the consultation to seek help drastically differ from the established Swedish middle class that many of the employees and volunteers represent. Applying the theoretical concept of the gift as developed by the sociologist and anthropologist Marcel Mauss,[7] where gift-giving—giving, receiving, and reciprocating a gift—is a fundamental to all human relations, it is not difficult to see that the consultation just described upholds unequal power positions, where the representatives of the church and the various organizations involved represent the powerful giver of the gift, while the undocumented migrants, as the recipients of the gift, are unable to recip-rocate that gift and thus remain in a powerless position.[8] In the words of Mauss, "[t]he unreciprocated gift still makes the person who has accepted it inferior, particularly when it has been accepted with no thought of return-ing it."[9] Thus, there are dynamics of power that are inherent to gift-giving, and clearly the dynamics look very different depending on the particular situation in which gift-giving takes place.

Christianity is impregnated by thoughts on giving, on helping your neighbor, and showing God's love and mercy by giving. To give is the duty of a Christian person.[10] In a study of missionary activities in Bolivia carried out by the Swedish Pentecostal church, the anthropologist Göran Johansson points at the central role of giving in mission work and how the giving leads to the maintenance and reproduction of asymmetrical positions between those that give and those that are the recipients of the gifts. If the asymme-try between the giver and the recipient would disappear, the whole mission

5. Wyller, "Becoming Human," 39.

6. Ibid., 42.

7. Mauss, *Gift*.

8. One can of course argue that the undocumented migrants *are* giving the em-ployees and the volunteers a gift, for instance by providing them with the chance of be-ing good citizens. The employees and the volunteers do not walk away empty-handed. However, it is not a gift that in any sense removes the unequal power dynamics that exist in that situation.

9. Ibid., 65.

10. A Bible verse that points at the centrality of giving is Acts 20:35: "In all this I have given you an example that by such work we must support the weak, remember-ing the words of the Lord Jesus, for he himself said, 'It is more blessed to give than to receive.'"

enterprise might cease to exist. Giving, Johansson continues, is crucial to Christian spirituality. It is by giving that the Christian person receives the blessings from God:

> The entire missionary enterprise is built up by a great and mul-tifarious gift-giving. A gradual elimination of the asymmetry in this pattern would, in practice, bring about a gradual liquidation of the Mission as we know it today. Such a process would entail a serious disturbance for the many gift-givers in the missionary's homeland. There the giving represents a vital part of the spiritual life, not to say a substitute for it. To whom would they give if not to the Mission? And where would the blessing otherwise be sought?[11]

However, to be the recipient of a gift is not always a blessing. Even if the intention is not to establish a power asymmetry, a continuous system of giving and receiving where both parts stay in their respective positions and where there is no prospect of altering those, might lead to a negative dependence on the part of the recipient of the gifts.[12] The theoretical framework of the gift shows that we develop dependencies in all social relations, dependencies that can be interpreted in terms of power, although we do not normally think in those terms when we bring a gift to a friend when we are, say, invited for a dinner party. The power dimensions are more obvious in a situation such as the consultation for undocumented migrants, where the differences between giver and receiver are so evident.

These two examples, the consultation for undocumented migrants and the mission work in Bolivia, point at different aspects of power at different levels. In each instance there are individuals acting within an organization, a given structure, in both cases churches and church organizations. These organizations with their particular role in society have a history—in one case CofS with its history of being a church with close connections to the political power centers, and in the other case a Swedish Pentecostal church, in which missional relationships to other churches around the world is a crucial part of its identity. Power dimensions come to the fore in relationships between individuals, as well as in organizational structures. Not least are acts performed by individuals within any organization interpreted in relation to what that specific organization represents and how it is understood in the wider society. These organizational dimensions are important to bear in mind since individuals that are acting within organizational structures—individuals that are striving to "do good"— might unintentionally reproduce

---

11. Johansson, *More Blessed*, 183.

12. Ibid., 192.

power asymmetries and inequalities maintained by the organization. Thus, there is a challenge to living a "Christian life," where giving is emphasized as being crucial, but where the goodness of giving might not be as self-evident as one would wish.

Perspectives on power and powerlessness are crucial to consider when analyzing processes of migration and diversity work. I mean that there are risks with a perspective that does not take structures of inequality into account; without knowledge and consciousness of how power operates such unequal structures easily continue to be reproduced. At the same time, power is not the only thing that needs to be analyzed in order to understand what "doing good" in various settings entails. With the consultation for undocumented migrants in mind, choosing *not* to help them would be much worse, bearing in mind the extremely vulnerable situation they live in. Thus, while I see the importance of analyzing power dynamics and unequal relationships, there are other perspectives that need to be incorporated in order to get a fuller understanding of human interactions such as this consultation. This leads me to reflect upon some perspectives on ethical acts, as described in the next section.

PERSPECTIVES ON ETHICAL ACTS

In order to make explicit how I look upon "ethics" and "ethical acts" I will draw upon the anthology *Ordinary Ethics*, where anthropologists, through different case studies, point at ethics as something that we *do* in our daily lives.[13] Several anthropologists state that ethical acts—instances of people striving to do what they find is right or good—need to be seen as integral to human condition and behaviour, speech and action, and not as separate entities in themselves. In the words of Michael Lambek, "the ethical is intrinsic to human action, to meaning what one says and does and to living according to the criteria thereby established. Ethics is a property of speech and action, as mind is a property of body. . . . Ethics is not a discrete object, not best understood as a kind or set of things."[14] Similarly, Webb Keane argues for an understanding of the ethical as embedded in materiality, in speech and action. For Keane, the ethical is something that is part of our everyday lives and our everyday interactions.[15]

In the same line Michael Jackson argues for an understanding of religion and of ethics not as "linguistically or conceptually . . . discrete domains," but as "questions of 'practical wisdom' (*phronesis*) in everyday

13. Lambek, *Ordinary Ethics.*
14. Lambek, "Toward an Ethics," 61.
15. Keane, "Minds," 82.

life when unprecedented situations arise, problems don't admit of any solution, perfection remains beyond our grasp, and virtue may reside less in achieving the good than in striving for it."[16] He emphasizes the practicality of everyday life, situations that appear that need to be handled, as the core of ethics and morality. This emphasis on the practicality is something I see to be crucial to my understanding and interpretation of what is happening in the churches that are part of my research project. As one of the deacons I have interviewed says: "To reinterpret every situation that emerges" and then act in relation to what is specific in that particular situation. That, she argues, is at the core of what it means to be a Lutheran church.

Jackson furthermore emphasizes the dynamics of intersubjectivity, "the everyday interplay of human subjects, coming together and moving apart, giving and taking, communicating and miscommunicating," as crucial to our understanding of the ethical.[17] He continues: "I suggest that we see our sense of the ethical as deriving less from normative maxims, categorical imperatives or cultural codifications than from our deep awareness that our very existence is interwoven with the existence of others, and that the reciprocal character of human relations gives rise, from the earliest months of life, to inchoate, conflicted and diffuse assumptions about fairness, justice, rightness and goodness."[18] Again, these perspectives on human relations are valuable in interpreting situations that emerge in the churches, such as the consultation for undocumented migrants described above, and how the employees approach these situations. It is through relationships with others, and in all kinds of situations in our everyday lives, that our ideas and understandings of what is right and good are being manifested.

Reflecting on how to understand and interpret the ethical in everyday life, and also criticizing a narrow perspective among social scientists on ethical acts, anthropologist Michael Lambek has this to say, based on his research and field studies:

> Very simply, the people I encountered have attempted, routinely—but also anything but routinely—to do what they think right or good, sometimes as a matter of course, sometimes in a struggle to know what the right path was, and sometimes ineffectively, infelicitously, inconsistently, incontinently, or not at all, but then with respect to what they or others think or have established as right or good. They also interpreted the actions and characters of others by criteria similar to those they applied

16. Jackson, "Ethics and Religion," 107.
17. Ibid., 107–8.
18. Ibid., 108.

to themselves. Put another way, they have acted largely from a sense of their own dignity; they have refused positions or attributions of indignity, and they have treated, or understood that they ought to treat, others as bearing dignity of their own. I do not think the Malagasy speakers I have met are exceptional in this regard, yet social theory has focused almost exclusively on rules, power, interest, and desire as forces or motivations for action.[19]

The way Lambek describes his informants very much accords with the way my informants are describing and negotiating what they are trying to accomplish. They are acting according to what they believe is right and good, and not least out of their conviction of how the Christian message ought to be lived out and expressed. Sometimes, they say, it is quite easy to know what a right or a good way to act is. Other times, it is not that easy. They are particularly challenged by the cultural and religious diversity that they are situated in; what they consider to be the right thing to do might be experienced in another way by the persons toward whom these acts are directed.

My informants note that they are motivated by their Christian faith to act out of love and compassion and not out of a desire to exercise power. At the same time some of those that I have interviewed say that they are aware of the unequal positions present in the consultation described above, a dilemma that they are struggling with as they attempt to overcome those inequalities. For instance, rather than putting foods and hygiene articles in bags and handing them out to the migrants—which would likely be more efficient—the employees and volunteers of CofS place foods and hygiene articles on tables, similar to a grocery store, so that the undocumented migrants can pick whatever they need themselves. The vicar in the parish says that it is a small way to show that the people that come to the consultation have the right to make their own decisions about what they need and want and to avoid a humiliating situation where a pre-packed bag is handed to them by one of the employees.

To conclude this section, what Keane, Jackson, and Lambek claim is that individuals' striving to perform ethical acts, to "do good," needs to be understood broadly, as intrinsic to the human condition, and thus cannot be reduced only to calculations or the interests of individuals. In the case of my informants, their Christian faith leads them to act, to involve themselves with the undocumented migrants, and to open the doors of the church.

---

19. Lambek, "Toward an Ethics," 40.

As a researcher one can choose what to emphasize in a situation like the consultation for undocumented migrants, the power dimensions inherent in the giving of gifts, or ethics and ethical acts as intrinsic to human nature, that is, the will of human beings to do good.

The comments I received at the seminar were rather one-sided and focused only on power dimensions and the interest of individuals as the motivating force to help others. This led me to ponder whether the fact that my informants are Swedish Christians, representing CofS, partly affected the views expressed at the seminar. Could it be something here that has to do with the historical aversion of anthropology in general toward the discipline of theology and Christianity? This might be speculative; however, I still want to raise the question for reflection. Furthermore, it is not the first time that I have encountered such reactions. My previous research among South African Pentecostals, both white and of color, occasionally caused reactions by some anthropologists, reactions that more than anything else revealed personal views on Christianity and Christians.[20] Thus, the reflections in the forthcoming section are based on experiences from several occasions.

ANTHROPOLOGY AND CHRISTIANITY— AN UNEASY RELATIONSHIP

Anthropology has a long history of studying groups of people that in, various ways, are in a vulnerable position: indigenous populations, groups of people that face urbanization and modernization, women, youth, etc. As such, anthropologists often side with the marginalized and least powerful in a society. Since most anthropological studies historically have been carried out in non-Western countries, the colonial situation has very much affected the studies, and Christianity has to a great extent been interpreted as an aspect of colonialism and of modernity.[21]

Generally speaking, Christianity has for many years been marginalized and even neglected as an object of study in anthropology. In the early days of anthropology, the study of Christianity was pushed to the margins, and it was considered the least urgent object of study. This was partly due to the close connections that in many ways existed between the early missionaries and the early anthropologists; both were often interested in the local cultural context in which they were involved, although the reason behind their presence differed. Because anthropology in the early days wanted to distance itself from religion and theology—emphasizing its rationality and scientific legitimacy, thus saying that theology was neither rational nor

20. Helgesson, "*Walking in the Spirit.*"

21. See for instance Comaroff and Comaroff, *Revelation*, vols. 1 and 2.

scientific—anthropology "has on the whole been less successful at considering Christianity as an ethnographic object than at considering any other
religion in this way."[22] The anthropologist Fenella Cannell argues that "the
topic of Christianity has provoked more anxiety than most other religious
topics. It has seemed at once the most tediously familiar and the most
threatening of the religious traditions for a social science that has developed
within contexts in which the heritage of European philosophy, and therefore of Christianity, tends to predominate,"[23] and that one has almost been
labeled as a "closet evangelist" if one has chosen to study Christianity.[24] A
bit ironic is, for instance, the fact that the term modernity, which so influenced early anthropology and implies an "irreversible break with the past,
after which the world is utterly transformed in mysterious ways," actually is
"modeled on the Christian idea of conversion."[25] Thus, despite the efforts of
early anthropology to distance itself from Christian thinking, Cannell argues that much anthropological theoretical understandings have been, and
may continue to be, unconsciously affected by forms of Christian thinking.

Although much has changed since those early days of anthropology
and the study of Christianity is not uncommon today, Cannell argues that
Christianity, particularly in the Western part of the world, is still an oc-
cluded object of study in the field of anthropology.[26] Christianity is seen as
important in other parts of the world but not in Europe or the United States.
When Christianity has been studied in the African context, it has often been
explained as a response to modernity and as a way for people to deal with
the social, political, and economic changes that come with modernity. The
last two decades have witnessed a growing interest among anthropologists
to various Pentecostal and neo-Pentecostal churches and questions of how
these churches' growth (not least in African, Asian, and Latin American
countries) is changing societies. Cannell writes: "Many anthropologists who
become interested in Christianity, then, do so almost against their will, initially seeing it as a kind of secondary phenomenon or top coat that has been
applied by external forces to the cultures they are studying."[27]

22. Cannell, "Introduction," 45.
23. Ibid., 3.
24. Ibid., 4.
25. Ibid., 39.
26. During the last two decades there is a growing research field, Anthropology of
Christianity, where anthropologists research the diversity of Christianity in a much
more conscious manner than previous generations of anthropologists. See Robbins,
"Anthropology."
27. Ibid., 12.

In a 1991 article, before the study of Pentecostalism and other charismatic Christian groups became common in anthropology, anthropologist Susan Harding argues that American Protestant fundamentalists are the "cultural 'others'"[28] in the academic discourse, as opposed to modernity; "[t]hrough polarities such as these between 'us' and 'them,' the modern subject is secured."[29] She goes on to describe how her choice to study evangelicals made her colleagues question her: "In effect, I am perpetually asked: Are you now or have you ever been a born-again Christian?"[30] They just could not comprehend her choice of study and suspected that there were other reasons behind her choice.

I have experienced similar reactions from some colleagues toward my Pentecostal informants in South Africa, especially my white South African informants. It was clear that some found it difficult to understand my choice of study. For some of my colleagues, my white informants' involvement with Israel, for instance, became an example of how unsympathetic they were. In the Swedish society, Pentecostal groups and other charismatic Christian groups, such as the neo-Pentecostal church Word of Life, are to a great extent the "cultural others," which should be taken into account when grappling with the reactions I met. Further, when these charismatic Christians were white South Africans, with all the attendant historical baggage, it was even more difficult to make interpretations of their beliefs and actions that were remotely understanding or sympathetic. The complexity within this group of white Pentecostals, where some for instance had been very much involved in the struggle against the apartheid regime, was difficult for some to take into account.

When it comes to the focus of my current research project, CofS, the history of the church as a church—with a powerful position in society and with historically strong links to political powers needs to be taken into account when it comes to reactions at the aforementioned seminar, with the one-sided emphasis on the necessity of raising perspectives on power. Also, not only is charismatic Christianity the "cultural other" in the Swedish society, but Christians overall are to some extent the "cultural others." Together with the long history of aversion from anthropology toward theology and Christianity, these are, I believe, background circumstances that affect choices of interpretation in relation to acts performed by Christians. Would the reactions expressed at the seminar have been different had my South African informants been black instead of white, or if the consultation for undocumented migrants had

28. Harding, "Representing," 375.
29. Ibid., 374.
30. Ibid., 375.

been run by a mosque instead of CofS? This is of course impossible to know, but these reflections point at the larger question of whether the way we as researchers interpret and represent the ethnographic material differs depending on who the informants are. On the one hand it goes without saying that interpretations and representations will differ, since who one's informants are, with their unique history and experiences, is crucial to the understanding of the ethnographic material. On the other hand there might be prejudices and leanings toward certain perspectives on the part of the researcher that come out more strongly depending on the identity of one's informants.

CONCLUDING REFLECTIONS—THE RESPONSIBILITY OF THE RESEARCHER

I began this chapter by asking how it is possible to make a fair representation of the ethnographic material gathered during field studies, a representation that builds on choices made when it comes to interpretation. To sum up my reflections, I have raised the issue of choice of interpretation based on the following: the example of the consultation for undocumented migrants; the question of how to understand and interpret ethical acts; and the tendency in anthropology to interpret people's striving to do good as motivated by power, interest, and desire. Lastly, I asked whether choice of interpretation has anything to do with who one's informants are, highlighting anthropology's long history of aversion toward Christianity and theology. These reflections finally lead me to some concluding thoughts regarding the responsibility of the researcher when it comes to choice of interpretation and representation, and the question of whether it is acceptable or not for an anthropologist to take a clear normative stand.

The theologian Mary McClintock Fulkerson raises the question of how to interpret and "read a situation correctly."[31] She states that a situation consists of "a variety of elements—not just Scripture, not just culture, or racial or gendered markers, but a complexity of elements, including power—that *converge* relationally."[32] She continues: "The task of framing a contemporary situation is not about its every detail, but the identification of certain patterns that characterize it."[33] If we once again return to the consultation for undocumented migrants, there are patterns and a structure that characterize that situation where undocumented migrants who are living in hiding and fear enter the church building and meet individuals from various organizations that represent the established society. There are historical, politi-

31. McClintock Fulkerson, "Interpreting," 127.
32. Ibid.
33. McClintock Fulkerson, *Places of Redemption*, 8.

cal, economic, social, and religious dimensions to that particular situation, dimensions that affect everyone involved, both those on the side of the giver and those on the side of the receiver.

The goal of coming as close as possible to what one is studying is at the core of the anthropological methodology, as is applying a holistic perspective on the matter studied, as McClintock Fulkerson notes. However, a bit contrary to what McClintock Fulkerson states, I would argue that the anthropological methodology sees the importance of details in situations that occur. Furthermore, it is a methodology that requires time and trust, that stays close to people's discourse and understandings of the world, and turning these experiences in "the field" into academic texts is a great challenge. For the researcher it is a balancing act not only to handle the trust in a responsible way that one's informants have given but also to analyze the ethnographic material with theoretical tools that are suitable and not shy away from perspectives that could be both critical and challenging. The text is always a reduction, no matter the ambition to provide a "thick description"[34] of the reality one has studied. There is always a choice to be made regarding what aspects from any particular situation to emphasize and what theoretical perspectives to apply. The analysis of the consultation, I argue, needs to involve perspectives that point at power asymmetries and hierarchies, as well as perspectives that take people's will to "do good" seriously. Otherwise the understanding of that particular situation is overly partial.

Anthropologists Erica Bornstein and Peter Redfield state the following regarding the role of anthropology, in this case in relation to the study of humanitarian action:

> [W]e suggest that anthropological analysis is unlikely to generate normative programs and mobile models ready for rapid transplantation. Nor is it likely to produce critiques dismissing all concern for suffering in clean categorical terms of political denunciation. . . . Anthropology's legacy, in contrast, recognizes the messy mass of lived experience, the "friction" of specific action that attends to the movement of people, ideas and things. Its classic strength therefore lies in unsettling, in reintroducing what was never quite left behind.[35] [. . .] As engaged and critical observers, however, we can suggest continued attention to its loose ends and their significance in actual practice.[36]

---

34. Geertz, *Interpretation*.

35. Bornstein and Redfield, "Afterword," 252–53.

36. Ibid., 253.

According to Bornstein and Redfield the role and strength of anthropology is to point at the frictions, cracks, ambivalences, and contradictions of human life, rather than to take a clear normative stand for or against something. My own passion for the discipline of anthropology is to a great extent based on just that, namely a curiosity and an interest in the complexity and contradictions of human life and the great variations of understandings and interpretations that a cross-cultural perspective offer. I experience the character of anthropology as both liberating and challenging, while I sometimes find normative positions taken as limiting and ethnocentric. However, in this research project I have experienced an urgency to say something more than pointing at contradictions and complexities.

The ethnographic material from my field studies within the network "The future lives with us" in many ways relates to current debates in society about refugees coming to Sweden and to debates about cultural and religious diversity. With refugees coming to Sweden and expressions of xenophobia and racism becoming more and more widespread in society, knowledge can be used in various ways by actors with different intentions. Thus, the question of representation becomes crucial. Bearing in mind the societal situation, what kind of knowledge should researchers emphasize in drawing from a research project such as mine? What does a one-sided focus on power and acts of solidarity as expressions of a neo-colonial order signal? It might be easy, and maybe also tempting, to end up with an analysis based in a hermeneutics of suspicion that depicts that what people are trying to accomplish is really rather about expressions of power and of individual desire. However, in the case of this research project such a one-sided analysis can also be used by those that do not think Church of Sweden should be involved with undocumented migrants.

When sympathizing with what these parishes are trying to accomplish, is it acceptable and maybe even a duty to take a clear normative stand? For me, bearing in mind the political situation described above, the answer is yes. However, each research project is unique and has its particular circumstances; as such, taking a normative stand is maybe not always the right thing to do and one should instead point at complexities and ambiguities. At the same time, taking a clear normative stand does not mean that complexities in the ethnographic material are not analyzed or that power dimensions and hierarchical orders are hidden. Rather, by highlighting the complexity of any situation—the fact that situations are embedded in, and affected by, among other things, history, politics, economics, and religion, factors that also affect the way individuals act—makes it possible as a researcher to contribute constructively, in this case, to an inclusive society.

18

Dilemmas of Representation—Response

EILEEN R. CAMPBELL-REED

We do not simply retreat into our minds to write theoretical
texts, but we create discourses and narratives that are themselves
entangled with the materiality and sensoriality of the moment
and of memories and imaginaries.[1]

R epresentation in any production of knowledge ushers the scholar
into a variety of dilemmas or *conundrums* that are not easily solved
or dismissed. Conundrums related to the issue of representation come
up perennially, and they are based in existential and/or material realities
of the complex, even paradoxical, limits of human experience.[2] Thus, the
problems we face when writing about the lives, experiences, and situations
of others—or about our own experiences for that matter—are inescapably
complicated. Yet the complexity does not mean we do not try. In fact we
must try. Whether we enter the conversation as theologians or as social scientists, or as people who operate in both worlds, the sheer human scale of
our subject matter, demands that we *re*-present what we know, what we are

1. Pink, *Doing Sensory Ethnography*, 47–48 [2nd ed.].

2. At the time scholars gathered in Sweden for the Scandinavian ecclesiology and
ethnography conference, another project in practical theology was coming together
that also speaks to many similar questions and dilemmas raised by authors in the
"representation" conversation of this book. See Miller-McLemore and Mercer, *Conundrums*, 2–4.

learning, and even what we do not know, for the sake of human flourishing. This is all to the say, representation is a significant aspect of what really matters in the work of ecclesiology and ethnography.

In response to four authors who lead the way into this conversation about representation, I want to gather up the concerns they raise into four conundrums or dilemmas of representation that both theologically-oriented and sociologically-oriented ethnographers face in the course of research and writing. Each author addresses several of the conundrums that I am suggesting in the list below.[3] As unsolvable puzzles, conundrums do require, if not solutions, then careful responses, in order that we might research, write, and construct meanings for theology and life.[4] Each of the tensions that animate the dilemmas of representation can either spark frustration or stultify writers into paralysis. However, the very same tensions also make space for creative negotiations in how to represent self, situations, and participants to our readers and conversation partners, as well as to a wider audience of people interested in who and what we study. For those new to the field of theological ethnography, I hope this heuristic exploration will be useful in allaying the anxieties that accompany beginnings, especially the writing task. Representation is:

* reductive *and* evocative

* descriptive *and* interpretive

* powerful *and* harmful

* contextual *and* skilled

I appreciate the questions raised by the four authors of this section of the book, and the thoughtful responses they offer to those questions. As a part of my exploration I will also lift up additional questions from each dilemma.

REPRESENTATION: REDUCTIVE AND EVOCATIVE

Subjects of study such as life, faith, family, congregations, on-line communities, and the like are irreducible, yet to convey our thoughts about them, we must find ways to speak and write about them. Several authors throughout this volume name the limits of language and writing, which are reductive to

3. The four authors also address other conundrums and dilemmas, but for the sake of space and opening up dialogue, I will explore just four and raise a few more questions to push thinking further.

4. Mercer and Miller-McLemore say "conundrums do not just confuse; they refuse easy answer." Mercer and Miller-McLemore, *Conundrums*, 2. These are not merely intellectual puzzles but also spill over into personal and emotional aspects of life and work.

the lives and situations about which we seek understanding. In her chapter, "Trying to Tell the Truth about a Life: The Problem of Representation for Ethnographic Theology," theological ethnographer, Natalie Wigg-Stevenson suggests two new tools to aid in circumventing the problem of reduction in ethnographic research and writing: autoethnography and performance ethnography. Each tool leans into the evocative and expansive side of representation. First at the stage of data collection, these approaches offer concrete and intentional ways to evoke the emotional and relational character of data collection. They move the researcher beyond observation and deeper into the waters of the situation itself. At the stage of writing, the novel tools offer freedom to think outside the boxes of style and form required by most academic journals and books.

In "Ethnography, Representation and Digital Media," digital ethnographer, Tim Hutchings suggests other ways of representing findings that evoke and even provoke both the participants of one's study and a variety of audiences who may be interested in the focus of his fieldwork, digital religion. He suggests a method of triangulation from which many ethnographic projects would benefit: "share preliminary representations with research participants, to solicit their responses" on the road to creating one's final report.[5] He also suggests creating and maintaining a "research blog," creating YouTube videos, and/or making an infographic. Each of these novel forms of representation, Hutchings cautions, should resonate with the situation under study. While novel forms of representation themselves do not eliminate the reductive character of the process or writing of ethnography, they offer more possibilities for expanding, evoking, and provoking readers and recipients of our ethnographic reports to imagine more, not less, of what we hope to convey.

REPRESENTATION: DESCRIPTIVE AND INTERPRETIVE

Too many theologians began making use of ethnographic and/or qualitative research tools in the 1990s without much reflection about what else they were adopting in the process. And far too many of the early proponents treated the tools for data gathering as neutral. Only after compiling the data and describing the situation under investigation, would they explicitly take up the task of theological reflection on that newfound information. Elsewhere I've argued, with my research partner Chris Scharen, about the inadequacy of this approach.[6] From the outset of a research program, through

5. See Hammersly and Atkinson, *Ethnography*, 230–32, for a discussion of triangulation.

6. Campbell-Reed and Scharen, "Ethnography," 235–43.

data gathering, in conversation with partners and informants in the field, and all the way through the writing process, theological ethnographers are making choices that not only describe, but interpret meaning and construct reality.[7] Each of the four authors in the present conversation about representation touch on the tension between representation as description and representation as interpretation. That precise conundrum rose to the level of crisis among anthropologists in the 1980s and 1990s. Wigg-Stevenson traces that history in her chapter, inviting theological ethnographers into that crisis, which presents an opportunity to take up new methods of research and writing. Rather than mire down in the crisis, we can learn from the previous attempts to navigate it. My chapter in this volume also addresses the same crisis in terms of reflexivity, exploring how the work of describing and interpreting both shapes and is shaped by the social location and voice of the researcher.

Thematizing data in fieldwork is tricky. Finding interpretive patterns in the data is among the aims in Sune Fahlgren's chapter "The Enacted and the Experienced Faith: Creating 'Stuff' on Baptist Spirituality in Sweden." The number and possible range of interpretations, even if researchers agree on the *patterns* of something like Baptist spirituality, remains even more complex. Fahlgren's chapter raises the question of how to write up findings in a way that they are set in a wider context for interpretation rather than leaving one's report at the level of summary or an account of the internal events of a community. For example, is there a wider shelf of Baptist history or Swedish religion in which the study of Baptist spirituality can be located? Fahlgren's project raises this kind of question for everyone doing ecclesial ethnography: What are the larger frameworks—social structures, national identities, historical theologies, cultural milieus, or religious groups in which we locate our particular fieldwork with specific people or situations? How do we dialog between the small scale and the large? Groups we study cannot be relied upon necessarily to articulate a high level of consciousness about their relationships with wider permeating cultures. It is our responsibility as researchers to place the particular situation in dialog with the larger interpretive frameworks.

Anthropologist of religion, Kristina Helgesson Kjellin explores the relationship between representation and interpretation in her chapter, "Choice of Interpretation and Representation—Reflections on Power, Ethics, and Normativity." She lays out the work of interpretation nicely in the following tasks:

7. Ibid., 236–37.

> [C]oming as close as possible to what one is studying . . . ap-
> plying a holistic perspective on the matter studied . . . [seeing]
> the importance of details in situations that occur . . . [staying]
> close to people's discourse and understandings of the world, and
> turning these experiences in "the field" into academic texts.[8]

The tasks, says Helgesson Kjellin, are "a great challenge." I would am-
plify her observations by noting that the work of interpretation requires
what scholar of nursing, Patricia Benner would call, *salience*.[9] Knowing
what is important and what should be in the foreground versus what to
leave in the background, is salience, a practical wisdom based in many years
of experience. This kind of knowing is embodied, relational, and embedded
in situations, such that it may feel intuitive, but is more likely the residue of
long years of practice. Researchers learn salience through trial and error, and
ideally when they are aided by thoughtful supervision. Even knowing how
description fits into an interpretive framework takes a sense of salience.[10]

REPRESENTATION: POWERFUL AND HARMFUL

Another crucial matter of salience is knowing when one's choice of
representation is doing harm, when it does something powerful or good,
and how representations hold potential to do both. Among Helgesson
Kjellin's provocative questions are these:

> How can anthropologists justly interpret and represent what
> people are doing when they are trying to "do good?" How can
> the actions and motives of people . . . be understood? Are their
> actions expressions of power that, regardless of intention, are
> upholding a neo-colonial and unequal order, in which "doing
> good" is usually problematic?

In her chapter, Helgesson Kjellin explores carefully the imbalances of
power between 1) "white, Swedish middle-class Christians," employees and
volunteers in her study, and 2) the vulnerable people, called by those with
power: "refugees and undocumented migrants." She concludes that power
should be examined and the possibility of harm considered carefully, yet

8. As we've seen with the other authors in this conversation, academic texts are
not the only kinds of representations that may result from ethnographic study, and in
any form, the work of interpretation and representation require the skills that could be
summed up in the concept of salience alone.

9. Endemic to any professional practice, salience is learned over time when one is
immersed in the hands-on work of the practice. Benner et al., *Educating Nurses*, 25–26,
49–52.

10. Ibid.

to stop there would miss far too much of the importance of the research moment.

Helgesson Kjellin shares an entry from her research diary following her visit to a weekly consultation with immigrants: "I am overwhelmed and deeply affected," she says, by the families who lack the most basic items, such as "diapers and oatmeal." The migrant families are at the brink of being "shattered" and Helgesson Kjellin herself seems to feel the shattering in her own emotional and cognitive dissonance between her privilege and the debilitating circumstances of the people she meets. Helgesson Kjellin watches vulnerability and commitment interact in the ecclesial space of the weekly migrant consultation. She acknowledges the structural inequities and implicit biases that work to reproduce social power imbalances and put migrants and refugees in harms way while helping white Christians feel more secure. Nevertheless, she also sees, in collaboration with anthropologist Michael Jackson, how everyday needs and unprecedented situations call for practical wisdom (phronesis) to respond adequately and fittingly. The response of Swedish Christians to undocumented migrants is a matter of acknowledging the "deep awareness that our very existence is interwoven with the existence of others."[11] To represent a narrow view of power dynamics in the migrant ministry would not only misrepresent the profound human interventions at work, it could also endanger the public perceptions of at much needed work.

Another mitigating strategy against the potential harms of representation is to collaborate more intentionally with those in the field. Hutchings shares fieldwork anecdotes showing how on occasion collaborations with participants could lead to more harm—both to his work as well as to the relationships among informants in his study. Well-intentioned remedies like collaboration do not unfortunately guarantee protection from all harms. Wigg-Stevenson suggests that performance ethnography invites theological reflection (the aim of her ethnographic projects) to be collaborative in a more helpful direction. After recounting the history of harm done by white feminist theology that unwittingly (and later more callously) offered white women's experience as universal while disregarding the experiences of women of color, Wigg-Stevenson offers up autoethnography as a way toward better representation and collaboration.

This does leave another stone unturned. Although I join my voice to the chorus of critics of white feminist claims to universal subject status, I find myself wondering if white feminists did not find value in their experience (and their writing about it), not simply for the power it maintains

---

11. Helgesson Kjellin is quoting Jackson, "Ethics and Religion," 107.

or the preservation of whiteness? Certainly feminist writing that does not acknowledge or deconstruct the power and privilege of whiteness has a devastating effect.[12] Yet hidden within the harm, and worthy of retrieval, is the power of the "universal particular." Something about the writing of concrete and detailed human experience does ring out for the universality of humanity itself. The problems arise when someone claims to represent the other without actually listening to or including the other, or when one's own reflexivity is thin or disregarded. Wigg-Stevenson provides us with an exemplar in *Proverbs of Ashes*, the prescient theological work by feminist theologians Rita Nakishima Brock and Rebecca Parker. As Wigg-Stevenson points out the book "deploys the personal to expose and unpack the cultural—and by extension the theological." While the prototype in *Proverbs of Ashes* does not portend to be universal, it holds out the possibility of "evoking transformative practice in its reader." Precisely because the narratives of Parker and Brock evoke particular universals the book holds tremendous power. Wigg-Stevenson points out that the time is ripe for theological ethnographers to take up exactly this kind of work. This brings us to two further questions. In juggling the potential harm and help in ethnographic representation, how can we pause to search for the particular universal in our work? How might we anticipate the goods and harms embedded in novel methodologies?

REPRESENTATION: CONTEXTUAL AND SKILLED

Representation is shaped by context *and* by ritual practices of research and writing. Tim Hutchings describes for us how brick and mortar churches and religious groups no longer need to feel threatened by the digital world of religion. This change in understanding about the lack of threat came largely from the field reports of ethnographers who investigated the new digital spaces, organizations, and people who populate religion online. The context when actually experienced in the field showed instead how digital religion (and digital culture broadly understood) is embedded in our everyday practices. Although Hutchings recommends the use of new media representations to share findings, he is not abandoning his training as a sociologist or ethnographer. The skills he and other contributors to this book developed in doctoral studies and while immersed in fieldwork have a particular coherence and shape. Scholars trained in sociology, anthropology, and even theological ethnography may trade tools and may push for new

12. This is a particular problem in European and North American settings where for too long those who benefit from "whiteness" have been able to enjoy those privileges relatively unscathed.

forms of representing the findings of their fieldwork, yet the training, skill, and adherence to practice—be that social science or theology—focuses the research gaze and shapes the way one organizes and represents findings.

In her chapter, Helgesson Kjellin concludes that both the complex situation and her perspective and skills as a researcher must shape the way she represents her findings. Although she admits how easy and tempting it could be "to end up with an analysis based in a hermeneutics of suspicion," she does not let her training or pressures of her professional guild override her embodied practical wisdom. Rather than abandon the hermeneutic of suspicion, she gives it its rightful place within, but not trumping, her representation and interpretations of meaning.[13] In his chapter Fahlgren' grapples with a different kind of formation in his training to examine historical texts and archive materials as a path to understanding the context of Baptist spirituality. His account raises the question of interdisciplinarity. How do we navigate multiple fields of academic training at any stage from project conception to final report? Additionally we can also ask: How might long-term skill development in theological ethnography cultivate practical wisdom in the researcher? How might theologians and social scientists understand their training as flexible and improvisational practices that serve the work of representation rather than falling captive to either skills or context?

The work of theological ethnography presents many gifts and challenges, among them the dilemmas of representation. And if indeed we are writing "the truth about life" as Mark Jordan and Natalie Wigg-Stevenson urge us, then we are writing about human experience that is irreducible. To "represent" life is not like charting maps or calculating formulas or even working out logical proofs. Instead when we go to the field and then turn to the page to write, we do what ethnographer Sarah Pink calls "emplaced practice" by representing what we have learned and experienced. She says, "we create discourses and narratives that are themselves entangled with the materiality and sensoriality of the moment and of memories and imaginaries."[14] This is the approach we need to navigate the tensions of representation that are reductive *and* evocative, descriptive *and* interpretive, powerful *and* harmful, and which depend on both context *and* skill. This is the approach we need to enrich our imaginations and language for representing life and love and tragedy and redemption.

---

13. In her chapter Helgesson Kjellin also raises this question: "is it acceptable as an anthropologist to take a clear normative stand in favor of acts of solidarity carried out by one's informants?" She concludes with a "yes" at the end of her chapter, pointing to an additional dilemma worthy of further exploration: representation as normative *and* aspirational. On a closely related topic, see Kaufman, "From the Outside," 134–62.

14. Pink, *Doing Sensory Ethnography*, 47–48 [2nd ed].

Bibliography

Adams, Nicholas, and Charles Elliott. "Ethnography Is Dogmatics: Making Description Central to Systematic Theology." *The Scottish Journal of Theology* 53 (2000) 339–64.

Adams, Tony E., Stacy Holman Jones, and Carolyn Ellis. *Autoethnography: Understanding Qualitative Research.* New York: Oxford University Press, 2015.

Afdal, Geir. *Researching Religious Education as Social Practice.* Münster: Waxmann, 2010.

———. "Teologi som teoretisk og praktisk aktivitet" [Theology as Theoretical and Practical Activity]. *Tidsskrift for teologi og kirke* 82 (2011) 87–109.

Ahmed, Sara. *On Being Included.* Durham, NC: Duke University Press, 2012.

Alcoff, Linda Martín. "The Problem of Speaking for Others." *Cultural Critique* 20 (Winter 1991–92) 5–32.

Aldén, Mats, and Johanna Gustafsson Lundberg. "Skapelsen som evangeliets förståelseshorisont: En ecklesiologisk erinran" [Creation as Hermeneutical Horizon for the Gospel]. *Svensk Teologisk Kvartalskrift* 90 (2014) 122–32.

Ammerman, Nancy T. "Lived Religion as an Emerging Field: An Assessment of Its Contours and Frontiers." *Nordic Journal of Religion and Society* 1 (2016) 83–99.

Aquinas, Thomas. *Summa Theologiae.* New York, NY: Benziger Brothers, 1911–1925.

Åqvist, Berit, ed. *Tro, frihet, gemenskap: Svensk baptism genom 150 år* [Faith, Freedom, Community]. Örebro: Libris, 1998.

Aristotle. *The Nicomachean Ethics.* Edited by J. L. Ackrill and J. O. Urmson. Translated by David Ross. Rev. ed. New York, NY: Oxford University Press, 1980.

Asad, Talal. *Anthropology and the Colonial Encounter.* Ithaca, NY: Ithaca Press, 1973.

Asdal, Kristin. "Returning the Kingdom to the King: A Post-Constructivist Response to the Critique of Positivism." *Acta Sociologica* 48 (2005) 253–61.

Bäckström, Anders, Ninna Edgardh, and Per Pettersson. *Religious Change in Northern Europe: The Case of Sweden: From State Church to Free Folk Church, Final Report.* Stockholm: Verbum, 2004.

Bäckström, Anders, et al. *Welfare and Religion in 21st Century Europe.* Vol. 1, Configuring the Connections. Farnham: Ashgate, 2010.

Balling, Jakob L., and Paul Georg Lindhardt. *Den nordiske kirkes historie* [The History of the Nordic Churches]. København: Nyt Nordisk Forlag Arnold Busck,1979.

Balsnes, Anne Haugland, Solveig Christensen, Jan Terje Christoffersen, and Hallvard Olavsson Mosdøl. *Gudstjeneste a la carte: Liturgireformen i Den norske kirke* [Worship a la Carte]. Oslo: Verbum, 2015.

Bardh, Ulla. *Församlingen som sakrament: Tro, dop, medlemskap och ekumenik bland frikyrkokristna vid 1900-talets slut* [The Congregation as Sacrament]. Uppsala: Uppsala universitet, 2010.

Barth, Karl. *Anselm: Fides Quaerens Intellectum*. London: SCM, 1960.

―――. *Det kristna dopet* [The Christian Baptism]. Stockholm: Westerberg, 1949.

Bass, Dorothy C., and Craig R. Dykstra. *For Life Abundant: Practical Theology, Theological Education, and Christian Ministry*. Grand Rapids, MI: Eerdmans, 2008.

Bauerlein, Valerie. "Church's Online Communion: Sacrament or Sacrilege? North Carolina Church's Virtual Plans Run Afoul of the United Methodist Hierarchy." *The Wall Street Journal*, November 15, 2013. http://www.wsj.com/articles/SB1000 142405270230486840457919442373425 1960.

Bergsten, Torsten. *Frikyrkor i samverkan: Den svenska frikyrkoekumenikens historia 1905–1993* [Free Churches in Cooperation]. Örebro/Stockholm: Libris/Verbum, 1995.

―――. "Svenskt perspektiv" [A Swedish Perspective]. In *Samfund i förändring: Baptistisk identitet i Norden under ett och ett halvt sekel*, edited by David Lagergren, 30–65. Tro & Liv Skriftserie 2. Stockholm: Teologiska högskolan Stockholm, 1997.

Bergsten, Torsten, Kjell Kyrø-Rasmussen, and Nils J. Engelsen. *Dopet, dåben, dåpen:Tre nordiska teologiska uppsatser*. [Baptism: Three Nordic Theological Essays]. Stockholm: Westerbergs, 1957.

Benner, Patricia E. *From Novice to Expert: Excellence and Power in Clinical Nursing Practice*. Menlo Park, CA: Addison-Wesley, 1984.

Benner, Patricia E., et al. *Educating Nurses: A Call for Radical Transformation*. San Francisco, CA: Jossey-Bass, 2010.

Berger, Peter, et al. *Religious America, Secular Europe? A Theme and Variations*. Aldershot: Ashgate, 2008.

Berggren, Henrik, and Lars Trägårdh. *Är svensken människa? Gemenskap och oberoende i det moderna Sverige* [Is the Swede Human]. 2nd ed. Stockholm: Norstedts, 2015.

Bernling, Tomas. "Att gå genom muren: Friginva långtidsdömda mäns livsberättelser efter en 30-dagarsretreat" [Passing Through the Wall]. Linköping, 2008.

Bevans, Stephen B. *Models of Contextual Theology*. Rev. and exp. ed. Faith and Cultures Series. Maryknoll, NY: Orbis, 2002.

Birkedal, Erling, Turid Skorpe Lannem, and Harald Hegstad, eds. *Menighetsutvikling i folkekirken: Erfaringer og muligheter* [Congregational Development within the Folk Church]. Oslo: IKO-Forlaget, 2012.

Bjørndal, Silje Kvamme. "The Church in a Secular Age: A Pneumatological Reconstruction of Stanley Hauerwas's Ecclesiology." PhD diss., MF Norwegian School of Theology, 2015.

Bornstein, Erica, and Peter Redfield. "Afterword: Humanitarianism and the Scale of Disaster." In *Forces of Compassion*, edited by Erica Bornstein et al., 249–54. Santa Fe: SAR, 2010.

Bourdieu, Pierre. *Outline of a Theory of Practice*. Translated by R. Nice. New York, NY: Cambridge University Press, 2006.

————. *The Weight of the World. Social Suffering and Impoverishment in Modern Society*. Cambridge: Polity, 1999.

Bourdieu, Pierre, and Loïc Wacquant. *An Invitation to Reflexive Sociology*. Cambridge: Polity, 1992.

Bretherton, Luke. "Generating Christian Political Theory and the Uses of Ethnography." In *Perspectives in Ecclesiology and Ethnography*, edited by Pete Ward, 145–66. Grand Rapids, MI: Eerdmans, 2012.

Brown, Leslie, and Susan Strega, eds. *Research as Resistance: Critical, Indigenous, and Anti-Oppressive Approaches*. Toronto: Canadian Scholars, 2005.

Browning, Don S. *Fundamental Practical Theology: Descriptive and Strategic Proposals*. Minneapolis, MN: Fortress, 1991.

Browning, Don S., et al. *From Culture Wars to Common Ground*. 2nd ed. Louisville, KY: Westminster John Knox, 2000.

Bruce, Steve, and David Voas. "Vicarious Religion: An Examination and Critique." *Journal of Contemporary Religion* 25 (2010) 243–59.

Buch-Hansen, Gitte, Kirsten Donskov Felter, and Marlene Ringgaard Lorensen. "Ethnographic Ecclesiology and the Challenges of Scholarly Situatedness." *de Gruyter Open Theology* 1 (2015) 220–44.

Burawoy, Michael, ed. *Ethnography Unbound: Power and Resistance in the Modern Metropolis*. Berkley, CA: University of California Press, 1991.

Burén, Ann af. "Living Simultaneity: On Religion Among Semi-Secular Swedes." PhD diss., Göteborgs universitet. Södertörns högskola, 2015.

Calvin, John. *Institutes of the Christian Religion*. Edited by John T. McNeill. Translated by Ford Lewis Battles. 2 vols. Philadelphia, PA: Westminster, 1960.

Cameron, Helen, et al. *Talking About God in Practice: Theological Action Research and Practical Theology*. London: SCM, 2010.

Campbell, Heidi. "Can Online Community Be Incarnational?" *When Religion Meets New Media* [blog], January 19, 2007. http://religionmeetsnewmedia.blogspot.com/2009/01/can-online-communty-be-incarnational.html.

Campbell-Reed, Eileen R. *Anatomy of a Schism: How Clergywomen's Narratives Reinterpret the Fracturing of the Southern Baptist Convention*. Knoxville, TN: University of Tennessee Press, 2016.

————. "The Power and Danger of a Single Case Study in Practical Theological Research." In *Conundrums in Practical Theology*, edited by Joyce Ann Mercer and Bonnie J. Miller-McLemore, 33–59. Boston: Brill Academic, 2016.

————. "Wisdom at the Crossroads (Proverbs 8:1–11)." In *This Is What a Preacher Looks Like: Sermons by Baptist Women in Ministry*, edited by Pamela R. Durso, 99–106. Macon, GA: Smyth & Helwys, 2010.

Campbell-Reed, Eileen R., and Christian B. Scharen. "Ethnography on Holy Ground: How Qualitative Interviewing is Practical Theological Work." *International Journal of Practical Theology* 17 (2013) 232–59.

————. "'Holy Cow! This Stuff is Real!': From Imagining Ministry to Pastoral Imagination." *Teaching Theology & Religion* 14 (October 2011) 323–42.

Cannell, Fenella. "Introduction: The Anthropology of Christianity." In *The Anthropology of Christianity*, edited by Fenella Cannell, 1–50. Durham, NC: Duke University Press, 2006.

Cartledge, Mark. *Testimony in the Spirit: Rescripting Ordinary Pentecostal Theology.* Aldershot: Ashgate, 2010.

Centrum för studiet av religion och samhälle. "The Impact of Religion: Challenges for Society, Law and Democracy." https://www.uu.se/digitalAssets/163/a_163564-f_imofr130520.pdf.

Chopp, Rebecca S. *The Power to Speak: Feminism, Language, God.* New York, NY: Crossroad, 1989.

Christiansen, Helle, Sabine Bech-Hansen, and Jakob Brønnum. "Præst i den Danske Folkekirke: Embedet og arbejdet" [Pastor in the Danish Folk Church]. In *Præsteforeningens Blad*, 210–17, København: Den danske Præsteforening, 2005.

Church of Norway, "Resources." https://kirken.no/nb-NO/church-of-norway/resources/plan-for-christian-education/.

——. "Basics and Statistics." http://kirken.no/nb-NO/church-of-norway/about/basics-and-statistics/.

Claesson, Urban, ed. *Folkkyrka nu? Samtal om utmaningar och möjligheter* [Folk Church Now?]. Uppsala: Svenska kyrkan, 2012.

Clifford, James, and George E. Marcus, eds. *Writing Culture: The Poetics and Politics of Ethnography.* Berkeley, CA: University of California Press, 1986.

Coakley, Sarah. *God, Sexuality and the Self: An Essay on the Trinity.* Cambridge: Cambridge University Press, 2013.

Collins, Suzanne. *The Hunger Games.* New York, NY: Scholastic, 2008.

Comaroff, Jean, and John Comaroff. *Of Revelation and Revolution.* Vol. 1. Chicago, Il: University of Chicago Press, 1991.

——. *Of Revelation and Revolution.* Vol. 2. Chicago, Il: University of Chicago Press, 1997.

Conquergood, Dwight. "Rethinking Ethnography: Towards a Critical Cultural Politics." *Communication Monographs* 58 (1991) 179–94.

Crenshaw, Kimberlé Williams. "Demarginalizing the Intersection of Race and Sex: A Black Feminist Critique of Antidiscrimination Doctrine, Feminist Theory and Antiracist Politics." *University of Chicago Legal Forum* 140 (1989) 139–67.

Daly, Mary, and Katherine Rake. *Gender and the Welfare State: Care, Work and Welfare in Europe and the US.* Cambridge: Polity, 2003.

Danbolt, Lars Johan, and Hans Stifoss-Hanssen. *Gråte min sang: minnegudstjenester etter store ulykker og katastrofer.* Cappelen Damm Høyskoleforlaget, 2007.

——. "Når kirkeledere blir samfunnsledere: Bisperollen i tida etter 22 juli" [When Church Leaders Turn into Denomination Leaders]. In *Den offentlige sorgen: markeringer, ritualer og religion etter 22. juli*, edited by Olaf Aagedal, Pål Ketil Botvar, and Ida MarieHøeg, 190–216. Oslo: Universitetsforlaget, 2013.

Danermark, Berth. *Explaining Society: Critical Realism in the Social Sciences.* London: Routledge, 2002.

Davie, Grace. *Religion in Britain since 1945: Believing without Belonging.* Oxford: Blackwell, 1994.

——. *Religion in Modern Europe: A Memory Mutates.* Oxford: Oxford University Press, 2000.

——. "Vicarious Religion: A Methodological Challenge." In *Everyday Religion: Observing Modern Religious Lives*, edited by Nancy T. Ammerman, 21–36. Oxford: Oxford University Press, 2007.

―――. "Vicarious Religion: A Response." *Journal of Contemporary Religion* 25 (2010) 261–66.

Demerath, N. J. "The Rise of 'Cultural Religion' in European Christianity: Learning from Poland, Northern Ireland, and Sweden." *Social Compass* 47 (2000) 127–39.

Den store danske. "Religionsfriheh." http://denstoredanske.dk/Samfund,_jura_og_ politik/Jura/Danmarks_statsforfatning/religionsfrihed.

Denzin, Norman K. "Confronting Ethnography's Crisis of Representation." *Journal of Contemporary Ethnography* 31 (2002) 482–90.

―――. *Interpretive Ethnography: Ethnographic Practices for the 21st Century*. Thousand Oaks, CA: SAGE, 1997.

―――. *Performance Ethnography: Critical Pedagogy and the Politics of Culture*. Thousand Islands, CA: SAGE, 2003.

Denzin, Norman K., Yvonna S. Lincoln, and Linda Tuhiwai Smith. *Handbook of Critical and Indigenous Methodologies*. Thousand Oaks, CA: SAGE, 2008.

Dietrich, Stephanie, ed. *Folkekirke nå* [Folk Church Now]. Trondheim: Verbum, 2015.

Dixon, Patrick. *Cyberchurch: Christianity and the Internet*. Eastborne: Kingsway, 1997.

Dulles, Avery. *Models of the Church*. New York: Image, 2002.

Dykstra, Craig R. *Growing in the Life of Faith: Education and Christian Practices*. 2nd ed. Louisville, KY: Westminster John Knox, 2005.

―――. "Reconceiving Practice." In *Shifting Boundaries: Contextual Approaches to the Structure of Theological Education*, edited by Barbara G. Wheeler and Edward Farley, 35–66. Westminster: John Knox, 1991.

Eckerdal, Jan. *Folkkyrkans kropp. Einar Billings ecklesiologi i postsekulär belysning* [The Body of the Folk Church]. Skellefteå: Artos, 2012.

Eco, Umberto, and Thomas A. Sebeok. *The Sign of Three: Dupin, Holmes, Peirce*. Bloomington, IN: Indiana University Press, 1983.

Edgardh Beckman, Ninna. *Folkkyrka—i solidaritet med kvinnor* [Folk Church—In Solidarity with Women]. Uppsala: Tro & Tanke, 1998.

Edgardh, Ninna. "(De)gendering Ecclesioiogy: Reflections on the Church as a Gendered Body." In *Ecciesiology in the Trenches: Theory and Method Under Construction*, edited by Sune Fahlgren and Jonas Ideström, 193–207. Eugene, OR: Pickwick, 2015.

―――. *Gudstjänst i tiden: Gudstjänstliv i Svenska kyrkan 1968–2008* [Worship through Time]. Stockholm: Verbum, 2010.

―――. "Social Agent—A Queer Role for the Church." In *For the Sake of the World: Swedish Ecclesiology in Dialogue with William T. Cavanaugh*, edited by Jonas Ideström, 65–85. Eugene, OR: Pickwick, 2010.

Ekman, Nils Gösta, and Josef Lundahl, eds. *Frontförkortning i ekumeniken: En debattbok* [Narrowed Fronts in Equmenism]. Stockholm: Gummessons, 1965.

Ekstrand, Thomas. *Folkkyrkans gränser: En teologisk analys av övergången från statskyrka till fri folkkyrka* [The Boundaries of the Folk Church]. Stockholm: Verbum, 2002.

Ellis, Carolyn, and Arthur P. Bochner. "Autoethography, Personal Narrative, Reflexivity: Researcher as Subject." In *Handbook of Qualitative Research*, edited by Norman K. Denzin and Yvonna S. Lincoln, 733–68. Thousand Oaks, CA: SAGE, 2000.

Elstad, Hallgeir. "Folkekyrkjeomgrepet—opphav og utvikling. Tysk og nordisk kontekst" [The Folk Church Concept—Origin and Development]. In *Folkekirke nå*, edited by Stephanie Dietrich, 21–33. Trondheim: Verbum, 2015.

Engedal, Leif Gunnar. "Fra fengselscelle til pilegrimsvei: En empirisk undersøkelse av innsattes pilegrimserfaringer" [From Prison Cell to Pilgrim Route: An Empirical Study of Inmates' Experiences of Pilgrimage]. Halvårsskrift for praktisk teologi 28 (2011) 59–73.

―――. "Retreat i Halden fengsel: Rapport om erfaringer fra retreat sommeren 2014" [Retreat in the Halden Prison]. 58, 2015.

Erlandson, David A., et al. Doing Naturalistic Inquiry: A Guide to Methods. Newberry Park, CA: SAGE, 1993.

Estes, Douglas. SimChurch: Being the Church in the Virtual World. Grand Rapids, : Zondervan, 2009.

Evagrius, Ponticus. The Praktikos and Chapters on Prayer. Kalamazoo: Cistercian, 1972.

Fabian, Johannes, and Vincent de Rooij. "Ethnography." In The SAGE Handbook of Cultural Analysis, edited by Tony Bennett and John Frow, 613–31. Thousand Oaks, CA: SAGE, 2008.

Fagermoen, Tron. "Et valg mellom visjoner? En analyse av ulike kirkesyn i kirkevalgkampen 2015" [An Election between Visions?]. Tidsskrift for praktisk teologi 33 (2016) 4–16.

―――. "Etter folkekirken? En kritisk diskusjon av neo-anabaptismen som veileder for de nordiske folkekirkene" [After the Folk Church?]. Tidsskrift for praktisk teologi 31 (2014) 24–35.

Fahlgren, Sune. "Baptismen och baptisternas gudstjänstliv" [Baptist's Worship life]. In I enhetens tecken: Gudstjänsttraditioner och gudstjänstens förnyelse i svenska kyrkor och samfund, edited by Sune Fahlgren and Rune Klingert, 249–87. Örebro: Libris, 1994.

―――. "Equmeniakyrkans ecklesiologiska äventyr: Kyrkovetenskapliga reflektioner kring nyckelord vid bildande av ny kyrka" [The Ecclesiological Adventures of Uniting Church of Sweden]. Svensk Teologisk Kvartalskrift 90 (2014) 133–48.

―――. "Från blandad kör till lovsångsteam: Historiska och teologiska perspektiv på frikyrkliga sånggrupper" [From Mixed Choir to Praise Team]. In Med skilda tungors ljud: Körsång och gudstjänstspråk, edited by Stephan Borgehammar, 23–76. Svenskt gudstjänstliv 88. Skellefteå: Artos, 2013.

―――. "Historieskrivningar från en kyrkobildningspraktik: En ecklesiologisk analys av kyrkospråk vid Equmeniakyrkans tillkomst" [Historiography from a Church Forming Practice]. In Ecclesiologica & alia: Studia in honorem Sven-Erik Brodd, edited by Erik Berggren et al, 145–70. Skellefteå: Artos, 2016.

―――. "När slutade läsarna att läsa? Historiska och ecklesiologiska perspektiv på bibelbruk" [When did the Readers Stop Reading?]. In Läsarna i distraktionernas tid: Bibel, kyrka och den digitala revolutionen, edited by Joel Halldorf, 123–45. Tro & Liv skriftserie 1. Örebro: Marcus förlag, 2014.

―――. Predikantskap och församling: Sex fallstudier av en ecklesial baspraktik inom svenska frikyrklighet fram till 1960-talet [Preachership and Congregation]. ÖTHrapport supplementserie 3. Uppsala: Uppsala universitet, 2006.

―――. Vatten tjockare än blod: En baptistisk kulturhistoria [Water is Thicker than Blood]. Studia Theologica Holmiensia 23. Stockholm: Teologiska högskolan Stockholm, 2015.

Fahlgren, Sune, and Jonas Ideström, eds. Ecclesiology in the Trenches: Theory and Method under Construction. Eugene, OR: Pickwick, 2015.

Fahlgren, Sune, and Odd Arne Joø. "Baptismens spiritualitet, speglad i dess gudstjänstliv" [The Spirituality of Baptism Mirrored in Its Worship Life]. In *Samfund i förändring: Baptistisk identitet i Norden under ett och ett halvt sekel*, edited by David Lagergren, 104–14. Tro & Liv Skriftserie 2. Stockholm: Teologiska högskolan Stockholm, 1997.

Farley, Edward. *Good and Evil: Interpreting a Human Condition*. Minneapolis, MN: Fortress, 1991.

———. *Practicing Gospel: Unconventional Thoughts on the Church's Ministry*. Louisville, KY: Westminster John Knox, 2003.

Felter, Kirsten Donskov. *Hvad vil det sige at være præst? En kvalitativ undersøgelse af danske præsters syn på embede og arbejde* [What does it Entail to Be a Pastor?]. Aarhus: Folkekirkens Uddannelses- og Videnscenter, 2016.

———. "Mellem kald og profession" [Between Calling and Profession]. University of Copenhagen, 2010.

———. "The Pastor: The Pastor's Role in the Evangelical Lutheran Church of Denmark." In *A Brief Guide to the Evangelical Lutheran Church in Denmark*, edited by Rebekka H. Svenningsen, 64–73. København: Aros, 2013.

Fiddes, Paul. "Ecclesiology and Ethnography: Two Disciplines, Two Worlds?" In *Perspectives on Ecclesiology and Ethnography*, edited by Pete Ward, 13–35. Studies in Ecclesiology and Ethnography. Grand Rapids, MI: Eerdmans, 2012.

———. *Participating in God: A Pastoral Doctrine of the Trinity*. Louisville: Westminster John Knox, 2000.

———. *Seeing the World and Knowing God: Hebrew Wisdom and Christian Doctrine in a Late-Modern Context*. Oxford: Oxford University Press, 2013.

———. *Tracks and Traces: Baptist Identity in Church and Theology*. Studies in Baptist History and Thought 13. Eugene, OR: Wipf & Stock, 2003.

Finn, Lise Cathrine, and Gro Lunde. "Rapport om retreat som metode: Fører Retreat til endring hos deltakerne?" [Report on Retreat as a Method:]. 20, 2015.

FKUV (Folkekirkens Uddannelses- og Videnscenter). "Kirkestatistik" [Church Statistics]. http://www.fkuv.dk/videnscenter/kirkestatistik.

Flaherty, Michael G. "The Crisis in Representation: A Brief History and Some Questions." *Journal of Contemporary Ethnography* 31 (2002a) 479–82.

———. "The Crisis in Representation: Reflections and Assessments." *Journal of Contemporary Ethnography* 31 (2002b) 508–16.

Flenser, Karin Kittelmann. *Religious Education in Contemporary Pluralistic Sweden*. Phd diss., University of Gothenburg, 2015.

Floyd-Thomas, Stacey M. *Mining the Motherlode: Methods in Womanist Ethics*. Cleveland: Pilgrim, 2006.

Flyvbjerg, Bent. "Fem misforståelser om casestudiet" [Five Misunderstandings About Case Studies]. In *Kvalitative Metoder*, edited by Svend Brinkmann and Lene Tanggaard, 463–87. København: Hans Reitzels, 2010.

———. *Making Social Science Matter: Why Social Inquiry Fails and How It Can Succeed Again*. Cambridge: Cambridge University Press, 2001.

Ford, David. "Introduction to Modern Christian Theology." In *The Modern Theologians: An Introduction to Christian Theology Since 1918*, edited by David Ford and Rachel Muers, 1–16. 3rd ed. Oxford: Blackwell, 2005.

Franzen, Bert. *Guds försprång: Om barnen och Guds rike* [God's Lead]. Örebro: Libris, 1991.

Frei, Hans. *Types of Christian Theology*. New Haven, CT: Yale University Press, 1992.

Fretheim, Kjetil, ed. *Ansatte og frivillige: Endringer i Den norske kirke* [Employees and Volunteers]. Oslo: IKO-Forlaget, Prismet Bok, 2014.

Fulkerson, Mary McClintock. "Foreword." In *Ethnography as Christian Theology and Ethics*, edited by Christian B. Scharen and Aana Marie Vigen, xi–xvi. London: Continuum, 2011.

——. "Interpreting a Situation: When is 'Empirical' also 'Theological.'" *Perspectives in Ecclesiology and Ethnography*, edited by Pete Ward, 124–44. Grand Rapids, MI: Eerdmans, 2012.

——. *Places of Redemption: Theology for a Worldly Church*. New York: Oxford University Press, 2007.

Gaarden, Marianne. "Den emergente prædiken: En kvalitativ undersøgelse af mødet mellem prædikantens ord og den situerede kirkegænger i gudstjenesten" [The Emergent Sermon]. PhD diss., Aarhus University, 2014.

——. "Den empiriske fordring til homiletikken" [Empirical Challenges for Homiletics]. *Tidsskrift for praktisk teologi* 2 (2013) 3–20.

——. *Prædikenen som det trejde rum* [The Sermon as the Third Room]. Frederiksberg: Anis, 2015.

——. *The Third Room of Preaching: The Sermon, the Listener, and the Creation of Meaning*. Westminster Homiletics Monograph Series. Louisville, KY: Westminster John Knox, 2017.

Gaarden, Marianne, and Marlene Ringgaard Lorensen. "Listeners as Authors in Preaching: Empirical and Theoretical Perspectives." *Homiletic* 38 (2013) 28–45.

Gallagher, Shaun. "Philosophical Antecedents of Situated Cognition." In *The Cambridge Handbook of Situated Cognition*, edited by Philip Robbins and Murat Aydede, 35–51. New York: Cambridge University Press, 2009.

Ganzevoort R. Ruard. "Van der Ven's Empirical/Practical Theology and the Theological Encyclopaedia." In *Hermeneutics and Empirical Research in Practical Theology: The Contribution of Empirical Theology by Johannes A. van der Ven*, edited by Chris A. M. Hermans and Mary E. Moore, 53–74. Leiden: Brill, 2004.

Garsten, Christina, and Anette Nyqvist. "Momentum: Pushing Ethnography Ahead." In *Organisational Anthropology*, edited by Christina Garsten et al., 241–50. London: Pluto, 2013.

Geertz, Clifford. *The Interpretation of Cultures: Selected Essays*. New York, NY: Basic Books, 1973.

Graham, Elaine. "Research Report: Is Practical Theology a Form of 'Action Research'?" *International Journal of Practical Theology* 17 (2013) 148–78.

Gregson, Jonathan. "The Richest Countries in the World." *Global Finance*, February 13 2017. https://www.gfmag.com/global-data/economic-data/richest-countries-in-the-world?page=12.

Gunaratnam, Yasmin. *Researching "Race" and Ethnicity: Methods, Knowledge and Power*. London: SAGE, 2003.

Gunnes, Gyrid. "Hvem er folkekirkens folk? Åpen mikrofon i Vår Frues kirke som diakonal utfordring til folkekirkeekklesiologien [Who Are the Folk of the Folkchurch? Open Microphone in the Church of Our Lady as Diaconal Challenge to Folkchurch Ecclesiology]." *Tidsskrift for praktisk teologi* 31 (2014) 12–23.

Gustavsson, Caroline. *Delaktighetens kris: Gudstjänstens pedagogiska utmaning* [The Crisis of Participation]. Skellefteå: Artos, 2015.

Haanes, Vidar L. "'I Jesu navn skal all vår gjerning skje': da Menighetsfakultetet ble opprettet" [All Our Deeds Should Be Done in the Name of Jesus]. Trondheim: Tapir akademisk forlag, 2008.

Habermas, Jürgen. "A 'Post-Secular' Society—What Does That Mean?" Paper presented at the Istanbul Seminars organized by Reset Dialogues on Civilizations in Istanbul. *Reset Dialogues on Civilizations: The Web Magazine for All the Tribes of the World*, June 2–6, 2008. http://www.resetdoc.org/story/00000000926.

Hagman, Patrik. "The Constantinianism of the Free Church Tradition and the Promise of a New Asceticism." In *Between the State and the Eucharist: Free Church Theology in Conversation with William T. Cavanaugh*, edited by Joel Halldorf and Fredrik Wenell, 102–13. Eugene, OR: Pickwick, 2014.

———. *Efter Folkkyrkan. En teologi om kyrkan i det efterkristna samhället* [After the Folk Church]. Stockholm: Verbum 2013.

Halldorf, Joel. *Av denna världen? Emil Gustafson, moderniteten och den evangelikala väckelsen* [Of This World?]. Skellefteå: Artos, 2012.

Halldorf, Joel, and Fredrik Wenell, eds. *Between the State and the Eucharist: Free Church Theology in Conversation with William T. Cavanaugh*. Eugene, OR: Pickwick, 2014.

Hammersly, Martyn, and Paul Atkinson. *Ethnography: Principles in Practice*. 2nd ed. New York, NY: Routledge, 1995.

Härdelin, Alf. "Den kristna existensen. Om spiritualitet och spiritualitetsforskning" [The Christian Existens]. In *Kyrkans liv. Introduktion till kyrkovetenskapen*, edited by Stephan Borgehammar, 305–17. Stockholm: Verbum, 1996.

Harding, Susan. "Representing Fundamentalism: The Problem of the Repugnant Other." *Social Research* 58 (1991) 373–93.

Hastrup, Kirsten. "Getting It Right: Knowledge and Evidence in Anthropology." *Anthropological Theory* 4 (2004) 455–72.

Hatch, Mary Jo, and Majken Schultz. "Relations between Organizational Culture, Identity and Image." *European Journal of Marketing* 31 (1997) 356–65.

Hauerwas, Stanley. *A Community of Character: Toward a Constructive Christian Social Ethic*. Notre Dame, IN: University of Notre Dame Press, 1981.

———. *With the Grain of the Universe: The Church's Witness and Natural Theology*. Grand Rapids, MI: Baker Academic, 2001.

Hawksley, Theodora. "What is Ecclesiology About? The Provenance and Prospects of Recent Concrete Approaches to Ecclesiology." PdD diss., University of Edingburgh, 2012.

Healy, Nicholas. *Church, World and the Christian Life: Practical-Prophetic Ecclesiology*. Cambridge: Cambridge University Press, 2000.

———. *Hauerwas: A (Very) Critical Introduction*. Grand Rapids, MI: Eerdmans, 2014.

Heelas, Paul, and Linda Woodhead. *Religion in Modern Times: An Interpretive Anthology*. Oxford: Blackwell, 2000.

Hegstad, Harald. "Ecclesiology and Empirical Research on the Church." In *Explorations in Ecclesiology and Ethnography*, edited by Christian B. Scharen, 34–47. Studies in Ecclesiology and Ethnography. Grand Rapids, MI: Eerdmans, 2012.

———. *Folkekirke og trosfellesskap: Et kirkesosiologisk og ekklesiologisk grunnproblem belyst gjennom en undersøkelse av tre norske lokalmenigheter* [Folk Church and Faith Community]. KIFO perspektiv ; nr 1. Trondheim: Tapir, 1996.

———. "Menighetsutvikling i folkekirken: Grunnlag og formål" [Congregational Development in the Folk Church]. In *Menighetsutvikling i folkekirken: Erfaringer og muligheter*, edited by Erling Birkedal, Turid Skorpe Lannem, and Harald Hegstad, 9–24. Oslo: IKO-Forlaget, 2012.

———. "Praktisk teologi som empirisk teologi: Forholdet mellom teologi og empiri hos Johannes A. van der Ven" [Practical Theology as Empirical Theology]. *Halvårsskrift for praktisk teologi* 15 (1998) 16–27.

———. *The Real Church: An Ecclesiology of the Visible*. Eugene, OR: Pickwick, 2013.

———. "Reflections on Understanding Ecclesiology." In *Ecclesiology in the Trenches: Theory and Method Under Construction*, edited by Sune Fahlgren and Jonas Ideström, 75–84. Eugene, OR: Pickwick, 2015.

Hegstad, Harald, Anne Schanche Selbekk, and Olaf Aagedal. *Når tro skal læres: Sju fortellinger om lokal trosopplæring* [When Faith is to Be Learned]. Trondheim: Tapir Akademisk, 2008.

Heimbrock, Hans-Günter. "Praktisk teologi som virkelighedsvidenskab" [Practical Theology as a Science of Reality]. *Kritisk Forum for Praktisk Teologi* 100 (2005) 13–32.

Helgesson, Kristina. *"Walking in the Spirit": The Complexity of Belonging in Two Pentecostal Churches in Durban, South Africa*. Uppsala: DICA, 2006.

Helgesson Kjellin, Kristina. *En bra plats att vara på* [A Good Place to Be At]. Skellefteå: Artos Academic, 2016.

Hellemo, Geir, ed. *Gudstjeneste på ny* [Worship Anew]. Oslo: Universitetsforlaget, 2014.

Henriksen, Jan-Olav, ed. *Difficult Normativity: Normative Dimensions in Research on Religion and Theology*. Frankfurt am Main: Peter Lang, 2011.

Hine, Christine. *Ethnography for the Internet: Embedded, Embodied, and Everyday*. London: Bloomsbury, 2015.

Holman Jones, Stacy, and Tony E. Adams. *Handbook of Autoethnography*. Walnut Creek, CA: Left Coast Press, 2015.

Holmqvist, Morten. "Learning Religion in Confirmation: Mediating the Material Logistics of Religion." PhD diss., MF Norwegian School of Theology, 2015.

Holtedahl, Øivind. "'Community,' 'God from Above' and 'God from Below': An Ethnographic Study of Religious Knowledge Practices in Two Youth Ministries in the Church of Norway." PhD diss., VID Specialized University, 2017.

Howe, Mark. *Online Church? First Steps Towards Virtual Incarnation*. Cambridge: Grove Books, 2007.

Hutchings, Tim. *Creating Church Online: Ritual, Community and New Media*. London: Routledge, 2017.

Ideström, Jonas. *Folkkyrkotanken—innehåll och utmaningar: En översikt av studier under 2000-talet* [Folk Church Thinking—Content and Challenges]. Uppsala: Svenska kyrkan, 2012.

———. "Implicit Ecclesiology and Local Church Identity—Dealing with the Dilemmas of Empirical Ecclesiology." In *Ecclesiology in the Trenches: Theory and Method under Construction*, edited by Sune Fahlgren and Jonas Ideström. Eugene, OR: Pickwick, 2015.

———. "It is That Loving Gaze." *Ecclesial Practices: Journal of Ecclesiology and Ethnography* 2 (2015) 108–19.

———. *Lokal kyrklig identitet: En studie av implicit ecklesiologi med exemplet Svenska kyrkan i Flemingsberg* [Local Church Identity]. Skellefteå: Artos, 2009.

———. "Mediators of Tradition: Embodiment of Doctrine in Rural Swedish Parish Life." *Ecclesial Practices: Journal of Ecclesiology and Ethnography* 3 (2016) 55–69.

———. *Spåren i snön* [The Tracks in the Snow]. Skellefteå: Artos, 2015.

———. "What's So Great About Being Different? A Folk Church Response to Exceptionalism." In *Between the State and the Eucharist: Free Church Theology in Conversation with William T. Cavanaugh*, edited by Joel Halldorf and Fredrik Wenell, 140–52. Eugene, OR: Pickwick, 2014.

Ideström, Jonas, and Tone Stangeland Kaufman. "Whose Voice? Whose Church? Using Action Research in Practical Ecclesiology." In *Mending the World?*, edited by Niclas Blåder and Kristina Helgesson Kjellin, 486–501. Eugene, OR: Pickwick, 2017.

Isasi-Díaz, Ada María. *En La Lucha: Elaborating a Mujerista Theology*. Minneapolis, MN: Fortress, 1993.

Jackson, Michael. "Ethics and Religion Avant la Lettre. The Perspective from Existential Anthropology." *Svensk Teologisk Kvartalskrift* 89 (2013) 107–15.

Johansen, Kirstine Helboe. "When Religion and Spirituality Converge in Ritual: Weddings Within the Church of Denmark." In *Complex Identities in a Shifting World: Practical Theological Perspectives*, edited by Pamela Couture et al., 53–63. Zürich: LIT Verlag, 2015.

Johansson, Göran. *More Blessed to Give*. Stockholm: Almqvist & Wiksell, 1992.

Johansson, Pernilla. "Spirituality within the Prison Walls: The Impact of a 30-Day Retreat at the Prison in Kumla." MA thesis, Mittuniversitetet, 2012.

Johnsen, Elisabeth Tveito. "Religiøs læring i sosiale praksiser: En etnografisk studie av mediering, identifisering og forhandlingsprosesser i Den norske kirkes trosopplæring" [Religious Learning in Social Practices]. University of Oslo, 2014.

———. "Teologi som ulike biter og deler: Ti år med trosopplæring i Den norske kirke" [Theology as Different Bits and Pieces]. *Prismet* 66 (2015) 125–45.

———. ed. *Gudstjenster med konfirmanter. En praktisk-teologisk dybdestudie med teoretisk bredde* [Worship with confirmands]. Oslo: IKO-Forlaget, Prismet bok, 2017.

Johnson, Elizabeth A. *She Who Is: The Mystery of God in Feminist Theological Discourse*. New York, NY: Crossroad, 1992.

Jones, Serene. "'Women's Experience' Between a Rock and a Hard Place: Feminist, Womanist and Mujerista Theologies in North America." *Religious Studies Review* 21 (1995) 171–78.

Jordan, Mark. "Writing the Truth." *Practical Matters* 6 (2013) 1–5.

Jørgensen, Dorthe. "The Experience of Immanent Transcendence." In *Transfiguration: Nordic Journal of Religion and the Arts*, 2010/2011, edited by Svein Aage Christoffersen, Martin Wangsgaard Jürgensen, and Nils Holger Petersen, 35–52. København: Museum Tusculanum, 2012.

Josefsson, Ulrik. *Liv och över nog. Den tidiga pingströrelsens spiritualitet* [Life and More than That]. Skellefteå: Artos, 2005.

Kauffman, Ivan J. *Follow Me: A History of Christian Intentionality*. Eugene, OR: Cascade, 2009.

Kaufman, Tone Stangeland. "From the Outside, Within, or Inbetween? Normativity at Work in Empirical Practical Theological Research." In *Conundrums in Practical Theology*, edited by Bonnie J. Miller-McLemore and Joyce A. Mercer, 134–62. Leiden: Brill, 2016.

———. "The Ignatian Exercises: A Life-Transforming Resource for Prisoners in Swedish Maximum Security Prisons." *Spiritus* 17 (2017) 19–39.

———. "Ignatiansk spiritualitet for lutherske prester? Jakten på en mer erfaringsnær spiritualitet [Ignatian Spirituality for Lutheran Pastors?]." In *Kristen spiritualitet: Perspektiver, tradisjoner og uttrykksformer*, edited by Knut-Willy Sæther, 147–66. Trondheim: Akademika Forlag, 2013.

———. *A New Old Spirituality: A Qualitative Study of Clergy Spirituality in the Church of Norway*. Oslo: MF Norwegian School of Theology, 2011.

———. "Normativity as Pitfall or Ally? Reflexivity as an Interpretive Resource in Ecclesiological and Ethnographic Research." *Ecclesial Practices: Journal of Ecclesiology and Ethnography* 2 (2015) 91–107.

———. "Pastoral Spirituality in Everyday Life, in Ministry, and Beyond: Three Locations for a Pastoral Spirituality." *Journal of Religious Leadership* 12 (2013) 81–106.

———. "A Plea for Ethnographic Methods and a Spirituality of Everyday Life in the Study of Christian Spirituality: A Norwegian Case of Clergy Spirituality." *Spiritus* 14 (2014) 94–102.

———. "The Real Thing? Practicing a Spirituality of Everyday Life." In *Between the State and the Eucharist: Free Church Theology in Conversation with William T. Cavanaugh*, edited by Joel Halldorf and Fredrik Wenell, 85–101. Eugene, OR: Picwick, 2014.

———. "The Researcher as Gamemaker." Paper presented at AAR 2016.

Kaufman, Tone Stangeland, and Jonas Ideström. "Why Matter Matters in Theological Action Research: Attending to the Voices of Tradition." *International Journal of Practical Theology* (2018) [Forthcoming].

Kaufman, Tone Stangeland, and Astrid Sandsmark. "Spaces of Possibilities: The Role of Artifacts in Religious Learning Processes for Vulnerable Youth." *Journal of Youth and Theology* 14 (2015) 138–54.

———. "Vilje til læring? Ungdom på institusjon i møte med trosopplæringens ekklesiologi og læringssyn [Willing to Learn?]." In *Trosopplæring for alle? Læring, tro og sårbare unge*, edited by Leif Gunnar Engedal, Tron Fagermoen, and Astrid Sandsmark, 79–102. Oslo: IKO-Forlaget, Prismet bok, 2015.

Kazubowski-Houston, Magdalena. *Staging Strife: Lessons from Performing Ethnography with Polish, Roma Women*. Montreal: McGill University Press, 2010.

Keane, Webb. "Minds, Surfaces, and Reasons in the Anthropology of Ethics." In *Ordinary Ethics*, edited by Michael Lambek, 64–83. New York: Fordham University Press, 2010.

Keller, Catherine. *From a Broken Web: Separation, Sexism and Self*. Boston: Beacon, 1986.

Kennerberg, Owe. *Innanför eller utanför: En studie av Församlingstukten i nio svenska frikyrkoförsamlingar* [Inside or Outside]. Örebro: Libris, 1996.

Kerdeman, Deborah. "Pulled Up Short: Challenging Self-Understanding as a Focus of Teaching and Learning." In *Education and Practice: Upholding the Integrity of Teaching and Learning*, edited by Joseph Dunne and Pádraig Hogan, 144–58. Malden, MA: Blackwell, 2004.

Kirkeministeriet. *Betænkning 1477: Opgaver i sogn, provsti og stift*. [Tasks in Parish, Rector, and Diocese]. København, 2006.

———. *Betænkning 1491: Folkekirkens lokale økonomi* [The Local Economy of the Folk Church]. København, 2007.

———. *Betænkning 1503: Uddannelse og efteruddannelse af præster* [Education and Traning of Pastors]. København, 2009.

———. *Betænkning 1527: Provstestillingen og provstiets funktion* [The Function of the Rural Deanery]. København, 2011.

———. *Betænkning 1544: Folkekirkens styre* [The Governance of the Folk Church]. København, 2014.

———. "Dåbstal" [Baptisms]. http://www.km.dk/folkekirken/kirkestatistik/daabstal/.

———. "Kirkelige begravelser" [Church Funerals]. http://www.km.dk/folkekirken/ kirkestatistik/kirkelige-begravelser/.

———. "Kirkelige vielser" [Church Weddings]. http://www.km.dk/folkekirken/ kirkestatistik/kirkelige-vielser-og-kirkelige-velsignelser/.

———. "Konfirmerede" [Confirmations]. http://www.km.dk/folkekirken/kirkestatistik /konfirmerede/.

Kjøde, Rolf. "Fra ellispe til sirkel: Om utviklingen i norsk kirkeliv, særlig sett i relasjon til forsamlingsvekst" [From Ellipsis to Circle]. *Dansk Tidsskrift for Teologi og Kirke* 38 (2011) 7.

Kohut, Heinz. *How Does Analysis Cure?* Edited by Arnold Goldberg and Paul Stepansky. Chicago: University of Chicago Press, 1984.

Kühle, Lene, et al. *Funktionspræster i Danmark: En kortlægning* [Pastors in Denmark: A Survey]. Aarhus: Aarhus Universitet og Folkekirkens Uddannelses- og Videnscenter, 2015.

Kvale, Steiner. *InterView: En introduktion til det kvalitative forskningsinterview* [An Introduction to the Qualitative Research Interview]. København: Hans Reitzels, 1997.

Lagergren, David. *Förändringstid: Kris och förnyelse. Svenska Baptistsamfundet åren 1933–1948* [Time of Changes]. Örebro: Libris, 1994.

Lagergren, David. "Intensiv och extensiv kristendom" [Intensive and Extensive Christianity]. *Tro & Liv* 54 (1995) 7–12.

Lagerkvist, Amanda. "Existential Media: Toward a Theory of Digital Thrownness." *New Media & Society* (2016) 1–15. http://nms.sagepub.com/content/early/2016/ 06/10/1461444816649921.full.pdf.

———. "Toward an Ethics of the Act." In *Ordinary Ethics*, edited by Michael Lambek, 39–63. New York: Fordham University Press, 2010.

Laghé, Birgitta. *Den evangeliska Mariavägen till enhet. En studie av Paulina Mariadotters spiritualitet* [The Evangelical Way of Maria to Unity]. Biblioteca theologiæ practicæ 73. Skellefteå: Artos, 2004.

Lambek, Michael (ed.). *Ordinary Ethics*, New York, NY: Fordham University Press, 2010.

Larsson, Mats. "*Vi kristna unga qvinnor.*" Askers Jungfruförening 1865–1903. Identitet *och intersektionalitet* [We Young Christian Women]. Studia historico-ecclesiastica Upsaliensia 48. Uppsala: Uppsala universitet, 2015.

Lassiter, Katherine E. *Recognizing Other Subjects: Feminist Pastoral Theology and the Challenge of Identity.* Eugene, OR: Pickwick, 2015.

Latour, Bruno. *Reassembling the Social: An Introduction to Actor-Network-Theory.* Clarendon Lectures in Management Studies. Oxford: Oxford University Press, 2005.

Law, John. *After Method: Mess in Social Science Research.* International Library of Sociology. London: Routledge, 2004.

————. *Organizing Modernity*. Oxford: Blackwell, 1994.

Leech, Geoffrey N. *Principles of Pragmatics*. New York, NY: Longman, 1983.

Leer-Salvesen, Paul. *Moderne prester* [Modern Ministers]. Oslo: Verbum, 2005.

Leganger-Krogstad, Heid. "Trosopplæringen som drivhjul i menighetsutvikling? Fellesskapslæring i kirken" [Christian Education as Sprocket in Congregational Development?]. In *Menighetsutvikling i folkekirken: Erfaringer og muligheter*, edited by Erling Birkedal, Turid Skorpe Lannem, and Harald Hegstad, 67–86. Oslo: IKO-forlaget, 2012.

Lerheim, Birgitte. "Lekmannsforsamlingar i endring" [Laymen Congregations Going Through Change]. In *Norsk bruksteologi i endring: tendenser gjennom det 20.århundre*, edited by Pål Repstad, 171–87. Trondheim: Tapir akademisk forlag, 2010.

————. "Vedkjenning og gjenkjenning: Refleksjonar i snittpunkta mellom kyrkjetenking og kyrkjepraksis" [Confession and Recognition]. PhD diss., University of Oslo, 2008.

Lindbeck, George. *The Nature of Doctrine: Religion and Theology in a Postliberal Age*. London: SPCK, 1984.

Lindström, Harry. *I livsfrågornas spänningsfält: Om P Waldenströms Brukspatron Adamsson: Populär folkbok och allegorisk roman* [In the Tensions of Existential Questions]. Stockholm: Verbum, 1997.

Livets Ord. *Årsredovisning 2014/2015* [The Word of Life]. http://www.livetsord.se/Portals/0/docs/ArsredovisningLO.pdf.

Lorentzen, Håkon, Kjetil Fretheim, and Sverre Dag Mogstad, eds. *Fellesskap og organisering: Frivillig innsats i kirkens trosopplæring* [Community and Organizing]. Oslo: Prismet Bok, 2016.

Louth, Andrew. *Maximus the Confessor*. London: Routledge, 1996.

Luhrmann, T. M. *When God Talks Back: Understanding the American Evangelical Relationship with God*. New York, NY: Vintage Books, 2012.

Manning, Peter K. "The Sky is Not Falling." *Journal of Contemporary Ethnography* 31 (2002) 490–98.

Marcus, George. "Ethnography in/of the World System: The Emergence of Multi-Sited Ethnography." *Annual Review of Ethnography* 24 (1995) 95–117.

Marcus, George E., and Michael M. J. Fischer. *Anthropology as Cultural Critique: An Experimental Moment in the Human Sciences*. Chicago: University of Chicago Press, 1986.

————. *Anthropology as Cultural Critique: An Experimental Moment in the Human Sciences*. 2nd ed. Chicago, Il: University of Chicago Press, 1999.

Markham, Annette. "Ethnography in the Digital Internet Era: From Fields to Flows, Descriptions to Interventions." In *The SAGE Handbook of Qualitative Research*, edited by Norman Denzin and Yvonna Lincoln, 650–68. London: SAGE, 2016.

Markie, Peter. "Rationalism vs. Empiricism." *The Stanford Encyclopedia of Philosophy* (Summer 2015 Edition). https://plato.stanford.edu/archives/sum2015/entries/rationalism-empiricism/.

Martinson, Mattias. *Postkristen teologi: Experiment och tydningsförsök* [Post Christian Theology]. Göteborg: Glänta, 2007.

Mason, Jennifer. *Qualitative Researching*. London: SAGE, 1997.

Mauss, Marcel. *The Gift*. London: Routledge, 1990.

McClendon, James W., Jr. *Systematic Theology: Ethics*. Nashville: Abingdon, 1986.

McFague, Sallie. *The Body of God: An Ecological Theology*. Minneapolis, MN: Fortress, 1993.

McGuire, Meredith. *Lived Religion: Faith and Practice in Everyday Life*. Oxford: Oxford University Press, 2008, TN

Medieakademien. *Förtroendebarometern 2016* [Barometer of Trust]. http://medieakademien .se/wp-content/uploads/2014/02/Fo%CC%88rtroendebarometern_2016.pdf.

Merton, Robert K. *Social Theory and Social Structure*. New York, NY: Free Press, 1968.

Meyendorf, John. *A Study of Gregory Palamas*. London: Faith Press, 1964.

MigrationsInfo. "Forskning och statistik om migration och integration i Sverige" [Research and Statistics on Migration and Integration in Sweden]. http://www. migrationsinfo.se/migration/sverige/historiskt/.

Miller, Daniel, and Heather Horst. "Introduction: The Digital and the Human." In *Digital Anthropology*, edited by Heather Horst and Daniel Miller, 3–38. London: Berg, 2012.

Miller-McLemore, Bonnie J.. *Also a Mother: Work and Family as Theological Dilemma*. Nashville, TN: Abingdon, 1994.

———. "The Living Human Web: Pastoral Theology at the Turn of the Century." In *Through the Eyes of Women: Insights for Pastoral Care*, edited by Jeanne Stevenson Moessner, 9–26. Minneapolis, MN: Fortress, 1996.

———. "Practical Theology and Pedagogy: Embodying Theological Know-How." In *For Life Abundant: Practical Theology, Theological Education, and Christian Ministry*, edited by Dorothy C. Bass and Craig Dykstra, 170–94. Grand Rapids, MI: Eerdmanns, 2008.

Miller-McLemore, Bonnie J., and Joyce Ann Mercer. "Introduction." In *Conundrums in Practical Theology*, edited by Joyce Ann Mercer and Bonnie J. Miller-McLemore, 33–59. Boston, MA: Brill Academic, 2016.

Morris, Charles W. *Foundations of the Theory of Signs*. Edited by Otto Neurath et al. Foundations of the Unity of Science 1. Chicago, Il: University of Chicago Press, 1938.

Moschella, Mary Clark. "Ethnography." In *The Wiley-Blackwell Companion to Practical Theology*, edited by Bonnie J. Miller-McLemore, 224–33. Malden, MA: Wiley-Blackwell, 2012., OH

———. *Ethnography as Pastoral Practice: An Introduction*. Cleveland, OH: Pilgrim, 2008.

———. *Living Devotions: Reflections on Immigration, Identity, and Religious Imagination*. Princeton Theological Monograph Series 78. Eugene, OR: Pickwick, 2008.

Mowry LaCugna, Catherine. *God for Us: The Trinity and Christian Life*. New York, NY: HarperCollins, 1991.

Murray, Paul. "Searching the Living Truth of the Church in Practice: On the Transformative Task of Systematic Ecclesiology." *Modern Theology* 30 (2014) 251–81.

Myerhoff, Barbara. *Number Our Days: A Triumph of Continuity and Culture among Jewish Old People in an Urban Ghetto*. New York, NY: Simon & Schuster, 1978.

Nahnfeldt, Cecilia. "Motstånd och poetiska fragment: En aktionsforskningsstudie om kunskaper och migration" [Resistance and Poetic Fragments]. *Tidskrift för Genusvetenskap* 36 (2015) 99–117.

Nakashima Brock, Rita. *Journeys by Heart: A Christology of Erotic Power*. New York, NY: Crossroad, 1988.

Nakashima Brock, Rita, and Rebecca Ann Parker. *Proverbs of Ashes: Violence, Redemptive Suffering and the Search for What Saves Us*. Boston, MA: Beacon, 2001.

Nämnden för statligt stöd till trossamfund. "Nämnden för statligt stöd till trossamfund" [The Committee for Government Support to Denominations of Faith]. http://www.sst.a.se/.

Niebuhr, H. Richard. *Christ and Culture*. San Francisco, CA: HarperSanFrancisco, 2001.

Nikolajsen, Jeppe Bach. *The Distinctive Identity of the Church: A Constructive Study of the Post-Christendom Theologies of Lesslie Newbigin and John Howard Yoder*. Eugene, OR: Pickwick, 2015.

Nordiskt Välfärdscenter. "Danmark" [Denmark]. http://nordisktvalfardscenter.se/sv/integrationnorden/Fakta/Landfakta/Landfakta—Danmark/.

————. "Norge" [Norway]. http://nordisktvalfardscenter.se/sv/integrationnorden/Fakta/Landfakta/Landfakta—-Norge/.

Nordström, Magnus. "Bakom dubbla murar: En sociologisk undersökning av klosterverksamheten vid Kumla-anstalten [Behind Double Walls]. Lunds Universitet, 2007.

Norheim, Bård Eirik Hallesby. "The Christian Story of the Body as the Ritual Plot for Youth Ministry." *Journal of Youth and Theology* 15 (2016) 88–106

————. "Cultivating a Vision of the Unseen: The Apophatic Mode in Ecclesiological Research." *Ecclesial Practices* 2 (2015) 40–56.

————. "Ministry as Womb and Tomb: Baptism as a Paradigm for Ministry." *Dialog* 53 (2014) 101–9.

————. *Practicing Baptism: Christian Practices and the Presence of Christ*. Eugene, OR: Pickwick, 2014.

Norheim, Bård Eirik Hallesby, and Knut Tveitereid. "Stemning har ikke noe med selve kirkerommet å gjøre: Unges utforming av gudstjenesterommet" [Atmosphere Does Not Have Anything to Do with the Sanctuary]. In *Skjønnhet og tilbedelse*, edited by Knut-Willy Sæther and Svein Rise, 229–45. Oslo: Akademika forlag 2013.

Nöth, Winfried. *Handbook of Semiotics*. Bloomington, IN: Indiana University Press, 1990.

Nygaard, Marianne Rodriguez. "Caring to Know or Knowing to Care? Knowledge Creation and Care in Deacons' Professional Practice in the Church of Norway." PhD diss., MF Norwegian School of Theology, 2015.

Palamas, Gregory. *The Triads*. Mahwah, NJ: Paulist, 1983.

Persson, Larsåke W. "Spiritualitet i Svenska Baptistsamfundet. PM till samtalsdelegationen SB/SvK" [Spirituality in the Swedish Baptist Union]. In the Baptist Archive, Bromma. *Varför inte i Svenska Baptistsamfundet? En omvänd ordlista från A till Ö* [Why Not the Swedish Baptist Union]. Stockholm: Svenska Baptistsamfundet, 1998.

Pettersson, Per, and Ninna Edgardh. "The Church of Sweden: A Church for All, Especially the Most Vulnerable." In *Welfare and Religion in 21st Century Europe*, edited by Anders Bäckström et al., 39–56. Vol. 1, Configuring the Connections. Farnham: Ashgate, 2010.

————. *Varför inte i Svenska Baptistsamfundet? En omvänd ordlista från A till Ö* [Why Not the Swedish Baptist Union]. Stockholm: Svenska Baptistsamfundet, 1998.

Pettersson, Thorleif, and Yilmaz Esmer. *Vilka är annorlunda? Om invandrares möte med svensk kultur* [Who Are Different?]. Integrationsverkets rapportserie 3. Norrköping: Integrationsverket, 2005.

Phillips, L. Edward. "Online Communion Conversation." *UMC Media*, 2013. http:// umcmedia.org/umcorg/2013/communion/online-communion-conversation.pdf.

Pike, Kenneth. *Language in Relation to a Unified Theory of the Structure of Human Behavior*. Glendale, CA: Summer Institute of Linguistics, 1954.

Pilario, Daniel Franklin. *Back to the Rough Grounds of Praxis: Exploring Theological Method with Pierre Bourdieu*. Leuven: Peters, 2005.

Pink, Sarah. *Doing Sensory Ethnography*. Thousand Oaks, CA: SAGE, 2009.

———. *Doing Sensory Ethnography*. 2nd ed. Thousand Oaks, CA: SAGE, 2015.

Piper, John. "What Are Your Thoughts About Being Part of an Online Church?" *Desiring God*, June 29, 2009. http://www.desiringgod.org/interviews/what-are-your-thoughts-about-being-part-of-an-online-church.

Plaskow, Judith, and Carol P. Christ, eds. *Womanspirit Rising*. San Francisco, CA: Harper and Row, 1979.

Pleizier, Theo. *Religious Involvement in Hearing Sermons: A Grounded Theory Study in Empirical Theology and Homiletics*. Delft: Eburon Academic, 2012.

Pontifical Council for Social Communications. "The Church and Internet." February 22, 2002. http://www.vatican.va/roman_curia/pontifical_councils/pccs/documents/rc_pc_pccs_doc_20020228_church-internet_en.html.

Prenter, Regin. *Kirkens embede* [The Ministry of the Church]. Aarhus: Universitetsforlaget i Aarhus, Ejnar Munksgaard, 1965.

Rabinow, Paul. "Representations Are Social Facts: Modernity and Post-Modernity in Anthropology." In *Writing Culture: The Poetics and Politics of Ethnography*, edited by James Clifford and George E. Marcus, 234–61. Berkeley, CA: University of California Press, 1986.

Rabinow, Paul, et al. *Anthropology of the Contemporary*. Durham, NC: Duke University Press, 2008.

Reckwitz, Andreas. "Toward a Theory of Social Practices: A Development in Culturalist Theorizing." *European Journal of Social Theory* 5 (2002) 243–63.

Reite, Ingrid. "Between Blackboxing and Unfolding: Professional Learning Networks of Pastors." *International Journal of Actor-Network Theory and Technological Innovation* 5 (2013) 47–64.

———. "Between Settling and Unsettling in a Changing Knowledge Society: The Professional Learning Trajectories of Pastors." PhD diss., MF Norwegian School of Theology, 2014.

Robbins, Joel. "The Anthropology of Christianity: Unity, Diversity, New Directions: An Introduction to Supplement 10." *Current Anthropology* 55 (2014) 157–71.

Rollins, Peter. *How (Not) to Speak of God*. London: Paraclete, 2006.

Rubin, Herbert J., and Irene S. Rubin. *Qualitative Interviewing: The Art of Hearing Data*. Thousand Oaks, CA: SAGE, 1995.

Said, Edward. *Orientalism*. New York, NY: Vintage, 1979.

Sainsbury, Diane. *Gendering Welfare States*. London: SAGE, 1994.

Saiving, Valerie. "The Human Situation: A Feminine View." *The Journal of Religion* 40 (1960) 100–112.

Sandsmark, Astrid, and Tone Stangeland Kaufman. "Landsby eller forstad? Konfirmasjon for unge på institusjon" [Village or Suburb?]. In *Trosopplæring for alle? Læring, tro og sårbare unge*, edited by Leif Gunnar Engedal, Tron Fagermoen, and Astrid Sandsmark, 55–78. Oslo: IKO-Forlaget, Prismet bok, 2015.

Saxegaard, Fredrik. "Realizing Church: Parish Pastors as Contributors to Leadership in Congregations." PhD diss., MF Norwegian School of Theology, 2017.

SCB (The Central Bureau for Statistics). *Personer efter hushållstyp, hushållsställning och kö*. http://www.scb.se/sv_/Hitta-statistik/Statistik-efter-amne/Befolkning/ Befolkningens-sammansattning/Befolkningsstatistik/#c_li_120253.

Scharen, Christian B., ed. *Explorations in Ecclesiology and Ethnography*. Grand Rapids, MI: Eerdmans, 2012.

———. "Judicious Narratives: Ethnography as Ecclesiology." *The Scottish Journal of Theology* 58 (2005) 125–42.

Scharen, Christian B., and Eileen Campbell-Reed. *Learning Pastoral Imagination: A Five Year Report on How New Ministers Learn Practice*. New York, NY: Auburn Studies, 2016.

Scharen, Christian B., and Aana Marie Vigen, eds. *Ethnography as Christian Theology and Ethics*. New York, NY: Continuum, 2011.

Schatzki, Theodore R., Karin Knorr Cetina, and Eike von Savigny, eds. *The Practice Turn in Contemporary Theory*. London: Routledge, 2001.

Schneider, Laurel C., and Cassie J. E. Trentaz. "Making Sense of Feminist Theology Today." *Religion Compass* 2 (2008) 788–803.

Schumacher, Lydia. *Divine Illumination: The History and Future of Augustine's Theory of Knowledge*. Oxford: Wiley-Blackwell, 2011.

Sigurdson, Ola. *Det postsekulära tillståndet: Religion, modernitet, politik* [The Post-Secular State of Things]. Munkedal: Glänta, 2009.

———. "The Return of the Body. Re-Imagining the Ecclesiology of Church of Sweden." In *For the Sake of the World: Swedish Ecclesiology in Dialogue with William T. Cavanaugh*, edited by Jonas Ideström, 125–45. Eugene, OR: Pickwick, 2010.

Snow, David A. "On the Presumed Crisis in Ethnographic Representation: Observations from a Sociological and Interactionist Standpoint." *Journal of Contemporary Ethnography* 31 (2002) 498–507.

Stark, Agneta. "Nej, svenskarna är inte världens ensammaste folk." [No, Swedes Are Not the Most Lonely People in the World]. *ETC*, April 8, 2016. http://www.etc.se/ledare/nej-svenskarna-ar-inte-varldens-ensammaste-folk.

Statistisk centralbyrå. "Den norske kirke." https://www.ssb.no/kirke_kostra.

Svenska kyrkan. "Statistik" [Statistics]. https://www.svenskakyrkan.se/statistik.

———. *Svenska kyrkans kommunikationsplattform* [The Church of Sweden's Communication Platform]. http://www.mynewsdesk.com/se/svenska_kyrkan/ pressreleases/naervaro-oeppenhet-och-hopp-ledord-foer-svenska-kyrkans-kommunikation-81478.

Sveriges Frikyrkoråd, *Gemensam väg* [A Common Way]. Stockholm: Sveriges Frikyrkoråd, 1968.

Sveriges Kristna Råd, *Dop, nattvard, ämbete: Grunddokument för samtal om kyrkans enhet. Den officiella texten från Faith and Order, den så kallade Lima texten 1982* [Baptism, Eucharist, Ministry]. Sveriges kristna råds skriftserie 20. Bromma: Sveriges kristna råd, 2014.

Sveriges Riksdag. "Lag om Svenska kyrkan 1998:1591" [Law on Church of Sweden]. In *Svensk författningssamling*.

Swinton, John, and Harriet Mowat. *Practical Theology and Qualitative Research*. London: SCM, 2006.

Tangen, Karl Inge. *Ecclesial Identification Beyond Late Modern Individualism? A Case Study of Life Strategies in Growing Late Modern Churches*. Global Pentecostal and Charismatic Studies. Leiden: Brill, 2012.

Tanner, Kathryn. *The Politics of God: Christian Theologies and Social Justice*. Minneapolis, MN: Fortress, 1992.

————. *Theories of Culture: A New Agenda for Theology*. Minneapolis, MN: Fortress, 1997.

Taylor, Charles. *The Malaise of Modernity*. Toronto: House of Anansi, 1991.

————. "Part VI. Reply and Re-Articulation: Charles Taylor Replies." In *Philosophy in an Age of Pluralism: The Philosophy of Charles Taylor in Question*, edited by James Tully and Daniel M. Weinstock, 213–57. New York, NY: Cambridge University Press, 1995.

Thornton, E. E. "Clinical Pastoral Education." In *Dictionary of Pastoral Care and Counseling*, edited by Rodney J. Hunter, 177–82. Nashville, TN: Abingdon, 1990.

Thurfjell, David. *Det gudlösa folket: De postkristna svenskarna och religionen* [The People Without a God]. Stockholm: Molin & Sorgenfrei Akademiska, 2015.

Torrance, Thomas F. *Theological Science*. Oxford: Oxford University Press, 1969.

Tuhiwai Smith, Linda. *Decolonizing Methodologies: Research and Indigenous Peoples*. New York, NY: Zed Books, 2012.

Turner, Victor. "Foreword." In *Number Our Days: A Triumph of Continuity and Culture Among Jewish Old People in an Urban Ghetto*, edited by Barbara Myerhoff, xiii–xvii. New York, NY: Simon & Schuster, 1980.

Tveitereid, Knut. "Pragmatics of Discipleship: A Study of Ambiguity on a Strategic Level in Norwegian Christian Youth Organizations." PhD diss., MHS School of Mission and Theology, 2015.

Underberg, Natalie, and Elayne Zorn. *Digital Ethnography: Anthropology, Narrative, and New Media*. Austin, TX: University of Texas Press, 2013.

van der Ven, Johannes A. *Practical Theology: An Empirical Approach*. Translated by Barbara Schultz. Kampen: Kok Pharos, 1993.

VID. "Cracks and In Betweens." http://www.vid.no/en/research/research-groups/cracks-and-in-betweens/.

Vikström, Björn. *Folkkyrka i en postmodern tid—tjänsteproducent i välfärdssamhället eller engagerande gemenskap?* [Folk Church in a Postmodern Time]. Åbo: Åbo Akademi, 2008.

Volf, Miroslav, and Dorothy C. Bass. *Practicing Theology: Beliefs and Practices in Christian Life*. Grand Rapids, MI: Eerdmans, 2002.

Wadel, Cato. *Feltarbeid i egen kultur: En innføring i kvalitativt orientert samfunnsforskning* [Fieldwork in One's Own Culture: An Introduction to Qualitatively Oriented Social Science Research]. Flekkefjord: SEEK, 1991.

Ward, Graham, John Milbank, and Catherine Pickstock. *Radical Orthodoxy: A New Theology*. London: Routledge, 1998.

Ward, Pete. "Blueprint Ecclesiology and the Lived: Normativity as a Perilous Faithfulness." *Ecclesial Practices* 2 (2015) 74–90.

————. *Liquid Church*. Peabody, MA: Hendrickson, 2002.

————. *Liquid Ecclesiology: Gospel and Church*. Leiden: Brill, 2017.

―――. *Participation and Mediation: A Practical Theology for the Liquid Church.* London: SCM, 2008.

―――, ed. *Perspectives in Ecclesiology and Ethnography.* Grand Rapids, MI: Eerdmans, 2012.

Watkins, Clare. "Reflections on Particularity and Unity." In *Ecclesiology in the Trenches: Theory and Method under Construction,* edited by Sune Fahlgren and Jonas Ideström, 139–53. Eugene, OR: Pickwick, 2015.

Watkins, Clare, et al. "Practical Ecclesiology: What Counts as Theology in Studying the Church?" In *Perspectives on Ecclesiology and Ethnography,* edited by Pete Ward, 167–81. Grand Rapids, MI: Eerdmans, 2012.

Weber, Max. *Wirtschaft und Gesellschaft: Grundriss der verstehenden Soziologie.* Tübingen: JCB Mohr/Paul Siebeck, 1980.

Webster, John. "In the Society of God: Some Principles of Ecclesiology." In *Perspectives on Ecclesiology and Ethnography,* edited by Pete Ward, 200–22. Grand Rapids, MI: Eerdmans, 2012.

Welzel, Christian. *Freedom Rising: Human Empowerment and the Quest for Emancipation.* New York, NY: Cambridge University Press, 2013.

Wennerström, Adrian. *Uppsala Baptistförsamling* [The Baptist Congregation of Uppsala], 1936.

Wiberg, Anders. *Det christliga dopet: Framstäldt uti Biblens egna ord och beledsagadt med förklarande anmärkningar samt wittnesbörd af utmärkta theologer* [The Christian Baptism]. Philadelphia, PA: Amerikanska baptist sällskapet för tryckning af christliga skrifter, 1854.

Wigg-Stevenson, Natalie. *Ethnographic Theology: An Inquiry Into the Production of Theological Knowledge.* New York, NY: Palgrave, 2014.

―――. "From Proclamation to Conversation: Ethnographic Disruptions to Theological Normativity." *Palgrave Communications: Radical Theologies.* 1:15024. doi: 10.1057/palcomms.2015.24.

―――. "Reflexive Theology: A Preliminary Proposal." *Practical Matters* 6 (2013) 1–19.

Williams, Delores. *Sisters in the Wilderness: The Challenge of Womanist God-Talk.* Maryknoll, NY: Orbis, 1993.

Williams, Rowan. *Resurrection: Interpreting the Easter Gospel.* London: Darton, Longman & Todd, 2002.

―――. *Silence and Honey Cakes: The Wisdom of the Desert.* Oxford: Lion Books, 2003.

Wilson, Shawn. *Research Is Ceremony: Indigenous Research Methods.* Black Point, NS: Fernwood, 2009.

Wingren, Gustaf. *Creation and Law.* Eugene, OR: Wipf & Stock, 2003.

―――. *Demokrati i folkkyrkan* [Democracy in the Folk Church]. Lund: Gleerups, 1963.

―――. *The Living Word: A Theological Study of Preaching and the Church.* Eugene, OR: Wipf & Stock, 2002.

Winter, Ralph D. "The Two Structures of God's Redemptive Mission." *Missiology: An International Review* 2 (1974) 121–39.

Winter, Ralph D., and R. Pierce Beaver. *The Warp and the Woof: Organizing for Mission.* South Pasadena, CA: William Carey Library, 1970.

Wittgenstein, Ludwig. *Filosofiska undersökningar* [Philosphical Investigations]. Stockholm: Bonniers, 1992.

World Values Survey. "World Values Survey, Findings and Insights." http://www.
worldvaluessurvey.org/WVSContents.jsp.
Wyller, Trygve. "Becoming Human: Compassionate Citizenship. An Interpretation of
a Project for Undocumented Migrants in Sweden." *Diaconia: Journal for the Study
of Christian Social Practice* 4 (2013) 34–44.
———. "The Undocumented Embodied: Shaping the Space Where the Sacred and the
Secular Intertwine." In *Secular and Sacred? The Scandinavian Case of Religion in
Human Rights, Law and Public Space*, edited by Trygve Wyller, Rosemarie Van
Den Breemer and Jose Casanova, 221–36. Göttingen: Vandenhoeck & Ruprecht,
2014.

www.ingramcontent.com/pod-product-compliance
Lightning Source LLC
Chambersburg PA
CBHW061002280326
41935CB00009B/807